the Complete Guide to

Kansas

FISHING

Amy Bickel
AND Jason Probst

trails books
NEENAH, WISCONSIN

Acknowledgments

Thanks to all the KDWP fisheries biologists,

whose help in putting this book together was incalculable,

and to *Kansas Wildlife and Parks* magazine editor Mike Miller,

who helped edit our manuscript, made suggestions,

and answered all of our questions.

To all the anglers who gave up their honey holes,

showed us their tricks, and took us fishing—we thank you.

Library of Congress Cataloging-in-Publication Data

Bickel, Amy.
Kansas fishing / Amy Bickel and Jason Probst ; [illustrations, Joe Tomelleri].
p. cm.
ISBN 978-1-934553-37-4
1. Fishing—Kansas. 2. Reservoirs—Kansas. I. Probst, Jason. II. Title.
SH497.B55 2011
639.209781—dc23
2011016689

Editor: Michael Bragg
Designer: Rebecca Finkel
Illustrations: © Joe Tomelleri
Photography: Jason Probst and Amy Bickel

Main cover photo: Jason Probst fishing for walleye at Cheney Reservoir dam, shot by Travis Morisse.
Cover images from left to right: Zac Udock holds a largemouth bass caught at Bone Creek Reservoir;
Jim Reid shows off a wiper caught at Glen Elder Reservoir;
Robin Blubaugh holds a walleye she caught at Kirwin Reservoir;
Nicholas Backencamp, of Lincoln, Nebraska, proudly displays a 15.5-inch crappie he caught and released
while fishing with Clyde "The Guide" Holscher at Coffey County Lake.

15   14   13   12   5   4   3   2

Printed in the United States of America

Trails Books, a division of Big Earth Publishing
3360 Mitchell Lane, Suite E • Boulder, Colorado 80301

This book is dedicated to our families—

Kim, Erica, and Mitchell Probst

and

John, Brett, and Kaci Young.

Thanks for letting us drag you along

through the heat, rain, wind, and bugs

during our statewide adventures.

Contents

Preface

It's hard to explain to an out-of-state angler just what it's like to spend a day, a weekend, or a week fishing in Kansas. Sometimes it's hard for them to understand, too, until they give it a try for themselves.

Kansas doesn't have awe-inspiring mountains or fast-running rivers and streams. Unlike some other states, it doesn't have giant reservoirs with scores of tournament anglers on the water week after week, month after month, nor does it have thousands of lakes. Sometimes the weather is hot, sometimes it's cold, and, more often than not, the wind is blowing harder than it should.

So what's so great about fishing in Kansas?

For starters, it is the best-kept secret on the Great Plains. The state boasts a range of sport fish and plenty of hot spots in which to find them. With 25 reservoirs and countless small waters and streams, Kansas has all the different kinds of structure that freshwater anglers need for a successful fishing trip.

Moreover, fishing in Kansas is fishing the way God meant it to be. In Kansas, fishing is for everybody, and our diverse collection of fishing holes—reservoirs, state and community lakes, rivers, creeks, and tiny little farm ponds—makes it easy to find a place to spend a spring or summer afternoon. You can enjoy Kansas lakes whether you have a high-dollar rig and the latest equipment or it is just you and a pole sitting on the bank.

If, by chance, the fish aren't biting, just sit back, relax, and scan the landscape. No, Kansas doesn't have the streams of Colorado or the lakes of Minnesota, but it isn't flat and barren, either.

Get off the interstate and take a slow drive down K-177, where the sky widens across a vast expanse of rolling prairie known as the Flint Hills—one of the last stands of tallgrass left in the world. The Flint Hills are also home to a few Kansas reservoirs, streams, and state fishing lakes.

Or, perhaps, take a gander at the stars that can be seen overhead on cloudless nights while fishing a reservoir's dam during the spring walleye spawn—thanks to the state's wide-open spaces. Maybe you'll slip a boat out on a body of water left a generation ago by coal miners, or on the cooling waters of a power plant.

Even the semi-arid, treeless landscape of western Kansas offers a beautiful oasis on the prairie—lakes that shockingly appear out of nowhere like sparkling mirages.

With most of Kansas' fishing waters surrounded by wildlife areas, it's not uncommon to walk up on a deer grazing in a field, hear a pheasant cackle in the morning, or see a group of turkeys playfully chasing each other.

If nothing else, set your eyes on the horizon—there are few places in the world that can rival Kansas' sunrises and sunsets.

Still, fishing in Kansas holds a deeper meaning than ending the day with a stringer full of fish or eye-catching scenery.

It's about freedom and the ability to wander around and not run into a mass of people or rows of buildings. It's about the older generation telling stories from their youth and sharing decades' worth of knowledge to up-and-coming anglers.

It's about kids leaving the house and not returning until dark—coming back home with a coffee can full of tadpoles or maybe a bucketful of catfish. And it's about parent and child, sitting on the shore, waiting for the red bobber to slip under the water with the pull of a fish.

It's about finding a fishing hole in the middle of the lake, or going so far up a winding creek bed that cell phones don't work, smart phones become useless, and the busyness of the world fades away—leaving your mind free to focus on the rippling water around your feet, the rustling sound of the cottonwood tree.

We grew up in Kansas—one in a small farm town in south-central Kansas, the other in the shadow of the Flint Hills—and we both spent a good part of our childhoods roaming the state's open areas and exploring small fishing holes. Those first youthful memories—a finicky catfish nibbling on a hunk of liver, a bluegill attacking a kernel of corn—have stayed with us well into adulthood. Today, we're passing these memories on to our own children, as well as helping them create their own childhood memories.

That's part of the reason for this book—to share Kansas' treasures with those who haven't yet found them. It might be a tail-water pit in western Kansas, an eastern Kansas river, or the rocky shoreline of a larger reservoir, but the treasures are there, and you'll find them once you take the time to see and experience them.

Kansas has everything you need to make that happen. Our hope is that this book can set you on the path to finding your own stories and memories to share, and that you'll learn to see all the wonder Kansas has to offer.

Introduction

The bulk of this book covers fishing in Kansas' large reservoirs. This is where the majority of the state's public-access fishing opportunities lie. To be sure, there is a wealth of fishing to be found in the smaller state fishing lakes, in community lakes, and in sections of rivers and streams throughout Kansas, and we have covered those, as well—though we unfortunately could not go into as much depth with those waters.

There are 25 large reservoirs in Kansas. Most were built for flood control, water supply, and recreation. Fishing, however, remains one of the main attractions for these state bodies of water. The reservoirs range in size from 1,200 to 16,000 surface acres. Most offer facilities, such as camping, boat ramp lanes, swimming beaches, and supplies.

According to the Kansas Department of Wildlife and Parks (KDWP), northeast Kansas reservoirs are known for producing crappie, white bass, and channel catfish. In the southeast part of the state, crappie, largemouth bass, white bass, and catfish are abundant. For central Kansas, reservoirs draw anglers searching out walleye, white bass, striped bass, wipers, and channel cats. In the west, anglers will find walleye, largemouth bass, wipers, and crappie.

Meanwhile, for anglers who prefer smaller waters, the KDWP manages more than 40 state fishing lakes. Another 200 community lakes are owned by local governments, and these gems can provide outstanding angling opportunities. The Community Fisheries Assistance Program has leased fishing rights to most of these lakes to allow fishing from the shore or a boat with no additional fees. Anglers just need a Kansas fishing license.

In all, according to the KDWP, less than 10 percent of community lakes still require daily or annual fees.

There are more than 10,000 miles of streams and rivers in Kansas, most of which are privately owned. There are three navigable rivers—meaning they are open to the public—the Arkansas, Missouri, and Kansas. A person, however, must have permission to access the river through private land. The rest of the streams are privately owned, but some reaches are leased by the department through the Fish Impoundments and Stream Habitats (FISH) Program, while other reaches are in public ownership. Also, there are more than 150,000 privately owned farm ponds that provide good fishing. These fishing holes allow anglers to hook largemouth bass, crappie, bluegill, and catfish. Permission must be granted from a landowner to fish any private water, except those waters enrolled in the FISH program.

Patterned after the state's successful walk-in hunting program, the KDWP introduced the Fishing Impoundments and Stream Habitats program in 1998, with the goal of increasing public fishing opportunities. It provides anglers with a place to fish while leaving the land in private ownership. The agency leases water bodies from landowners—paying roughly $42 an acre for ponds and $500 to $1,000 for each stream mile. About 75 percent of the payment comes from the Federal Aid in Sport Fish Restoration Act, funded through the purchase of fishing equipment. In 2009, the state had 229 FISH properties, which included 1,172 acres of ponds, 90 miles of streams, and 8 stream access sites, according to the KDWP.

Who Needs a License?

If you are a Kansas resident age 16–64, you need a fishing license present while fishing in Kansas. Non-residents 16 or older must have a nonresident license.

Anyone residing in Kansas who is at least one-sixteenth American Indian by blood, and is certified by the Bureau of Indian Affairs, can apply for a free fishing license, which the angler must have in his/her possession when fishing. All other laws and regulations apply to American Indians.

> **Fishing license prices***
> **Resident:** $20.50 annual permit
> **Youth Multi-year (age 16–20):** one-time purchase $42.50
> **Non-resident:** $42.50 annual permit
> **Five-day fishing (nonresident):** $22.50
> **24-hour permit:** $5.50
> **Trout permit:** $12.50
> **Paddlefish permit:** $12.50
> **Youth Paddlefish permit:** $7.50
> **Hand fishing permit:** $27.50
> **Bass Pass (for tournaments):** $12.50
> **Three-pole permit:** $6.50
>
> *Prices as of the printing of this book

Camping

Much of the camping at the larger reservoirs in Kansas is on state park land and is managed by the KDWP. Campers are limited to a stay of 14 consecutive days. Quiet hours are 11:00 p.m. to 6:00 a.m. Consumption of 3.2 beer is permitted unless otherwise posted. Regulations that apply to these locations include:

- A current motor vehicle permit is required for every motorized vehicle entering the state park.

- Motor vehicles are restricted to maintained roads and parking areas only, unless otherwise posted, and are limited to a 25-mile-per-hour speed limit.

- Fires are allowed in fireplaces, fire rings, and cooking grills. Fires must be completely extinguished prior to leaving the area.

- Swimming is allowed in designated areas. Liquor and beer are prohibited on swimming beaches or in waters designated by buoys or other markers as swimming areas. For other beverages, only shatterproof containers are allowed.

- Pets must always be restrained by a camper, cage, hand-held leash, or tethered chain no longer than 10 feet. They are not allowed on swimming beaches or swimming areas that are delineated by buoys or other markers or in public buildings or structures. Dogs participating in authorized activities or assisting the visually or hearing impaired are not subject to these restrictions.

- A special event permit is required for any event involving entrance fees, exclusive use of an area, sales, organized competition, amplified sound, use of temporary structures (does not include common camping gear or blinds), or reservation of a specific site or facility. Check with the park office for details.

- Hunting is allowed only on remote portions of a few state parks, as posted. Be sure to check with the state park office before hunting.

- Fishing is prohibited on boat ramps, swimming beaches, and in swimming areas marked with buoys. In state parks, fish may only be cleaned at designated fish cleaning stations or other locations as posted. Trotlines and setlines are prohibited in the waters of state fishing lakes, Crawford State Park, Meade State Park, and Scott State Park.

- Only livestock used for riding are allowed in state parks. Horses and other such livestock are restricted to maintained roads and designated riding trails, and may only be stabled in designated areas.

- Fireworks are allowed only at designated times and in designated areas.

- Litter must be put in trash containers, if provided. Where containers are not provided, park users must carry their trash out with them.

- Digging holes, removing geological formations, archeological relics or ruins, or vegetation (except for noncommercial use of edible wild plants, wild fruits, nuts, or fungi) is prohibited.

- No person may advertise or solicit sales.

- Firearms may only be discharged in areas specifically designated for hunting or target practice.

State Parks vehicle permit prices*

Daily permit: $3.70 off-season (October to March), $4.20 in prime season (April to September)

Annual permit: $19.70 off-season, $24.70 in prime season

Second vehicle permit: $12.20 off-season, $14.70 prime season

Senior/Disabled daily permit: $2.60 off-season, $2.85 prime season

Senior/Disabled annual permit: $11.10 off-season, $13.60 prime season

State park camping permit prices*
(separate from state vehicle permit)

Daily camping: $7.50 off-season (October to March), $8.50 prime season (April to September)

14-day camping: $87.50 off-season, $101.50 prime season

Prime site fee: additional $2.50

Annual camping: $202.50

One utility: $7.00

Two utilities: $9.00

Three utilities: $10.00

Rent-A-Camp: $15.50

Overflow camping: $6.50

Group camping: $1.50 per person, plus $1.50 per site

Youth camping: $4.00 per camping unit

Campsite reservation: $12.00, call individual state park

*Prices as of the printing of this book

Several state parks have cabins available for rent, and more are being added every year. The cabins are moderately priced, and most are designed to sleep up to 6–8 people, and include a stove and refrigerator, utensils, bedding, and cleaning supplies.

State parks with cabins include: Keith Sebelius, Prairie Dog, Lovewell, Glen Elder, Webster, Cedar Bluff, Scott, Wilson, Ottawa, Kanopolis, Kansas State Fairgrounds, Cheney, Kingman, Tuttle Creek, Milford, McPherson State Fishing Lake, El Dorado, Fall River, Cross Timbers, Melvern's Eisenhower State Park, Pomona, Clinton, Perry, Atchison State Fishing Lake, Crawford, and Mined Land Wildlife Area. Prices vary on cabins, but they generally cost $45–$95 per night. To view a complete list of available cabins and make a reservation, visit https://reserve.ksoutdoors.com/reservations/complete-cabin-list.

Many reservoirs in Kansas also have camping areas that are maintained by the U.S. Army Corps of Engineers. In those areas, KDWP vehicle and camping permits are not valid. Fees at Corps parks may vary, but typically a day use fee of $1 per person is charged for access to developed swimming beaches. The Corps also charges $3 per vehicle for use of boat launching ramps. Camping fees vary by location, and range from

$10 for a campsite without electrical hookups to $20 for an improved campsite.

Legal Equipment

Each angler is limited to two lines with not more than two baited hooks (single or treble) or artificial lures per line. A third line can be used with the purchase of a $6.50 third-pole permit.

In addition to two lines, a fisherman may set one trotline with not more than 25 hooks or, instead of a trotline, an angler can use eight setlines containing not more than two hooks each. Unattended lines must be checked at least once every 24 hours and must be tagged securely and plainly with the angler's name and address.

Trotlines and setlines are prohibited on all department-managed waters under 500 surface acres, as well as in the waters at Crawford, Meade, and Scott State Parks.

Except where snagging paddlefish and non–sport fish is permitted, legally caught fish are ones that are hooked in the mouth. If hooked anywhere else, the fish must be returned to the water.

Other Fishing

Besides a rod and reel, the Kansas Department of Wildlife and Parks offers these alternatives in some areas of the state, depending on the time of year.

Hand Fishing: Hand fishing is legal from sunrise to sunset June 15 through August 31. Locations include the flowing portions of the Arkansas River from its origin downstream to the Kansas–Oklahoma border; the flowing portions of the Kansas River from its origin downstream to its confluence with the Missouri River; and all federal reservoirs from 150 yards away from the dam to the upper end of the federal property. Those with hand fishing permits also must fill out a questionnaire that must be submitted no later than 30 days after the close of the hand-fishing season.

Spearfishing, Gigging, and Bowfishing: Unless otherwise posted, spear guns, without explosive charge, can be used to take non-sport fish in waters posted "open to scuba and skin diving." Spears must be attached to a spear gun or person by a line. Non–sport fish also can be taken by gigging in waters not posted as closed to gigging.

Meanwhile, all waters are open to bowfishing, unless posted otherwise. Some bowfishing is permitted at city, county, township, or private lakes, but regulations vary, so bowfishermen should consult local rules. Crossbows are legal. Arrows must have barbed heads, and each arrow must be attached by a line to the bow and must be shot from the bow. Waters within 50 yards of an occupied boat dock or ramp, occupied swimming area, occupied picnic site or camping area, and other public-use areas are closed to bowfishing. Only non–sport fish can be taken with a bow.

Paddlefish Snagging: A special paddlefish snagging season runs March 15 through May 15 on posted areas inside city parks on the Neosho River in Chetopa and Burlington; the Neosho River at Iola downstream from the dam to the city limits; the Marais des Cygnes River below Osawatomie Dam downstream to the posted boundary; the Marais des Cygnes River from the upstream boundary of the Marais des Cygnes Wildlife Area downstream to the Kansas–Missouri border; and the Browning Oxbow Lake of the Missouri River.

The paddlefish permit includes six carcass tags. The daily creel limit is two fish. Anglers can snag them using pole and line with not more than two single or treble hooks. Anglers also can snag non–sport fish (carp, drum, grass carp, threadfin and gizzard shad, goldfish, gar, suckers including carpsucker and buffalo, goldeye, and bowfin) during the paddlefish season in posted waters. There are no limits on non–sport fish.

A few other rules

- There is a 24-inch minimum length limit on paddlefish in Missouri River boundary waters and a 34-inch minimum length limit on the Marais des Cygnes River.

- Barbless hooks must be used in Chetopa City Park. Catch and release is allowed in Burlington, Chetopa, and Iola; however, once attached to a stringer, a fish becomes part of the daily creel limit.

- Immediately upon harvest, anglers must sign a carcass tag, record the county, date, and time of harvest, and attach the carcass tag to the lower jaw of the paddlefish taken.

- Anglers must stop snagging once the daily limit of paddlefish is reached.

Floatline Fishing: Started in 2009, KDWP's three-year pilot program allows anglers a season to jug, or floatline fish. The season is during daylight hours from July 15 through September 15 at selected Kansas reservoirs. They are: Hillsdale, Council Grove, Tuttle Creek, Kanopolis, John Redmond, Toronto, Wilson, and Pomona.

Anglers are allowed no more than eight floatlines or eight setlines, with no more than two hooks attached to each line, or one trotline with no more than 25 hooks attached. Each trotline, setline, tip-up, floatline, and unattended fishing line shall have a tag or label securely attached, designating the name and address of the operator. No trotline, floatline, or setline shall be set within 150 yards of any dam. All floatlines must be under immediate supervision of the angler and must be removed from the water when fishing ceases.

Material for floats is restricted to closed-cell devices made of plastic, wood, or foam; metal or glass floats are not allowed. A floatline permit is required.

Trout

Kansas might not have those crystal-clear streams like Colorado. However, just like the mountain waters of the neighboring Rockies, the Sunflower state does have trout. Indeed, for those who don't want to sit by a hole on the ice and fish for crappie (or even if you do), trout fishing opportunities abound across Kansas, whether it's a stream near a reservoir or a state or city lake.

From October 15 through April 15, the Kansas Department of Wildlife and Parks stocks rainbow trout about every two weeks in roughly 25 areas throughout the state. While most locations stock rainbow trout, several waters contain brown trout.

To fish for trout, a $12.50 trout permit is required.

A trout permit is required to fish for trout on the waters listed below from January 1 through December 31. Trout fishing at Mined Land Wildlife Area #30 (Cherokee County) and Tuttle Creek Reservoir Seep Stream, where trout survive through the summer, requires a trout permit year-round.

The daily creel limit is 5 trout. The possession limit is 15.

Trout Permit Required for All Anglers

- Auburndale Park, in Topeka
- Cedar Bluff Stilling Basin
- Cimarron Grasslands Pits
- Garnett Crystal Lake
- Glen Elder State Park Pond
- Gun Park Lake, in Fort Scott
- Kanopolis Seep Stream
- KDOT East Lake, in Wichita
- Mined Land Wildlife Area #30
- Lake Charles, in Dodge City
- Lake Henry, in Clinton State Park
- Pratt Centennial Pond
- Sandsage Bison Range and Wildlife Area Sandpits (Periodically Dry)
- Vic's Lake and Slough Creek, in Sedgwick County Park
- Walnut River Area, in El Dorado State Park
- Webster Stilling Basin
- Willow Lake, at Tuttle Creek Reservoir

Trout Permit Only Required for Trout Anglers

- Cameron Springs, in Fort Riley
- Dillon Nature Center Pond, in Hutchinson
- Great Bend Veterans Memorial Park Lake
- Lake Shawnee, in Topeka
- Lakewood Lake, in Topeka
- Moon Lake, in Fort Riley
- Moss Lake and Horseshoe Lake, in Sedgwick County Park
- Scott State Fishing Lake
- Scott State Park Pond
- Smoky Gardens Lake, in Sherman County
- Solomon River between Webster Reservoir and Rooks County #2 Road

Statewide Creel and Length Limits

The following length and creel limits govern all fishable waters in Kansas, unless special regulations are posted at individual locations. Length and creel limits may be subject to change as the KDWP adjusts to changing conditions. For up-to-date limits, check the KDWP website (http://www.kdwp.state.ks.us/news/Fishing/Fishing-Regulations/Statewide-Creel-Length-Limits).

Species	Creel limit	Min. length
Channel and blue catfish		10
Walleye, sauger, saugeye (combination)	5	15
Rainbow and brown trout (combination)	5	
Black bass (largemouth, smallmouth, spotted, in combination)	5	15
Flathead catfish	5	
Northern pike	2	30
Striped bass	2	
Wiper	2	
Crappie	50	
White bass	no limit	
Bullhead catfish	no limit	
Bluegill	no limit	
Sunfish	no limit	
Paddlefish	2	34
Other legal species	no limit	

Education Programs

The Kansas Department of Wildlife and Parks provides a number of educational opportunities around the state for those who want to learn more about Kansas outdoors.

The Pratt Education Center is near US 54, on 25th Ave., two miles east and one mile south of Pratt, and offers displays, dioramas, and exhibits that showcase the wildlife of Kansas. The Aquarium Room features

Seth Way's Catfish

Watching as competitors weighed catfish at the annual Ducks Unlimited catfish tournament at John Redmond, John Way leaned over to ask me something. He wondered if I knew how the whiskered species became a prosperous Kansas sport fish.

I didn't, I said. I had thought catfish were always in Kansas' waters. As Way informed me, however, while there were some catfish in Kansas beforehand, there wasn't the abundance that there is today.

Way, an outdoorsman himself, told me his grandfather led the way for channel cat reproduction. In fact, his grandfather's pioneering system for culturing catfish is still used nationwide today.

Seth Way, John's grandfather, was just a teenager without much formal education when he was hired by the Pratt hatchery in 1922. Not that his age or education mattered.

"Way, he had a natural aptitude," said Don Patton, a former manager of the Kansas Department of Wildlife and Parks' Pratt Hatchery who learned under Way. "He was basically self-taught."

Born in 1903, Way worked at the State Fish Hatchery in Pratt for 46 years, serving as the hatchery manager for most of that time. While he had little advanced education, he did have hands-on knowledge from fishing the rivers around his little town of Murdock, in Pratt County. There, he'd watch male catfish fan their eggs.

It was through research based on those experiences that Way developed a channel catfish incubation system, Patton said. Previously, it had been difficult to achieve good numbers of catfish in the state's small impoundments through natural spawning. Larger fish oftentimes ate the small fry, which didn't have much of a place to hide in lesser waters. Catfish reproduction had been experimented with at Pratt for several years before Way's employment, but with limited success.

Way took over when his boss left in 1925.

Way placed old cream cans or similar containers in the Pratt ponds. Channel cats deposited their masses of eggs in the can, which were retrieved by fisheries staff. The eggs then were placed in screened baskets situated in a long wooden trough where water would flow—acting as an improvised incubator.

Knowing he had to keep the water agitated over the eggs, Way asked the state commission for a motor to run the pump, Patton said. The commission, however, didn't want to budget any money. "Someone suggested, 'Why don't you power it by a water wheel,'" Patton said. "So the first attempt was to actually use the current of the river."

Way published the basic design in 1927, according to the American Fisheries Society's National Fish Culture Hall of Fame, into which Way was inducted in 1995, thanks to a nomination by Patton.

Meanwhile, his grandfather's concept is still used as the accepted method of egg incubation in state, federal, and private hatcheries across the nation, John Way said, noting that a model of the incubating trough is on display at KDWP's Pratt Education Center.

Through his work, Way was able to hatch and rear millions of catfish fry and fingerlings that were eventually stocked into Kansas' small lakes, as well as a few reservoirs. And it's just one of the stories that have helped evolve Kansas fishing.

Kansas fish, as well as the history of the Pratt Hatchery, including a working model of Seth Way's incubation system. Hours are 8:00 a.m. to 4:30 p.m. Monday through Friday, except holidays. Admission is free.

The Milford Nature Center, at 3415 Hatchery Dr. in Junction City, is located near Milford Reservoir and features a number of live animal exhibits—including snakes, lizards, prairie dogs, and raptors. Nature trails near the center showcase natural habitat, and demonstrate how to attract wildlife to your backyard. The Milford Fish Hatchery sits nearby and is also available to tour after 1:00 p.m. on weekends, or by appointment. Nature center hours are 9:00 a.m. to 4:30 p.m. Monday through Friday, and 1:00 p.m. to 5:00 p.m. on weekends from April through September. The center is closed weekends October through March. Admission is free.

The Great Plains Nature Center is located at 6232 E. 29th St. in Wichita and provides an opportunity to enjoy nature in the heart of Kansas' largest city. The center's signature event, Walk with Wildlife, takes place the second Saturday in June and attracts approximately 1,500 visitors. The center is open 9:00 a.m. to 5:00 p.m. Monday through Saturday, except holidays.

The Olathe Prairie Center is a 300-acre tallgrass preserve within minutes from the metro area. Located at 26235 W. 135th St., the center contains trails that meander through natural tallgrass, native wildflowers, and woodlands. No public buildings are available here, and the site is open from dawn to dusk, seven days a week.

The Kansas Wetlands Education Center sits on the edge of a key stop for waterfowl traveling the Central Flyway—Cheyenne Bottoms. Located at 592 NE. K-156, near Great Bend, the center gives visitors a glimpse into the wildlife that roams the waters of this marshy lowland area. After visiting the center, drive across the street to the nearly 20,000-acre Cheyenne Bottoms, where birds, waterfowl, deer, and eagles take advantage of this unique ecosystem. Admission is free to the center, which is open 8:00 a.m. to 5:00 p.m. Tuesday through Saturday and 1:00 p.m. to 5:00 p.m. on Sunday.

Additionally, the Kansas Department of Wildlife and Parks has an active hatchery and stocking program that annually stocks roughly 40 million fry, 3.5 million fingerling and 385,000 intermediate-sized fish in Kansas. Those stocked fish include walleye, largemouth bass, smallmouth bass, channel catfish, blue catfish, bluegill, striped bass, wiper, rainbow trout, crappie, paddlefish, sauger, and saugeye.

The KDWP operates four hatcheries: Farlington, Meade, Milford, and Pratt. The KDWP also operates a rearing pond at Woodson State Fishing Lake.

The Farlington Fish Hatchery, north of Girard in Crawford County, produces channel catfish, bluegill, redear sunfish, hybrid sunfish, striped bass, wiper, walleye, sauger, saugeye, and grass carp. Tours of the hatchery are available by calling 620-362-4166.

KDWP Contact Info

Office of the Secretary, 785-296-2281
Pratt Operations Office, 620-672-5911
Region 1 office (northwest), 785-628-8614
Region 2 office (northeast), 785-273-6740
Region 3 office (southwest), 620-227-8609
Region 4 office (southcentral), 316-683-8069
Region 5 office (southeast), 620-431-0380
Emporia Research and Survey Office, Emporia, 620-342-0658
Kansas City District Office, Shawnee, 913-422-1314
Operation Game Thief hotline, to report wildlife crimes, 877-426-3843

Fisheries Biologists

Steve Price, Region 1 and 3 supervisor ...785-628-8614
Chuck Bever, Region 2 supervisor 785-273-6740
Tom Swan, Region 4 and 5 supervisor...316-683-8069
Scott Waters, Downs District..............785-545-3345
Tommie Berger, Ellsworth District 785-658-2465
Dave Spalsbury, WaKenney District......785-726-3212
Mark Shaw, Stockton District.............785-425-6775
Ely Sprenkle, Manhattan District.........785-539-7941
John Reinke, Milford District 785-238-6465
Andy Jansen, Kansas City District...913-422-1313, x111
Richard Sanders, Lawrence District 785-832-8413
Kirk Tjelmeland, Atchison District.......785-246-4514
Lowell Aberson, Dodge City District 620-227-8609
Craig Johnson, El Dorado District 316-322-7513
Jessica Mounts, Wichita District..........316-683-8069
Jeff Koch, Cheney District.................620-459-6922
Carson Cox, Fall River District 620-342-0658
Rob Friggeri, Pittsburg District 620-231-3173
Don George, Mound City District.......913-795-2218
Leonard Jirak, New Strawn District 620-364-5552
Tom Lang, Pratt District...................620-672-5911
Sean Lynott, Independence District 620-331-6820

Master Angler Program

While a number of anglers dream of landing a new state record fish, few ever will. The Kansas Master Angler program offers a suitable alternative, though. Anglers who catch a noteworthy fish, albeit not quite a state record, can receive recognition for their skill by applying for a Master Angler Award.

A close up photo of the fish is required for application, as well as a completed application form signed by a witness to the measurement. Applications and mailing address can be found in a current copy of the Kansas fishing regulations summary.

Seth Way's footprint also is on the state's white bass, his grandson said, although he noted that might not be good for publication. However, after digging through newspaper archives, I found a column by Clelland Cole, an outdoor writer for *The Hutchinson News*, who wrote in 1974 that Way, along with another state employee some time roughly 20 years earlier, took a hatchery truck, loaded up some minnows, and went fishing in Oklahoma, bringing back about 100 white bass, which they unloaded into Fall River. After a second trip, a load was taken to Kanopolis.

And, today, there are millions of white bass across most Kansas reservoirs.

Minimum Measurements for Master Angler Award
(in inches)

Largemouth bass	23
Smallmouth bass	18
Spotted bass	18
Striped bass	35
White bass	16
Wiper	25
Blue catfish	37
Bullhead catfish	15
Channel catfish	33
Flathead catfish	41
Crappie	15
American eel	30
Paddlefish	41
Sauger	20
Saugeye	24
Walleye	27
Yellow perch	12
Northern pike	34
Bigmouth buffalo	30
Smallmouth buffalo	30
Carp	30
Drum	25
Gar	48
Goldeye	15
Grass carp	34
Shovelnose Sturgeon	25
Bluegill	10
Green sunfish	11
Hybrid sunfish	12
Redear sunfish	11
Warmouth	10
Brown trout	20
Rainbow trout	20
Yellow bass	11

Are My Fish Safe to Eat?

The Kansas Department of Health and Environment and the Kansas Department of Wildlife and Parks have fish consumption advisories in place for fish caught at certain locations. The advisories identify species that should be eaten in limited quantities or, in some cases, avoided altogether because of contamination found in tested fish.

The advisories include guidelines for mercury and polychlorinated biphenyls (PCBs) in fish, perchlorate in fish and other aquatic life and lead and cadmium in shellfish. Data from most Kansas long-term monitoring sites show a decrease in PCB levels and no trend in mercury concentrations, according to KDHE. PCBs have not been in use in the U.S. since the 1970s, and chlordane use was discontinued in 1988.

Chlordane levels have declined dramatically statewide, and PCB levels are expected to follow. PCBs and chlordane degrade slowly, so it takes decades for them to be completely removed from the environment, even after use is discontinued.

State officials recommend not eating specified fish or aquatic life from the following locations:

- The Kansas River from Lawrence (below Bowersock Dam) downstream to Eudora at the confluence of the Wakarusa River (Douglas and Leavenworth counties) for bottom-feeding fish (carp, blue catfish, channel catfish, flathead catfish, freshwater drum, bullheads, sturgeons, buffalos, carpsuckers and other sucker species) because of PCB levels

- Horseshoe Lake located in units 22 and 23 of the Mined Lands Wildlife Area (Cherokee County) for all forms of aquatic life in addition to all fish because of perchlorate levels

- The Spring River from the confluence of Center Creek to the Kansas/Oklahoma border (Cherokee County) for shellfish (mussels, clams, and crayfish) because of lead and cadmium levels

- Shoal Creek from the Missouri/Kansas border to Empire Lake (Cherokee County) for shellfish because of lead and cadmium levels

In addition, officials recommend a limit of one 8-ounce serving per month, or twelve 8-ounce servings a year, on the consumption of bottom-feeding fish from the following locations due to PCBs:

- The Arkansas River from the Lincoln Street dam in Wichita downstream to the confluence with

Cowskin Creek near Belle Plaine (Sedgwick and Sumner counties)

- Cow Creek in Hutchinson and downstream to the confluence with the Arkansas River (Reno County)

Due to mercury contamination, officials recommend a limit of one 8-ounce serving per week for adults or one 4-ounce serving per week for children (12 years or younger) of any species of fish from the following locations:

- The Little Arkansas River from the Main Street Bridge immediately west of Valley Center to the confluence with the Arkansas River in Wichita (Sedgwick County)

- The main stem of the Blue River from U.S. 69 Highway to the Kansas/Missouri state line (Johnson County)

According to KDHE, Kansas counties with current fish consumption advisories include: Cherokee, Douglas, Johnson, Leavenworth, Reno, Sedgwick, and Sumner Counties.

For other consumption advisories, including for children and pregnant women, visit www.epa.gov/fish advisories/advice/1-meal-per-week.pdf. Information on the FDA/EPA commercial fish advisory is available at: www.epa.gov/fishadvisories/advice/.

Information on the Kansas Fish Tissue Contaminant Monitoring Program can be found at: www.kdheks.gov/befs/fish_tissue_monitoring.htm.

Aquatic nuisance species

For information on aquatic nuisance species, or to report an aquatic nuisance species specimen found in uninfected waters, call Jason Goeckler, Aquatic Nuisance Species Coordinator, 620-342-0658.

Several aquatic nuisances have surfaced in the last decade. Aquatic nuisances can have a detrimental effect on bodies of water used for fishing, recreation, water supply, and power generation. Among those species, two have surfaced in Kansas as the most prolific—the white perch and the zebra mussel.

White Perch: The white perch is a native of the Atlantic coastal region. It is a voracious feeder, and has been associated with a decline in walleye and white bass numbers in those waters where it has been introduced. White perch have the ability to out compete game fish for forage, and they are known to prey on the eggs of walleye and white bass.

In Kansas, the white perch has been found in Cheney, Wilson, and El Dorado Reservoirs; the Ninnescah, Arkansas, and Saline Rivers; Hoover Pond in Kingman, Kingman State Fishing Lake, Lake Afton in Sedgwick County, Sedgwick County Park Lakes, and Carey Park Pond in Hutchinson.

The white perch closely resembles a small white bass, but there are several ways to tell the difference between the two. A white perch's spiny and soft dorsal fins are connected, and both will stand up when the spiny fin is erected. The dorsal fins on a white bass are not connected. White perch also don't possess lines or stripes like a white bass, and are generally silvery green in color.

Human activity is the primary means by which white perch spread. Do not release a white perch once it's been caught, and don't take it to another body of water. In Kansas, it is illegal to possess a live white perch. Anglers who catch a white perch at an infected body of water should dispose of the fish properly. If a white perch is caught at an uninfected water, seal it in a plastic bag, freeze it, note the date and location, and contact the Aquatic Nuisance Species Coordinator at 620-342-0658.

Zebra Mussels: Native to the Black and Caspian Seas, the zebra mussel arrived in the U.S. Great Lakes region in 1988. Since then, the mussel has spread throughout much of the central U.S., where it has caused millions of dollars in damage to developed waterways.

In Kansas, zebra mussels have been found in Council Grove City Lake, Milford Reservoir, Wilson Reservoir, Marion Reservoir, Perry Reservoir, Cheney Reservoir, El Dorado Reservoir, Winfield City Lake, and Lake Afton. The mussels are also established in the rivers that flow out of these impoundments.

Zebra mussels are small, usually the size of a dime, with yellowish-brown shells that feature alternating dark and light stripes. The danger with zebra mussels is multi-faceted. For fisheries biologists, the mussel presents a danger because of its prolific filter feeding. The mussels consume plankton through this filtering process—the same plankton that larval game fish rely upon for their survival. Additionally, the mussels leave the water clearer, which can allow algae blooms to flourish and UV rays to penetrate to deeper depths, damaging fish eggs laid during the spawning season. Furthermore, according to Jason Goeckler, research has shown that zebra mussels also retain some toxins in their body tissue, which has been linked to waterfowl deaths in the Great Lakes region.

Aside from the fisheries concerns, zebra mussels wreak havoc on water systems by forming colonies on pipes and water control structures, which inhibits the flow of water. Nationally, it costs about $145 million each year to control zebra mussels in electric generating plants.

Like the white perch, the spread of zebra mussels is primarily due to human activity. Zebra mussels produce larvae called veligers, which are so small they can't be seen without the aid of a microscope. These veligers float in the water for up to five weeks before growing large enough to search for a hard surface on which to cling. It's during this stage that zebra mussels are able to hitch a ride with boaters, anglers, and skiers—through bilges, livewells, bait buckets, or any water-holding container.

If a zebra mussel is found in a body of water that's not listed as an affected lake, save it, note the date and location, and contact the Aquatic Nuisance Species Coordinator at 620-342-0658.

Asian Carp: Another emerging nuisance in Kansas is the Asian carp. While not as prolific as the white perch or the zebra mussel, the Asian carp is another species capable of outcompeting native fish for food. This fish reproduces quickly and, when young, closely resembles a gizzard shad, which is a popular bait fish. Goeckler said anglers should not transport bait from one body of water to another to avoid introducing this species into untainted fisheries.

Clean, Drain, and Dry

Zebra mussels cannot be controlled, and chemicals that could be used to kill them would also affect fish and other native wildlife. The best hope to stop the spread of zebra mussels is to enlist the help of boaters and educate them to clean, drain, and dry their watercraft when leaving a body of water.

"Any time (anglers) go to any lake, they should follow clean, drain, and dry every time," says KDWP fisheries biologist Craig Johnson. Boaters should inspect their boat and trailer to ensure no mussels are attached to the craft. Clean your equipment before you leave the lake. Remove any mussels that are found. Drain all livewells, bilges, and bait buckets before leaving the area. Afterward, the boat should be washed with water that is at least 140 degrees F. As an alternative, the boat can be cleaned with a 10-percent chlorine solution, or allowed to dry for at least five days before traveling to another body of water. Additionally, fish and plants should never be taken from one body of water to another.

White Bass

Striped Bass

17

Illustrations: © Joe Tomelleri

Wiper　　　　　　　　　**White Perch**

18

Largemouth Bass

Smallmouth Bass

Spotted Bass

White Crappie

20

Blue Catfish, adult

Flathead Catfish

Channel Catfish

Sauger

Saugeye

Walleye

23

Rainbow Trout

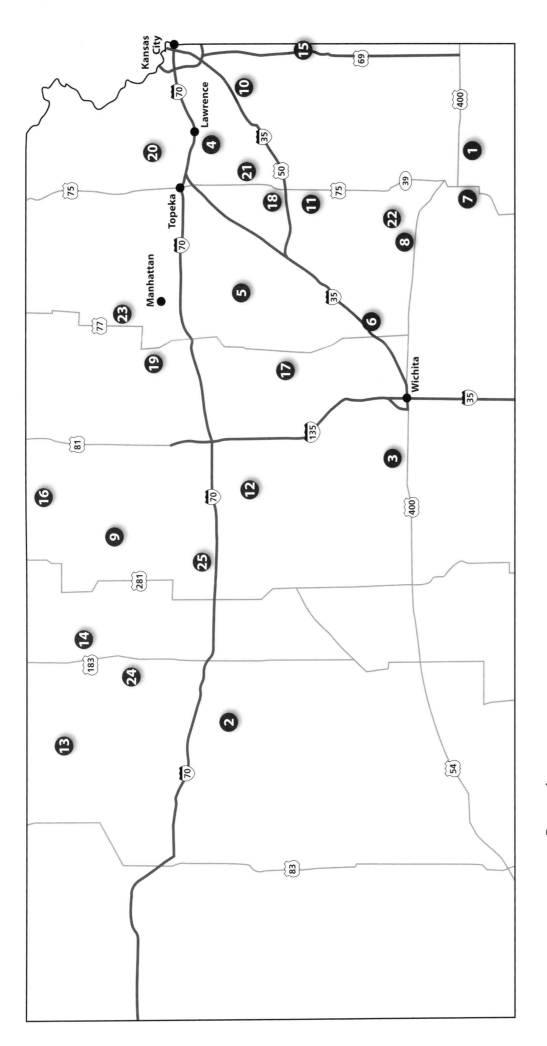

25

Reservoirs

1. Big Hill Reservoir
2. Cedar Bluff Reservoir
3. Cheney Reservoir
4. Clinton Reservoir
5. Council Grove Reservoir
6. El Dorado Reservoir
7. Elk City Reservoir
8. Fall River Reservoir
9. Glen Elder Reservoir
10. Hillsdale Reservoir
11. John Redmond Reservoir
12. Kanopolis Reservoir
13. Keith Sebelius (Norton) Reservoir
14. Kirwin Reservoir
15. La Cygne Reservoir
16. Lovewell Reservoir
17. Marion Reservoir
18. Melvern Reservoir
19. Milford Reservoir
20. Perry Reservoir
21. Pomona Reservoir
22. Toronto Reservoir
23. Tuttle Creek Reservoir
24. Webster Reservoir
25. Wilson Reservoir

Big Hill Reservoir

SIZE: 1,240 acres

LOCATION: About 5 miles east of Cherryvale, Kansas, which sits just east of K-169.

CONTACT: Mound Valley Gate House, 620-328-2050

FEATURE FISH: Largemouth Bass, Smallmouth Bass, Spotted Bass, Crappie, White Bass

DAILY CREEL LIMIT/MINIMUM LENGTH:
Largemouth Bass: 6 fish, 21 inches • Smallmouth Bass: 6 fish, 18 inches • Spotted Bass: 6 fish, 15 inches • Channel Catfish: 10 fish • Flathead Catfish: 5 fish • Crappie: 50 fish • Walleye: 5 fish, 18 inches

Big Hill isn't big (or particularly hilly), but it's big where it really matters—the numbers, size, and variety of angling opportunities. This federal fishing lake in southeast Kansas' Labette County is one of the best largemouth and smallmouth bass fisheries in the state. And the fishing for just about everything else isn't too bad, either.

"It has everything a guy could want in a lake," local angler and tournament bass angler Matthew Smoot, of Chanute, says about Big Hill. "The lake has some good smallmouth fishing, very good largemouth, crappie, and channel cat. Tons and tons of trees, and most of the banks are fairly rocky."

I had driven by Big Hill many times throughout the years, but never stopped to fish the lake until recently. It's an easy lake to overlook on the map, but it's definitely a body of water that should be explored.

Despite the stories I had heard about Big Hill, I was stunned to see the lake in person. The water was clear

enough to see fish cruising along the shoreline. The rocky outcrops and wooded banks of the lake added to the dramatic scene.

While many other lakes in southeast Kansas are subject to seasonal fluctuations in water levels due to heavy spring rains, Big Hill's depth seldom changes. Scan Lynott, fisheries biologist for Big Hill, says that's because the lake was built primarily for recreation, unlike other lakes that serve as flood control tools. "Big Hill is like a state lake on steroids," Lynott says.

Few lakes can offer what Big Hill offers to anglers. The clear water and rocky shoreline create great fish habitat throughout the water for both boat and shore anglers. Additionally, much of the timber in the lake was left standing when the lake was constructed. The combination of good habitat, stable water levels, and low turbidity

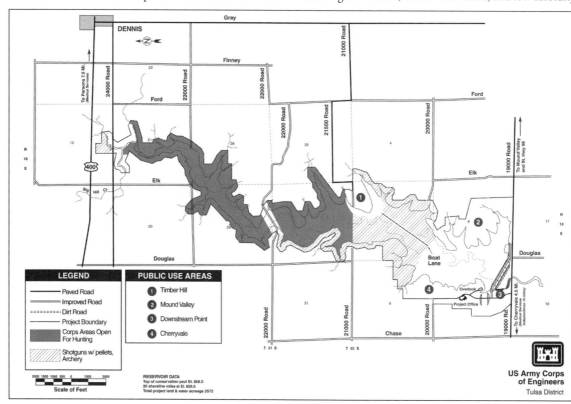

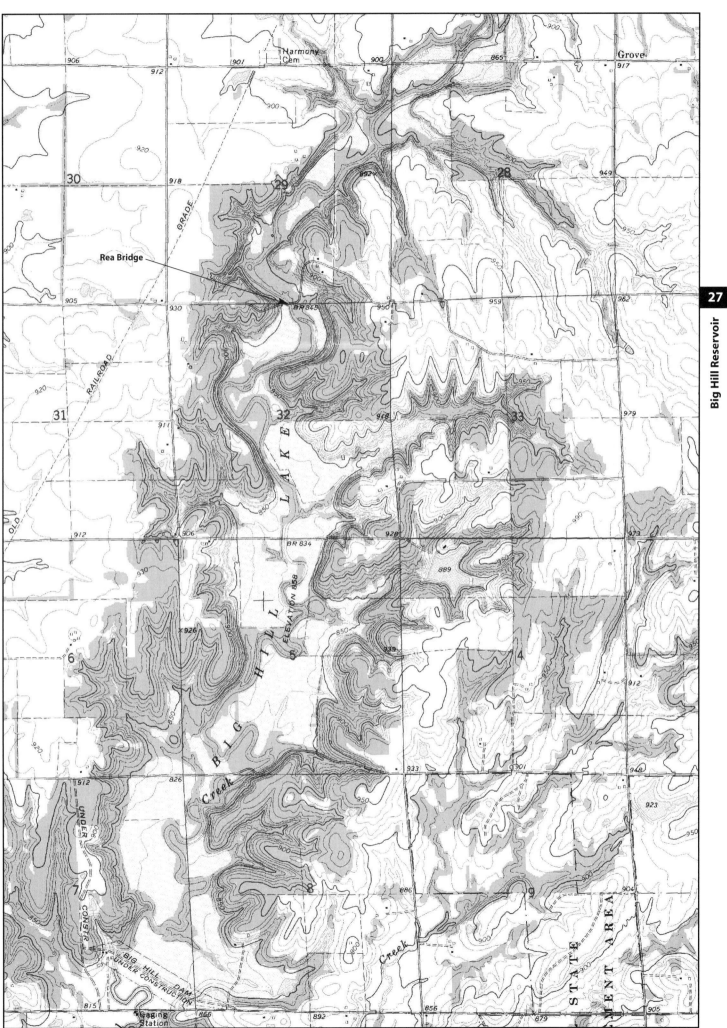

creates a successful environment for reproduction, which, according to Lynott, leads to good yearly recruitment and a stable fish population.

I haven't been able to visit this remarkable lake as often or for as long as I'd like, but the images and ideas of what this lake offers have been etched in my mind. Talking to the people who regularly fish Big Hill only confirmed what I had imagined: this is an incredible fishing lake, designed and managed with the avid angler at its core. Any trip through the southeast part of Kansas isn't complete without a stop at Big Hill—even if it's just for a picnic or a quick rest from the road.

Feature Fish

Black bass: According to the U.S. Army Corps of Engineers, a shoreline stabilization project began in 1996 to decrease the effects of erosion at Big Hill. The Kansas Department of Wildlife and Parks began planting water willows along the shoreline, and today approximately 80 percent of the lake's shores are filled with living fish attractors. The lake's bass and sunfish populations thrive in the water willows, according to the Corps. That ample shoreline habitat, coupled with the standing timber that was left in approximately 80 percent of the lake, makes Big Hill one of the most popular lakes in the area for bass tournaments.

Smoot says the lake is filled with both standing timber and "laydowns," or trees that have fallen and offer good hiding places for fish. According to Smoot, the lake has four distinct zones. The area near the dam, for the most part, is open water with fewer trees. The riprap along the dam, however, is a popular place for smallmouth anglers.

The second area, just to the north of Downstream Point, is characterized by fairly heavy underwater timber. Buoys mark a clear boat lane through the area and will lead boaters to Timber Hill, toward the northeast. Smoot says the area around the Timber Hill boat ramp offers a lot of good fishing holes, and a separate pond behind the Timber Hill boat ramp cove is worth trying.

"A lot of fish come out of there," he says.

The area between Timber Hill and the Rea Bridge spanning the lake makes up the third zone. Smoot says there are a lot of deep water areas to fish, where anglers find some smallmouth, but primarily largemouth and spotted bass. The area is heavily timbered, and the shoreline is marked by rocky bluffs, adding to the fish-holding qualities of the area.

But the area isn't without its dangers. "If you don't know where you're going, you better take it slow," Smoot says. He should know—he once lost a lower unit in his boat to an underwater tree stump in this area.

The last zone of the lake is from the Rea Bridge, in the northern part of the lake, to the entry point of the Big Hill Creek that feeds the lake. Smoot said the bridge is a

"hot spot" for both bass and crappie. The water is generally shallow—less than 20 feet deep—and Smoot again warns anglers to idle their way through the area because of the heavy timber in this location.

In the spring, Smoot heavily fishes the area around the bridge, where he says a lot of crappie have been caught along the bridge pilings. The area north of the bridge offers anglers several coves that hold fish, as well as additional ponds that are available for fishing. The water becomes much more shallow in this area—sometimes as shallow as 5 feet—but the fishing in this area might just be worth dodging the timber. "They hammer some good fish up there in the spring," he says.

Mark Kirkpatrick, of Wichita, who fishes Big Hill as part of the American Bass Angler tournament circuit, also praises the lake's productivity. "It's really a great lake to fish," he says. While many tournament anglers head toward the river in the spring, Kirkpatrick stays in the main lake, targeting smallmouth along the dam and off rocky points, or along the spawning grounds in the coves. Often, he'll look for weed beds in the coves or adjacent to rocky areas and find the fish he's looking for—that's the method he used to land first place in the November 2009 ABA tournament at Big Hill.

Once he finds a pattern, Kirkpatrick knows he'll be catching fish all day. Black and blue jigs are "primary" colors at the lake, but other favorites include green, pumpkin, and red or orange plastics, often with a beaver tail–patterned tube jig.

During the summer—and even into the fall—Kirkpatrick says the topwater action shouldn't be overlooked. The fish will hit a topwater popper or a floating crankbait in the early morning or evening hours, and the smallmouth will still strike on minnow patterned lures. The key, Kirkpatrick says, is to try different patterns until you can learn how the fish are holding and what they're hitting. "There are so many fish and so much cover—you just have to find the pattern," Kirkpatrick says.

Lynott confirmed that evidence of largemouth bass virus has been found, though there are no human implications and the virus hasn't yet created any sort of fish kill. The virus can be spread through water, however, so KDWP suggests following the same practice used to stem the spread of zebra mussels—clean, drain, and dry your boat and anything that comes in contact with the water.

Recent sampling at the lake shows that 5 percent of largemouth are over 20 inches long. In the spring, Lynott suggests looking for largemouth in shallow water—depths of 1–6 feet—and working the deeper areas along those shallow spots. Early in the season, traditional baits such as spinnerbaits and jigs will work, but Lynott warns that these fish learn quickly and many are caught and released—making them savvy to traditional baits. Later in the season, switch to "finesse" baits and plastics to pull largemouth out of their timber hiding spots.

Anglers at Big Hill enjoy quality smallmouth bass fishing that's not found in many places in southeast Kansas. An 18-inch length limit is in place, and recent samples show good-sized fish, with one weighing in at 4 pounds. Lynott suggests fishing for smallmouth along the riprap of the dam or in other rocky areas, casting crawfish imitations from April through June. Later in the year, he recommends shad imitations, fishing for suspended fish in deeper water. The always-exciting topwater lures are successful in the early morning and late evening hours, and Lynott says blue and white have recently been successful colors. If you wait until Memorial Day to hit Big Hill, you'll likely miss out on some of the best fishing of the year. According to Lynott, smallmouth aren't as active once the summer season begins.

White Bass: The white bass population at Big Hill has been climbing since 1991, and now it appears that the population has stabilized. Lynott's sampling shows that 30 percent of the whites are more than 12 inches long. One popular area is around the Timber Hill campground, and Lynott suggests using shad imitations throughout the year for these voracious feeders. During the summer months, whites can be found chasing schools of shad near the surface, and casting just about anything that looks like a shad is sure to hook a fish.

Crappie: According to the KDWP's 2008 creel survey, anglers most preferred to catch crappie at Big Hill. Lynott estimates about 30,000 crappie were taken from the lake in 2009, with an average length of 10 inches. According to the recent biologist's sampling, more than 54 percent of the crappie population is over 10 inches in length, and Lynott says he's never seen the crappie population as healthy as it is right now. He suggests looking for spawning crappie in the spring along the rocky shoreline, using small jigs and minnows cast toward weed beds. In the fall, the fish are likely to be found in deep-water brush and timber.

Other Fishing: While the bulk of anglers spend their time looking for bass and crappie, Big Hill offers great opportunities for other species as well. Sunfish can be caught from the fishing docks and around the water willows along the shoreline. The lake also has a good population of channel cats and flatheads, both of which are hard-fighting fish that will give anglers a memorable battle.

Facilities

In addition to the excellent fishing at Big Hill, the area around the lake is breathtaking. Big Hill sits in an area of Kansas known as the "Little Ozarks" and is one of the few places in Kansas where deciduous trees cover the landscape, including much of the lake's shoreline. The Corps area includes the 17-mile **Big Hill Horse Trail,** which offers a variety of terrain and striking views for horseback riders. Additionally, the **Ruth Nixon Memorial Trail** is about a mile in length and follows a series of birdhouses. Both trails wind their way through scenic areas and offer a great chance to enjoy Kansas wildlife.

For those looking for a longer stay, this Corps-managed lake provides plenty of camping areas, all open March 26–November 1. The **Mound Valley North and South** campground areas and the **Timber Hill** areas offer boat ramps. Check local postings for more information, as there is a daily launching fee for use of boat ramps in Corps-managed areas.

Timber Hill camping area: approximately 20 non-electric sites, drinking water, restrooms, trailer dump station, boat ramp, boat dock, fishing dock, and horse trail.

Cherryvale Park camping area: approximately 23 electrical hookups and no primitive sites, group campsite available for $120 and can be reserved in advance, drinking water, restrooms, showers, trailer dump station, fishing berm, hiking trail, horse trail, playground, and ball field.

Mound Valley camping area: approximately 64 electrical hookups and no primitive sites, includes some ADA accessible sites, drinking water, restrooms, showers, trailer dump station, boat ramp, boat dock, fishing dock, hiking trail, playground, and swimming beach with change house.

Shopping/Supplies

G&W Foods sells licenses, tackle, and supplies. Open 7:00 a.m. to 8:00 p.m. daily. 1007 S. Commercial St., Oswego, 620-795-4431. **3 Weiner Dogs Bait and Tackle Shop,** 324 W. Main St., Cherryvale, 620-891-0194. **Jump Start,** open 24 hours a day, 120 S. 3rd St., Chetopa, 620-236-7200.

Cedar Bluff Reservoir

SIZE: 6,870 acres

LOCATION: 13 miles south of I-70 Ogallah Interchange (Exit 135) on K-147

CONTACT: KDWP Cedar Bluff area office, 785-726-3212

FEATURE FISH: Largemouth Bass, Smallmouth Bass, Spotted Bass, Crappie, Walleye, White Bass, Wiper

DAILY CREEL LIMIT/MINIMUM LENGTH:
Largemouth Bass: 5 fish, 15 inches • Smallmouth Bass: 5 fish, 15 inches • Spotted Bass: 5 fish, 15 inches • Channel Catfish: 10 fish • Flathead Catfish: 5 fish • Crappie: 50 fish • Walleye: 5 fish, 18 inches • Wiper: 2 fish

What Cedar Bluff Reservoir has needed more than anything else in recent years is water. Once one of Kansas' premier bass fisheries, the western Kansas lake has suffered low water since 2001, which has altered the lake's ecology and created challenging conditions for black bass. In 2009, the lake was 17 feet below conservation pool level—and while that might seem disturbingly low, consider that in 1991 the lake was 52 feet below conservation pool.

During the early part of the 1990s, Cedar Bluff was 11 feet deep at its deepest level; today the depth finders will mark 55-foot water in some areas near the dam. After several years of decent rainfall, the water level has stabilized and anglers are returning to the lake to some success. What they're fishing for, however, has changed slightly since the days when tournament anglers used to roam the waters.

"This is a boom or bust lake," Kansas Department of Wildlife and Parks fisheries biologists Dave Spalsbury says. "The water level and water history determine every-thing." Spalsbury says the lake still holds a decent number of largemouth and smallmouth bass, but anglers now spend more time chasing open-water fish like wipers, white bass, and walleye.

That's what La Crosse resident and superintendent of the local school system Bill Keeley spends his time in search of. "The wipers are kind of our specialty," he says. Keeley, who grew up in Dodge City, has been fishing Cedar Bluff since he "was in diapers." Over the years, he's seen the changes in the lake and the fish population, and adjusted his fishing accordingly. When he was a young-ster, the lake was full of water. By the time he was in high school, the water had dropped steadily.

But then rain and flooding in 1993 and 1994 recharged the lake. That sparked an explosion in the num-ber of largemouth in the lake, and turned Cedar Bluff into one of the best tournament lakes in the Midwest during the 1990s. As the '90s moved to the new millennium, however, the water levels began to drop again, until rains returned in 2007.

What occurred during those years of drought, though, plays an important role in catching fish today. Parking lots were built with rocky abutments, roads were created, and campgrounds were established. Today those features that made the lake usable in the 1980s are under-water and make the lake more fish-able today.

"We call it the paper route," Keeley says. "There are about 30 spots that we hit, and the fish are usually biting at one of them. On that lake, it's old parking lots and roads and fire pits. We'll tell a guy to cast over there by the bush, you'll come over some rocks. The people in the boat

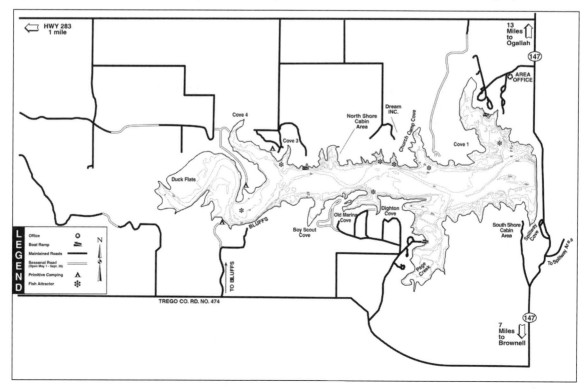

will look at you like you're joking. Sure enough, they'll get a bite and they think you're a genius, but we just know the lake so well."

• • •

I never got the chance to fish Cedar Bluff during its heyday, but I remember the stories about massive largemouth, and plenty of them, being pulled from the water. It's a lake I always wanted to visit, but I didn't get a chance to until well after the boom of the '90s was a distant memory.

Yet, the lake still made an impression on me. The water is clear, and there is plenty of structure to fish, even for an angler who doesn't know all of Keeley's hotspots. My most recent trip to Cedar Bluff didn't yield an amazing number of fish, but it was enough to keep me maneuvering around the shorelines, looking for the next fish.

The lake's biologist suggested fishing the rocky area under the lake's namesake—the Cedar Bluffs. The limestone cliffs reach down into the water and are a striking sight from the water or land. Cedar Bluff is a scenic and inviting body of water by any standard, and the contrast to the windswept high plains makes the lake even more remarkable.

Cedar Bluff will become a regular stop for me in the future, and I'm hopeful that the largemouth population will return to its former glory. In the meantime, however, there's still plenty of fun to be found at this remarkable high plains lake.

Feature Fish

Black Bass: With adequate water levels, Cedar Bluff now provides plenty of habitat for fish to thrive. The lake's shoreline provides a considerable amount of rocky structure that serves as habitat for smallmouth bass. After nearly a decade of low water levels, the lake now includes ample underwater timber, as well as flooded salt cedar trees, just under the surface near many parts of the lake.

In addition to the existing structure, biologists have worked to establish several deep-water brush piles to serve as fish attractors at Cedar Bluff. One such site is the Bluffs—the sheer limestone bluffs that rise above the lake's southern rim. Other brush piles are set up at the mouths of several coves along the lake, including Dighton Cove and Church Camp Cove. Most of the brush piles are easy to spot thanks to marker buoys placed by the KDWP.

Spalsbury says smallmouth bass often can be caught near the dam, under the bluffs, or along other rocky shorelines, particularly along the south shoreline. He suggests looking for eroded boulders in the water, which often hold smallmouth nearby.

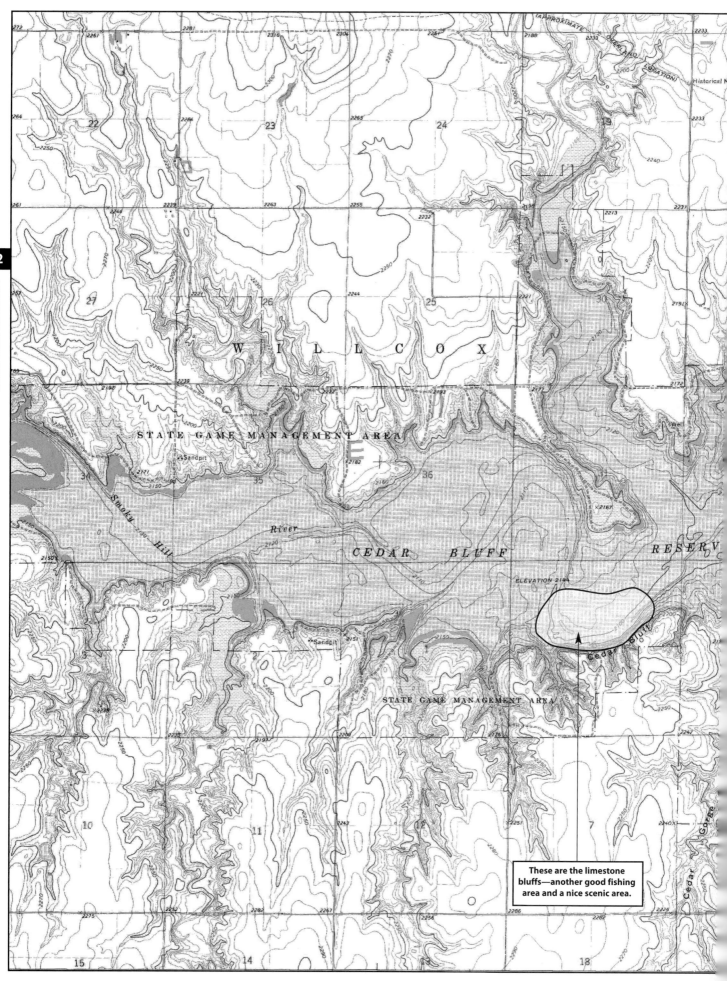

These are the limestone bluffs—another good fishing area and a nice scenic area.

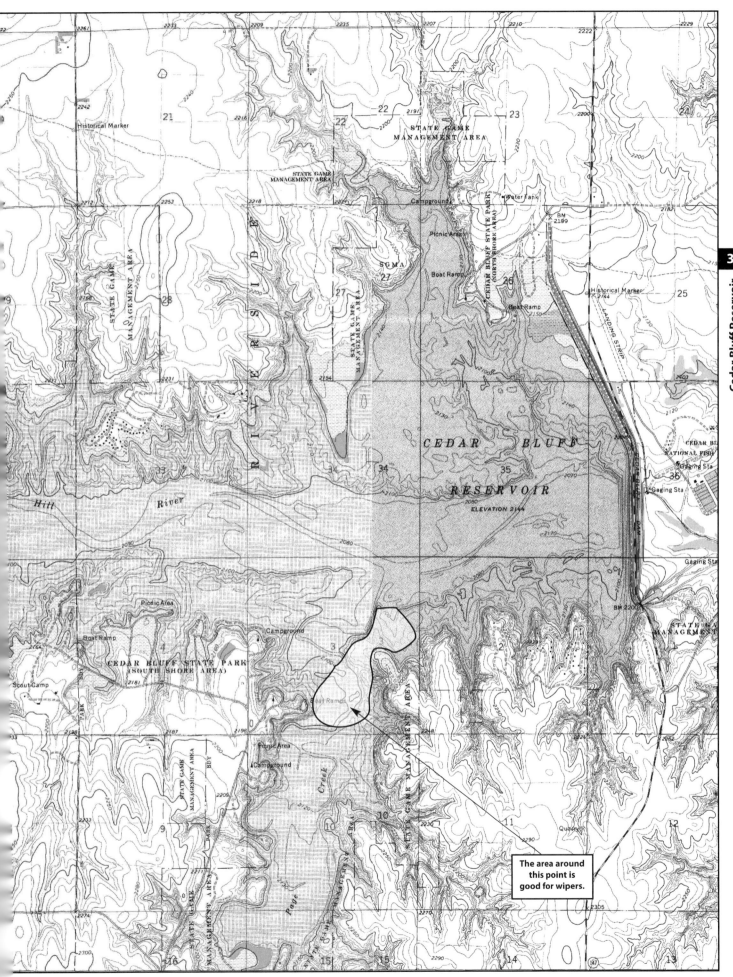

The area around this point is good for wipers.

Largemouth and spotted bass numbers continue to hold up well, although larger fish are harder to find. With plenty of flooded timber and vegetation in the lake, anglers can generally find success pulling spinnerbaits or a jig and pig through the brush. The state of black bass fishing tends to mirror the status of the water level, with the best time to catch the fish in the spring.

Look for largemouth and smallmouth around aquatic vegetation and rocky areas, such as the limestone bluffs. Brushy habitat in the spring offers the best chance for black bass, though rocky shorelines and points with rock bottoms provide cover for spotted and smallmouth bass. The population has suffered from low water levels, but should improve, as the water level has remained steady in the past few years. The face of the dam also offers good prospects for smallmouth fishing.

Wiper/White Bass: Anglers can find wipers in just about any part of the lake, but one key area is found along the southern shoreline, near the mouth of the Page Creek cove. The Page Creek channel works its way to the main body of the lake, creating an ideal location for wipers near the mouth of the cove—where the deep creek bed runs alongside the more shallow shoreline. Additionally, any windblown point along the lake, particularly in shallow water, is a good bet during the spring months.

Trolling shallow shad-imitation baits or casting bucktail jigs both work well in the spring. As summer sets in, the wipers move to deeper water, and Spalsbury says they can be caught with live bait, such as shad or sunfish. As the mercury rises, and the shad in the lake become readily available, top water baits can attract wipers looking for an easy meal.

Keeley follows seasonal patterns when looking for wipers. In the early part of spring—April and May—there's a short period of time when Keeley will catch wipers on topwater baits cast into the salt cedar trees in shallow areas. The adult shad spawn in the cedars, and the wipers follow. The period lasts only about two weeks, Keeley said, and he uses larger Zara Spook topwater plugs—generally 6–8 inches long—to land wipers ranging from 8 to 12 pounds.

As spring gives way to summer, Keeley changes his approach by fishing with live bait in 30–35 feet of water. Many anglers at Cedar Bluff use sunfish, perch, carp, goldfish, or live shad rigged to a heavy weight—1–1½ ounces—to keep the bait near the bottom. Most often, Keeley will anchor in one location, but sometimes he'll slowly pull the bait using an electric trolling motor.

During this time of year, setting up off of windblown points offers the best chance of success, as the Kansas wind pushes bait fish toward the windward shore. Often, however, the wind blows too hard in Kansas to anchor a boat, in which case it's best to search for structure along the leeward shoreline. "Sometimes it's so windy you just fish where you can," Keeley says.

Another successful method is slabbing. Keeley says some people prefer to tie on a large spoon or slab—something big, with a flash—and drop it down in front of a school of fish located on a fish finder, which should appear as arches about 25 feet down. Quickly lift the rod tip to raise the bait about two to three feet, then let it flutter its way back down. If the fish are eating, the fluttering flash should trigger a strike.

But Keeley offers two warnings. First, look for a school of fish on the finder when slabbing—a fish here or there isn't enough for this approach. Second, know that sometimes the fish just won't hit, no matter how close you put that bait in front of them. "The most frustrating thing is when we're sitting over a school, and on the screen there are hundreds of wipers," Keeley says. "And we've got the bait in front of them, and they won't bite. That will make a grown man cry. It makes you want to stick your head in the water. Fortunately, that doesn't happen too often."

During the hotter part of the summer—in late July and August—Keeley again changes his approach by looking for signs of schooling fish that are chasing shad toward the surface.

During the spring, it's not uncommon to hook into a wiper while fishing for walleye, Keeley says. The walleye move toward the dam during the spawn in early spring, but move toward hard-bottomed points and old road beds later in the spring. The normal jig and crawler rig is productive during this period.

Keeley says he takes the rig over some of his well-known memorized fishing holes—the old campground parking lot, roadways, and rock piles. To find those, however, you'll have to fish the lake as long as he has fished it. "Knowing the lake helps," Keeley said. "We've fished it so long, we know where to find the rocks, and what types of rocks they are. Mostly, we know what was there."

Facilities

Cedar Bluff State Park spans 1,100 acres divided between two areas. Bluffton is on the north shore of Cedar Bluff. **Page Creek** is on the south side and offers a lot of primitive camping in addition to electric sites. In total, the park offers: 121 utility campsites; 10 sites with water, sewer and electric; 91 sites with water and electric; 20 sites with electric only; 300 non-utility sites; a group campground with 12 utility sites; 5 cabins; 5 shower houses; 3 dump stations; 4 shelter houses; 11 boat ramp lanes; 5 courtesy docks; a marina; 2 fish cleaning stations; and 1 swimming beach. Camping is also allowed in designated areas on the wildlife area.

Shopping/Supplies

Sport Haven offers fuel, fishing tackle and bait, camping and boating supplies, food, boat repair, boat sales, and storage. Located on K-147, near the entrance to the state park, 785-726-4457.

Mr. Quick Bait, 1003 Main St., Hays, 785-628-1865; **Southside Convenience,** 703 Vine St., Hays, 785-628-2411.

Generally, where there are wipers, there are bound to be white bass, Spalsbury says of the late spring and early summer pattern. Keeley looks for the schooling whites—marked by an area of surface breaking by shad—and knows that the bigger wipers are lurking underneath waiting for a free meal.

"If you want to catch whites, throw something small," Keeley says, adding that during a white bass feeding frenzy, an angler can catch the fish on a "beer can with a hook." For the wipers, though, he'll throw out a larger Rapala minnow or cast a large Zara Spook and walk it through the feeding area. The white bass might tap the lure, but they won't take it. An explosion on the water, though, is a sure sign that the larger wipers have moved up after your bait.

Crappie: Another popular method of fishing for white bass and crappie at Cedar Bluff is night fishing with floating lights, Spalsbury says. The lights attract insects, bait fish, and eventually the bigger fish anglers are seeking.

Cedar Bluff has suffered from low numbers of crappie in past years, though the population has stabilized and is showing some signs of growth. The best chance for successful crappie fishing is in the spring, around the spawning beds in April, or in the deep water brush piles in the fall.

Walleye: Though Cedar Bluff isn't known for its walleye population, recent biologist sampling data shows an increase in the walleye population during the past several years. Keeley says his crew finds success with a floating jig head and a nightcrawler. He generally ties on a swivel, with a weight and a two-foot leader to the jig head. The leader, coupled with the floating jig, keeps the worm off the bottom and in easy view of hungry walleye.

Cheney Reservoir

SIZE: 9,950 acres

LOCATION: 24 miles west of Wichita on US 400/54. Turn north on K-251 and travel 4.5 miles to County Road 556. Follow to the west into the state park.

CONTACT: Cheney State Park, 316-542-3664

FEATURE FISH: Channel Catfish, Crappie, Walleye, White Bass, Wiper

DAILY CREEL LIMIT/MINIMUM LENGTH:
Largemouth Bass: 5 fish, 15 inches • Blue Catfish: 5 fish, 35 inches • Channel Catfish: 10 fish • Flathead Catfish: 5 fish • Crappie: 50 fish, 10 inches • Striped Bass: 2 fish, 21 inches • Walleye: 2 fish, 21 inches • Wiper: 2 fish, 21 inches

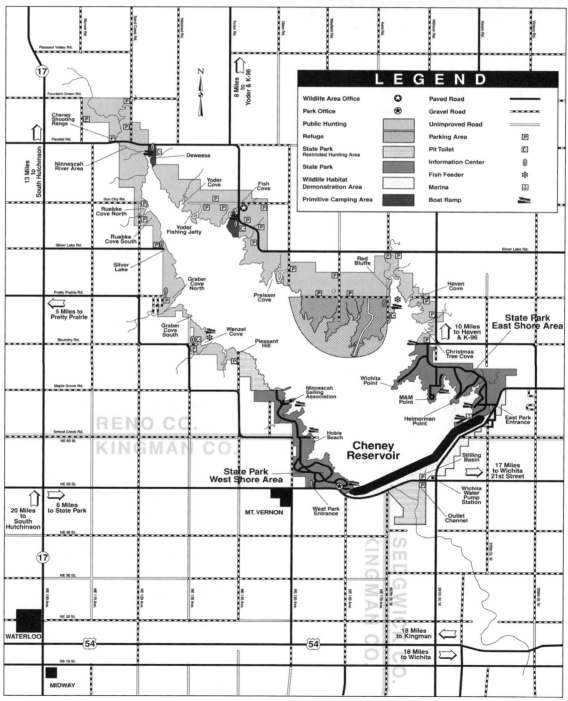

The remarkable thing about Cheney is that it's strikingly unremarkable. Unlike some of Kansas' more scenic lakes, Cheney Reservoir, which sits less than a half hour west of Wichita, doesn't offer scenic cliffs or crystal-clear water. It's not loaded with row after row of standing timber or fish holding vegetation. But that's not altogether bad.

"The thing about Cheney is that there's not much structure," Mike Cook, who owns Wichita's Four Lake Guides, says. "So when you find structure, there's a good chance you'll find fish." And Cook says it doesn't take much structure at Cheney to hold fish. A single lay down, a small hump, or an old ditch will do the trick. "The fish will be there, even if that structure is just a blip on the graph."

Cheney is one of my favorite Kansas lakes to visit in the early spring—generally before March 15—to fish the dam for big spawning walleye. The weather is still cool, and late winter storms can still move into the area, but Cheney's big walleye are worth it.

I'll walk over the backside of the dam with a head lamp, plenty of floating Rapala crank baits, and a warm winter coat. After dark, the walleye move up to the shore of the dam, where they can be seen rolling in just inches of water. I've caught some big walleye along Cheney's dam by casting a crank bait parallel to the dam—but outside of that, few things are certain. Sometimes a fast retrieve is the trick; other times a slow retrieve is what's needed. Eventually, though, something will hit that crank bait—and it's likely to be big.

This sort of fishing should come with a warning, however. It's dark, it's on uneven surfaces, and the wind usually blows from the north, across the lake and straight into your face. I've tangled up lines and then had to untangle them in the dark. A friend of mine accidentally tossed his fishing pole into the lake when his hands were too numb to hold it—only to catch it later with a different rig and pull it to shore. On more than one occasion, I've fallen into the icy waters, courtesy of the dam's concrete embankment, which becomes incredibly slick when soaked with water.

And if you, too, happen to fall in, remember this advice: crawl out, don't try to stand up and walk. Trust me, I know.

Feature Fish

Walleye: Jon Stein, who worked until mid-2009 as the fisheries biologist at Cheney, says the walleye population has enjoyed several good year classes that are keeping high numbers of big fish in the lake. During a recent fish sampling, current fisheries biologist Jeff Koch found that 46 percent of walleye were 15–20-inches long. "The fishing is spectacular," says Koch. Recent angler creel surveys showed that one in six fish caught by Cheney anglers measured longer than the 21-inch length limit at Cheney.

The invasive white perch was accidentally introduced into the lake in the mid-1990s, and in 2002 a white perch management plan was put in place. That plan included an aggressive length and creel limit for two of the lake's most voracious eaters—walleye and wiper. As a part of the effort to build up the number of predators in the lake, each has a 21-inch length limit and a 2 fish creel limit.

In 2008, efforts to curb the white perch population got a helping hand from an especially cold winter. A large number of white perch died and washed downstream, and today anglers can catch perch in the 8–12-inch range—a dramatic change from the smaller fish that once overpopulated the lake and made fishing with a worm almost impossible. The coming years should offer strong fishing, as well—many of the fish measured 11–15 inches long, indicating a strong and healthy class of fish for the future.

Hit the face of the dam in early to mid-March, casting a 4-inch or longer Rapala crankbait—Firetiger is the color most used by anglers. Post-spawn, the walleye move toward the islands near Fish Cove, and around other structure in the lake. A jig and crawler works well if you can keep the white perch out of your way. While some anglers anchor around the islands or drift over them, others stick with trolling crankbaits around the structure.

Stein says the best way to learn where the fish are biting is to look for boats. "There's always boats on them on the weekends," he says of the walleye hot spots in the lake.

Wiper: Mike Cook spends much of his time in search of the big wipers at Cheney, and though they can be caught year-round, the approach changes with each season. During the summer months, the wipers can be found chasing shad to the surface—mainly in July and August. "I'll start throwing a Kastmaster—but it doesn't really matter what it is—and rip back on it until a fish stops it," Cook says. Another method is to troll around the islands—located near Fish Cove—or off the face of the dam with a brightly colored crankbait.

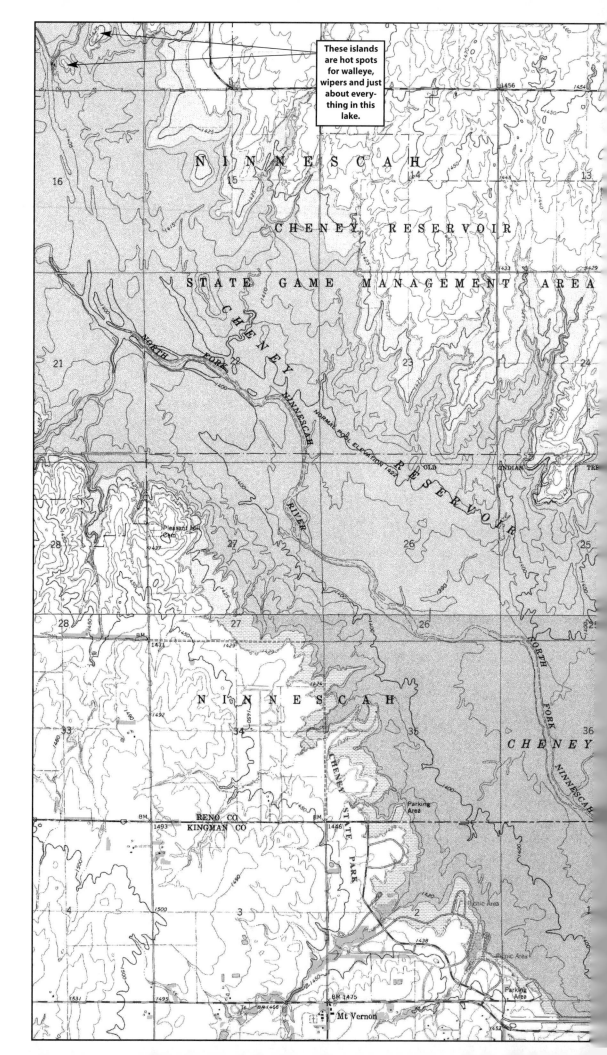

These islands are hot spots for walleye, wipers and just about everything in this lake.

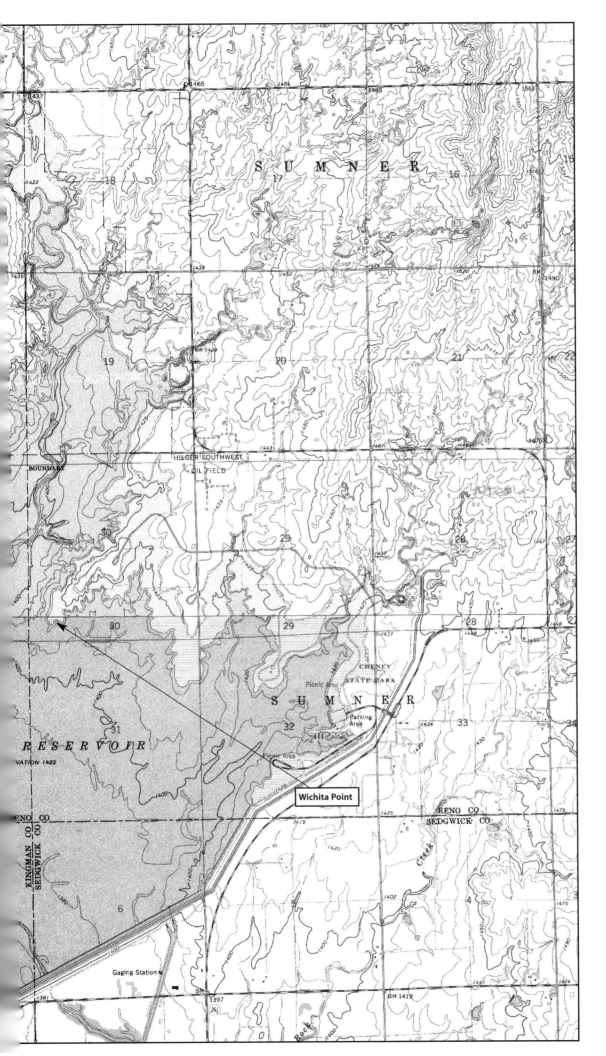

Wichita Point

Most of the time, however, Cook fishes the wind—if it's out of the south, he fishes the north, and vice versa. Cheney offers several points on which anglers can position their boats—Wichita Point, M&M Point, Heimerman Point, and Refuge Point among them. In the spring, the wipers tend to run into the shallower water, but by November, Cook says, the wipers can be found 20–25 feet deep.

As big as the walleye are known to get at Cheney, the lake holds even bigger wipers. Stein caught a wiper that topped 15 pounds during recent fish sampling. The anglers he talked with also indicated that they were hooking large fish—some of which were snapping lines before they could make it to the boat.

The proof, however, can be found on the Snyder's Marina website (www.snyderscheneymarina.com), where Tammera Snyder posts photos of proud anglers. "You have to know where the habitat is," Snyder says.

Catfish: As the weather heats up in July, start looking for channel catfish, which can be found throughout the lake. "A lot of people are catching them up in the Ninnescah," says Candice Black, owner of Shorty's Lakeside Country Store. She says any sort of stink bait, or shrimp, will attract the cats, while Snyder says many people will fillet a caught white perch from head to tail and use the meat for bait.

Like his wiper fishing method, Cook uses the wind when fishing for catfish. The windier it is, the more shallow he'll fish—sometimes in as little as two feet of water. "I've caught 25-pound catfish in two foot of water," Cook says. The wind pushes dead fish and other food to the windward side of the lake, Cook explains, just as small shad are pushed into coves and points by the wind. If a cove or other structure doesn't produce fish, Cook wastes little time in moving to another location—knowing that the cats are somewhere patrolling for food.

"A guy told me one time that a catfish's job, whether he likes it or not, is to clean the bottom of the lake," Cook says. "So I fish the wind, and I fish structure."

Look for catfish in the Ninnescah River, in the upper end of the lake and in the coves opposite the wind. Stinkbaits and liver work well. Cut bait is another favorite choice, and since Cheney has so many white perch, there's no need to buy any—just catch the perch and fillet your own bait.

Crappie: Cheney is beginning to experience a resurgence in angling for crappie—a species that held a high ranking in the lake prior to the white perch infestation. More anglers are looking for crappie, and some are finding success in the early spring while the fish are spawning in coves with timber or vegetation. Black says that, while some are being caught, many aren't big enough to keep—giving hope that the crappie population in the years to come will offer an additional opportunity at the lake.

Look for crappie in the spring as they head to the coves to spawn. Tube jigs and beaver tail patterns work well. At other times of the year, look for underwater structure and brush piles. The crappie fishing is just beginning to pick up steam and should improve in the coming years.

White Bass: Cheney used to be known for legendary white bass runs up the Ninnescah River, but the white perch population out-competed the white bass for food. Recent gill net samples showed relatively few numbers of white bass, though some large fish were netted. "Hopefully, we'll get a good year class here in the next year or two, or the white bass fishing might be slim for awhile," Koch says.

Look for white bass on the windward side of points—such as Refuge, M&M, Wichita, and Heimerman—during the early spring. In the later spring, fish around the islands near Fish Cove, and in the summer look for these fish to chase schools of shad to the surface. Trolling brightly colored crankbaits works well around the islands and points. Throw something flashing when they're chasing shad. The Ninnescah River above the lake is also a good spot in April, when they make the annual spawning run.

The best advice from Stein for anglers new to Cheney is to find the top of an island, or similar change in water level, and fish around that structure. "There are about seven or eight species that hang out there that can be caught on a jig and crawler," Stein says.

Cook's suggestion is to pay attention to the wind, and to fish in shallower water than you think you should. "Cheney is different than other lakes to fish, due to the slope," Cook says. "When you're fishing Cheney, fish shallow, and when you find structure, you'll find fish."

Facilities

Cheney Reservoir crosses three counties—Sedgwick, Kingman, and Reno. The park covers 1,900 acres in two areas on the east and west sides of the lake, and includes Giefer Creek and Spring Creek nature trails. In total, the park offers: 223 campsites with water and electric; 274 non-utility sites; 7 rental cabins; 9 shower houses; 4 dump stations; 4 shelter houses; 22 boat ramp lanes; 3 courtesy docks; 2 fish cleaning stations; and 4 swimming beaches.

Shopping/Supplies

Shorty's Lakeside Country Store carries some boating and fishing supplies, and bait, including minnows. Beer, soft drinks, packaged foods. Some menu items, including biscuits and gravy on weekend mornings. Closed Mondays. Open 8:00 a.m.–6:00 p.m. Tuesday and Wednesday; 8:00 a.m.–9:00 p.m. Thursday–Sunday. Kitchen menu available until 6:00 p.m. most days. Hours may vary based on season and business level. 15541 N.E. 60th St., Cheney, 316-542-9924. **Snyder's Marina** offers boating supplies, fishing tackle and some bait. Packaged food, beer, soft drinks, camping/cookout needs. Slip rental available; winterization service available, but no mechanic on duty. Open March 15–October 15. Call ahead for days and hours. East Side Cheney State Park, 316-542-0163.

Don's Bait Shop, 16 E. Ave. D, South Hutchinson, 620-662-1407; **Heartland Outdoors**, 1 Heartland Dr., South Hutchinson, 620-664-6103; **L&D Tackle**, 129 E. 4th Ave., Hutchinson, 620-259-7015; **Oliver's Carry Out - Burgers and Bait**, 1228 E. 4th Ave., Hutchinson, 620-669-8639.

Clinton Reservoir

SIZE: 7,000 acres

LOCATION: 4 miles west of Lawrence on K-10

CONTACT: Clinton Project Office, U.S. Army Corps of Engineers, 785-843-7665

FEATURE FISH: Largemouth Bass, Smallmouth Bass, Blue Catfish, Channel Catfish, Flathead Catfish, Crappie, Walleye, White Bass, Wiper

DAILY CREEL LIMIT/MINIMUM LENGTH: Largemouth Bass: 5 fish, 18 inches • Smallmouth Bass: 5 fish, 15 inches • Blue Catfish: 10 fish • Channel Catfish: 10 fish • Flathead Catfish: 5 fish • Sauger: 5 fish, 15 inches • Striped Bass: 2 fish • Wiper: 2 fish, 18 inches

Chat "Crappie" Martin has a secret that he doesn't mind sharing with just about anyone he meets. Crappie can be caught in the hottest of weather—even in July and August, when most crappie anglers put away their gear and spend their time looking for catfish.

What's more, those fish aren't found in deep water or sunken brush piles—they're found in just a few feet of water and can be brought into the boat by the angler who has the knowledge to find those summertime crappie and the patience to entice them into hitting. "Every tree has one crappie on it," Martin says. "It's his territory, and he's there guarding it."

Martin's home lake of Clinton Reservoir, which sits just outside of Lawrence, is loaded with the sort of trees he's looking for. And by extension, it's full of the crappie he's looking for, too.

Clinton is fed by Rock Creek and the Wakarusa River, and the lake offers plenty of habitat for not only crappie, but bass, walleye and a variety of other sportfish. Construction on the dam began in 1971, and the U.S. Army Corps of Engineers began filling the lake in 1977. Clinton Lake serves as flood control for the Wakarusa River Valley downstream, and helps control flooding in the Kansas, Missouri, and Mississippi Rivers. The lake has 85 miles of shoreline, and provides up to 10 million gallons of water each day to the nearby city of Lawrence, according to the Corps. Additionally, the land around the lake is carefully managed for the benefit of local wildlife.

Unfortunately for me, my trip to Clinton occurred during an unexpected heat wave that kept the temperatures near the 90s, even through the night. And while the summer air was miserable, my family and I had decided to set up camp in a tent, which only made the heat worse. We couldn't even enjoy a proper campfire because it only made the temperature even more unbearable.

However, in the early morning hours I found a crappie every now and then just as Chat Martin described—hovering around a lonely tree to which I had tied off the boat. The fishing for me didn't last long on those mornings—I was generally off the water by 11:00 a.m.—but it served as a nice distraction from impending heat that was sure to strike by early afternoon.

Fishing aside, though, Clinton is a lake of many uses. It has a sizeable network of trails that wind their way around the lake. The swimming beach in Clinton State Park can accommodate a large number of people. Its location, tucked into a cove and hidden behind a grove of trees, makes it feel as if one has stepped away from this traditionally busy lake and entered a secret lagoon.

With its proximity to the college town of Lawrence, Clinton experiences times of high traffic. It's a popular camping location, and several big events take place throughout the year. The marina is a hot spot during the summer, with fishing boats, ski boats, and monstrous party barges all sharing the water. Timing—

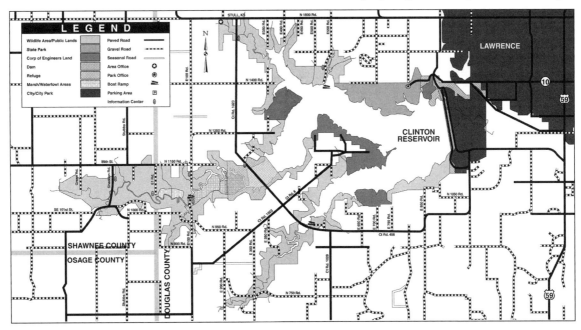

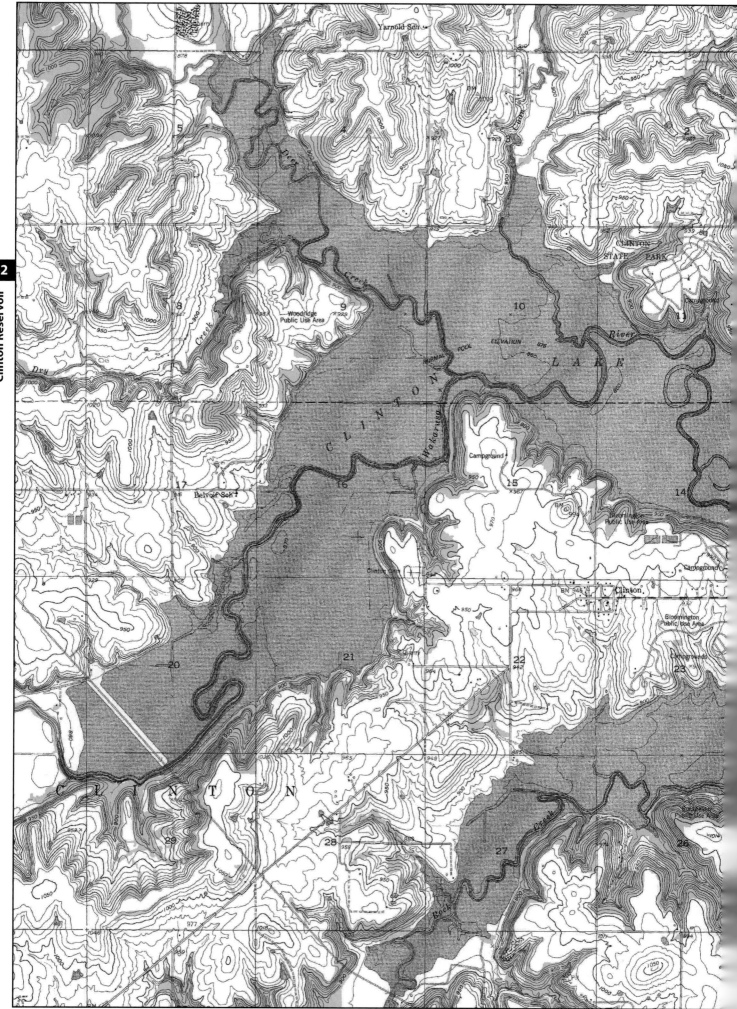

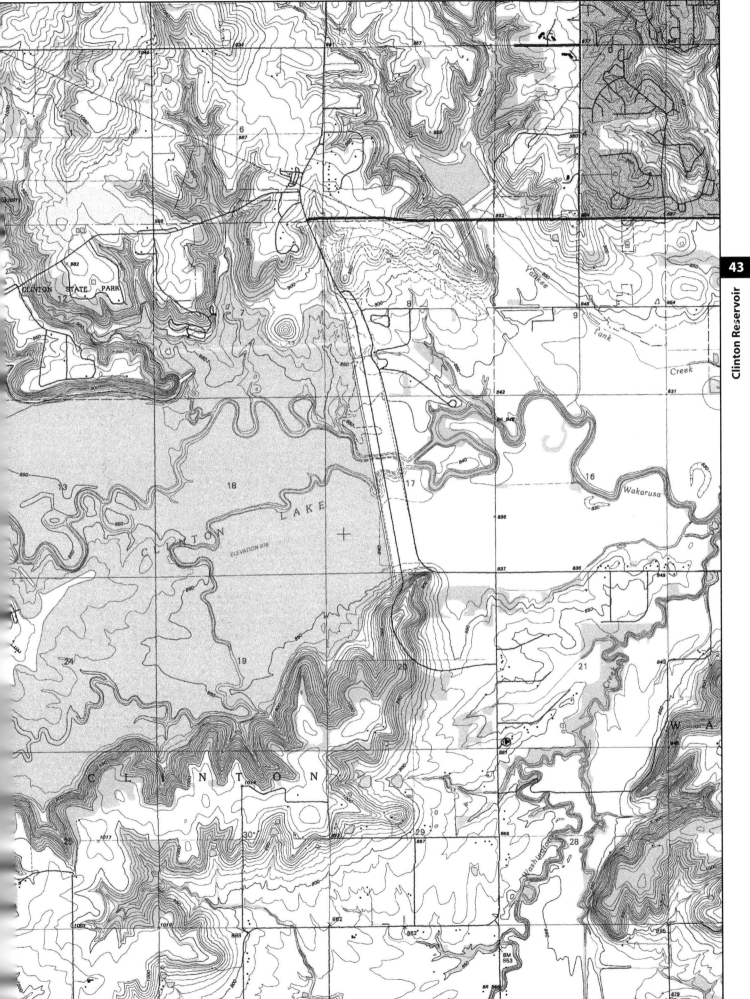

throughout the year and throughout the day—is an important element for anglers to remember during a trip to Clinton.

Feature Fish

Crappie: Martin's method for summertime crappie fishing involves the smallest of tackle, a 1/32 or 1/16 oz. jig head, tipped with a minnow. When he finds a tree or underwater brush, he'll dip the jig near the tree and wait. A slight tap lets him know that the crappie he's looking for is there, but patience is needed to catch crappie with this method.

Martin explains that the first several taps are simply the crappie's way of chasing this intruding minnow out of the area. If tapping doesn't work, however, the fish will simply eat the minnow to get rid of it. When the line moves "out, back, or to the side," he knows the crappie is carrying the minnow in its mouth.

These summer crappie aren't hungry, Martin explains, but they are territorial. Consequently, many of the crappie caught in this fashion will be large fish—ranging from 12 inches or more. When he catches one on a standing tree, it's time to move on to another—and contrary to common knowledge about summertime crappie fishing, these slabs are found in only a few feet of water.

Look for Clinton crappie among the standing timber and brush piles. Those fish will move to the shallow water to spawn in the early spring. Give Chat Martin's method for summertime crappie a try by dropping a small jig near a shallow-water stump. In the fall, look for those fish to move to deeper water and congregate on the brush piles and other standing timber.

Richard Sanders, Clinton's KDWP fisheries biologist, says crappie is among the most popular species for anglers at the lake, but channel catfish, walleye, and wipers are also targets for local anglers.

Walleye: Sanders says he's struggled to keep the walleye population high at the lake, but adds that fish can be found along the breaks around the main island. The popular sportfish, however, is a little more of a challenge at Clinton. Martin maintains that the fish are there, but that anglers simply can't figure out how to catch the sometimes elusive fish.

Sanders says those anglers looking for walleye will do best around the dam and along the breaks along the peninsula that forms in the middle of the lake, where the lake's "arms" split to the north and south. Typical of walleye angling in Kansas, the fish will usually hit on trolled crankbaits or on a jig tipped with a night-crawler or minnow. Drifting along the breaks, or using a trolling motor at a slow speed, with a chartreuse twister tail grub will yield the best success.

Look for walleye off of rocky points and the dam during the early spring spawning season. Through the rest of the spring and into the summer, these fish will move to the mud flats near river channels, where they can be found in water from 5–15 feet deep on the flats,

and from 15–30 feet when they move to the river channels. Try different live baits hooked on a jig, such as worms, leeches, and minnows.

White Bass/Wiper: Clinton dam might seem like an unlikely place for flyfishing anglers to gather. After all, the lake doesn't have trout, and there's no undulating mountain stream nearby. But there are wipers and white bass, and for members of the Free State Flyfishers there's nothing quite like the sound of a big wiper stripping line from a fly reel.

What began as an accident in 2006, when a group of the fly anglers were bored and wanted to practice their casting, has become an annual spring event for the club. "It's one of those things," says Ronn Johnson, owner of Yager's Fly Shop in Lawrence and member of Free State Flyfishers. "Kansas doesn't have moving waters but guys still want to go fly-fishing. Now it's a yearly thing, and when it's on, it's on."

During the spring, members of the Free State Flyfishers gather on Clinton dam and cast woolly buggers, Clouser minnows, and nymphs into the water. Most of the fish are taken on wet flies that somewhat resemble baitfish and run below the surface. Popular colors include chartreuse and white, with sizes ranging from an eight up to the bigger 2/0 size.

"They're aggressive and fight like the devil," says Johnson. "I caught one the other night that took me to my backing. It's a hoot."

In addition to the springtime jaunts to Clinton Dam, Johnson says those anglers with a boat also fly-fish for whites and wipers in much the same way traditional anglers approach these fish—by following their surface feeding around the lake. The anglers will watch the gulls and look for the explosion of shad on the surface—and then creep up on the fish and cast to the edge of the action.

Like the walleye, wipers and whites also congregate off rocky, windblown points and the dam, and can be spotted in the summer chasing shad toward the surface. Although wiper stocking only began in 2003, Sanders says the species has taken off well at the lake, and anglers are finding success—both in the number of fish they're catching and in the size, with some fish reaching upwards of five pounds. This burgeoning population of wipers is gaining in strength and popularity at the lake. Spinners, spoons, and jigs work well any time of year.

Catfish: Later in the year, as the water temperature warms to the mid-70s, Clinton's ample catfish population begins to move toward shallow water for the spawning season. During this season, anglers find success with nightcrawlers and liver on shorelines adjacent to deep water breaks. Sanders said fish feeders can be found on the lake, with two located along the shoreline in Clinton State Park.

Anglers interested in catfish will find another species lurking in Clinton's water: the legendary blue cat. This species, which is capable of reaching sizes of more than 100 pounds, was introduced into the lake in 2006, with additional stocking in subsequent years. Sanders says the first year class is now around 15 inches in size and over two pounds in weight. According to Sanders, the blue cats will be stocked for several more years, with the hope that the population will continue to do well and sustain itself.

Look for catfish on the bottom of coves and in the upper end of the creek channels—and don't forget to try the stilling basin behind the dam. Catfish can be caught on a variety of baits, including shad sides, liver, stink bait, and worms. Cat fishing peaks in June, when the water reaches 70° F.

Black Bass: Clinton Reservoir splits into two arms west of the "island," and bass will locate to standing timber along the old river channels in each arm of the lake. Closer to the dam, the fish will hang out near the rocky areas and points.

Those looking for spawning crappie or hungry walleye should consider making the trip to Clinton in the early spring. During the heat of the summer, when the fish slow down, the action at Clinton heats up as hundreds of recreational boats take to the water. During the fall season, the crappie begin to school up again, just in time for summertime activity on the lake to taper off.

Brush pile GPS locations	
1) N38 55.755	W095 24.146
2) N38 56.444	W095 24.466
3) N38 56.283	W095 23.465
4) N38 56.014	W095 23.096
5) N38 55.036	W095 22.568
6) N38 56.011	W095 23.085
7) N38 55.073	W095 22.565
8) N38 55.785	W095 22.235

Facilities

Clinton State Park is 1,500 acres in one area on the north shore. In total, the area offers: 500 total campsites; 240 sites with water and electric; 70 sites with electric; 220 non-utility sites; 4 shower houses; 2 dump stations; 6 shelter houses; 16 boat ramp lanes; 8 courtesy docks; marina; 1 fish cleaning station; and 1 swimming beach. Boat rental is available. Other features: an archery range, trout pond, kids' fishing pond; area for mountain biking; well-known and established trail system for hikers; and park staff that works closely with the University of Kansas.

With more than 10 boat ramps along Clinton Reservoir, there's plenty of access for anglers to reach the water. The state park provides plenty of camping spaces for both tent and RV camping. The lake's proximity to the college town of Lawrence makes it a popular recreation lake, with thousands of people traveling to the lake each year for hiking, boating, wildlife viewing, and camping.

The U.S. Army Corps of Engineers manages five campgrounds: Cedar, Walnut and Hickory in the Bloomington East Park, Rockhaven Park, and Woodridge Park.

Shopping/Supplies

You'll find the **Submarina Deli** in the Clinton Marina. It is generally open starting weekends from Memorial Day weekend to Labor Day weekend, and serves breakfast, lunch, and dinner. Closed Mondays, except holidays. Open Tuesday–Thursday 8:00 a.m.–5:00 p.m.; Friday–Saturday 8:00 a.m.–6:00 p.m.; Sunday 8:00 a.m.–5:00 p.m. The marina features slips for lease, storage, and rental of fishing or pontoon boats; packaged food, drinks, and beer; clothing, boating, fishing, and ski gear; and bait, including minnows. 1329 E. 800 Rd., Lawrence, 785-749-3222.

Yager's Fly Shop, 2311 Wakarusa Drive, Suite B, Lawrence, 866-359-7467, yagersflies@swbell.net, www.yagersflies.com. Clinton Reservoir sits near the college town of Lawrence, and several retail outlets and sporting good stores are available in town.

Council Grove Reservoir

SIZE: 3,280 acres

LOCATION: 1 mile north of Council Grove on K-177

GPS LOCATION: N38 41 6.11 W96 30 17.37

CONTACT: Council Grove Lake office, 620-767-5195

FEATURE FISH: Channel Catfish, Flathead Catfish, Crappie, Saugeye, Wiper, White Bass

DAILY CREEL LIMIT/MINIMUM LENGTH: Largemouth Bass: 5 fish, 15 inches • Spotted Bass: 5 fish, 15 inches • Channel Catfish: 10 fish • Flathead Catfish: 5 fish • Crappie: 20 fish • Saugeye: 5 fish, 15 inches • Walleye: 5 fish, 15 inches • Wiper: 2 fish, 18 inches

Crappie is some of the best eating, at least, in my opinion. But when it comes to cooking them up, I defer to my husband. You see, I can't cook. I admit it. My husband, on the other hand, can cook a yummy meal of any sport fish whether at the lake or at home.

But while I may not be great at cooking crappie, I do like to catch them. And crappie, happily, are found in just about every reservoir in Kansas. In fact, they bite year-round, but spring brings them close to shore, where they spawn in shallow water. This makes great fishing for anyone with a hook and line—plus, there is no need for expensive fishing rigs.

We hit the crappie spawn about right when we ventured to Council Grove Reservoir in early May. It had been a cold spring, but water temperatures had finally warmed to near 60 degrees, which is the temperature range at which crappie move to rock and brush piles, cattails and rocky shorelines, as well as areas around marina slips and boat ramps.

We jigged for crappie from the shore and from our boat using ultra-light rods with a 6–pound test line. We fished using a bobber with jig suspended about 2 feet. We found success using blue and white, as well as chartreuse and red, tube jigs, reeling in groups of crappie during an early morning outing, as well as at nearby Council Grove City Lake at dusk. And, thankfully, we left our girls at

home, and thus we didn't have to worry about their loud voices and heavy feet spooking any fish—which helped make our trip even more prosperous.

Council Grove isn't a secret, however; it's just a matter whether one wants to make the drive. Bob Butts, who we met at the reservoir's marina, said he doesn't mind the trip from his home, north of Topeka, to a lake as beautiful as Council Grove. Besides, he added, there's plenty of fish to be caught in these Morris County waters. "It's a nice lake, not real crowded," he said as he chatted with marina owner Bill Berns. "And it has some pretty good fishing."

• • •

We got to Council Grove Reservoir on a Friday evening, after spending the day fishing at nearby Marion Reservoir. And, had we taken the twins, we couldn't have found a more family-friendly lake. The lake had great locations for primitive camping—ours was a hilltop location surrounded by shade trees with a nearby spout for running water. Also, the area shower facility was the best of I've seen from all the Kansas lakes: a family sized individual shower with toilet that included a heater for this cold Kansas night.

Moreover, it's a lake of utter beauty, located in Kansas' Flint Hills region—one of the last expanses of tall-grass prairie in North America. The reservoir is located about one mile north of the Santa Fe Trail town of Council Grove, at the north end of the Flint Hills National Scenic Byway. Set on the Neosho River, surrounded by rolling bluestem hills and outlined by trees, the reservoir is truly a gorgeous place to fish.

"It's just a beautiful lake—one of the reasons people come here to camp," says Rick Ross, a Council Grove native who has fished the area all his life for everything from catfish to crappie.

According to the U.S. Army Corps of Engineers, the Flood Control Act of 1950 authorized the Council Grove Project. Construction began in 1960, and the project was placed in full flood control operation in October 1964. The wildlife area consists of 2,638 acres of land and water at the upper ends of the reservoir. During the spring, it attracts migrating waterfowl, as well as bald eagles. Hunters find populations of upland birds, turkey, and deer. And twelve months of the year there are people fishing, says Craig Johnson, the fisheries biologist with Kansas Department of Wildlife and Parks.

Feature Fish

Crappie: Johnson says the best time to catch crappie is the spring spawn, which normally occurs from the end of April and into May—when the water temperatures range from the upper 50s to lower 60s. "Look along shallow spawning banks," he says. "If you can find areas of cover, brush, things like that, that's even better."

Also, according to the KDWP, find them in April in the channel of Munkers Creek and the Neosho River above the lake, as well as along the face of the dam. Small gravel-bottomed coves and the Church Camp peninsula are often good locations.

Avid anglers can find crappie well into the fall and winter, Johnson says. During this season, look for crappie along the dam, creek channels, points in the main lake, and other breaks. That includes an area by the tower where the water is deep. Crappie jigs are a popular winter crappie bait. Johnson advises changing colors and sizes of jigs until a "hot combo is found."

"Crappie can be found in large schools, and catching can be fast and furious when they are located," Johnson says. Also, Butts says to look for them schooling around bluffs and along the dam and breaks in 10–12 feet of water. Most use tube jigs or minnows fished under a bobber, though Butts recommends trying different colors to attract those finicky fish.

Deep-water brush piles sometimes are productive during the winter season, just as they can be other times of the year. The trick, Butts says, is finding the depth of the fish—which can be a few feet to more than 30 feet deep.

Numbers had been down in the early part of the 2000s, Johnson says. Populations, however, have been improving since that time. According to marina owner Berns, the area always has been known for crappie. And on this spring day, "they're biting like the dickens," he says. However, he notes, the lake also has a smorgasbord of other species.

Catfish: Catfish anglers have always been successful at Council Grove, Butts says. He suggests finding them on the edge of drop offs, as well as on the mud flats on the upper ends of the lake. The west side of Church Camp Point is also good for catfish. Another spot he recommends is on creeks during inflows.

For flatheads, Johnson notes anglers should try Munkers Creek and the Neosho River. That's where some of the bigger fish are found. Catfish can also be found along shorelines if you enjoy fishing from a campground, Johnson says.

"We've been using fresh shad," he says, "which there are a ton of in this lake. Leopard frogs and striped frogs work well, too." Also, Council Grove is one of the lakes approved for jug fishing, which runs from July 15–September 15. See the Kansas Fishing Regulations summary for restrictions and requirements on float-line fishing in Kansas waters.

White Bass: White bass numbers have increased since 2008, Johnson says, thanks to some productive spawning years. "We have a good number of white bass," Johnson says. "Sizes are good, but we don't have a lot of the jumbo fish that anglers like to have."

Whites spawn upstream during the spring, but in the summer anglers are productive trolling with crankbaits or casting and jigging shad-imitating baits and jigs along the dam and points.

Saugeye: Anglers should expect good saugeye fishing at Council Grove, Johnson says. The reservoir is one of four in the state stocked with saugeye each year—the first Kansas lake to be part of KDWP's saugeye program, according to the Corps.

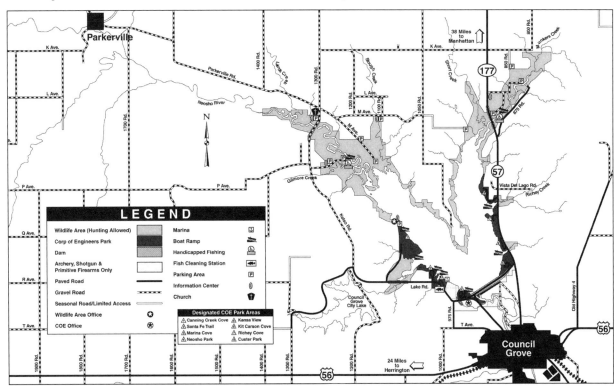

Council Grove Reservoir

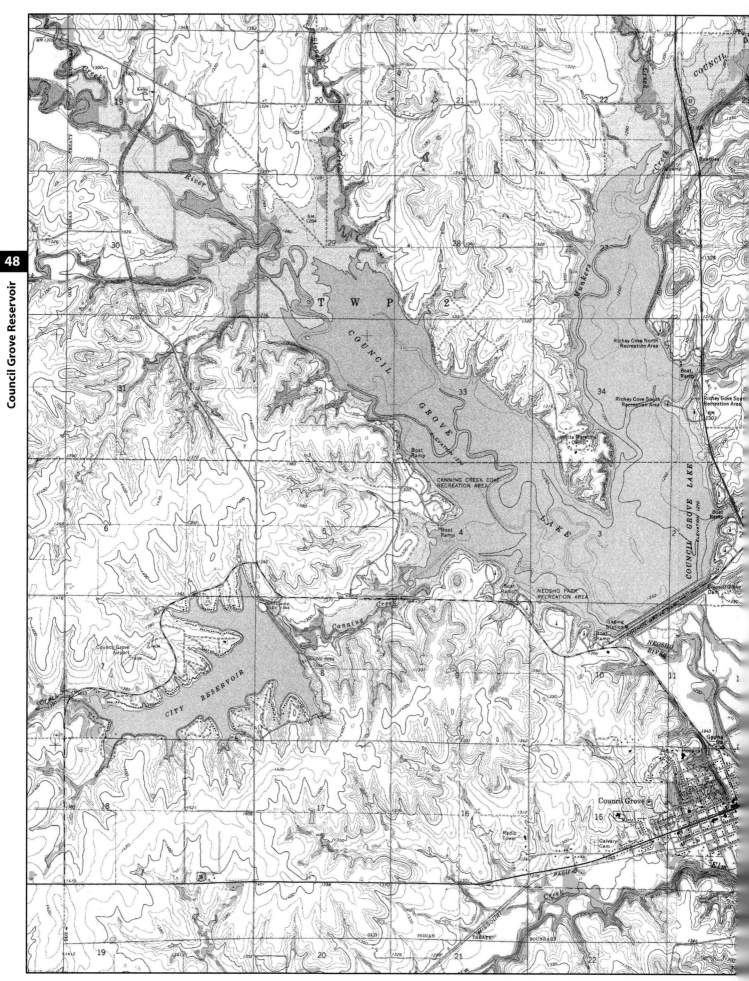

Some anglers hit the lake's stilling basin, catching them in the river below. However, Johnson says with numbers climbing lake-wide, anglers can find saugeye along rocky shorelines, creeks, and the back of coves. In late winter, saugeye start showing up along the face of the dam and on rocky breaks. When the water begins warming, anglers will also find them at the back of coves in shallow areas.

"They don't have problems getting in trees and flooded timber," Johnson says. He also says those trying to fish for saugeye like they fish walleye probably won't have luck. Most anglers tend to fish too deep for the saugeye. Saugeye are usually occupying much shallower water than walleye, so if you aren't getting bites, try fishing shallower water.

"The big problem is trying to find these fish," he says. "But at Council Grove, don't be afraid to go too shallow to look for these things. Even during those clear blue-bird-sky days, high sun, these fish don't have a problem being in two or three feet of water." And, if you find them, he says, "there are some really quality fish out there."

Wiper: Wiper, a white bass–striper hybrid, was stocked in Council Grove in 2008. During the summer of 2010, some of these wipers were already 14-inches long, and Johnson hoped to find some fish nearing 18 inches in length during the fall 2010 netting. "We are going to manage this as a trophy fishery," he says. "They get bigger than the white bass and pull a little harder, as well, so we're anxious to see the results."

> **Council Grove Reservoir's name** comes from the nearby town of the same name, one of the main stops along the Santa Fe Trail. As early as the 1820s, the place where Council Grove now stands was mentioned by travelers, according to the Council Grove Chamber of Commerce. Local legend includes a story of Kit Carson cutting the name "Council Grove" on a buffalo hide and nailing it to the huge oak tree under which the treaty with the Osage Indians that established the trail was signed in 1825.
>
> The marked stump of the Council Grove Oak is still visible on the north side of Main Street in Council Grove. Post Office Oak, where letters were left for caravans passing through the area between 1825 and 1847, also remains.
>
> The city has been designated a National Historic Landmark with several historic attractions: Kaw Methodist Mission; Last Chance Store, built in 1857; Farmers and Drovers Bank, built in 1892; The Hays House restaurant, built in 1857; and Custer Elm, under which General George Custer and his famous 7th Cavalry camped in 1867.

Facilities

Hiking trails include the **Pioneer Nature Trail,** which offers a 0.63-mile loop. The **Richey Cove Trail** is a 0.25-mile trip one-way. The lake includes 8 developed parks for camping, picnicking, a nature trail, fishing, sightseeing, and countless other activities. The lake has several developed parks run by the U.S. Corps of Engineers for camping and picnicking. In total, the park offers: 142 campsites with water and electric, with more than 170 total sites. Campsites include **Canning Creek Cove Park, Custer Park, Kansas View Park, Kit Carson Cove Park, Marina Cove Park, Neosho Park, Richey Cove Park** and **Santa Fe Trail.** There is also a swimming beach, and **Berns' Marina** has supplies as well as boat rentals.

Two good fishing streams, **Munkers Creek** on the east and the **Neosho River** on the west, feed the lake. Two boat ramps and handicap accessible sidewalks provide access to these streams. Corps boat ramps are at **Canning Creek, Richey Cove, Kit Carson Cove, Custer Park, Marina Cove,** and **Neosho Park.** A public fish cleaning station is located in the **Marina Cove** area. There are no free boat ramps at the park. A swimming beach is located at **Richey Cove.**

> **GPS Locations**
>
> **Canning Creek area and boat ramp:**
> N38 41.320 W96 31.957
>
> **Neosho Park Marina Cove boat ramp:**
> N38 40.946 W: 96 31.338
>
> **Neosho Park Boat Ramp:**
> N38 40.692 W96 30.696
>
> **Neosho River Boat Ramp and handicap accessible fishing:** N38 43.080 W096 33.326
>
> **Munkers Creek Boat Ramp and handicap accessible fishing:** N38 43.549 W096 29.471

Shopping/Supplies

Ace Hardware, 415 W. Main St., Council Grove, 620-767-6805; **Adams Lumber Home Store,** 203 E. Main St., Council Grove, 620-767-5818; **Cottonwood Mercantile,** 328 Broadway St., Cottonwood Falls, 620-273-8100 ; **Council Grove Marina,** 1025 Lake Rd., Council Grove, 620-767-5924; **Morris County Clerk,** 501 W. Main St., Council Grove, 620-767-5518; **R & J Bait,** 1594 S. 1300 Rd., Council Grove, 620-767-3252.

Contacts

Council Grove Lake Office, U.S. Army Corps of Engineers, 945 Lake Rd., Council Grove, 620-767-5195, 620-767-6745 (Canning Creek Cove Gate House), 620-767-5800 (Richey Cove Gate House), 620-767-7125 (Santa Fe Trail Gate House); **Council Grove Wildlife Area,** 1130 Lake Rd., Council Grove, 620-767-5900.

El Dorado Reservoir

SIZE: 8,000 acres

LOCATION: About 7 miles northeast of El Dorado on I-35

CONTACT: Eldorado State Park, 316-321-7180; U.S. Army Corps of Engineers, 316-321-9974

FEATURE FISH: Largemouth Bass, Smallmouth Bass, Spotted Bass, Channel Catfish, Flathead Catfish, Crappie, Trout, Walleye, Wiper, White Bass

DAILY CREEL LIMIT/MINIMUM LENGTH: Largemouth Bass: 5 fish, 18 inches • Smallmouth Bass: 5 fish, 18 inches • Spotted Bass: 5 fish, 18 inches • Blue Catfish: 5 fish, 35 inches • Channel Catfish: 10 fish • Flathead Catfish: 5 fish • Crappie: 50 fish • Trout: 5 fish • Walleye: 2 fish, 21 inches • Wiper: 2 fish, 21 inches

AQUATIC NUISANCE SPECIES ALERT: White Perch and Zebra Mussels (unlawful to possess alive)

I've met some interesting folks on these fishing trips. Some have had nicknames centered on their love of fishing. Some have been professional anglers whose job centers on finding a lake's hatchery. And then there are those salt-of-the-earth types, those friendly anglers who might not get paid to fish, but you'll find them at the lake any off-hour they have, between their work schedule and life's added events.

So it didn't seem out of the norm to find an avid angler like area resident Jason Teeter fishing for catfish at El Dorado Reservoir on an early summer afternoon, despite the fact his close relative's wedding would commence in just a few hours. The way Jason Teeter saw it, he still had a bit of time to squeeze in some fishing. So, on a hot summer day, he cast his hook baited with liver into the spillway at El Dorado Reservoir's outlet area, hoping to catch a few catfish to take home.

He didn't come alone, either, bringing several members of his family for a pre-wedding get together. And a few of them, including Teeter, had stringers of fish ready to be cleaned before the evening affair.

After all, he questioned, is there a better lake nearby? Like any lake diehard, many days of the week he can be found at the reservoir, whether he is setting trotlines or fishing with his rod and reel. Catfish is typically his fish of choice this time of year—he notes he even caught a 58 pounder once around the "old Chelsea Cove" area (located along with the boat ramp on northeast Cole Creek Road, about a mile north of 50th on Durechen Creek). "It's really good fishing," Teeter said, adding with a grin that his relative was getting married at 5 p.m. that evening, and he didn't want to call it quits while the fishing was hot. "I think we can fish until at least four o'clock."

• • •

El Dorado Reservoir is nestled on the edge of Butler County's Flint Hills, just north and east of the city of El Dorado. Construction of the reservoir was completed by the U.S. Army Corps of Engineers in 1981. At conservation pool, the reservoir features 98 miles of shoreline. Like many other reservoirs across the state, management of the reservoir's resources has been granted to the Kansas Department of Wildlife and Parks. El Dorado State Park is Kansas' largest state park, offering 8,000 acres. About 4,500 acres are managed by KDWP, including a 4,000-acre wildlife area permissible for hunting.

The reservoir has a combination of steep, rocky shoreline and shallow mudflats. Maximum depth reaches 60 feet. It is the site of a number of annual fishing tournaments and other events, such as Outdoor Kansas for Kids Day. The Walnut Valley Sailing Club offers sailing lessons and holds several regattas during the year. It's also a popular lake close to Wichita for boaters and jet skiers.

• • •

Big Hill Reservoir

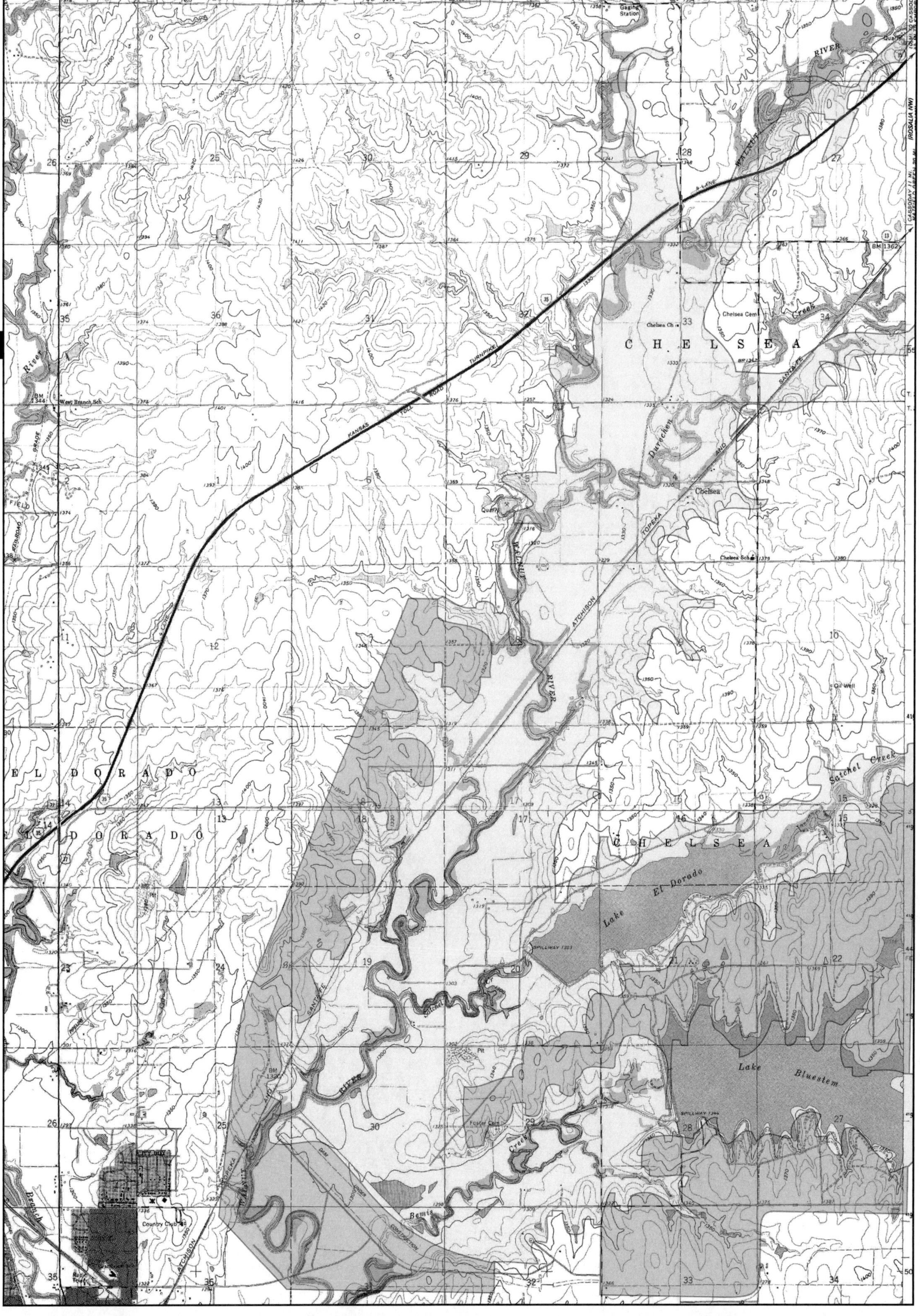
Gaging Station
WALNUT RIVER
KANSAS TOLL ROAD TURNPIKE
West Branch Sch
Chelsea Ch
Chelsea Cem
C H E L S E A
Chelsea
Chelsea Sch
ATCHISON TOPEKA AND SANTA FE
Oil Well
Satchel Creek
E L D O R A D O
Lake El Dorado
SPILLWAY 1323
Lake Bluestem
SPILLWAY 1344
Foster Cem
Bemis
Country Club
DAM UNDER CONSTRUCTION

Jim Keller, an angler from Douglas, says El Dorado has a variety of fishing opportunities. When I caught up with him, he was searching for wipers. Keller noted he had a good morning of luck when it came to pinpointing this fighting fish. However, he notes, the avid anglers also can find walleye, largemouth bass, smallmouth bass, white bass, channel catfish, flatheads, crappie, and blue cats.

Some of the hotspots include riprap on the face of the dam and the railroad right-of-way on the north end of the lake. Other potentials are old submerged railroad beds, river channels, a rock quarry, fish attractors, and standing timber. And, of course, the fishing area at the reservoir outlet is a popular spot for finding fish, including Teeter's catfish.

Craig Johnson, the reservoir's fisheries biologist with the KDWP, says much of the timber in the lake was left standing during construction to serve as fish habitat. The lower half of the lake has a steep, rocky shoreline. The rocky shorelines hold a variety of fish species.

After talking to Keller, John and I headed out with our twin girls, Brett and Kaci, hoping to find some of the hotspots Keller and Teeter talked about. We were able to hook into some catfish, but never found any of Keller's wipers. No worries, however. Deciding to head to a smaller body of water where the girls could play on the embankment while we cast away, we loaded up the pickup and went northward to Chase County State Lake, where little Kaci caught her first fish ever, a little drum.

Feature Fish

Black Bass: El Dorado has all three species of black bass—largemouth, spotted, and smallmouth. Populations vary year to year. But those looking for black bass can find them if they know where to look.

Anglers don't have to look very far to find smallmouth bass at the lake, but the larger ones are harder to come by. The lake had good numbers of 8–12-inch smallies in 2010.

On the largemouth population, Johnson says, "It used to be a pretty good lake. But it has gotten aging reservoir syndrome over the years—fish habitat degrades over time and bass population goes down, as well." The largemouth bass' usual whereabouts during spawn include shallow flats and the backs of bays and coves. Post-spawn bass will often suspend in and around timber, rock points, as well as water willows in late spring.

Look for smallmouth and spotted bass in rocky areas, along the dam, and in the riprap along causeways. Keller also recommends a rock quarry area by the Sail Boat Marina. It's good for bass fishing, as well as finding other species.

Walleye: Walleye fishing, of course, is good along the face of the dam during the spring spawn. Johnson says, however, that the best action is during May or June when they move to the flats. And, according to Johnson, there are flats all over the lake. A few good spots include El Dorado and Bluestem Points, as well as the old submerged railroad bed that runs north and south under the lake. This railroad bed can act as a highway for fish, as they use it to travel from one part of the lake to the other. Many depths can be found along the old railroad bed, making it an attractive area for fish—and anglers.

"Many anglers prefer to drift with live bait such as a jig-and-crawler combo over the larger flats, while others will work smaller locations, vertical jigging," Johnson says. Trolling can be very productive, especially after the gizzard shad have spawned and the walleye have switched over to a shad diet.

El Dorado Point might be one of the most popular areas, but Johnson notes that doesn't mean there aren't walleye in other areas of El Dorado. "Sometimes there will be 12 or 15 boats off of El Dorado Point, and other productive areas aren't being fished at all," he says. "Everyone has honey holes, but look around and try different spots. There are a lot of different spots that are underfished for walleye."

In response to the discovery of white perch at El Dorado in 2009, Johnson has a 21-inch minimum length in place, with a creel limit of two walleye a day, in an effort to keep perch numbers controlled.

Catfish: Fishing for catfish typically is decent lakewide, including the spillway, says Teeter. He also recommends checking out the creeks, especially during inflow events. He's caught some big channel cats and flatheads in this area off summertime trotlines. Johnson says flathead fishing is good in a variety of areas, especially Old Bluestem Lake.

Meanwhile, El Dorado has a fledgling blue cat population. Johnson has been stocking the lake with 16,000 blue cats a year since 2004. Blue cats are slow growing, usually taking seven years to mature. The reservoir has a 35-inch minimum length limit on the species.

In 2005, biologists released 600 tagged fish, ranging from 10–23 inches in length. The tag is located at the base of the dorsal fin and is yellow in color. Those catching a tagged blue cat should write down the number on the tag and get a length, then report it to Johnson's office. "Hopefully we can get them established in the reservoir and provide an opportunity for some trophy-sized catfish," he says.

Crappie: Anglers have caught up to 17-inch crappie in El Dorado. "We don't have a high density, but the fish are quality," Johnson says.

There is good action in March and April for crappie if one looks in coves and creeks, including Durechen, Satchel, Bemis, Walnut River, and Cole. The crappie spawn is usually in full swing during late April through mid-May. Crappie can be caught from shore on jig-and-bobber or jig-and-minnow combos in near-shore areas with brushy cover.

Ice fishing anglers will fish about anywhere the ice is safe, Johnson says, but notes a few popular spots are Walnut River and Durechen Creek arms. "They've had decent crappie action through the ice," he says. "After the ice comes off, anglers also will find pre-spawn crappie still in deep-water winter haunts near channel breaks with woody or rocky cover."

White Bass/Wiper: Wipers were first stocked in 2003 and did very well the first couple of years. With shad numbers down in 2006, wipers didn't fair as well, but Johnson says populations are increasing. In 2010, wiper fishing was hit or miss—with the species not staying in one spot for long. Surface action typically takes place early or late in the day. For success, try along windblown shorelines and also off the main lake points.

Productive baits are anything that looks like shad, according to biologists, but try to match the size of the lure to the shad. As part of the effort to keep white perch numbers controlled, wiper must be 21 inches in length to keep, with a limit of two a day.

Fishing should be good for white bass, as well, Johnson says. Depending on the weather, whites will spawn up in the creeks in April, about the time the water temperatures reach about 58 degrees. However, some years, whites won't make the run due to low flow rates in the creeks, and they will instead stage on the riprapped causeways.

Normally, just like for wipers, lake visitors can find white bass by looking for shad and watching the birds. Johnson says some years when there are good numbers of shad, whites can be caught up into November in a foot or two of water. Along with wipers, windblown shallow shorelines are ideal places to find fall white bass feeding up on shad.

Trout: Like several other Kansas reservoirs, El Dorado offers trout angling opportunities throughout the winter. Trout are stocked in the Walnut River area of El Dorado State Park bimonthly. The season runs October 15–April 15, and a trout permit is required.

Aquatic Nuisances

The bad news about fishing El Dorado? **Zebra mussels.** First introduced into the lake in 2003, they have spread into other recreational lakes, thanks in part to boaters spreading the aquatic nuisance. El Dorado also has a **white perch** problem.

To keep the problems at bay, Johnson promotes "Clean, Drain and Dry." See "Aquatic Nuisances" in the Introduction, p. 15. Other efforts, including the length and creel limit changes and increased stockings of walleye and wipers, might help keep the problem from getting as bad as some Kansas lakes, including Cheney Reservoir.

Facilities

El Dorado State Park features 7 nature trails that offer opportunities for hiking and biking, including 1 specifically for horseback riding. In total, the park offers: more than 1,000 campsites; 10 cabins, including 5 deluxe cabins; 10 boat ramps, including 3 that provide access to waters near the upper ends of the reservoir; full service marina (Shady Creek); sailboat marina; picnic shelters; a laundry facility; and swimming areas.

GPS Locations

Bolder Bluff area Boat Ramp (south): N37 51.052 W96 49.590

Bolder Bluff area Boat Ramp (north): N37 53.550 W96 48.154

Shady Creek Boat Ramp (West): N37 50.449 W96 46.832

Shady Creek Boat Ramp (east): N37 50.761 W96 46.567

Shady Creek Marina: N37 50.422 W96 46.771

Quail Run Boat Ramp: N37 51.223 W96 46.986

Goose Cove Boat Ramp: N37 52.075 W96 46.078

Shopping/Supplies

Bluestem 4 Bait Shop, Bluestem Point, 316-321-5052; **Dillons,** 700 N. Main St., El Dorado, 316-321-0332; **El Dorado Ace Hardware,** 609 N. Main St., El Dorado, 316-322-7500; **Lucky Bait and Tackle,** 1220 N. Main St., El Dorado, 316-321-3443; **Maynard's Bait Service,** 2743 SE Conner Rd., El Dorado, 316-321-9675; **Midwest Tackle Service,** 8630 E. Longlake St., 620-683-0018; **Orscheln Farm and Home,** 2354 W. Central Ave., El Dorado, 316-321-4004; **Rent-a-Wave (rentals),** 618 NE Bluestem Rd., El Dorado, 316-320-9283; **Shady Creek Marina,** 1000 NE Marina Rd., 316-321-0943, www.shadycreek.com; **Sutherlands,** 2850 W. Central Ave., El Dorado, 316-322-7788; **Walmart,** 1618 N. Ohio St., Augusta, 316-775-2254; **Walmart,** 301 S. Village St., El Dorado, 316-322-8100; **Zeiner's Bass Shop,** 737 S. Washington St., No. 6, Wichita, 316-265-5551, www.zeiners.com; **Zeiner's Fishing Headquarters,** 540 E. 37th St. S., Wichita, 316-524-3217.

Guide Service

Four Lake Guides, Mike Cook, 316-655-1541, www.kansasangler.com/fourlakeguides.html; **Hook'Em Guide Service,** El Dorado, 316-323-0010, www.hookemguide.com.

Elk City Reservoir

SIZE: 4,450 acres

LOCATION: About 4 miles west of Independence on US 160

CONTACT: U.S. Army Corps of Engineers, 620-331-6820

FEATURE FISH: Channel Catfish, Flathead Catfish, Crappie, White Bass

DAILY CREEL LIMIT/MINIMUM LENGTH: Largemouth Bass: 6 fish, 15 inches • Channel Catfish: 10 fish • Flathead Catfish: 5 fish • Crappie: 50 fish • Saugeye: 5 fish, 15 inches

Debbie Puryear spends most of her time during the week working as the tourism director for the Independence Chamber of Commerce, where she helps inform people about the things to see and do in this small southeastern Kansas town. But on the weekends, Puryear trades in her office digs for a rod and reel and spends much of her time fishing for crappie at Elk City Reservoir.

"When the weather is perfect, the crappie spawn is great," Puryear says. "Years ago, we used to get up at 5:00 a.m., load up the boat, and start fishing at the crack of dawn. We caught hundreds of crappie doing that, and we ate every one of them."

Elk City Reservoir was part of the Flood Control Act of 1941, and construction on the dam began in 1962 and was completed in 1966. The reservoir serves primarily as a flood control impoundment on the Verdigris River drainage system. Due to the heavy silting, the reservoir has an average depth of 7 feet, though there are areas that offer deeper water—particularly around the dam. Its role in flood control means that it's largely susceptible to rainfall and drainage—and the fishing conditions change drastically with the onset of spring rains. "You have to understand that it was built for flood control, not recreation," Puryear says. "When it rains, it floods."

I traveled to Elk City Reservoir in the fall of 2009, and the lake was just recovering from the flooding that had taken place during 2007 and 2008. The park rangers I visited with told me that the water level had just then receded to a level that would allow camping. The boat ramps had been underwater, and access to the lake had been greatly restricted.

Record floods hit the area in 2007, and it has taken Elk City several years to rebound. Nevertheless, I spent an afternoon fishing in the Card Creek area, where the campground area was still slightly soggy and flooded in areas.

I didn't have any luck, but then, with the water conditions as they were, I didn't really expect much luck. Those who fish the area regularly suggest fishing the spillway during the times of high water, and there's no doubt in my mind that's the right approach. A flooded lake is frustrating, but at least one known variable is that lots of water—and fish—are leaving at the lake's tailwaters.

When the rain doesn't fill the lake to flood level, and the temperatures hold steady, the fishing at Elk City Reservoir can be remarkable. That's what happened during the spring of 2010, when a mild spring season left the lake stable, the crappie population with plenty of spawning beds, and anglers with a lot of choices in how to reach them. "This year has been phenomenal," Kansas Department of Wildlife and Parks fisheries biologist Sean Lynott said. "This has been one of the top two years in the past 16 years, with a lot of fish in the 2-pound range."

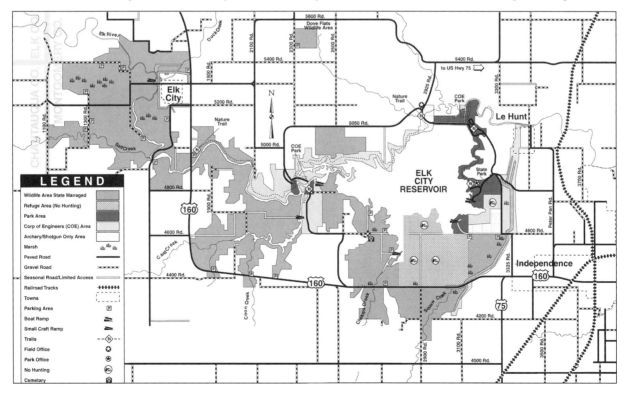

LEGEND

Wildlife Area State Managed
Refuge Area (No Hunting)
Park Area
Corp of Engineers (COE) Area
Archery/Shotgun Only Area
Marsh
Paved Road
Gravel Road
Seasonal Road/Limited Access
Railroad Tracks
Towns
Parking Area
Boat Ramp
Small Craft Ramp
Trails
Field Office
Park Office
No Hunting
Cemetery

Elk City Reservoir

Although crappie anglers saw nearly unparalleled success in 2010, Lynott says even in those years that test anglers' patience, the fish flourish in the up-and-down waters of Elk City Reservoir. "Even in bad years, the lake produces good numbers of quality fish," Lynott says. "But in years like this, when we have good temperatures and less rain, the spawn stays on for three weeks instead of a week. I'm kind of excited to see what 2012 and 2013 produces."

While many anglers use a boat to navigate the reservoir and upstream in the Elk River and Card Creek, fishing at Elk City can be just as good from shore. Puryear says several areas around the lake offer excellent access to shore-bound anglers, as well as access to some of the hottest fishing waters on the lake. According to Puryear, the area to the north and south of the swimming beach in the Elk City State Park is a good place to jig for crappie. The state park also features several jetties from which anglers can fish.

Feature Fish

Crappie: There's little doubt that it's the crappie that monopolizes anglers' attention at Elk City. The lake, which is fed by the Elk River and Card Creek, contains some shoreline

rocks and vegetation that facilitate springtime spawning. Additionally, Elk River and Card Creek both offer habitat that is capable of holding these fish throughout the year.

Puryear, who lives about a mile and a half away from the lake with her husband, says they look for the crappie to move into the "ski" coves during the spawn, which generally occurs in the later part of April and into May. "You don't have to have a boat to catch fish," Puryear says. "There are berms that come out into the water." The main coves at the lake include the two southern arms, where Chetopa Creek and Squaw Creek enter the reservoir. Lesser coves, such as those in the KDWP state park on the southeast side of the dam, are also productive areas for crappie anglers.

That's where you're likely to find Diane Hight, administrative assistant at Elk City State Park, fishing along the

shoreline with a long crappie pole. Some days she hits the lake before her workday begins, as well as during her lunch break and for an hour or so at the end of her workday. In fact, she spends so much time jigging for crappie, some locals have dubbed her the "Crappie Queen."

"Some of the regulars that come here latched it on to me," Hight said. Despite her moniker, and her reputation as an effective crappie angler, Hight says she prefers to keep it simple when fishing Elk City—just a long rod, light and small jig balanced just above the shoreline brush. "I don't do anything fancy," Hight said. "I don't spend a lot of money. I just want that bump."

Lynott says one of the most fished areas is at the eastern corner of the dam, just below the Memorial Overlook. In this area, the riprap of the dam provides good spawning habitat for crappie, and the nearby channel of the Elk River also serves to draw in crappie.

Puryear says Elk City Reservoir is home to "monster" crappie that top the 2.5–3 pound range. But for Puryear and her husband, most of their crappie come from nearby Card Creek—where they can fish around submerged and standing timber.

Many crappie anglers at Elk City prefer to use jigs—generally shaded yellow or white—and find plenty of fish with this method. On the other hand, Puryear says she doesn't like to jig fish. "I get tangled up every single time," she says, "so I just use minnows."

In the fall, the crappie school up and can be found in the main body of the lake, holding on brush piles or other underwater structure, such as the Elk River channel. Puryear says that, at this time of year, the lake is more popular for fall waterfowl hunting than it is for fishing—so would-be cool weather anglers should be aware of key hunting areas in the lake, most of which rest on the south end of the reservoir.

Despite the lake's inconsistent nature, and its tendency to ebb and flow with local rainfalls, Puryear thinks the lake is home to some great crappie fishing. "You can go out on any given day and catch a crappie," she says. "It just depends on the day."

Lynott echoes Puryear's thoughts, adding that at Elk City, the timing of a fishing trip will determine its successfulness. "Elk City has the best and worst you could ask for," Lynott says. "But when it's good, you've got to be Johnny on the Spot. … If you want to catch big crappie, go to Elk City. You won't take home 50 fish, but almost everything you catch will be a pound and a half to two pounds."

White Bass: As at many lakes in Kansas, the white bass run up the reservoir's feeding river is an annual right of passage—a sure sign that spring is truly in full swing. Puryear says she often finds white bass in the spring mixed in with the crappie for which she's usually fishing.

On County Road 1550, near where Salt Creek enters Elk River, white bass and crappie anglers find success by fishing around the bridge that spans the waterways. To the south of the Elk River is where Card Creek enters the lake, and this is another stretch of water in which white bass move to spawn.

Tim Rasmussen, the lead U.S. Army Corps of Engineers park ranger for Big Hill, Toronto, Elk City, and Fall River, says anglers can fish this stretch of water for about 4 miles above the Card Creek campground. After that, the water becomes too thin and shallow for boats to pass through. "There's no charge on the boat ramp at Card Creek," Rasmussen says. "It doesn't get a lot of use and there's good fishing on the river."

Puryear says that anglers fishing for white bass in the rivers generally toss white or chartreuse jigs and Roadrunners. After the spawn, the white bass return to the lake, where they follow the typical Kansas pattern of holding off of windblown points, chasing shad. Rasmussen said anglers often troll crank baits around those points to elicit strikes. This pattern generally reaches its peak in June, but lasts throughout the summer, until the fish begin to migrate toward deeper water for the winter.

Catfish: Elk City contains a lot of silt thanks to the seasonal flooding that brings debris and mud into the lake. While this natural occurrence has reduced the reservoir's water level, it also makes Elk City a productive catfish fishery.

The north end of the lake, where the Elk River and Card Creek flow in, is a popular location for catfish anglers. Most use dough baits or shad sides, and tossing out set lines is another common method for local anglers.

During the spawning season when the water temperature nears 70 degrees, Lynott says, the western edge of the dam is among the best locations to catch cats, which move into the shallow water to feed and release their eggs. Throughout the spring and summer, Lynott recommends that anglers try drift fishing in the central part of the lake, slightly south and west of the dam, between ¼ and ½ mile south of the northern shore.

The channel cat might reign supreme when it comes to numbers, but the catfish that dominates this lake by its size is the flathead catfish. "There have been record flathead caught at Elk City," Puryear says. "There are some pretty big fish in here." Puryear isn't alone in vouching for the size of the Elk City flatheads. In 1998, Ken Paullie, of Caney, Kansas, caught a state record flathead that weighed a whopping 123 pounds—with a rod and reel and a jig and a minnow. It's a record that has remained on the books for more than 12 years.

Facilities

Waterfowl hunting, camping, and hiking are all popular pastimes at Elk City Reservoir. The reservoir is also home to one of the longest and most scenic shoreline trails in Kansas. The 15-mile Elk River Hiking Trail follows the northern shoreline of the reservoir, with trailheads at the Elk City Fish and Wildlife Office, north and west of the Card Creek area, at the dead end of County Road 2350, and to the south of the town of Elk City, off of US 160. The trail takes hikers through hardwood forests, sheer rock cliffs, and overhangs and offers a great view of the lake. Additionally, the Table Mound Hiking Trail and the Squaw Creek Trail offer hikers a scenic view of the eastern

side of the reservoir. Behind the dam, mountain bikers will enjoy the Eagle Rock Mountain Bike trail.

Elk City State Park is located west of Independence, in Montgomery County, with 857 acres in one area with well-shaded campgrounds. The park features a nationally recognized trail system. Various attractions include the Eagle Mountain bike trail, 6 miles of hiking/nature trails, and a frisbee golf course. In total, the park offers:; 11 sites with water, sewer, and electric; 86 sites with water and electric; 53 non-utility sites; 2 shower houses; 2 dump stations; 3 shelter houses; 3 boat ramp lanes; 2 courtesy docks; 1 fish cleaning station; and 1 swimming beach. Also features an ADA fishing dock.

The U.S. Army Corps of Engineers operates the **Card Creek campground** on the shores of Card Creek, to the west of Elk City Reservoir. This area is described as a place for those who enjoy riverbank camping, and want to get away from the crowds. The campground includes: 15 sites with electric only; non-utility sites; fresh water; shower houses; restrooms; a dump station; a boat ramp and boat dock; and a playground.

Shopping/Supplies

Cessna Employees Club Independence, 1 Cessna Pl., Independence, 620-332-0139; **Elk City State Park,** 4825 Squaw Creek Rd., Independence, 620-331-6295; **Pumpn Petes,** open 6:00 a.m. to 10:00 p.m. daily, 109 S. Olive St., Cherryvale, 620-336-2240; **Walmart,** 1863 County Rd. 5300, Coffeyville, 620-251-2290; **Walmart,** 121 S. Peter Pan Rd., Independence, 620-331-5805.

Fall River Reservoir

SIZE: 2,500 acres

LOCATION: About 2 miles west of Fall River on US 400

CONTACT: U.S. Army Corps of Engineers, 620-637-2213

FEATURE FISH: Largemouth Bass, Channel Catfish, Flathead Catfish, Crappie, White Bass

DAILY CREEL LIMIT/MINIMUM LENGTH: Largemouth Bass: 5 fish, 15 inches • Spotted Bass: 5 fish, 15 inches • Channel Catfish: 10 fish • Flathead Catfish: 5 fish • Crappie: 50 fish

An autumn outing on Fall River Reservoir in Greenwood County is likely to show anglers a side of Kansas that's not often seen by even those who live in the state. Nestled in the transition zone between the rolling Flint Hills and the wooded areas to the east, Fall River offers visitors a blend of forests, plains, and tallgrass prairies. But most of the people who visit Fall River during this remarkable time of year come not for the turning tree leaves or the moderate fall temperatures—they come for the crappie fishing, which bursts with activity from the middle of September until the cold of January.

"The fish in this lake grow really fast and get really big," Kansas Department of Wildlife and Parks fisheries biologist Carson Cox says. During annual sampling of the fish population, Cox has captured crappie that nearly top the scales at four pounds—a monster fish in any water. That reputation for large crappie, and plenty of them, has drawn the attention of out-of-state anglers, park manager Kim Jones says.

The secret to the lake's large number of big crappie, as well as a healthy population of several other species, lies above the lake, in the Fall River itself. When the river swells in the spring as rain covers the nearby countryside, it brings food, nutrients, and structure into the lake. This annual rise in the river, however, doesn't come without drawbacks. "One thing to know about this lake is that it flashes really bad," Cox says of the spring water levels. "It can increase 20 to 30 feet in a short time, and then go back down really fast, too."

This rise and fall means that anglers will have to change their tactics accordingly and should do some advance research before heading to Fall River Reservoir. A spur of the moment trip immediately after a localized rainfall could leave would-be anglers stranded on the banks of a reservoir that's filled to flood-control level, without access to boat ramps or camping areas.

However, like neighboring lakes Toronto Reservoir and Elk City Reservoir, the water that the lake holds back to prevent downstream flooding eventually is released—along with thousands of fish. "When we're releasing water from the spillway," Cox says, "the fishing there is really good for flatheads and channel cats."

The spillway is where I found Larry Johnson and Gary Branham, both of Neodesha, fishing for channel catfish with worms and stink bait. I had just set my line in the roiling waters of Fall River, and I noticed these guys reeling in another nice channel cat that they added to their stringer of fish.

We talked for a while about fishing around the area, and the two men told me that they liked fishing in both the Fall River and the Verdigris River, and that they spent most of their fishing time looking for cats.

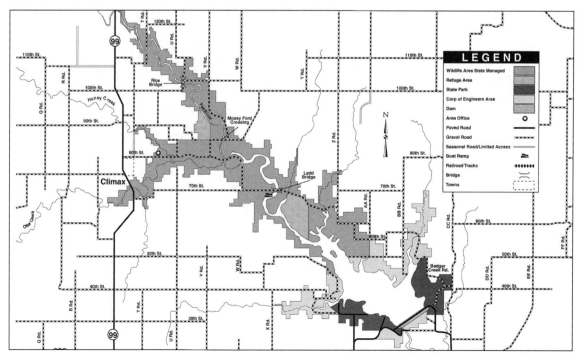

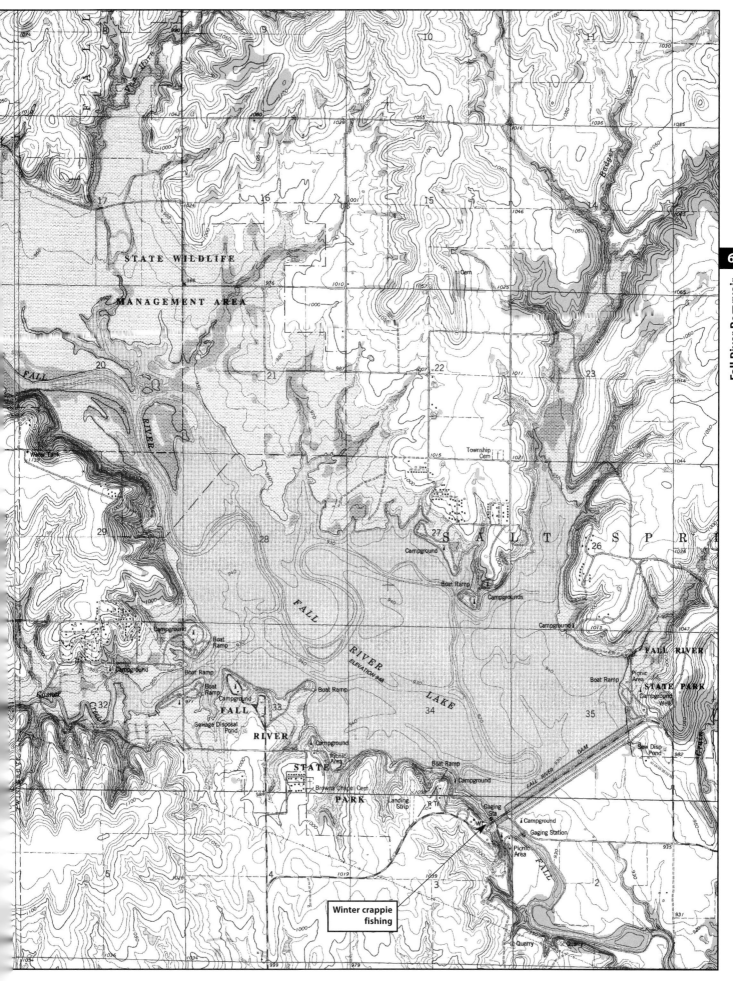

STATE WILDLIFE

MANAGEMENT AREA

Water Tank

FALL RIVER

Township Cem

Campground

Boat Ramp

Campgrounds

SALT SPR

Campground

Boat Ramp

Campground

Boat Ramp

FALL RIVER

Campground

FALL RIVER

LAKE

ELEVATION 948

STATE PARK

Picnic Area

Campground Well

Boat Ramp

Boat Ramp

Campground

FALL

RIVER

Sewage Disposal Pond

Campground

STATE

Picnic Area

Browns Chapel Cem

Boat Ramp

Campground

PARK

Landing Strip

Sew Disp Pond

Gaging Sta

WT

Campground

Gaging Station

Picnic Area

FALL

Winter crappie fishing

Quarry

Quarry

"And I know where a lot of the underwater piles are, and if I don't pick up action at one, I'll move on to another."

According to Cox, the river channel of Fall River plays an important role for crappie, which orient to the channel throughout the year and throughout the length of the reservoir. Cox said after mid-September, when the lake has generally finished its turnover and the entire depth of the water is oxygenated, the crappie will move into a fall pattern in which they move up and down the underwater river channel. From this deeper water of 12–20 feet deep, the crappie will move to the shallower water along the channel breaks to chase shad and baitfish.

As the water and air temperature cools, the crappie migrate south along the channel toward the outlet gates of the dam. According to Jones, who manages the state parks for both Fall River and Toronto Reservoirs, anglers line the walkway on the southeast corner of Fall River Dam in January to enjoy some of the best, if not unusual, crappie fishing the state has to offer. "The moving water keeps it from freezing in that area," Jones says. "But you have to bring a bucket or basket of some kind to get your fish out—it's a long way from the bridge to the water."

Cox says this part of the lake presents the best, and hottest, action for crappie on the lake at any time of year. "I've seen two guys in a boat catch 100 crappie a day," Cox says about the January fishing in this location.

Yet after two separate creel surveys spread out over 10 years, Cox says he's never seen evidence that the fish are being over harvested. The inflow of the Fall River is partly responsible for this resilient crappie population. According to Cox, the lake has very high recruitment, or fish reproduction, because of the fertile waters carried down from the Fall River. It's also the reason the fish here grow so fast. Crappie that begin their second year at 7.5 inches balloon to 13.4 inches long by their fifth year. By their sixth year of life, the average crappie in Fall River Reservoir will measure 15 inches or better.

During the winter fishing near the dam, Cox says anglers typically fish between 15 and 20 feet deep with jigs. "I don't hear about a lot of guys bouncing bottom," Cox says. He recommends that anglers look for the channel break in the southeast corner of the lake, where the water drops from 22 feet to around 30 feet deep. Sometimes the fish run in shallower water, but they'll often locate near the channel break.

At the opposite end of the seasons, when the heat is at its highest, Cox says the best crappie fishing can be found in the Fall River, near the Ladd Bridge area northwest of the lake. "The water is cool, it's oxygenated, and there are deep holes, with timber and willow trees on both sides of the river that provide shade," Cox says. "You'll find the fish under those trees hiding in the shade."

This is where Cook spends most of his time fishing for crappie, using red and chartreuse or pink and

Both told me the same thing that I had heard from biologists—that when the gates of the dam are open and flowing, the fishing in the spillway is at its best.

They held up a stringer of channel cats that they caught in just a few hours. "The river fishing is pretty good here, in the Verdigris, and in Fall River," Johnson said.

I wasn't really set up to do much cat fishing because I expected to spend most of my time tossing jigs and crank baits from shore. Nevertheless, I enjoyed the chance at Fall River to hook on a worm, find a split tree branch to lean my fishing pole against, and lie back to enjoy some easy fishing.

Feature Fish

Crappie: When it comes to fishing Fall River Reservoir for crappie, most of the action can be found in the river above the lake. "There are brush piles all over the place," says Mike Cook, with Four Lakes Guide Service.

chartreuse jigs to attract the large crappie for which this lake has become known. He's always willing to change up his presentation, however, if the fish aren't responding to his regular baits. White, chartreuse, and an assortment of dark-colored jigs often fill in for his more popular colors.

"You're still going to catch small crappie," Cook says about Fall River fishing. "But you'll catch a 3-pound crappie, too. And nothing will make your pole shake like a 3-pound crappie."

In the late winter or early spring, Cox says anglers often return to the river after the fishing near the dam has tapered off a bit. Until the spring spawning season, however, the fishing is somewhat sporadic and unpredictable. "It can be good one day, and no good the next," Cox says. "Then in the spring, the river floods and they disappear." Once spring arrives, Cox suggests searching for spawning crappie in the back of Rock Ridge Cove, near the state park on the south side of the lake, and in the back of Engineer Cove, to the northeast end of the lake, on the U.S. Army Corps of Engineers area.

Another popular, although seasonal, spot for crappie anglers is Quarry Bay. This detached body of water north of the main reservoir is where crews removed the stone needed to construct the dam. In the spring, when the lake floods, Quarry Bay connects to the reservoir. When the water drops, Quarry Bay stands alone as a separate body of water, although the crappie that moved into the area remain. Cox says a lot of good fish are taken from Quarry Bay, but only during late winter and early spring.

White Bass: Like crappie, the white bass in Fall River Reservoir also grow rapidly and thrive in the nutrient-rich waters of the lake. Cox says when the water level is stable, the white bass in the reservoir live longer and are capable of reaching upwards of 3 pounds. The 2010 spring season didn't bring the flooding of previous years, which should produce several years of good white bass fishing at Fall River Reservoir.

Water temperatures in the mid-50s spark the white bass' annual migration upstream to spawn, and Fall River is home to some key locations for this exciting spring fishing. Cox said the spawning period at Fall River lasts about 30 days, and one of the best locations is where Otter Creek meets up with Fall River, to the north and west of the Ladd Bridge boat ramp. The convergence of these two waters creates a riffle that provides the agitation egg-laying white bass seek out.

Unlike other lakes, where the spawn generally doesn't begin until April, Cox says his research shows that the whites begin to move toward the warmer water of the river as early as February. "I couldn't find a fish in the lake," Cox says of a recent spring fish sampling. "They really keyed in on that riffle."

Cook says he generally finds the white bass mixed in with the crappie, but adds that an angler fishing for whites can find success with a Beetle Spin, roadrunners, and crappie jigs.

Despite the long season and the high numbers of fish, Fall River doesn't experience the fishing pressure that can be found at other lakes during the white bass run. "For Fall River, about 24 cars with a couple of

guys each is busy," Cox says. "And that's about all they get in the white bass spawn, too."

After the spawn ends, Cox says the whites return to the body of the reservoir, chasing shad on the flats near Fredonia Bay and on the north end of the lake, near the mouth of the river. Successful presentations include bright colored jigs, as well as Rattletraps when the water is murky due to high inflow from the river.

Catfish: Several elements combine to make the cat fishing at Fall River a memorable experience. The water that flows in from Fall River brings all the things that catfish want and need, which draws them toward the upper end of the lake. What the river doesn't provide, Kansas' famous southerly summer winds provide—making the upper end of Fall River Reservoir one of the best locations for summer channel cat fishing.

Cox says many anglers will use shad sides when fishing this area. Deploying set lines in this relatively shallow area is also very popular.

Cook says there are a lot of laydowns of timber in the area, and that he's hooked large catfish amongst that structure. "I don't catch the numbers there," he says, "But I've caught big, big cats."

Like Toronto Reservoir to the east, Fall River also employs a water management plan that begins on July 4 of each year and lasts until the water level returns to conservation level. During this period, the lake collects water during the week, and releases water on the weekends. When the water is flowing out of the lake, anglers can catch a variety of species in the spillway.

"This is very successful for people fishing in the spillway," Cox says. "When we're releasing water from the lake, the fishing is good for flathead and channel cats. People will also catch crappie and whites this way, and it's really good on the weekends when the water is coming out."

Largemouth Bass: Fall River doesn't have a high density of largemouth bass, but the bass that are found in the clear water of the river above the lake are quality fish that grow fast and large. "Don't bother fishing in the reservoir for bass," Cox says. "They're all in the river."

While the density of bass in the river isn't remarkable, Cox says there are enough to make for an exciting outing, and that catching a 5-pound largemouth out of the river isn't uncommon. Cox suggests fishing for largemouth in the timber filled waters above Ladd Bridge, where the bass look for shad.

In the summer, Cox says a plastic worm can pull bass out of the slumber, but a jig and pig is a deadly combination in the spring. Most of the time, however, the angler that throws a crankbait or a Rattletrap that resembles a shad will have the best success.

Recently, officials with KDWP and researchers from Kansas State University collaborated on a habitat project for spotted bass in Otter Creek, north of Fall River Reservoir. The team constructed 12 "lunker structures" which were designed to mimic undercut riverbanks—a preferred hideout of large predator fish. To help track the use of the structures, biologists placed radio transmitters on 26 spotted bass and recorded their movements over two years.

The results showed that every bass carrying a transmitter utilized the artificial structure—a better return than the brush piles and root wads that also were placed in Otter Creek for this experiment. Furthermore, the lunker structures remained in place during high water, while the root wads collected debris and washed down stream. In fact, those structures still remain in Otter Creek, attracting both fish and anglers.

Facilities

The **campground** is 981 acres over 3 areas. Campsites can be reserved. In total, the area offers: 45 campsites with water and electric; 93 non-utility sites; 3 shower houses; 1 dump station; 14 shelter houses; 4 boat ramp lanes; 4 courtesy docks; 1 fish cleaning station; hiking trails; and 1 swimming beach.

Shopping/Supplies

Hilltop Bait/Grocery sells food, bait, camping supplies, and "a little bit of everything." Also home of the Hilltop Café. Several cabins are available for rent—call ahead for information or reservations. Open 8:00 a.m. to 8:00 p.m. Thursday through Tuesday, 8:00 a.m. to 2:00 p.m. on Wednesday. 153 Westshore Rd., Toronto, 620-637-2700. **Country Junction** sells bait, tackle, groceries, fuel, and deli food, open 7 a.m. to 7 p.m. daily, 153 US 54, Toronto, 620-637-2384.

Alco, 501 W. US 54, Eureka, 620-583-7076; **DJ Sporting Goods,** 200 W. River St., Eureka, 620-583-5211; **Fall River State Park,** 144 K-105, Toronto, 620-637-2213; **Johnson's General Store,** 205 W. River St., Eureka, 620-583-5672; **Johnson's General Store,** 201 W. Mary St., Yates Center, 620-625-2538; **Main Street Mini Mall,** 226 W. Main St., Madison, 620-437-2441.

Glen Elder Reservoir (Waconda Lake)

SIZE: 12,586 acres

LOCATION: About 12 miles west of Beloit on US 24

CONTACT: Glen Elder State Park, 785-545-3345

FEATURE FISH: Smallmouth Bass, Channel Catfish, Flathead Catfish, Crappie, Walleye, White Bass, Wiper

DAILY CREEL LIMIT/MINIMUM LENGTH: Largemouth Bass: 5 fish*, 18 inches • Smallmouth Bass: 5 fish*, 18 inches • Spotted Bass: 5 fish*, 15 inches • Channel Catfish: 10 fish • Flathead Catfish: 5 fish • Crappie: 50 fish • Striped Bass: 2 fish • Walleye: 5 fish, 18 inches • Wiper: 2 fish

* Largemouth, Smallmouth, and Spotted Bass in combination

• • •

One word is all that's really needed to describe Glen Elder Reservoir: full. After several years of drought and low water levels, the north central Kansas lake is back to its original form and is full of water. It's full of crappie, which provide anglers a year-round supply of fishing excitement. It's full of walleye, the lake's signature species. White bass and wipers? Full. Catfish? Full. Black bass? Full, and growing fuller all the time.

Glen Elder Reservoir is one of the state's premier lakes and is poised to become even better as the fish populations there continue to explode, thanks to favorable climate conditions and effective fisheries management. Scott Waters, the Kansas Department of Wildlife and Parks fisheries biologist for Glen Elder, has found a number of signs for encouragement.

Before 2008, drought had left the lake roughly 10 feet below conservation level, and, consequently, the fish population struggled. After several years of good rain, however, the coves filled with water, and the fish—particularly crappie—have returned to their spawning habitat, creating an abundant population for anglers.

While working on this book, Glen Elder became my new favorite lake. If I felt like catching crappie, I caught crappie—by the livewell full. If I felt like catching walleye, they weren't hard to find. Whatever I wanted to catch, Glen Elder provided it in ample numbers.

And it doesn't take a pro to find them. With a little understanding of structure and the way fish hold to it, any angler can find fish at Glen Elder. There are rocky shorelines, submerged brush piles, mud flats, and coves filled with underwater vegetation—and any one of those structures is likely to have some fish. And as if the structure and the volume of fish weren't enough, Glen Elder's water is remarkably clear.

Perhaps the best thing about Glen Elder, though, is the people. From Wayne Jay, the president of the Waconda Lake Association (Waconda is the Native American name for the hot springs originally located where the lake was built, as well as the former name of the lake), who gladly took me to his favorite fishing holes, to the bait and tackle store owner, the people around Glen Elder are genuinely happy to help visitors have a successful fishing trip. The Waconda Lake Association hosts several fishing tournaments, a weekend kids' fishing derby, and multiple cookouts throughout the year.

If you travel to Glen Elder, you're not likely to be disappointed—by either the fish or company you'll find there.

Feature Fish

Crappie: Crappie numbers "are way up" according to Waters. "This is a good population that should sustain

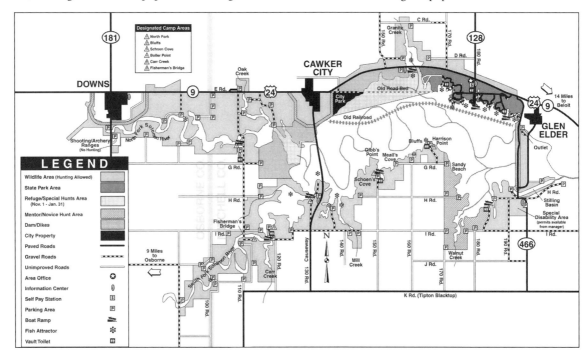

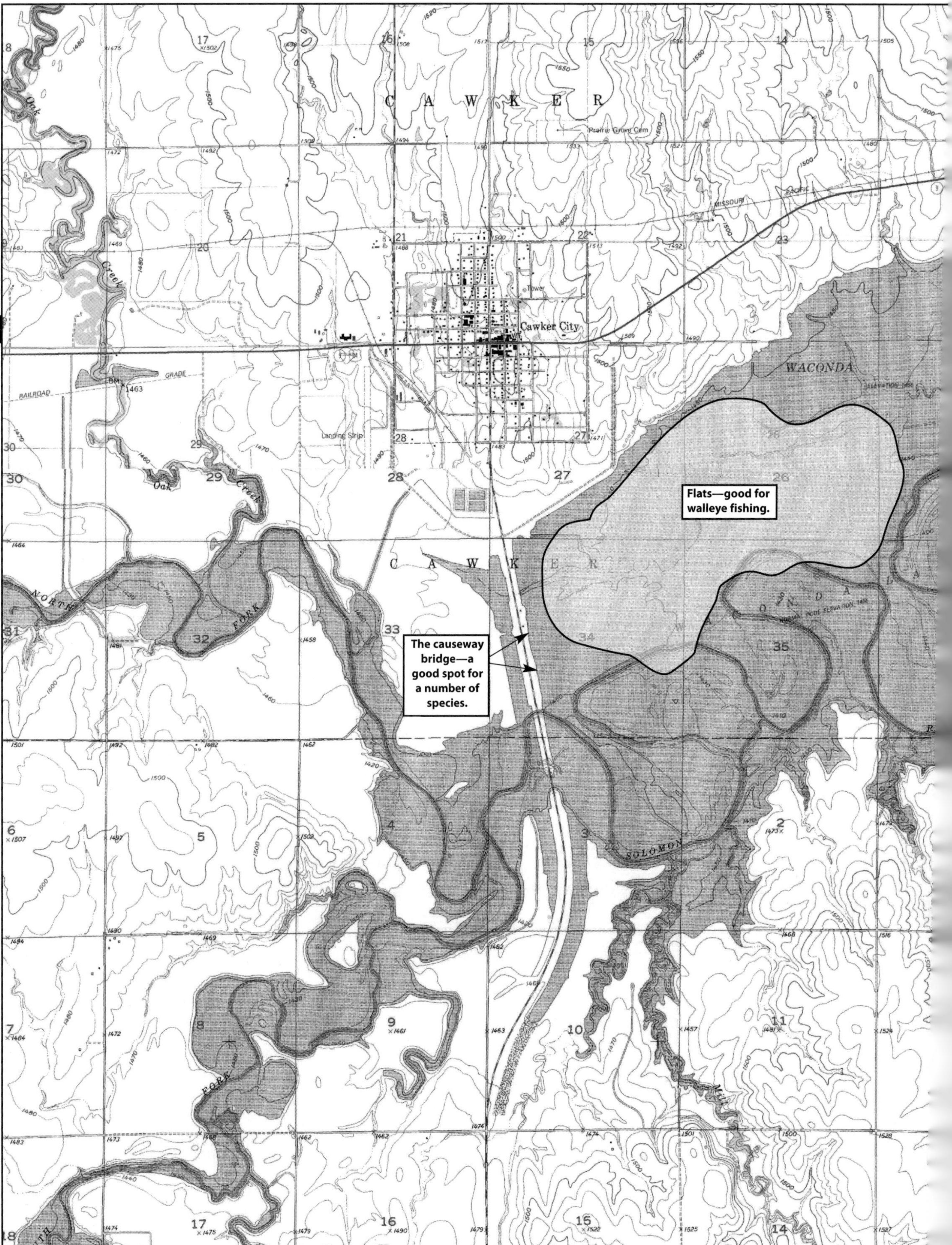

C A W K E R

Prairie Grove Cem

Tower

Cawker City

WACONDA

Flats—good for walleye fishing.

The causeway bridge—a good spot for a number of species.

C A W K E R

NORTH FORK

Oak Creek

RAILROAD GRADE

Landing Strip

SOLOMON

SOUTH FORK

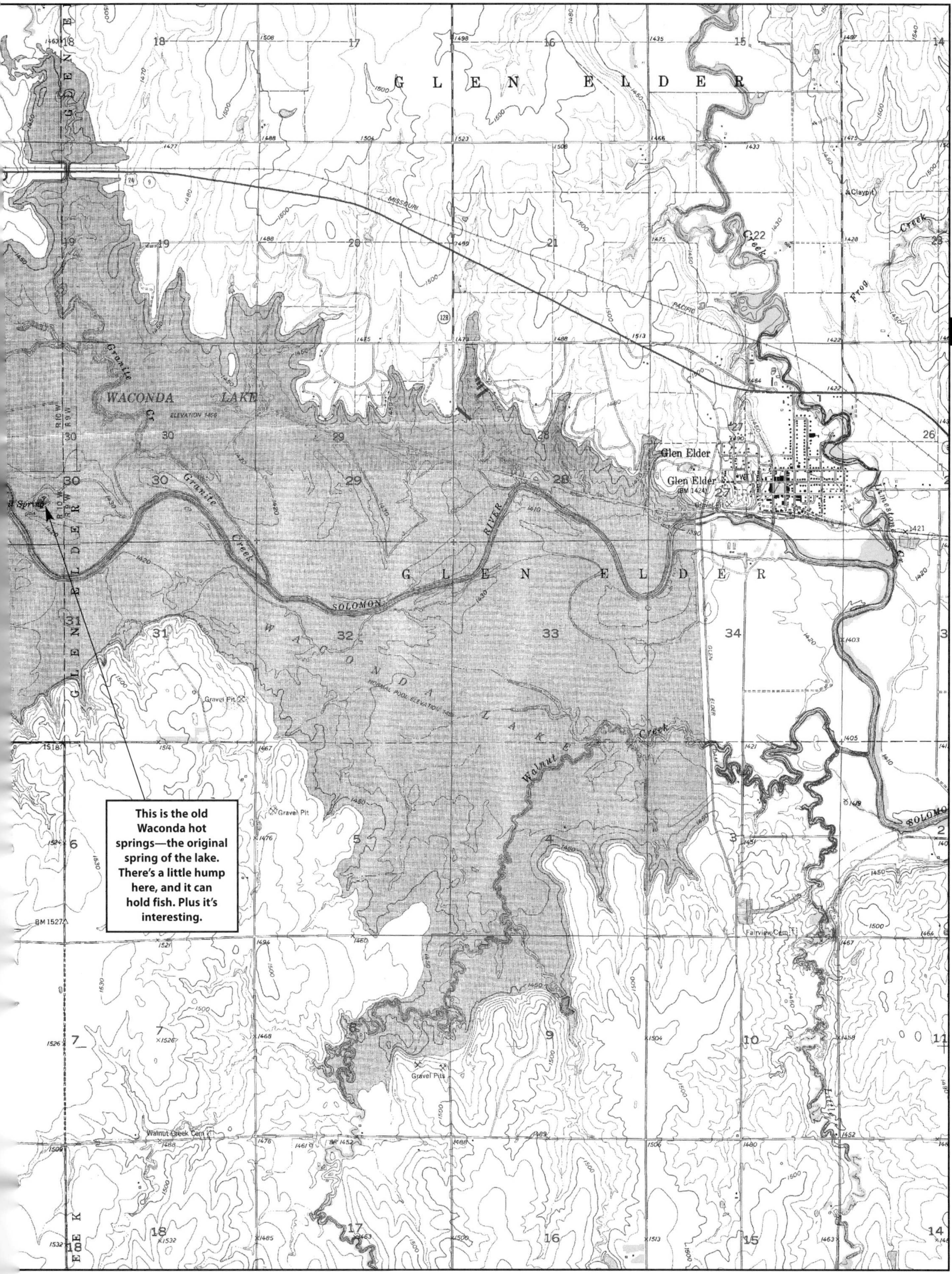

Glen Elder Reservoir (Waconda Lake)

This is the old Waconda hot springs—the original spring of the lake. There's a little hump here, and it can hold fish. Plus it's interesting.

GLEN ELDER

WACONDA LAKE

ELEVATION 1468

Glen Elder

Glen Elder
BM 1424

GLEN ELDER

SOLOMON RIVER

WACONDA LAKE

MISSOURI

PACIFIC

Granite Creek

Walnut Creek

Limestone Cr

Frog Creek

Gravel Pit

Gravel Pit

Gravel Pits

Gravel Pits

Fairview Cem

Walnut Creek Cem

BM 1527

Spring

SOLOMON

R 10 W
R 9 W

R 9 W
R 8 W

itself," he says. Though Glen Elder is primarily a silt and mud bottom lake, the impoundment has plenty of rocky shoreline to attract crappie and other fish—including the south shore bluffs and the riprap created by the causeway embankment near Cawker City, where the confluence of the North and South Forks of the Solomon River enter the lake. Look for spring crappie along the bluffs, or in the lake's numerous coves.

Wayne Jay lives in the nearby town of Glen Elder and fishes the lake more often than he doesn't—and most of the time he's chasing crappie. "You can catch crappie just about anywhere," Jay says. "Last year we caught them right up to the dog days of summer."

As the water temperature reaches the mid-60s in May, Jay heads to the numerous brush piles and underwater timber located near rocky shorelines. KDWP staff at Glen Elder consistently work to improve habitat in the lake, and both deep water and shallow brush piles are abundant.

Jay prefers to dip tube jigs in shallow water with a long pole in areas between the brush and the shoreline, generally using 1/8-ounce jigheads with a chartreuse tube, beaver tail or twister tail jig. In the spring, though, color doesn't matter much at all as the spawn-mode crappie will hit just about anything that's put in front of their noses.

Walleye: Though the crappie fishing has exploded in the past several years, the lake is better known for its walleye fishing—and there are plenty of walleye in the lake. During the 2010 spring fishing season, anglers were catching plenty of walleye, but the better part of the fish population fell below the 18-inch length limit at the lake. "There are lots of 15-, 16-, and 17-inch walleye," Jay said. "A lot of throwbacks."

According to Waters' recent sampling of the fish population, about 3 out of 25 walleye will measure more than 18 inches. The good news, however, is that the fish thrown back in the lake during 2010 will be keepers in the coming years. Waters estimates that 76 percent of walleye population in 2010 landed between 12 and 16 inches, with another 6 percent around 17 inches. "A lot of these should be keepers in 2011," Waters says.

The jig and crawler combination is an exceptional method for landing post-spawn walleye, with orange and chartreuse twister tails being the preferred colors and bait. But much like the crappie, the color isn't nearly as important as tipping the jig with a worm and finding the location.

After the spawn, which generally occurs in late March through early April, the walleye hide out for a while before moving toward the mud flats to feed. Many anglers spend their day drifting across the area between the Solomon River and the Granite Creek causeways. Look to the north for the Cawker City golf course, and you'll know that you're in the right location. Another popular location is along Gibbs Point, on the south side of the lake near Schoen's Cove, where another smaller mud flat is located.

White Bass/Wiper: When the walleye stop their voracious feeding frenzy, and the crappie move out to deeper water, anglers still have plenty of reasons to head to Glen Elder. The lake features a healthy white bass and wiper population, which can be found just about any time of year. Waters said the white bass are abundant in the lake, and the wiper population continues to grow both in numbers and size, with some fish coming in over 22 inches long and weighing upwards of 7 pounds.

Whites and wipers can be caught on crankbaits or jigs along the rocky shoreline of the causeway and the sandy beach area near Harrison Point, on the lake's south side.

Black Bass: When it comes to bass, there's also something happening at Glen Elder that not many people have figured out yet: It's starting to become a good fishery for black bass, specifically for smallmouth.

According to Waters' 2010 sampling, Glen Elder ranks third in Kansas for its density of smallmouth bass, and Waters says anglers are landing some fish

ranging 12–15 inches, with some reports of fish weighing up to 6 pounds. Even though he's trying to spread the word about the smallmouth bass fishing at Glen Elder, as of 2010 many anglers hadn't yet discovered the lake's potential for these popular sport fish.

Spring crappie anglers often find the smallies mixed in with crappie near the rocky areas and in the brush piles, as the two species, along with largemouth, head to the spawning grounds around the same time of year. Waters says the bigger smallmouth have been found in deeper water near the rocky shorelines. Popular baits include jigs and swimbaits, as well as shad- or crawfish-colored crankbaits.

Although smallmouth are the dominant black bass in Glen Elder, Waters sees encouraging signs for an up-and-coming largemouth population, largely thanks to improved water levels at the lake in recent years.

Catfish: During the summer months, some anglers begin their pursuit of channel and flathead catfish, and Glen Elder has no shortage of those fish. Waters began stocking blue catfish in the lake in the fall of 2010, and those massive fish will add another fishing opportunity for anglers at Glen Elder.

Jay advises that a popular catfish method is to throw a cast net for shad, and drift for channel cats during the night. "It's kind of like fishing for walleye, only for cats," Jay says.

Waters' figures show a numerous and healthy population at the lake, with 1 in 5 channel cats in his net sampling coming in over 20 inches long. While anglers can find cats just about anywhere in the lake, some of the more popular fishing areas include the south shore near the dam, around the bridge to Granite Creek, and along the bluffs and the sandy beach area on the lake's south shore. Some anglers, however, venture past the Solomon River causeway near the North Fork boat ramp on the upper end of the lake.

Whatever the species, and whatever time of year, anglers are likely to find success at Glen Elder for something. "Everybody's catching fish," Waters says. If it's too hot during the summer days, try fishing at night. And as fall sets in and the temperature cools, anglers will again find active fish roaming the lake's waters.

Facilities

The lake's rich history—it once was the location of a hot springs used by Native Americans for its healing properties—can be explored at **Glen Elder State Park.** Local supporters maintain the old Hopewell Church, which is often used to house events and dinners, and visitors can hike up a scale version of the original hot springs near the church.

Cawker City is home to the "World's Biggest Ball of Twine," and the wildlife area surrounding the lake is filled with pheasant, turkeys, deer, and a variety of other wild species.

For lake visitors, the park area includes 11 different campgrounds with a mixture of primitive and RV camping. Many campsites at the lake are close to the water and offer a spectacular view of the lake and easy access to shoreline fishing. Glen Elder also has a total of 8 boat ramps, making access to the water relatively easy.

Glen Elder State Park, spanning 1,391 acres in one area, was honored as one of the top five best parks by *Field & Stream* in 2004. Scenic trails in the park are under development. In total, the park offers: 112 campsites with water, sewer, and electric; 8 sites with electric only; 240 non-utility sites; 3 shower houses; 2 dump stations; 1 shelter house; 6 boat ramp lanes; 2 courtesy docks; boat rental available at marina; 1 fish cleaning station; 1 swimming beach.

Shopping/Supplies

Glen Elder is a lake that's a little unlike any other in Kansas. The active **Waconda Lake Association** sponsors an annual contest as a fundraiser for the organization, which assists KDWP staff in many lake projects. The annual **Fish-A-Thon** contest begins on May 1 of every year and generally runs through the end of Labor Day weekend. For a $10 entry fee—which covers an entire family—anglers can redeem tagged fish that they catch for cash prizes, which in 2010 totaled $9,500 for approximately 325 tagged fish. Entry forms must be purchased before you catch a tagged fish, and they can be bought at Wayne's Sporting Goods, and Waconda Boats in Glen Elder, at the Glen Elder Marina on the lake, the KDWP park office, Lakeside Convenience on US 24, and Lakeside Lodge and The Little Bait Shop in Cawker City.

Bait shops and fishing supply stores are also abundant around the lake. At **The Little Bait Shop** in Cawker City, Marty White takes special care to ensure that her bait is fresh and ready for the lake. Marty cleans her massive stainless steel bait tanks twice a week and feeds the fish twice a day. The shop offers worms, minnows, catfish bait, salties—a mix between goldfish and perch—perch, and crawfish. Marty places bait orders on Wednesday mornings, so if anglers need something specific or a large order for the upcoming weekend, a call on Tuesday is advised. Open every day 7:00 a.m.–7:00 p.m. March 1–October. 1017 9th Ave., Cawker City, 785-781-4246, www.littlebaitshop.com.

Waynes Sporting Goods sells live bait, tackle, guns and ammo, hunting supplies, clothing, basic hardware and plumbing supplies, camping gear, beer, and groceries. Hours are 8:30 a.m. to 6:30 p.m. Monday through Saturday, noon to 5:00 p.m. on Sunday. 129 S. Mill St., Glen Elder, 785-545-3333, http://members.nckcn.com/wayneshdwe/waynes.htm.

Nearby Beloit, about 12 miles east of Glen Elder Reservoir, has lodging, tackle, and full service restaurants and shopping areas.

Glen Elder Marina, 306 N. Broadway Ave., Beloit, 785-545-3251; **Waconda Boats,** 408 N. Center St., Glen Elder, 785-545-3545.

Hillsdale Reservoir

SIZE: 4,580 acres

LOCATION: From Olathe, a southwestern suburb of Kansas City, travel south on US 169 about 13 miles to 255 St. Turn west, and travel about 2 miles to the entrance to Hillsdale State Park.

CONTACT: Hillsdale Lake Project Office, U.S. Army Corps of Engineers, 913-783-4366

FEATURE FISH: Largemouth Bass, Bluegill, Channel Catfish, Flathead Catfish, Crappie, Walleye, White Bass

DAILY CREEL LIMIT/MINIMUM LENGTH: Largemouth Bass: 5 fish, 18 inches • Channel Catfish: 10 fish • Flathead Catfish: 5 fish • Crappie: 20 fish, 10 inches • Walleye: 5 fish, 18 inches

There are several ways to tell if you're fishing at a crappie lake. Plenty of standing timber, ample shoreline vegetation, and a consistent water level all help make a body of water in which crappie can thrive. But you really know you're at a crappie lake when it's not unusual to see a fisherman's boat and truck emblazoned with the label "Uncle Crappie."

Roger "Uncle Crappie" Cameron, of Edgerton, spends as much time as he can fishing at northeast Kansas lakes, but you're most likely to find him at Miami County's Hillsdale Reservoir. "I fish down here every day," Cameron says, adding that he can usually "pick up some fish in the deep brush piles" even in the heat of summer.

Hillsdale contains excellent habitat for both crappie and walleye—the two species most anglers in the area spend their time chasing. Biologists are quick to point out, however, that the lake offers a variety of opportunities for bass and bluegills. Kansas Department of Wildlife and Parks biologists rated Hillsdale good for white bass, crappie, and walleye in the 2010 fishing forecast. Additionally, the lake resists seasonal fluctuations in the water level, which aids in fish spawning and recruitment and keeps the water relatively clear throughout the year.

Dave Spalsbury, who previously worked as the KDWP fisheries biologist at Hillsdale before moving to Cedar Bluff, says the lake is one of the newest in Kansas. Construction on the lake finished up in 1982, and the KDWP began fisheries management shortly thereafter. Most of the standing timber in the valley was left in place and remains standing today, providing a seemingly endless supply of holes for anglers to fish. It's not uncommon to see boats tied off to a tree, with anglers dancing a tube jig or minnow off the side, or maneuvering through the dense timber stands looking for lurking crappie.

Current fisheries biologist Andy Jansen, who took over management of the lake in early 2009, credits Spalsbury with adding to the lake's habitat by installing a lot of deep water brush piles throughout the lake, giving fish—and anglers—a place to gather in the summer and winter.

> **I was surprised by a school of bluegill** while drifting off of Hillsdale Point one summer day. I had a worm harness on the end of my line while fishing for walleye. Suddenly, a scrappy bluegill attacked the worm, providing a fun fight on a hot afternoon. I kept drifting through the area and picked up several more bluegill—which is never a disappointment.
>
> What impressed me the most about Hillsdale was that this is a lake built for anglers. I was amazed at the amount of standing timber available to fish. If that isn't enough to impress you, the water is home to dozens of brush piles that attract fish. Whatever it is—rocky shorelines, mud flats, or sandy beaches, Hillsdale has the structure to fish and the fish you want to catch.

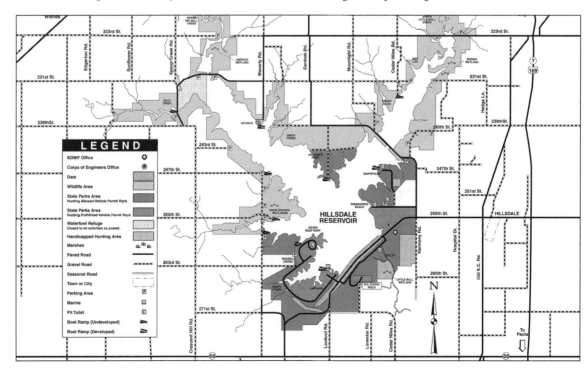

What I found in Hillsdale is a true fishing lake—it practically begs you to stop and put your boat in the water. And once on the water, there's a long list of potential fishing holes that are all worth dropping a line in.

Feature Fish

Walleye: In addition to the timber and brush piles, Hillsdale Reservoir has a lot of rocky shoreline and bottom areas that create ideal structure for walleye. Aggressive stocking and good retention and recruitment are working to make Hillsdale among the state's best walleye lakes. Biologists collected nearly 4 million walleye eggs during their 2009 hatchery collection at Hillsdale, and Jansen says the lake has had several good year classes of walleye recently, which should keep walleye anglers busy in upcoming fishing seasons.

Like nearly all large lakes in Kansas, the walleye will move toward the riprap of the dam in the early spring to spawn, and then move toward the mud flats in May and June. Look for walleye off of Hillsdale Point when they move on the flats to feed. In addition to the dam's riprap, look for walleye to gather around other rocky areas around the lake, including the shoreline's many points. Other popular areas for walleye anglers include anywhere in the spreads of standing timber and the riprap along the Tontzville causeway bridge on the northern arm of the lake, toward the Marysville boat ramp and camping area.

Jansen says the jig and worm works well for walleye, and Cameron says he hits the mud flats with a 3/8 or 1/2 ounce jig tipped with a nightcrawler.

Crappie: Crappie fishing dominates Hillsdale, with the fall fishing reaching near legendary levels. The crappie fishing slows during the early fall, when the lake turns over, but improves once the water has settled—and remains good for the rest of the winter. Look for crappie to gather over deep water brush piles in the fall—beginning in October as the temperatures begin to cool, and continuing well into November, which Spalsbury says is the best time of year for crappie fishing at the lake.

Try a small jig tipped with a minnow—red and chartreuse are among the most popular colors at Hillsdale. Many crappie anglers use this method along one of the creek beds in the lake.

Cameron says he spends much of his time searching out the lake's brush piles, and often finds the fish in 12–15 feet of water. One, just south of the causeway, is an enormous collection of cedar trees that is easy to spot on a depth finder. He prefers to use a slip bobber to maintain a consistent depth, and his standby colors are red and chartreuse and black and chartreuse.

Black Bass: While Hillsdale may have gained fame as a walleye and crappie lake, Jansen said the lake is a "fair bass fishery."

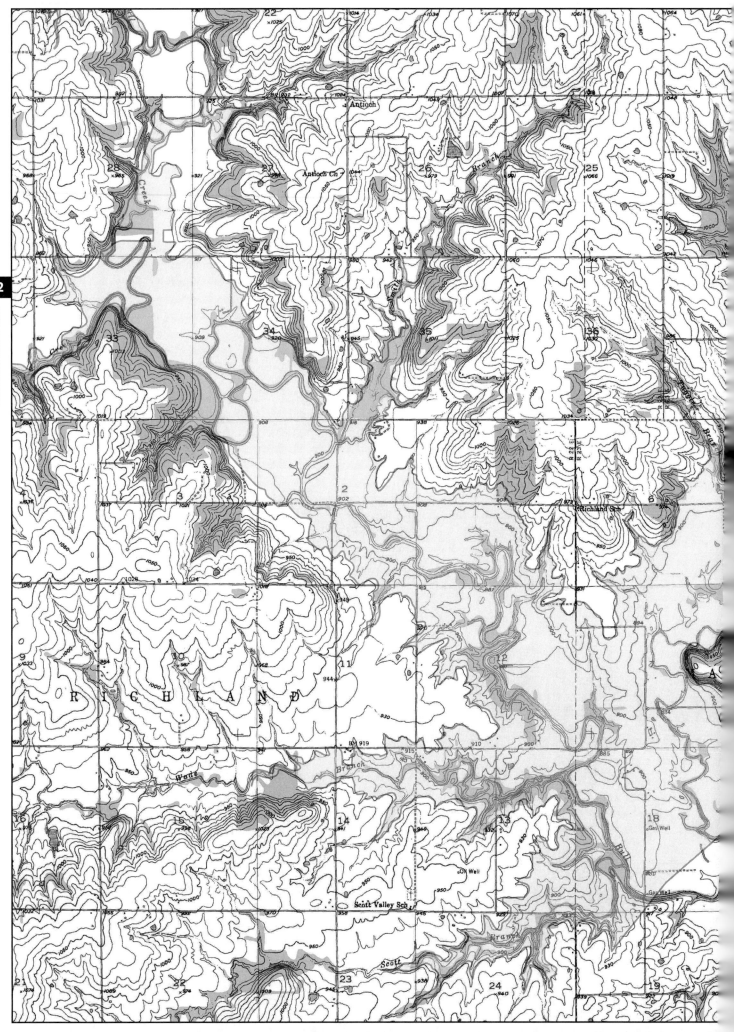

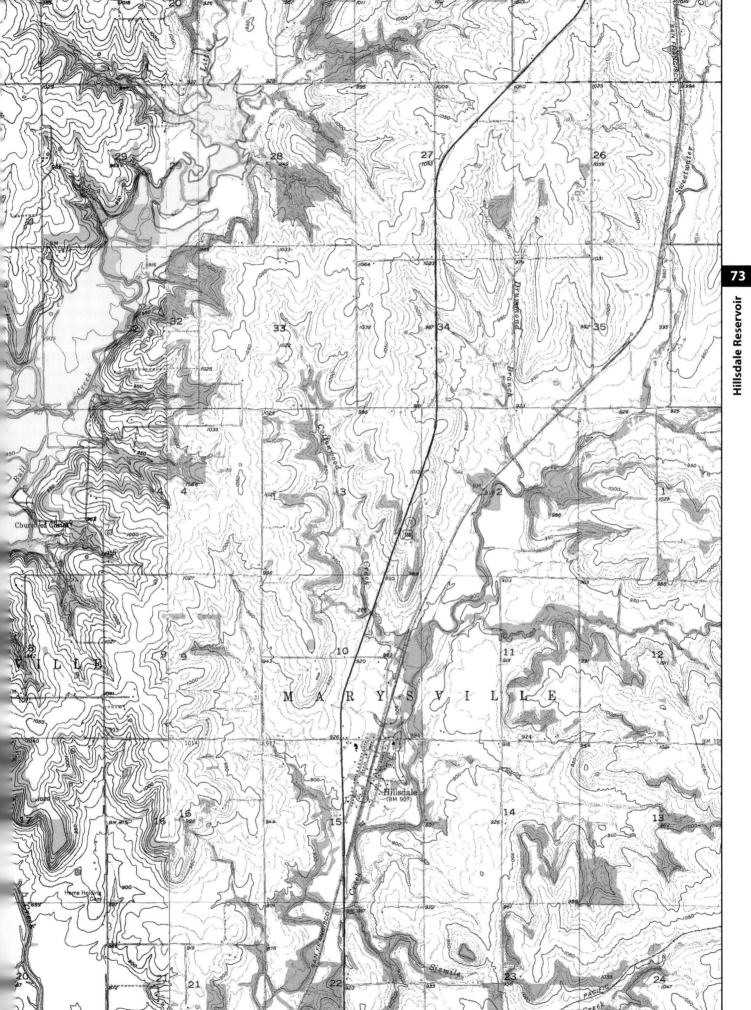

In 2009, the KDWP launched a research project aimed at improving the largemouth bass population. This project included the planting of water willows along the shoreline to create more habitat for largemouth bass. The early spawned largemouth come from the hatchery in Meade, Jansen said. Biologists there artificially change the photoperiod, or length of daylight, to trigger spawning by adults in March and April. The fish are then transplanted to Hillsdale in the hope that they'll find food and grow faster and reach greater sizes than naturally spawned bass.

Specifically, biologists have recently been working in the Scott Cove area, near the southwest edge of the dam, to increase bass habitat. Hillsdale's improving bass population has caught the interest of local tournament organizers, who have used the lake more in recent years as the site for annual tournaments.

Spalsbury says the most popular bait is a spinnerbait or a jig and pig combination. Try fishing for black bass around shallow timber and vegetation in the spring season, and in deeper timber as the water warms.

Catfish: The ubiquitous channel catfish provides another angling opportunity at Hillsdale, and Jansen says the lake contains both high numbers of cats, as well as many large ones that will put up a fight. Most of the cat fishing at Hillsdale is done in the upper ends of the reservoir, using dough baits or shad sides, fished along the windblown banks that generally face Kansas' southerly summer wind. Aside from the rod and reel, many anglers opt to set up limb lines in this part of the lake. Spalsbury

says anglers shouldn't overlook the chance to hook into a giant flathead at Hillsdale.

White Bass: Hillsdale is also home to one of the most abundant game fish in Kansas—the white bass. In mid-April, look for the whites to migrate upstream to spawn. Anglers searching for spawning whites should start on the west side of the Tontzville causeway bridge, on the northeast arm of the reservoir, near the Marysville campground. Jigs and small spinners are productive this time of year. Post-spawn, these fish will set up around some of the lake's main points—including Hillsdale Point, Wade Branch, and Marysville State Park—as well as the Tontzville causeway bridge. Many anglers rely on jigs or crank baits that imitate shad. Jansen says there are good numbers of white bass in Hillsdale, and that most fish measure between 12–15 inches.

Bluegill: Hillsdale is home to a "moderate abundance" of bluegill, according to Jansen, and some of those fish measure up to 8 inches in length. Most anglers specifically fishing for bluegill find them along the shoreline, using a small jig or live bait fished under a bobber. Productive areas include Scott Cove, on the lake's southwest edge, and the Marysville camping area.

Boaters need to be cautious as they navigate the waters. Standing trees cover a large amount of the lake, and in some cases the timber is just below the surface, ready to wreak havoc on props and lower units. Watch for trail markings on your way in and out of the boat ramps, and pay particular attention to marker buoys.

Hillsdale Reservoir Brush Pile GPS Coordinates in Decimal Degrees, Map Datum NAD83		
Name	**Longitude**	**Latitude**
bp1	W094.93048	N38.64805
bp2	W094.93014	N38.64744
bp3	W094.93223	N38.64613
bp4	W094.93239	N38.64601
bp5	W094.93257	N38.64593
bp6	W094.93297	N38.64557
bp7	W094.93325	N38.64539
bp8	W094.93337	N38.64528
bp9	W094.93371	N38.64509
bp10	W094.93403	N38.64495
bp11	W094.89748	N38.67773
bp12	W094.89828	N38.69222
bp13	W094.89741	N38.69251
bp14	W094.89702	N38.69279
bp15	W094.94708	N38.69250
bp16	W094.94691	N38.69360
bp17	W094.94704	N38.69379
bp18	W094.94713	N38.69395
bp19	W094.94722	N38.69413
bp20	W094.94779	N38.69478
bp21	W094.94782	N38.69492
bp22	W094.94421	N38.69326
bp23	W094.94534	N38.69457
bp24	W094.94288	N38.69476
bp25	W094.94215	N38.69504
bp26	W094.94205	N38.69519
bp27	W094.93699	N38.66412
bp28	W094.94645	N38.66321
bp29	W094.94644	N38.66343
bp30	W094.94643	N38.66366
bp31	W094.94641	N38.66384
bp32	W094.94634	N38.66403
bp33	W094.94635	N38.66417
bp34	W094.94640	N38.66433
bp35	W094.94645	N38.66451
bp36	W094.90004	N38.67656
bp37	W094.89887	N38.67613
bp38	W094.89917	N38.67590
bp39	W094.89849	N38.67479
bp40	W094.89835	N38.67491
bp41	W094.89771	N38.67667
bp42	W094.89577	N38.67619
bp43	W094.89524	N38.67595
bp44	W094.89519	N38.67651
bp45	W094.89592	N38.67677
bp46	W094.89638	N38.67762
bp47	W094.89677	N38.67734
bp48	W094.89712	N38.67773
bp49	W094.89818	N38.67848

Facilities

Hillsdale offers an abundance of recreational opportunities outside of angling. **The Saddle Ridge** horse camping area and trailhead provide access to more than 30 miles of horseback trails. Behind the dam, to the west of the outlet area, is an established radio-controlled airplane flying field, which is popular in the area. The U.S. Army Corps of Engineers land around the lake provides hunters and outdoors enthusiasts more than 7,000 acres of land that is home to deer, waterfowl, and other game birds.

Hillsdale offers plenty of camping areas managed by the KDWP. Hillsdale State Park, 2,830 acres in five areas, encompasses the area around Scott Cove and includes the Crappie Cove, Quail Run, Rabbit Ridge, and Scott Creek campgrounds. To the north, across the dam, you'll find Windsurfer Beach, which is open from sunrise to sunset, and the Saddle Ridge horse camping area. The lake also features 9 boat ramps in various locations along the shoreline. In total, the state park offers: 175 campsites with water and electric; 40 non-utility sites; 3 shower houses; 1 dump station; 9 shelter houses; 10 boat ramp lanes, with five ramps improved with concrete ramps and loading docks; 5 courtesy docks; boat rentals available; marina available; and 1 swimming beach.

Shopping/Supplies

Hillsdale is serviced by **Jayhawk Marina,** located in the southern part of the lake, near the mouth of Scott Cove. Aside from a full service marina and bait shop, the Jayhawk Marina offers a floating cabin available for rent—which includes its own boat slip. The cabins are furnished with two full-size bunk beds, air conditioning, a table and four chairs, shelving, and clothing hangers. There's also an indoor fishing dock for cold weather fishing. The marina store is well stocked with boating and fishing supplies, packaged food, soft drinks, and beer. 0.5 mile past the entrance to Hillsdale State Park, 913-557-9900.

K M S Lake N Dale sells fuel, food and features barbeque meals daily, with breakfast on Saturday and Sunday. Open 5:00 a.m. to 9:00 p.m. daily. 25495 Old KC Rd., Hillsdale, 913-783-4684.

Alco Discount Store, 1220 W. Amity St., Louisburg, 913-837-1431; **Circle C Country Supply,** 136 Fairlane Dr., Louisburg, 913-837-1440; **Jayhawk Marina,** 26353 Jayhawk Dr., Paola, 913-686-2319; **Orscheln Farm and Home,** 1160 W. Amity St., Louisburg, 913-837-4566; **Ozmart,** 503 E. Main St., Osawatomie, 913-256-3130; **Rands Louisburg,** 304 S. Metcalf Rd., Louisburg, 913-837-2416; **Rands,** 25500 Old KC Rd., Hillsdale, 913-783-4411; **Walmart,** 310 Hedge Ln., Paola, 913-294-5400; **Walmart,** 310 Hedge Ln., Paola, 913-294-5400.

Contacts

Miami County Clerk, 201 S. Pearl, Suite 102, Paola, 913-294-3976; **Hillsdale State Park,** 26001 W. 255th St., Paola, 913-783-4507.

John Redmond Reservoir

SIZE: 9,400 acres

LOCATION: 2.5 miles north of Burlington on US 75

GPS LOCATION: N38 13 55.82 W95 46 28.18

CONTACT: U.S. Army Corps of Engineers, 620-364-8613

FEATURE FISH: Channel Catfish, Flathead Catfish

DAILY CREEL LIMIT/MINIMUM LENGTH: Largemouth Bass: 6 fish, 15 inches • Smallmouth Bass: 6 fish, 15 inches • Spotted Bass: 6 fish, 15 inches • Blue Catfish: 10 fish • Channel Catfish: 10 fish • Flathead Catfish: 5 fish • Crappie: 50 fish • Paddlefish: 2 fish • Sauger: 5 fish, 15 inches • Saugeye: 5 fish, 15 inches • Striped Bass: 2 fish • Walleye: 5 fish, 15 inches • Wiper: 2 fish

Call this the big muddy. Typically not much more than six feet deep, at best, this is John Redmond Reservoir in Coffey County, which is located in an area known as the Catfish Capital of the World—a title encouraged by local anglers, and bait store owners.

Catfish is what's for dinner in Burlington, a town crowned Catfish Capitol by its residents. "We've always had good cat fishing, even before John Redmond was built," says Loy Hall, an avid catfish angler who owns The Bait Shop in Burlington.

And catfish is exactly what I found when I ventured to Redmond on one of its busiest days of the year, the annual Ducks Unlimited Catfish Tournament. Well, perhaps I should clarify what I mean by "found."

We went to the tournament weigh-in, where I watched as angler after angler brought their five heaviest fish to the scales, hoping they had enough poundage to be one of the tournament winners.

That included Jeremy Way of Emporia, who hoisted more than 37 pounds of catfish onto the scales during the event. "We actually didn't do too bad this year," Jeremy's father and fishing partner, John Way, said with a grin as the two headed back to their boat with the stringer with their heaviest five fish, including one that weighed 9.16 pounds.

But, alas, it wasn't enough to win the $500 payout, which was awarded to Ryan Gnagy of Tecumseh, whose five fish weighed a total of 55.5 pounds. In total, nearly 600 pounds of catfish crossed the scales that day from the 40 boats that graced the waters, proving John Redmond is just as prolific with catfish as locals say.

Yet, says Bob Hammond who helps plan the annual tournament, while it would seem simple to find catfish in this shallow of water, the lake isn't necessarily easy fishing.

That's what my husband John and I found when we ventured here the summer before the DU tournament. It was hot. There was no wind. Brett and Kaci were hot and whiney. We didn't catch a lick, and it didn't look like the only other boat on the lake that July afternoon was having any luck, either.

But, obviously, after spending an afternoon with some expert cat fishers, there's plenty of catfish to be reeled from this Coffey County lake.

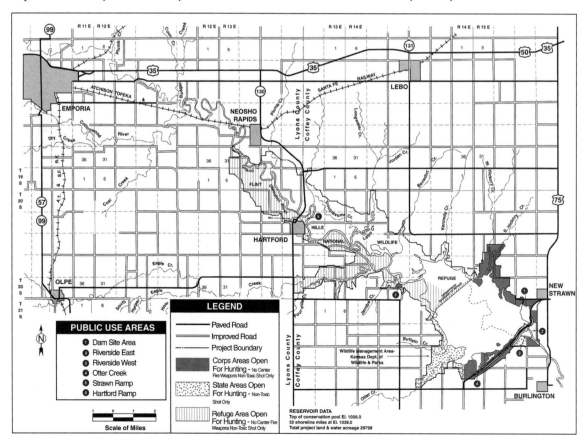

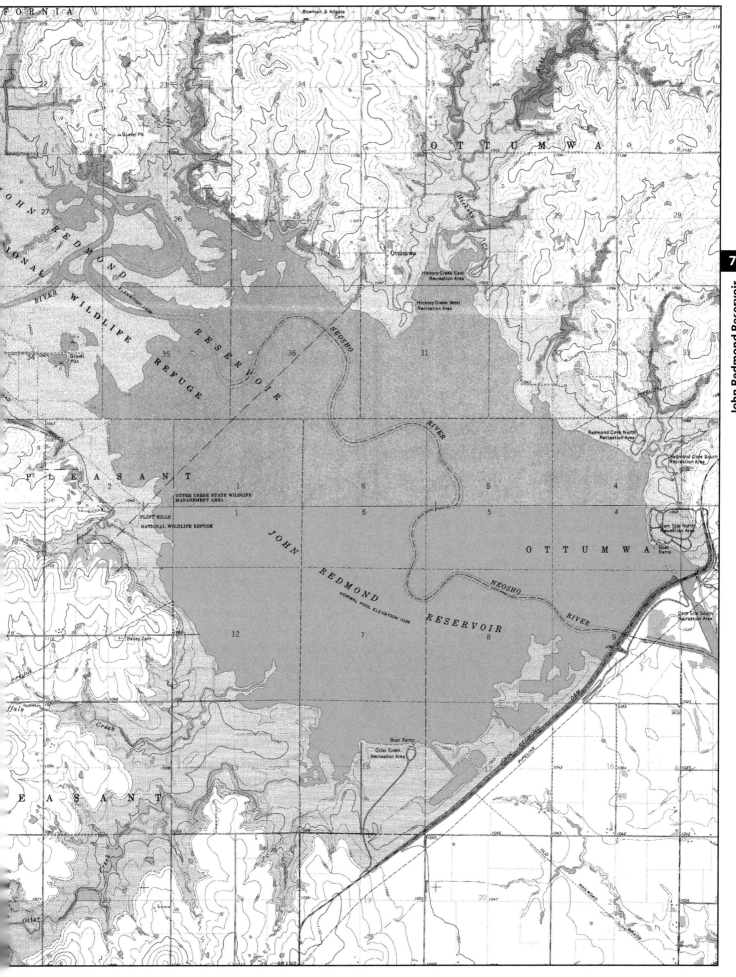

• • •

Before the reservoir was built, according to the U.S. Army Corps of Engineers, the Neosho River Valley was flooded 57 times in 34 years. In the worst flood, "floodwaters ran 30 feet deep at the dam site and one-third million acres were under water."

The reservoir, which sits in the Neosho River Valley, was originally approved by Congress in 1950 as "Strawn Dam," and in 1958 lawmakers renamed it after *Burlington Daily Republican* Publisher John Redmond. Redmond was one of the first to champion flood control and water conservation along the Neosho River.

Construction on the reservoir began in 1959. According to the Kansas Water Office, the town of New Strawn was relocated six miles east on higher ground when the dam was constructed. Part of "Old Strawn" is now underwater.

About 3,000 square miles drains into the lake, according to the KWO. However, sedimentation has taken a toll at Redmond. In 2010, capacity loss due to sedimentation was 37 percent, according to the KWO.

Feature Fish

Catfish: Sedimentation issues and the muddy waters have left this lake a prime channel and flathead catfish water body, says Leonard Jirak, a fisheries biologist with the Kansas Department of Wildlife and Parks. According to Jirak, when water temperatures creep into the 70s, the catfish spawn begins, which draws anglers to the reservoir's dam. Yet, this isn't the only time to catch catfish.

Each year in late July, New Strawn resident Bob Hammond helps plan the Ducks Unlimited Catfish Tournament at John Redmond, which draws 40 to 50 boats, depending on the year. Of the reservoir, Hammond, who fishes for catfish when it is not duck hunting season, says, "It's like a big saucer. It's a lot different than the other lakes that are deeper, clearer, and have good walleye and other fish."

Some anglers can catch white bass in the spillway, and sometimes crappie in nearby Lebo and Eagle creeks. Indeed, the state record white bass was caught in the river above John Redmond. Marvin Gary, of Peculiar, Missouri, used a rod and reel with a roadrunner lure to bring in a 5.67-pound, 20⅜-inch white bass in April of 2002.

However, Hammond says, most drift the lake for catfish. The best time to fish is a few days after a good rain. "Some get up to the Strawn Flats and catch the runoff," he notes. Of course, that's only if the water in the northern area of the lake is plentiful.

Anglers also are allowed to use float lines during daylight July 15–September 15, according to KDWP. This fishing method provides an additional angling opportunity on reservoirs with untapped channel catfish populations.

Coffey County's rivers, including the Neosho, are hot for fishing channels and flatheads, as well. Hall fishes the Neosho River downstream of Redmond. A logjam in the river at the head of the lake is a good spot, according to Hall. He adds that Redmond catfish anglers can cast net the abundance of shad in the lake for bait. Others try cut bait, goldfish, stink bait, and shrimp. "If you stick with it, you can catch a few in John Redmond," he says. "Where you catch a catfish today, you won't catch there tomorrow."

He noted the town of Chetopa also considers itself a catfish capitol—an area of Kansas where anglers also can catch lunker catfish. The two towns used to have a contest, with a trophy given to the town that caught the biggest catfish that year. "[Chetopa] would swipe it from Burlington, and Burlington would swipe it back from them," Hall says, adding that, at one time, the trophy was sitting on a shelf in the Jaycee's building in Burlington.

"I can't honestly tell you where it is today," he says, but adds Burlington's claim to fame "is on the city sign when you enter town."

Facilities

The lake attracts visitors for camping, fishing, and birding, since it is located in the middle of the Central Flyway.

The lake offers several amenities, including 96 utility campsites, as well as non-utility camping, group shelters, several boat ramps, and swimming beaches.

Trails include the **Otter Creek All-Terrain Vehicle Area,** 140 acres of trails for dirt bikes and ATVs, and **Hickory Creek Trail,** a multiple-use trail for hikers, horseback riders, and mountain bikers.

Shopping/Supplies

Coffey County Clerk, 110 S. 6th St., Burlington, 620-364-2191; **Lakeview Bait & Tackle,** 203 N. Main St., New Strawn, 620-364-8354; **Pamida,** 300 Cross St., Burlington, 620-364-2924; **Sundance Bait & Tackle,** 8145 W. 325th St., Lebo, 620-256-6061.

Guide Service

Catdaddy Guide and Tour, 1308 NW. Logan St., Topeka, 785-357-0934, www.catdaddyguideservices.com.

Kanopolis Reservoir

SIZE: 3,550 acres

LOCATION: From Salina, travel 32 miles southwest on K-140/K-14 to the Kanopolis State Park entrance. Continue south to reach the south shore entrance.

CONTACT: U.S. Army Corps of Engineers, 785-546-2294

FEATURE FISH: Channel Catfish, Crappie, Saugeye, Trout, Walleye, White Bass, Wipers

DAILY CREEL LIMIT/MINIMUM LENGTH: Largemouth Bass, 5 fish, 15 inches • Channel Catfish: 10 fish • Flathead Catfish: 5 fish • Crappie: 50 fish • Saugeye: 5 fish, 15 inches • Trout: 5 fish • Walleye: 5 fish, 15 inches • Wiper: 2 fish

Most anglers have a place they call "home." It might be a local farm pond, a stretch of creek, or a reservoir that's easy to visit after a day of work or every weekend. For me, Kanopolis is that place.

My dad and I spent many weekends at this reservoir in Ellsworth County. We fished from the shore, before moving up to a canoe mounted with a 2.5-horsepower outboard motor and eventually a full-size fishing boat. Today, it's the lake I still visit most often, and I know it better than I know any other lake—though others still know it much better than me.

But I've fished Kanopolis Reservoir enough to know it's a lake full of options. Anglers who like to fish for walleye head to the lake in March, right after ice out, and know to hit Loder Point for hungry pre-spawn fish. Those who like white bass know to hit the lake in April as the fish migrate toward the upper end in preparation for their annual trip up the Smoky Hill River. Catfish anglers know where the "chumming hole" can be found, and anglers without a boat know that the spillway always provides a chance to catch something—even if it's a massive drum.

"The fish are always biting," says George Dickinson, who with his wife Connie owns the Smoky Hill Trading Post, which sits to the south of the dam. "It's a good fishing lake."

And while it's not unexpected that a local store owner would make the case that the hometown fishing hole is always worth going to, he's not really stretching the truth too awful much. Local anglers have been saying the same thing for the past several years, and their anecdotal stories about buckets full of fish being hauled out of the lake are largely true—as corroborated by the research of fisheries biologist Tommie Berger.

Prior to 2007, Kanopolis suffered from low water levels, even dropping to the point in 2006 that the official boat ramps at the lake were unusable. During that time, however, trees and vegetation took hold around the lake's shoreline—and when the lake refilled in 2007, fish suddenly found an ample supply of cover.

The result has been a fishing resurgence at Kanopolis, the likes of which haven't been seen at the

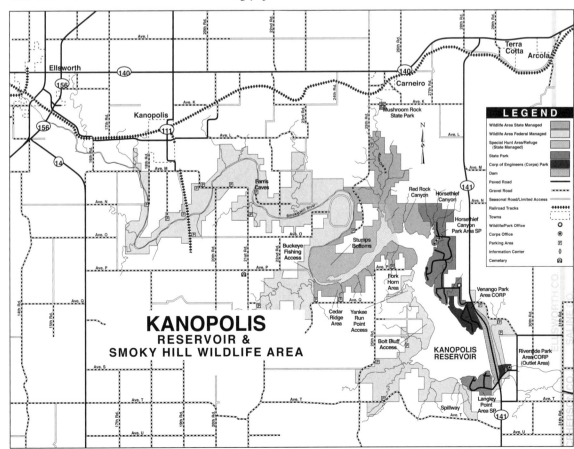

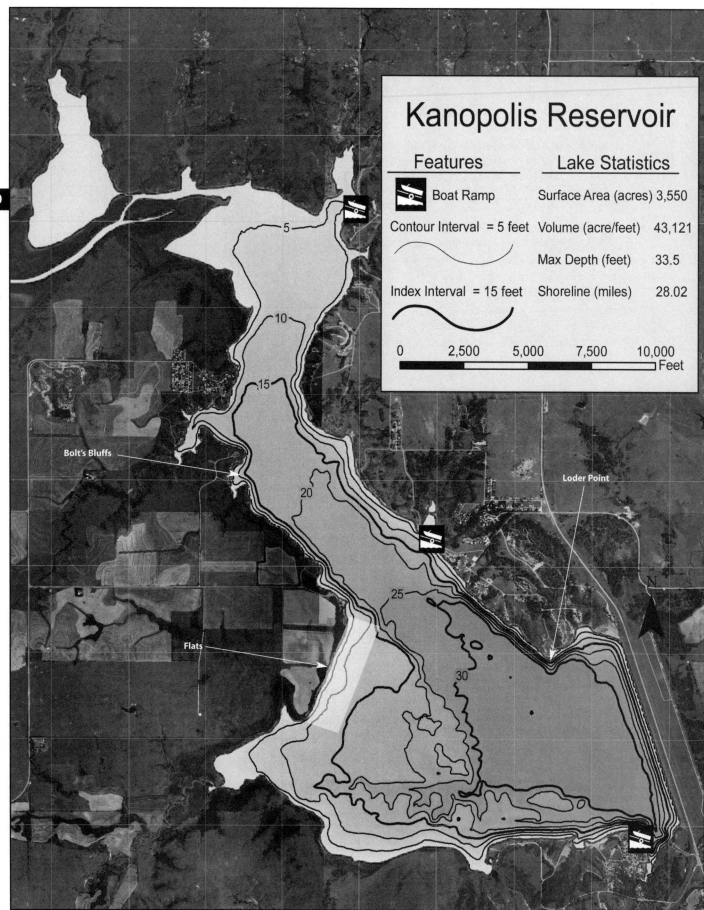

Kanopolis Reservoir

Features

| Boat Ramp |
| Contour Interval = 5 feet |
| Index Interval = 15 feet |

Lake Statistics

Surface Area (acres)	3,550
Volume (acre/feet)	43,121
Max Depth (feet)	33.5
Shoreline (miles)	28.02

0   2,500   5,000   7,500   10,000
Feet

5

10

15

Bolt's Bluffs

Loder Point

20

25

Flats

30

N

lake for a number of years. "I am surprised the lake didn't go down a foot or more from just the fish that were removed," Berger wrote in his annual fishing forecast for 2010. "You guys hauled fish out of the lake in record numbers."

The lowest rating Berger gave any species in Kanopolis for 2010 was "fair" for wipers and walleye—though his sampling indicates that wipers are on the way up, not the way down. And when the walleye population is viewed alongside the saugeye population, the two species together garner a "good" rating. "The wiper numbers are up," Berger said. "Anglers are catching a lot more wipers and lots and lots of whites."

Feature Fish

White Bass/Wiper: Derek Wixson of Hutchinson has fished Kanopolis since he was a kid, but it's the Smoky Hill River above the lake that draws him each spring. In mid-April the white bass make their run up the river, and anglers who are willing to brave the still-chilly waters of the river generally leave with all the white bass they'd care to clean. "A guy can sit in the river and catch fish all day," Wixson says.

During the annual run, Wixson looks for an area that sits about halfway between the broken bridge, which is near the town of Kanopolis, and the lake itself, in a spot lined with white bluffs. It's there that the river turns and starts to get a little deeper, and where a curly tailed jig will draw the attention of the hungry white bass.

Wixson says the weather plays a big role in how the fish behave. As the temperature warms, and spring brings a few 75–80 degree days, the white bass will increase in activity. After a rain storm or a sudden cool down—something that's not uncommon during April—the fish will shut down for several days, and fishing will be a struggle at best.

Berger reminds anglers that not all of the white bass head upstream during this season, and that plenty of fish can still be caught along the Boldts Bluff and Yankee Run areas, as well as off the face of the dam and along other sandy shores in the lake. Those are areas I hit every March and April, when I'm itching to get the boat on the water. And more often than not, I'll find the whites in one of these early hot spots.

As spring gives way to summer, the whites and wipers return to the lake and continue their seemingly year-round feeding frenzy. One anonymous angler—who fishes the lake nearly every day of the year—says during the summer the whites tend to gather near where the water drops from the shallow flats on the west end of the lake to the deeper water of the river channel. "Those fish sit in there, and they're looking up," he says. "Anything that comes over that ridge, they're going to smack it."

He notes that if other local anglers knew he had shared the lake's best fishing information, they'd "throw rocks at me when I'm on the lake."

Wixson says he'll also spend time looking for the whites as they chase shad to the surface during the evening and morning hours, when the wind is down and the lake's at its stillest. He'll move along the dam until he sees the tell-tale sign of active white bass—the bubbling surface water and shad trying desperately to escape. "There's a real good shad population," Wixson says. "When the whites start chasing them, it looks like a meat grinder."

If the ice gets thick enough in the winter, anglers will catch whites around deep water brush piles. Trolling works well throughout the year, and whites are often caught by walleye anglers drifting worms around the flats.

Walleye/Saugeye: It's the walleye and saugeye fishing that gets most local anglers' blood flowing. The lake has a strong population of both fish, and the water is full of fish-holding structure that makes it fairly easy to find to success.

Just after the ice melts away—generally in late February or early March—the walleye and saugeye head to Loder Point, a rocky peninsula on the north side of the lake. The water is fairly shallow, but drops suddenly about 30 yards from the shoreline, depending on the water level. Kimble Point, to the west, is another productive area, and often anglers will fish between Loder and Kimble to find the fish staging for the spawn.

Wixson says his preferred bait is a chartreuse curly tail jig fished just off the bottom. Other popular colors include orange, white, and yellow. While many anglers will anchor their boats close to the ridge, others simply wade out in the shallow water and cast their bait as far as possible. Both methods have produced good numbers of early spring walleye.

During the spawn, walleye make their way to the dam. After the spawning season, the walleye are for the most part dormant for several weeks, but then reappear along the flats on the west side of the lake between Bluff Creek and the Boldt's Bluff area. It's here that the water drops from between 5–7 feet to 12–15 feet, and it's here that the walleye congregate in search of an easy meal. Drift fishing with a jig and crawler is the most common method, though many anglers will anchor off in the area and cast a crawler away from the boat. "I like to drag a worm on a white jig," one angler said. "But only hook about an eighth of the tip of that worm on the hook, and let the rest dangle out there."

The fish are harder to catch in the summer, but can be found in the river channel, and in the deeper water off Loder Point.

Catfish: Kanopolis can't be discussed without mention of one of the longest standing secrets at the lake—the chumming hole. During the dog days of summer, scores of anglers will anchor off about 300 yards north of the rock jetty near the South Shore boat ramp. For nearly 20 years, anglers have been gathering here during the year's hottest days to catch catfish.

Those cats, however, aren't simply coming to this spot in the middle of the lake all on their own. For years, local anglers have been tossing cups full of soured grain—the most popular is soybean—into the water in an effort to attract fish to a single hump in the deep water.

Local anglers say the hump is about 28 feet deep on one side, but then curves up to roughly 16 feet on the other side. Anchor off when you find this spot—

use a front and rear anchor so you don't swing around—and toss about two scoops of chum into the water alongside the boat. Dip baits and chicken livers—sometimes scented with garlic powder overnight—are the preferred baits, and many anglers simply tie on a hook, a split shot weight, and drop the bait straight down to the bottom.

If the fish aren't biting in about 15 minutes, toss a couple more scoops of chum into the water and keep waiting. The catfish in Kanopolis know to come to this hole, and anglers leaving the lake with their limit of catfish isn't only common, it's the norm.

During the spawning season, look for cats in the shallow waters of the lake's coves and around rocky points and jetties. The most popular cat fishing spot is the chumming hole

Crappie: For all the fishing options that Kanopolis offers, there's yet another that's emerging and gaining attention from anglers: crappie. After the high water of 2007, and the availability of shoreline vegetation, the crappie in Kanopolis have experienced a rebirth that really began to take hold in 2010. "The crappie fishing is getting better, but the crappie aren't," one local angler said, adding that while the numbers of crappie are encouraging, most fish are fairly small.

Berger's sampling placed the lake at number two in the state for crappie. He rated the crappie fishing as good, but said he'd have marked it excellent had the fish been a little larger. The fish are on an upward cycle, Berger said, and the next several years hold great promise for crappie anglers—thanks to healthy looking fish and an abundant shad population.

The future of crappie fishing at Kanopolis was revealed to anglers during the early months of 2010, when an unusually cold winter covered the lake in thick ice and gave die-hard anglers a chance to enjoy some productive ice fishing. "It was one of the best years I've ever seen for ice fishing," Wixson says. "We'd drill holes around the brush piles near the tower and fish them until we narrowed it down to two holes."

My own ice fishing experience wasn't as encouraging. I don't ice fish often, but the long, cold winter of 2010 put enough ice on the lakes to convince me to go. My first mistake, however, was thinking that I could drill through a foot of ice with a dull auger. Thanks to a friendly nearby angler with a power auger, my son and I had a couple of fishable holes. The fish, however, wouldn't cooperate; a day of jigging yielded nothing but frozen lines and frostbitten noses.

In the spring, look for crappie at the backs of coves—try Bluff Creek Cove, Marina Cove, and Buzzard Bay Cove. In the fall, before the ice sets in, local anglers suggest looking for schooling crappie in deep water brush piles, which can be found throughout the lake. While some anglers will toss out a minnow and bobber, most prefer small jigs tipped with crappie nibbles or some other small scented bait. Depth matters more than anything when fishing for crappie, but you'll have to get the bait right in front of them if you have any hope of success.

A minnow and bobber always works well, but many anglers prefer to use a small jig, sometimes tipped with a scented nibble bait. Some anglers prefer small spoons or Kastmasters during the colder months. Popular brush piles are located near the spillway tower, outside of Buzzard Bay, and off of Loder Point.

If, for some reason, the catfish aren't eating chum, the walleye aren't eating worms, the crappie aren't tapping on jigs, and the whites aren't chasing shad, Kanopoplis offers yet another option that's so simple, and effective, it's easy to overlook. "We'll catch 11 or 12 pound drum in the spillway," a local angler says. "Talk about something that will make your pole moan."

Aside from the drum, which many consider to be a junk fish, yet some consider to have a meat that rivals white bass, any species that can be caught in the lake can be caught in the water behind the lake, where the Smoky Hill River returns to its winding path.

Trout: And then there's the trout fishing—which can be found in the seep stream that runs parallel to the dam before making its way to the spillway. Cool water from deep in the lake fills the seep stream channel, creating a viable water for trout to thrive. While the state's trout season runs from October 15 through April 15, with trout being stocked throughout the season, Berger continues to work to create habitat that will allow the trout to over-summer in the stream.

"The brown trout didn't over-summer well in the main stretch of the stream, but we did find some rainbows and browns that made it through June," Berger says. "We're going to put in more habitat and structure that will provide more shade and keep the water cooler."

Both rainbow and brown trout have been stocked in the water. Local anglers land trout with a variety of methods—Yum minnows slowly retrieved on a gold hook and Powerbait are among the most popular, as well as Rooster Tails and small spoons. Some anglers even break out the fly-fishing gear and work the retention pools that have been built along the stream.

The seep stream trout fishing is a great addition to the sometimes bleary Kansas winters. The stream is easy to reach, easy to fish, and it has the feel of a small mountain stream. I love taking a trip to the seep stream in February, after much of the hunting season is over, and spring fishing hasn't really heated up. I like to toss a Little Cleo spoon or a small Rooster Tail into the

water, but something as simple as salmon eggs and a hook will do the trick, too. That, and a bobber, is all my son used to catch a 5–plus-pound trout from the stream several years ago.

Note that a special trout permit is needed (see introduction, p. 12). Special rules are in place at the seep stream, so be sure to check local postings before fishing the area.

Facilities

Kanopolis State Park, launched in 1959, was the first state park in Kansas. This 1,585-acre park features an area to the south and the larger Horsethief area. The park features more than 27 miles of multi-use trails. In total, the park offers: 16 campsites with water, sewer, and electric; 44 sites with water and electric; 223 sites with electric only; 23 rental cabins; 3 shower houses; 3 dump stations; 5 shelter houses; 6 boat ramp lanes; 2 courtesy docks; 2 fish cleaning stations; and a swimming beach.

The U.S. Army Corps of Engineers also manages two parks at the lake—Venango, on the north shore, has camping areas, a boat ramp, and a swimming beach. The spillway park behind the dam also has camping areas and offers access to the spillway.

Shopping/Supplies

Worms and other fishing supplies are available at **Smoky Hill Trading Post.** Fuel, licenses, and park permits are sold here. Homemade food sold during the day, as well as packaged food, beer, and soft drinks. Storage units are available. Open 7:00 a.m.–7:00 p.m. weekdays, 7:00 a.m.–9:00 p.m. weekends, and 7:00 a.m.–5:30 p.m. in the winter. Located just south of Kanopolis Dam, 785-546-2665.

The **Tower Harbor Marina** is a full service marina, with fuel available both on the slips and on land. Worms and other tackle available, and permits and licenses are sold here. Some boating and camping supplies available. Marina can refill propane bottles. Most emergency supplies can be found at Tower Harbor. Open April 1–October 15. April: open 9:00 a.m.–5:00 p.m. on weekends; May–September: open 9:00 a.m.–5:00 p.m. Monday through Thursday, 9:00 a.m.–9:00 p.m. Friday, 8:00 a.m.–9:00 p.m. Saturday, and 9:00 a.m.–5:00 p.m. Sunday; September–October (after Labor Day weekend): open 9:00 a.m.–5:00 p.m. on weekends. Dixie Barrow, who runs the Marina store, says she's sometimes working at the store even when it's closed, and she will help anglers and boaters who find her even in off hours. Turn toward the Little Bluestem camping area in the Langley area of South Shore State Park, and stay right; 785-546-2324.

Popular brush pile GPS locations (NAD83)	
North	West
1. 38 37.441	97 58.764
2. 38 37.565	97 58.989
3. 38 37.609	97 59.043
4. 38 38.142	97 59.591
5. 38 39.815	98 00.087
6. 38 39.598	98 00.111
7. 38 39.470	98 00.241
8. 38 38.874	98 00.878
9. 38 38.228	98 00.471
10. 38 38.446	98 00.382
11. 38 37.924	98 00.213
12. 38 36.525	97 59.517
13. 38 36.471	97 58.608
14. 38 36.482	97 58.054
15. 38 37.924	97 59.462
16. 38 37.886	97 59.502
17. 38 37.831	97 59.542
18. 38 37.807	97 59.601

Keith Sebelius (Norton) Reservoir

SIZE: 2,300 acres

LOCATION: About 3 miles southwest of Norton on US 36

GPS LOCATION: N39 48.757 W99 57.794

CONTACT: Bureau of Reclamation, Prairie Dog State Park/Norton Wildlife Area, 785-877-2953

FEATURE FISH: Largemouth Bass, Spotted Bass, Channel Catfish, Crappie, Saugeye, Walleye, Wiper

DAILY CREEL LIMIT/MINIMUM LENGTH: Largemouth Bass: 5 fish, 15 inches • Spotted Bass: 5 fish, 15 inches • Channel Catfish: 10 fish • Flathead Catfish: 5 fish • Crappie: 50 fish • Saugeye: 5 fish, 18 inches • Walleye: 5 fish, 18 inches • Wiper: 2 fish

This journey is not for the tepid angler. At 220 miles from the mid-Kansas city of Hutchinson, the closest large city to my hometown, northwest Kansas' Keith Sebelius Reservoir probably seems like the end of the Earth to some. But, then again, those folks haven't met the famous "Bobber" Bill Klein.

I called old Bobber one late spring evening, asking him if I could chat with him about hotspots on the lake near his hometown of Norton, population 3,012.

"You want me to take you fishing?" he asked.

I was not about to turn down guide service from a guy who goes by Bobber. Besides, I have heard that, despite the distance, an angler can find excellent fishing at Sebelius. So, in the middle of a long weekend at Webster Reservoir, which is just a few counties away, I left my twin girls in the care of their daddy for a little wiper action with one of Sebelius's expert anglers.

I wasn't sure what to expect in this area of Kansas. Prairie Dog Creek feeds Sebelius, and Bobber says upfront it's not typically a gusher. Yet, like a mirage on the desert, a roughly 2,300-acre lake appeared, where, instead of a wealth of jet skis and speedboats, I found a lake full of anglers—all of whom knew Bobber on a first-name basis.

Moreover, after an afternoon of fishing, I can truly tell you that those who venture this far west will find a worthwhile haven. One that includes the wiper, that hard-fighting hybrid—and saugeye, says Bobber. "There are days I could catch a hundred myself in saugeye," Bobber says, but adds there is nothing better than the good fight of a wiper.

He can prove it, too.

From his fishing boat on this early summer day, he cast a handmade bucktail jig into one of his favorite spots—the concrete remains of a structure submerged deep into the water. He danced it across the water as evening began to set in. And it didn't take long for wipers and saugeye to take the bait.

"They're proven," says Bobber. After all, he made the bucktails himself on cold winter nights when the fishing was slow—bleached white deer tails on multicolored lead heads. Bobber added some more proof as he reeled in several wipers and saugeye, as well as a few drum—a species Bobber says "tastes just like white bass."

So, as dusk approached, I left Sebelius with a few wipers, a saugeye, and even a drum for my family's evening supper.

• • •

This spot where Sebelius stands today was just a puddle until 1964, when the lake was built. And Bobber recalls fishing the lake with his dad about a year later, not much older than age 9 or 10. Now he fishes Sebelius almost exclusively. In fact, on this day, he had fished 17 out of the past 20 days.

Bobber says the water levels have experienced substantial fluctuation over the years. Recreational opportunities there also have varied, declining in dry years when inflows to the lake didn't provide enough water for recreation.

Mark Shaw, the reservoir's Kansas Department of Wildlife and Parks fisheries biologist, says while these days Sebelius is known for its wipers and saugeye, it also is a good place for sport fish such as walleye, largemouth bass, crappie, and channel catfish. Other fish present include flathead catfish, spotted bass, and bluegill.

Shaw says there are plenty of angling opportunities for fish in Sebelius. Habitat includes old bridges and railroad beds, as well as the tree structures that populate much of the lake.

Feature Fish

Saugeye/Walleye: The saugeye, a cross between a walleye and a sauger, has been successfully stocked in reservoirs where walleye populations are difficult to maintain. The state record saugeye, weighing 9.81 pounds and measuring 28½ inches long, was caught at Sebelius by Raymond Wait, of Norton, in 1998. The reservoir typically is rated number one in the state for its saugeye population.

Shaw says anglers will find saugeye and walleye along the dam in March and April before the fish move to the Marsh Flats in the later part of April. Other prime spots include the old South Shore Road and the sandpit area (N39 47.271' W99 59.079'), as well as a 30-foot hump just off the middle of the dam. In late summer, good spots include Concrete Cove, the Marsh Dike (located around N39 47.582' W99 58.948'), and the river channel, using night crawlers on the bottom.

Some of the chosen lures include casting jigs, roadrunners, crank baits, and, of course, bucktails.

Catfish: Catfish can be found off the public fishing dock when they congregate around the fish feeder; around Leota Cove and the north end of dam; up west by the Marsh Dike; and around the sandpit. Other spots for channels include the east side of Schoen's Cove, out on the point, as well as around Concrete Cove, Shaw says. Catfish can also be caught along the dam and rocky areas while spawning in June.

Baits to use include shad sides and gizzards, night crawlers, stink bait, or shrimp.

Black Bass: Sebelius typically ranks in the top five in the state for its density of largemouth bass. Density of spotted bass also is generally in the top five.

Anglers searching for largemouth should try the shoreline and submerged cover. Popular lures include spinners and other artificial lures in Leota Cove, along the dam, and Schoen's Cove. Shaw says another opportunity might be the sandpit area, although it's not necessarily a prime location. He also recommends fishing the rocky areas for the spots.

Spotted bass spend most of their time in the rocks along the dam.

Crappie: According to Shaw, Crappie are typically found around the public fishing dock, marina slips, fish attractors, or up in the coves using jigs or jigs tipped with minnow under a bobber or small slab spoon. Other hot spots: Marsh Dike, the sandpit area, Schoen's Cove, and Concrete Cove. "You'll find them in Leota Cove clear up in the cove, as well," Shaw says. The railroad trestle past the marina slips to the north is also a popular spot.

Wiper: Sebelius was one of the first lakes stocked with wipers back in the late 1970s. That's about when Bobber began chasing wiper. Today, wiper density in the lake ranks in the top ten. Shaw recommends bucktail jigs cast into the wind while wade fishing on the north side of the dam and the mouth of Leota Cove, along with fishing with night crawlers and shrimp on the bottom up into Leota Cove. Live bait fished over the drop-offs outside the Leota Cove and Concrete Cove is also effective.

Additional angling opportunities are available in the stilling basin below the dam.

Bobber, however, has his own hot spots for wipers, as well as his own techniques. He knows the lake like the back of his hand, after all, and there aren't many spots that wipers can hide. And when he's on a spot, his Terrova I-Pilot trolling motor control system allows him to keep his boat in one location using a global positioning system instead of an anchor. That's a big help when he gets to what he considers the popular hangouts for wipers.

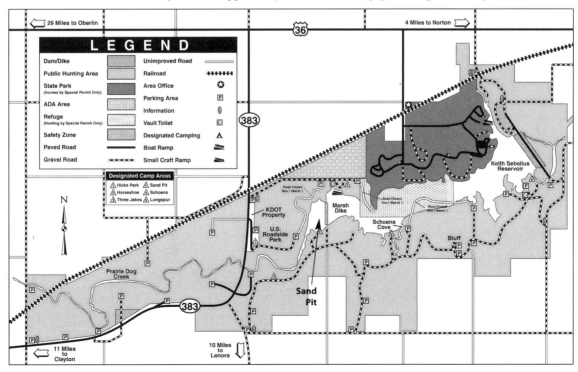

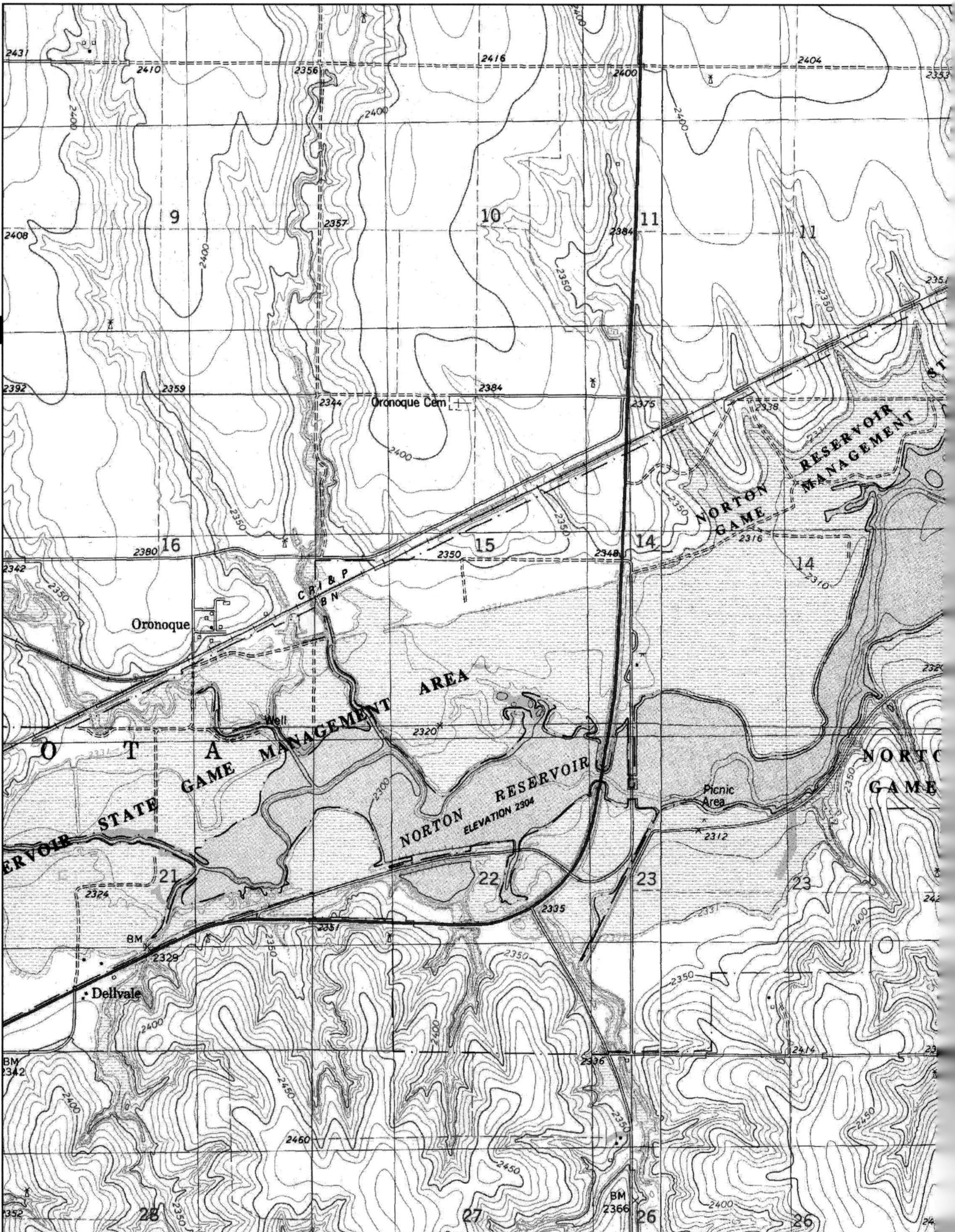

Keith Sebelius (Norton) Reservoir

Oronoque Cem

Oronoque

NORTON GAME RESERVOIR MANAGEMENT

OTA STATE GAME MANAGEMENT AREA

RESERVOIR

Well

NORTON RESERVOIR
ELEVATION 2304

Picnic Area

NORTO GAME

9

10

11

11

16

15

14

14

21

22

23

23

BM 2329

Dellvale

BM 2342

28

27

BM 2366

26

26

CRI&P BN

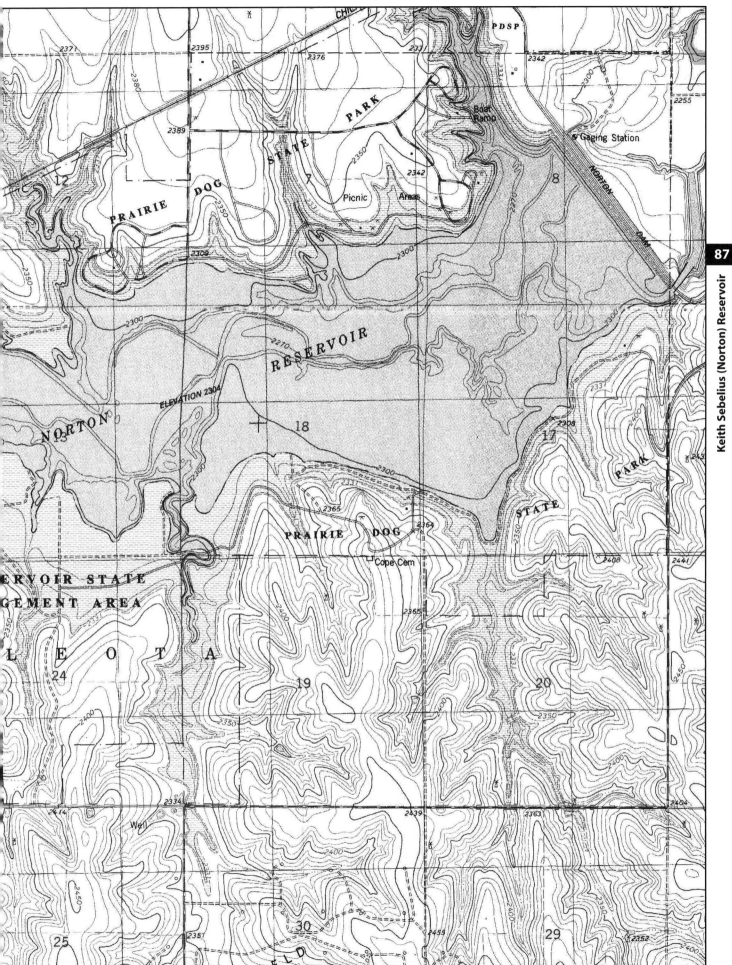

Bobber says to look along the South Road bed, the Marsh Dike, and even around the old sand pit. On this day, he was catching wipers and saugeye near the willows that are situated across sections of the lake. And his favorite areas include around old submerged structure, but Bobber is a little more tight lipped about giving out his hot spots.

Besides his toys, as well as his knowledge of the lake, Bobber credits much of the successes to his choice of bait, which he tailors to the seasons. In the spring and early summer, he casts his bucktails—proven fish catchers. There probably was a time when bucktails were found in every tackle box. Moreover, bucktails can be fished at any depth if you choose the right weight head.

In the spring and fall, Bobber uses 4-inch chartreuse-and-white Berkley gulp shiner minnows, which he calls a magnet for fish like wipers, saugeye, and drum. He also uses a lighter test weight, usually 6 pounds. The lighter test weight is a key element, according to Bobber. "You wouldn't believe how many fish we caught in September and October," he says, adding, "The wipers just slam it and take off."

He uses gulp in deep water breaks. Those who use it have to find the right rhythm, he says. The wrong rhythm can mean getting skunked. Bobber tells of a time he and his fishing buddy were on his boat fishing, and Bobber kept reeling in the fish while his friend didn't have any

luck. The difference between their success rates was their rod motion and rhythm.

"Instead of fishing slow on the bottom, jerk it up and let it fall to the bottom," Bobber says.

Usually, he uses a 1/8 to a 1/4 size jig head and a longer shank hook. He prefers Gamakatsu Eagle Claw—a long shank hook—saying that, while more expensive, he finds a good hook is preferable. Another good lure is Lytle's Tail Spinner, which he also uses in the fall.

But his name comes from his expertise at fishing using a bobber. Bobber perfected a technique for using live green sunfish below an inflated balloon bobber when the fish are suspended in depths of 10–16 feet. When the fish hit the bait, the balloon pops off, he says.

This is how he caught a near–state record breaker. He once reeled in a 20.9-pound wiper at Sebelius using quarter- to half-pound live shad under a balloon. The giant wiper ended up just a few pounds shy of the state record.

Facilities

The shores of this prairie lake showcase an enclave of natural Kansas history. Sebelius is home to **Prairie Dog State Park** and **Norton Wildlife Area,** which are operated by the Kansas Department of Wildlife and Parks under licenses from the U. S. Bureau of Reclamation.

Prairie Dog State Park occupies 1,150 acres. The park is home to a thriving prairie dog colony and is the site of the last remaining adobe house in Kansas. The renovated adobe house was built on the site in the early 1890s and is just one of a handful of historic buildings preserved, including two vintage nineteenth-century buildings and a one-room school. A 1.4-mile nature trail, complete with interpretive signage, runs through the area. In total, the park offers: 60 utility campsites; more than 130 primitive sites; and 2 cabins.

GPS Points
Lenora Boat Ramp GPS: N39 78.0126 W99 99.7864
Spillway Boat Ramp: N39 78.0126 W99 99.7864

Shopping/Supplies
Endzone Sports Office Supplies, 102 S. 2nd Ave., Norton, 785-877-2611; **Jamboree Foods,** 117 N. 2nd Ave., Norton, 785-877-2551; **Pamida,** 505 W. Holme St., Norton, 785-877-3363; **T & D Bait Shop,** 307 E. Penn St., Norton, 785-874-4687.

Kirwin Reservoir

SIZE: 5,000 acres

LOCATION: About 16 miles southeast of Phillipsburg on US 183 and K-9

GPS LOCATION: N39 40 2.71 W99 7 53.54

CONTACT: U.S. Fish and Wildlife Service, Kirwin National Wildlife Refuge, 785-543-6673

FEATURE FISH: Channel Catfish, Crappie, Walleye, White Bass, Wiper

DAILY CREEL LIMIT/MINIMUM LENGTH: Largemouth Bass: 5 fish, 15 inches • Channel Catfish: 10 fish • Flathead Catfish: 5 fish • Crappie: 50 fish • Walleye: 5 fish, 15 inches • Wiper: 2 fish

Dee and Robin Blubaugh of Phillipsburg have fished many a lake in their lives as walleye wranglers on the competitive fishing circuit—including the Cabala's National Team Championship in 2008, where they took 56th out of 250 entries. However, there is no place they'd rather be when it's time to go fishing than Kirwin Reservoir—a northwest Kansas lake surrounded by farmland and pastures and far from heavily populated cities.

It's also a lengthy venture to the far west from my little central Kansas hometown. But after a phone conversation with Dee on a late summer day, and an invite for a guided tour of the Blubaugh's favorite fishing spot, I headed northwestward with my family on a 400-mile round trip that took us by more than a few ghost towns before entering Phillips County near the Nebraska border.

This little spot, I soon would realize, is heavenly if you like fishing. Kirwin, after all, is a lake that has been touted by pro angler Jimmy Houston as a well-kept secret crappie hot spot. Dee and Robin agree, saying the fish in these waters are lunker crappie. "We're catching some that are 15–16 inches," says Dee Blubaugh, who also is president of the Friends of Kirwin Lake Association. He notes that one spring day they caught 34 crappie, including one that was 17½ inches long.

With guides like the Blubaughs, there wouldn't be anyone leaving empty-handed on this fishing trip.

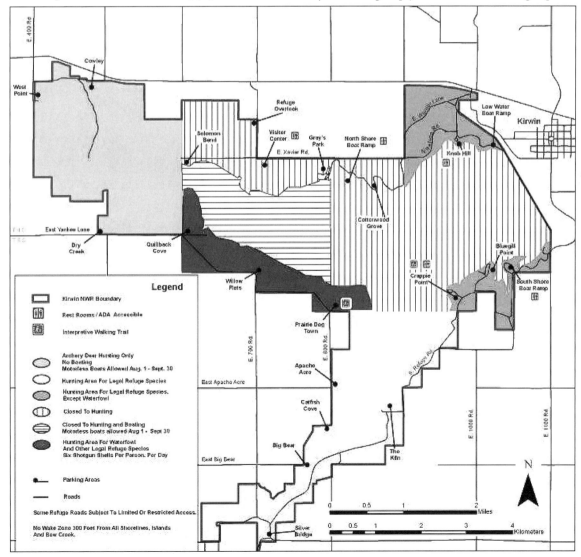

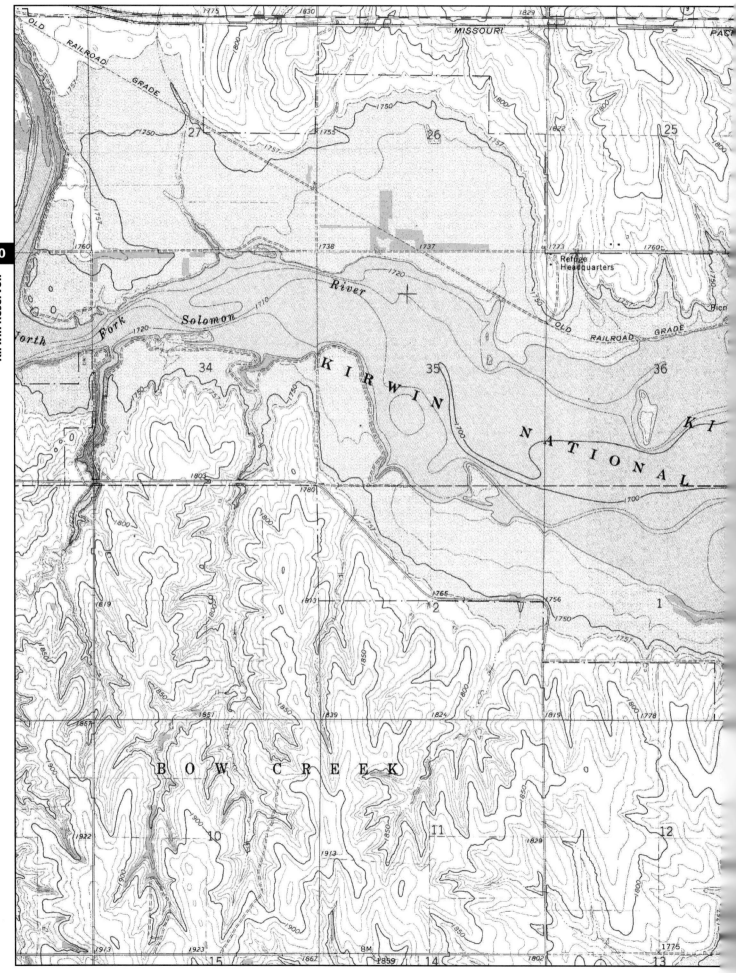

Railroad flats

Kirwin Cem

Campgrounds

Picnic Area

WT

Kirwin

Landing Strip

Landing Strip

Siphon

Gaging Station

Boat Ramp

Boat Ramp

Campground

Campground

30

29

28

28

31

32

33

33

RESERVOIR

ELEVATION 1729

N

WILDLIFE

REFUGE

Bluegill Point

Boat Ramp

Picnic Area

Picnic Area

Picnic Area

Crappie Point

Picnic Area

WT

VALLEY

Bow Creek

KIRWIN RESERVOIR ELEV. 1729

KIRWIN NATIONAL WILDLIFE REFUGE

KIRWIN DAM

6

5

4

4

7

8

9

9

16

16

17

18

• • •

Located in the rolling hills of the narrow North Fork of the Solomon River Valley in southeastern Phillips County, Kirwin Reservoir was established in 1954 as an overlay project on a Bureau of Reclamation irrigation and flood control reservoir. The reservoir is fed by the North Fork of the Solomon River and Bow Creek. Both are intermittent streams, thus the reservoir water levels fluctuate from year to year, depending upon precipitation.

The reservoir is part of Kirwin National Wildlife Refuge, the first national wildlife refuge in Kansas. The primary purpose of the 10,778-acre refuge is to provide a haven for birds, including upland game birds and waterfowl. According to the U.S. Fish and Wildlife Service, the bureau owns the land and controls reservoir water levels. The Kansas Department of Wildlife and Parks stocks and manages the waters. This means different rules from other Kansas reservoirs, said Steve Price, KDWP's Fisheries and Wildlife Division regional supervisor. The FWS bans camping, fires, swimming, and jet skis on this lake.

Per another rule, the west end past the buoy is closed to fishing much of the year, except for a period in the fall. Fishing is permissible by rowboat or other non-motorized boat during a select period, usually early fall.

"It would be nice to have public access back," Dee Blubaugh says, adding that camping and outdoor recreation that surround it "could really help these little towns."

• • •

Most of the reservoirs in the western part of Kansas, including Kirwin, were built for irrigation use and flood control. But western Kansas' semiarid terrain means less precipitation for lakes like Kirwin—quite a different scenario than for eastern Kansas waters. Yet, after multiple years of very low water levels, Kirwin was full of water when we made the trek northward, thanks to rains in the late 2000s.

Mark Shaw, KDWP fisheries biologist for Kirwin, said the reservoir is known as a good fishing spot for those who make the drive. Besides crappie, fishing at Kirwin can mean catching black bass, wipers, catfish, and white bass, as well as the Blubaughs' prized walleye. In fact, some of the best fishing for many of the state's game fish can be found at this small lake.

Moreover, the years of low water levels, just like at Keith Sebelius and Webster Reservoirs, allowed shoreline vegetation to grow—vegetation that has now created a fishing haven of flooded timber extending from the shore into the lake.

These submerged trees, along with underwater structure such as rock points and brush, as well as a number of brush-pile fish attractors, make this lake one of the state's hot spots.

One such site is the Crappie Point fish attractor, located at GPS: N39 38' 55.58" W99 08' 31.70" on the lake. The brush pile fish attractor is in 25–35 feet of water at conservation pool, and consists of about seventy-five 10–20-foot cedar tress that are weighted down with concrete weights attached to the trees by wire, according to the KDWP. The attractor is maintained with new trees every three or so years, and it is marked with a buoy.

• • •

As for the Blubaughs, Kirwin is the main lake you'll find them on most summer days. Dee has fished western Kansas reservoirs all his life. He's also fished lakes across the United States. But when it comes to fishing, he says, as the old saying goes, there's no place like home. "I've fished every inch of this lake," he says. "It's kind of hard to go anywhere else when you have good luck here."

Our morning of fishing with the Blubaughs began early, before 7:00 a.m. We unloaded the boat and tried many of the lake's recommended spots, including Prairie Dog Town, Bluestem and Crappie Points, and the Cottonwood Grove area. Yet, after casting around several spots on the lake to no avail, Dee piloted over to the Railroad Flats, where Robin pointed out the pronounced ledge on the fish finder.

It ended up being the day's hot fishing spot.

Fishing commenced, with the Blubaughs demonstrating the technique called slabbing. Using only artificial lures, they vertical jig a slab spoon in hopes of catching walleye—as well as other species. It's a technique that works well along dropoffs, points, flats, and submerged brush.

"We use from quarter-ounce to three-quarters of an ounce and some use up to an ounce," he says of the spoons. Some use chartreuse and white, others chartreuse and red. He sticks with black and silver—his favorite.

He also makes his own spoons. "I've bought some, but mostly, I make my own," he says, noting he's had plenty of bites even using a magic marker to make the eyes.

We all reeled in several fish at Railroad Flats—largely crappie, walleye, and a few wipers. I only got snagged on some deeper timber a few times, and luckily I was able to get free using Robin's Hound Dog Retriever tool, which must be able to get the toughest snag free.

Feature Fish

Walleye: Walleye at Kirwin are rated in the top five in density among Kansas reservoirs. And on this late-summer day, the Blubaughs are catching walleye after walleye, as well as crappie, off an old submerged railroad bed area dubbed Railroad Flats. "This is one of the good fishing spots on the lake," Dee says. "There are several areas that are good here."

Railroad Flats is also a spot where he catches 16- to 19-inch crappie off the ledges, he says. Walleye, however, is some of the best fish to catch, at least in Robin's point of view. And, on our fishing excursion, the Railroad Flats were productive for walleye.

During March and April, look for walleye to spawn along the dam. Shaw recommends using jigs, roadrunners, and crankbaits.

After the spawn, Dee says, the fish begin to move to the flats and dropoffs, such as the Railroad Flats area and the flats around Prairie Dog Town. Robin also recommends the Cottonwood Grove area, as well as along ledges. Railroad Flats, located at N39 39.936 W99 09.130, and Cottonwood Grove are also good spots after dark. And anglers, she says, also "shouldn't overlook the submerged parking areas and roadbeds."

There is a dropoff at Bluegill Point that can have walleye, but Shaw suggests spots just outside Crappie Point where there are 30-foot dropoffs. "You can catch white bass, wipers, and everything there," Shaw says. "It is a pretty good spot."

During spawn, Dee says, crappie will hit the edge of the tree lines on the north side of the reservoir, suspended on ledges 6–15 feet deep. As a rule of thumb, the crappie will spawn on the ledges and on the mud in the spring around the last weekend of April and into May. "It all depends on how fast the weather warms up," he adds.

During the spawn, some anglers also caught crappie in coves along Grays Park and along the buoy line, where the east side of the ledge is 27 feet up to 4–5 feet.

According to Dee, walleye tend to congregate in the fall around the river channel near Railroad Flats, suspended anywhere from 18–26 feet on the taper of the dropoff. "There are two ledges south of Railroad Flats were Bow Creek meets the Solomon," he says.

Some anglers use orange jigs or twister tails and do well in this location, Dee says. Others are successful using all-white jigging spoons. Dee and Robin prefer silver jigging spoons with black on them. "Try different things to attract them," Dee says. "Some were catching crappie with minnows. Others had a jig and a minnow and were doing well. You might catch them in 35-foot of water, but you might try different spots. Fish either the top of an island or a taper where there is a ledge."

> In 1967, a remote portion of the **Kirwin National Wildlife Refuge** was designated as a research natural area. The area consists of bluestem and grama prairie grasses, according to the U.S. Wildlife Service. Kirwin has also been identified as significant for world bird conservation. The American Bird Conservancy officially designated Kirwin as one of 500 "Globally Important Bird Areas."

Catfish: According to Shaw, "The overall supply of channel catfish is pretty fair, with fish scattered over a wide size range."

As the water starts warming up, these fish will move shallow to feed, he says. The catfish can be caught in the upper ends of coves and shallow areas. When catfish spawn in the first part of June, Shaw recommends looking for them along the dam, rocky areas, and the bluffs, as well as Crappie Point. He adds that the outlet area also is a good spot, and in the spring anglers can catch them up in the river channels. For instance, he says that when there is water coming into the lake, "the channels should be up in Bow Creek and the North Fork of the Solomon River."

A few of the baits anglers use include shad sides, gizzards, shrimp, and stink or dip baits.

Wipers: Kirwin ranks in the top ten for density of wipers. Fish in the 15–20-inch range were plentiful in 2010. "The supply is strong and the quality of this fishery is back up," Shaw says.

Shaw said to try casting bucktail jigs into the wind along either side of the dam; on the north side information shelter, Knob Hill, which is an old sand beach between Bluegill and Crappie Points; and around Cottonwood Grove.

Also, of course, there are the Blubaugh's Railroad Flats, which Dee says will land several different species of fish, including walleye, wipers, and crappie. Another good location for fishing opportunities is below the dam when the government is releasing water.

White bass: "They're going to be in the same spots as wipers, but it all depends on the direction the wind is in," Shaw says. "Fish on the side of the wind, around the coves and points." Watch the gulls, he adds, noting that they will tell anglers where the fish are chasing shad. Trolling diving lures is also a good technique to catch white bass and wipers.

In the fall, fishing along the south side of the lake has proven successful, according to Shaw. "It's been really good," he says. "They catch them right and left all fall."

Of course, there are Railroad Flats, Dee notes, but adds the white bass are still growing. "It seems like every fifth or sixth white bass caught is keeper size."

Crappie: Kirwin's density for crappie ranks in the top ten for state reservoirs, and fourth in the state for black crappie in 2010. Decent water levels have allowed successful spawns each spring since 2001.

Shaw said crappie should be concentrated around the north and south shore fish attractors and dropoffs and can be caught using jigs, jigs tipped with minnows, or small slab spoons. During the spawn, crappie also can be caught up in the shallows of coves and off the dam using jigs or jigs tipped with minnows under a bobber. Dee Blubaugh also suggests the north side of the lake, as well as area with timber, rock piles, and other structure.

"Find your ledges," Dee says. There are the ledges on Railroad Flats, for starters, he says. There is a dropoff at Bluegill Point and a more pronounced area outside Crappie Point where there are 30-foot dropoffs. Another good spot is just south of the Prairie Dog Town area.

GPS Locations
Kirwin Fish Attractors
N 39 40.14083 W 99 8.30116
N 39 40.20783 W 99 8.53666
N 39 39.05716 W 99 8.31083
Crappie Point:
N 39 38.92633 W 99 8.52833
(The four fish attractors at Kirwin are all marked with buoys)

"Crappie Point, we've caught some of our crappie there," he says, noting with the deeper water the past few years, the fishing has changed a little. "You still will catch some crappie there, but you can also catch quite a few catfish in there, too. Marina Cove (or Concession Cove) is a good spot, as well as the south shore boat ramp area."

Dee and Robin say they are hoping that, with the higher water levels and submerged structure, crappie numbers and sizes will grow like they did in 1993. That year, Dee recalls, it only took 16 crappie out of Kirwin to fill a five-gallon bucket. Most of those crappie were 17–18 inches long. "They weighed up to 3 pounds, and some were over 3 pounds," he says. "That is not exaggerating."

Facilities

Kirwin has several boat ramps, including **South Shore Boat Ramp, North Shore Boat Ramp** and **Low Water Boat Ramp.**

Shopping/Supplies

Alco, 1401 State St., Phillipsburg, 785-543-6776; **Harold's Bait & Tackle,** 241 SE. 1st St., Kirwin, 785-543-5048; **Hillbilly Inn,** 301 SW. 2nd St., Kirwin, 785-543-5993; **Logan Hardware,** 202 W. Main St., Logan, 785-689-7592; **Philips County Clerk,** 301 State St., Phillipsburg, 785-543-6825; **Sawyers Ace Hardware,** 341 F St., Phillipsburg, 785-543-5017; **Whites Foodliner,** 934 3rd St., Phillipsburg, 785-543-5412.

La Cygne Reservoir

SIZE: 2,600 acres

LOCATION: About 60 miles south of Kansas City on US 69

CONTACT: Kansas Department of Wildlife and Parks, 913-795-2218

FEATURE FISH: Largemouth Bass, Flathead Catfish, Crappie, White bass, Wiper

DAILY CREEL LIMIT/MINIMUM LENGTH: Largemouth Bass: 5 fish, 18 inches • Smallmouth Bass: 5 fish, 18 inches • Blue Catfish: 10 fish • Channel Catfish: 10 fish • Flathead Catfish: 5 fish • Crappie: 50 fish, 10 inches • Striped Bass: 2 fish, 18 inches • Wiper: 2 fish, 18 inches • Walleye: 5 fish, 15 inches

The La Cygne Reservoir is a small lake, even by Kansas standards. The fish that swim its waters, however, aren't following suit. Bruce Holt, park manager for Linn County Park, says the lake is home to some of the biggest fish in the state. He has seen a nearly 11-pound largemouth pulled from its waters. Wipers rapidly grow to monstrous size, and white bass roam the lake constantly searching to feast on a school of shad.

And flathead catfish grow to terrifyingly big sizes. "There have been a lot of big blues and flats taken out of here," Holt says. "Sixty-two pounds is the biggest I've caught, but the biggest I've seen weighed eighty-five pounds."

The secret to La Cygne's reputation as a monster-producing fishery lies to the east, where the twin smokestacks of the Kansas City Power and Light's power generating station rise above the landscape. The coal-powered electrical plant provides power to Kansas City and the surrounding suburbs, but the lake's water serves as a coolant for the generators, with the warm water being released back into the lake. The result is a body of water that never completely freezes, in which bait fish remain plentiful throughout the year, and game fish remain active through the winter. "La Cygne has it all, with its many good populations of fish and warm water," Kansas Department of Wildlife and Parks fisheries biologist Don George says of the lake.

La Cygne's bottom is made up largely of mud and doesn't feature many undulations or variations in depth in the main body of the lake. Before its construction in 1967, the flooded area that now makes up La Cygne Reservoir was largely farm fields. Most of the timber in the area was removed before the lake's infill to prevent loose timber from making its way into the power plant's cooling system. However, to improve the habitat, fisheries biologists have submerged many trees in numerous locations for fish attractors.

The maximum water depth is roughly 30 feet, near the dam, which also draws fish into the riprap and cooler deep water—particularly in the warmer summer months.

• • •

When planning a trip to La Cygne, forget what you know about what the water temperature should be during any given time of year. Because of the power plant's steady release of heated water, the lake's surface temperature seldom drops below 60 degrees, even in the winter. In the summer, it's not uncommon for the surface temperature to reach the 90s, which stifles even the heartiest appetite of man or fish.

"July through mid-September is the slowest fishing of the year because the water's so warm," Holt says. "November through May, the fishing is really hot. In the summer, the fish get sluggish, just like the rest of us."

I found this out firsthand during my trip to La Cygne. My family and I didn't plan our camping trip to coincide with the hottest week of the year, but that's how it worked out. A week or more of 100-plus degree temperatures, coupled with the warm water outlet of the generation station, had the water temperature at La Cygne reaching well into the 90s. That meant there was little action on the water during my time at La Cygne, but that doesn't mean I didn't find a lot to like at this lake.

Toward the north end of the lake, there's some vegetation-lined shore that I'm sure would've been productive during a cooler time of year. I also found a couple of nice coves close to the dam that looked like they'd be real hot

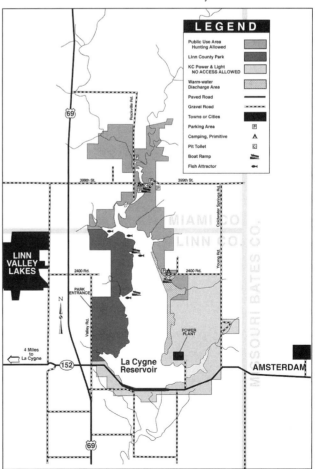

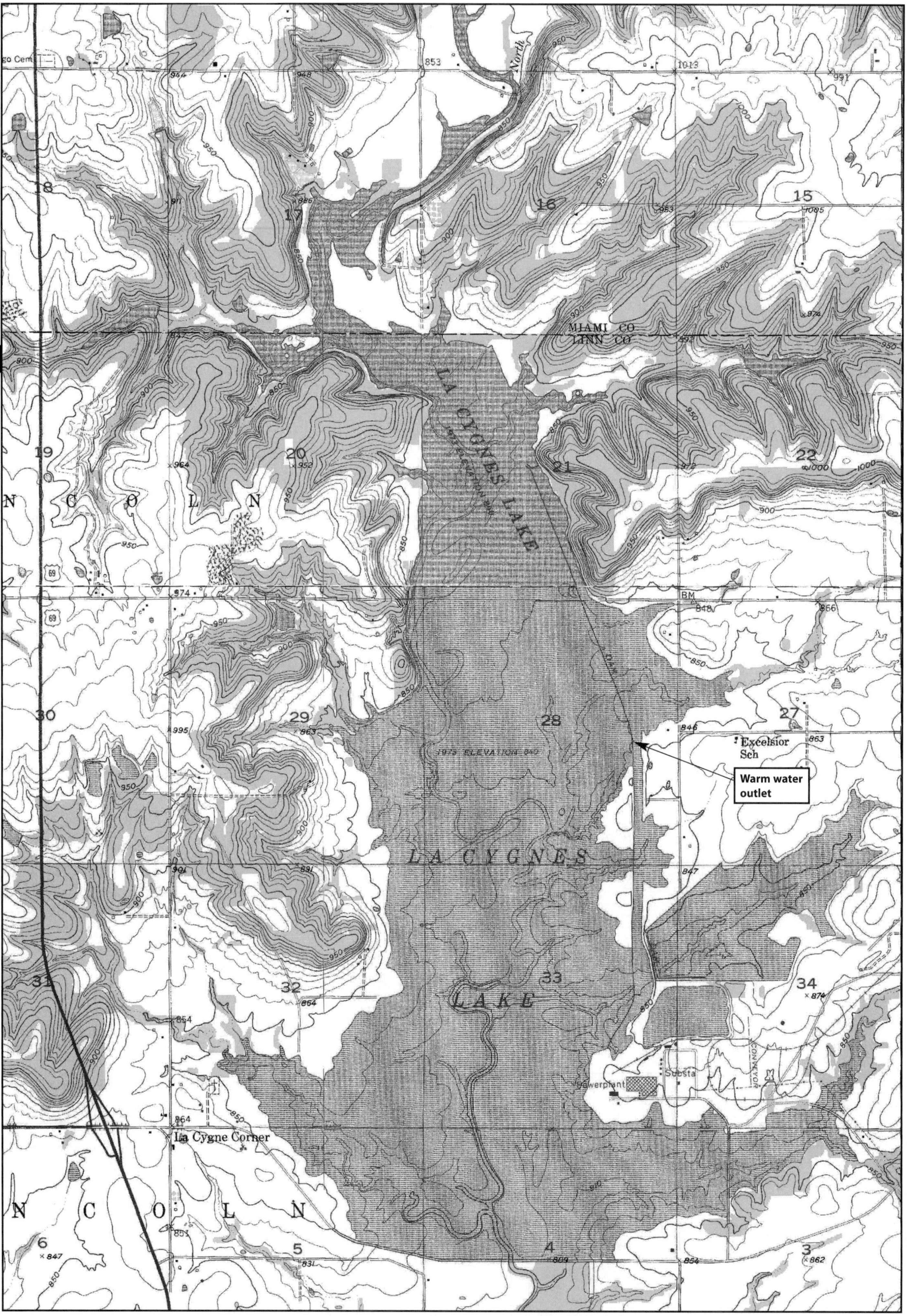

LA CYGNES LAKE

LA CYGNES LAKE

MIAMI CO
LINN CO

Warm water
outlet

Excelsior
Sch

1973 ELEVATION 840

La Cygne Corner

Powerplant   Substa

spots when it wasn't quite so hot. Additionally, in the early morning hours, the white bass still chased shad to the surface—which is an exciting time no matter how hot the weather. While casting toward a weed bed for largemouth early one morning, I found myself surrounded by a school of white bass chasing shad up to the water's surface. Using a Gulp Alive minnow on a 1/8 ounce jig head, I landed a couple of nice whites while following their feeding frenzy into a nearby cove.

Any trip to La Cygne is going to be more productive during the fall, winter, and spring than during summer. If it's a summer trip you plan to take, however, consider packing up the night fishing gear and looking for channel cats around one of the lake's fish feeders. The fish know to hang out in this area, and the cooler night time temperatures will make the experience more tolerable for both fish and fisherman.

• • •

According to George, the fall through April season is the best time to fish the hot water outlet on the lake's east side—and anglers should be ready to catch a mixed bag of fish. "During the cooler months, this warm water attracts large numbers of gizzard shad and other forage fish species," George says. "This abundance of food attracts many game fish, such as largemouth bass, crappie, wipers, striped bass, and channel, blue, and flathead catfish. In this area of concentrated fish, an angler could really catch different species of predators with any cast."

George adds that anglers can find success in this area either from a boat or by walking in from the parking lot on the east side of the lake—and it's this area in which most of the larger fish at La Cygne have been caught.

While the lake doesn't have much in the way of submerged timber, La Cygne offers plenty of other fish-holding structure for anglers. There are some old dropoffs in the lake—particularly around the original creek channel—where fish can be found. There's also the outlet tubes located at the main entrance road to the power

plant, where water moving underneath the road attracts many fish, such as crappie, white bass, and wipers. Other areas, such as mud flats, weed beds, and the upper end of the lake, where Sugar Creek feeds the lake with fresh rainwater, all draw and hold fish.

Additionally, the lake offers miles of shoreline riprap, which is where Holt says wipers, largemouth, and catfish can be found in mid-June and July by trolling or casting a crankbait. Otherwise during the summer months, anglers move to the dam, where the water is deeper, and the upper end of the lake, where fresh water enters the lake.

I found Ed Maloney, a former professional angler who operates the "Fishin with Ed" guide service out of Kansas City, loading his tournament boat after a hot summer morning of fishing. He found the fish to be relatively inactive. However, his client had landed three "tournament keepers" before the heat of the day began to set in. "The smaller fish have more places to hide," Maloney said. "And the temperature is so hot, there's not much hitting."

George says traditional and favored baits, such as spinnerbaits, jigs, and plastic baits, used by bass anglers generally are successful, but as the water warms up the best fishing can be found in the early morning and late evening hours—tossing surface lures and topwater baits into bass habitat.

Because La Cygne was built primarily as a cooling pool for the power plant, there are restrictions for boaters and anglers. No swimming or skiing is allowed at the lake, and some areas around the power plant have restricted access. Be sure to check with the park manager for up-to-date information about any changes to the regulations.

Despite the power plant's presence and use of the water, Holt says the lake water is tested regularly for contaminants and that the fish are safe to eat. "Kansas City Power and Light takes water samples every day to make sure there are no contaminants," Holt said. "It's monitored more than just about any other lake in the state."

Feature Fish

Crappie: The numbers of crappie in the lake continue to flourish and grow, providing another exciting opportunity for visitors to La Cygne. During the peak of spawning season in May, look for these fish to move to shallow coves adjacent to vegetation, where they'll attack jigs. As the temperatures warm in the spring, look for crappie away from the warm water in the power plant outlet—such as the dam and the upper reaches of the lake. In the fall and winter, look for crappie to congregate around the outlet.

Biologist Don George said crappie anglers have had a good year, thanks to an abundance of fish in La Cygne. Don't overlook shoreline fishing at La Cygne, either. The east side of the reservoir has a walk-in trail that provides access to the shore near the outlet tubes. Additionally, the lake offers miles of riprap shoreline that can hold fish.

Crappie anglers have success at La Cygne using dark colors, such as green or black, as well as brighter colors like white and chartreuse.

Catfish: Catfish at La Cygne grow large and remain active throughout the entire year. To catch the giant flatheads in the lake, Holt suggests using a live bluegill fished along the old creek channel. Many anglers find the biggest catfish by setting out underwater trot lines and by fishing at night.

According to George, Catfish anglers can do well with rod and reel combinations using prepared baits, worms, or liver, and most of the larger fish are caught on set lines in the lake. "Because of the warm water in the winter, cats in this lake are more active, and set lines can produce many pounds of fighting fish," George says.

On the west side of the Lake, in Linn County Park, several fish feeders regularly toss food to the surface, which attracts large numbers of catfish and carp for shoreline anglers. George says these fish feeders are productive areas where young anglers can enjoy a day of steady action.

Some of the larger catfish, in particular the larger flatheads, can be caught on trotlines set in the lake. Park manager Bruce Holt has a technique that allows him to set deepwater trotlines near the river channel—generally in the spring and into the first part of May. Holt uses heavy anchors—around 50 pounds—to hold the lines underwater, and he marks them with jugs or buoys on the water surface. The gear used for this sort of setup has to be heavy-duty in order to handle the strain of pulling the anchors out of the mud. Holt said he'll span the trotline over a drop-off or creek channel. He'll bait the lines with green sunfish, though bluegill or small catfish will work as well. Both trotline anglers and line anglers will have better luck catching flatheads overnight, when the fish are more active.

Black Bass: Maloney says La Cygne has become well known for its big largemouth bass, and as a result the lake has been fished heavily by both tournament and recreational anglers. While that's made the fishing tougher in recent years, Maloney says he still takes accomplished anglers to the lake looking for bass that regularly top five pounds.

There's plenty of shoreline vegetation around La Cygne, particularly in the coves and the upper end of the lake, that hold bass in the spring. Additionally, anglers will hit the bluffs along the western shore of La Cygne, where the river channel cuts a deep path. But the place that has given La Cygne its fame is the warm water outlet area of the power plant, where baitfish congregate in the moving water, which in turn attracts predatory game fish. Other active areas include mud flats, old dropoffs, and the creek channel on the upper end of the lake, where cool rain water drains into the lake. During the winter months, fish and anglers gather around the warmer water, regardless of the air temperature outside.

Remember that these fish eat all year, so some are capable of growing quite large. Shad serve as the primary food source at La Cygne, and anglers can find success with crank baits, Rattletraps, swim baits, and topwater lures. George said that avid bass anglers have their own preferences on baits and lures, but that most anglers can

find success at La Cygne with whatever bait they prefer. As the temperatures warm, George says topwater baits offer the best, and most exciting, action early in the morning and late in the evening.

Don't forget to fish along some of the rocky shorelines, and around the dam, which hold fish throughout the year, particularly when the water gets too warm to fish the outlet area.

White Bass/Wiper: White bass and wiper are also thriving in LaCygne's warm water. The wiper and white bass follow similar patterns to other fish, particularly when it comes to moving toward the hot water outlet. Unlike largemouth bass, however, the wiper and white bass are open-water fish and can be found unattached to structure, chasing shad. In the early morning and late evening hours, watch for schools of shad breaking the water's surface.

Once located, these hungry fish will hit on a variety of lures, including soft plastic shads, jigs, spoons, and crank baits. Topwater baits work well also.

Anglers often find these fish while fishing for largemouth bass at La Cygne, but both species are attracting anglers fishing specifically for these fish. Part of their popularity, aside from their reputation as hard-fighting fish, stems from the growing population of wipers and white bass at La Cygne, and the chance for anglers to hook into a well-fed lunker. Like other predator fish, look for white bass and wipers to gather around the hot water outlet in search of shad and other baitfish.

Facilities

The **Marais des Cygne** waterfowl area is located just a few miles south of the reservoir, and the Marais des Cygne massacre site is a historically rich area where visitors can learn more about Kansas' role in the Civil War. Further south on US 69, **Fort Scott,** a National Historic Site, is home to some of the original buildings used by the U.S. Army when Fort Scott was a military outpost. Fort Scott was an important outpost during the turbulent years of the Civil War, in which the state earned the name "Bleeding Kansas."

La Cygne is home to 1,100-acre **Linn County Park,** managed by Linn County. The park features about 25 miles of trails for those who enjoy horseback riding and have their own horses. In total, the park offers: 115 campsites with electric, some with water and sewer; 6 cabins; non-utility sites on the northern end of the lake offer shoreline access to entry point of La Cygne River; 2 group shelters; marina; bait shop; swimming pool open Thursday to Sunday during the summer months; and a supply store. 913-757-6633, www.linncountyks.com (click on "recreation").

Shopping/Supplies

Wades Bait and Tackle, 22157 Valley Rd., LaCygne, 913-757-2542.

Lovewell Reservoir

SIZE: 2,986 acres

LOCATION: 4 miles east and 10 miles north of Mankato on US 14

GPS LOCATION: N39 53 25.20 W98 1 41.48

CONTACT: Kansas Department of Parks and Wildlife, Lovewell State Park, 785-753-4971

FEATURE FISH: Channel Catfish, Flathead Catfish, Crappie, Walleye, White Bass, Wiper

DAILY CREEL LIMITS/MINIMUM LENGTH: Largemouth Bass: 5 fish, 15 inches • Channel Catfish: 10 fish • Flathead Catfish: 5 fish • Crappie: 50 fish • Walleye: 5 fish, 18 inches • Wiper: 2 fish

Each year, for several weeks in the spring, Dave Bowlin moves from Nebraska to Kansas. But not just anywhere in the Sunflower State. Since 1984, the retired Lincoln, Nebraska, firefighter and his pals have set up camp by tree-lined Lovewell Reservoir, where, he says, he always finds good spring fishing for walleye, white bass, and crappie.

I found Bowlin sitting in the Lovewell Marina and Grill on a spring day. He's such a lake regular, in fact, he was preparing to help the owner smoke meat out back. He had already been out on an early morning outing, on which he reeled in two walleye, a catfish, a couple white bass, as well as wipers and crappie—showing there are a diversity of fish in this Kansas lake. He's fished other spots in Kansas and Nebraska, but something brings him back to Lovewell each year. "This is just a good lake," Bowlin says. "The fishing is good, and we love it, which is probably why we come back here every year."

• • •

My father, Gary Bickel, quipped an old fishing proverb before my husband, John, and I headed out for our fishing trip to Lovewell. "Wind in the north, fish don't go forth," he said.

It had been a week of warm weather in mid-May. Fishing reports showed anglers were hot on walleye at Lovewell's flats. We left the girls in the safe care of Grandma and Grandpa Bickel, and despite my dad's advice, John and I headed northward to Jewell County, where we set up camp in hopes for an early morning stringer of fish.

It was a good thought anyway.

Temperatures began to turn frigid Friday afternoon—cold enough that we needed a heater to stay warm overnight. That good fishing on the flats had shut off. Bowlin, who knows Lovewell like the back of his hand, said knowing a few of the lake's other hotspots was one reason he was so successful on this cold Kansas morning.

Still, we found Lovewell to be one of the more beautiful and serene lakes in Kansas. Located in the northern part of Jewell County, Lovewell Reservoir is nestled amid the Chalk Hills region of the Smoky Hills of north-central Kansas and fed by White Rock Creek. Surrounded by a 1,100-acre state park filled with oak-covered hillsides and upland prairies, it is well known to avid anglers who, for years, have beaten a path to the boat ramps and shorelines.

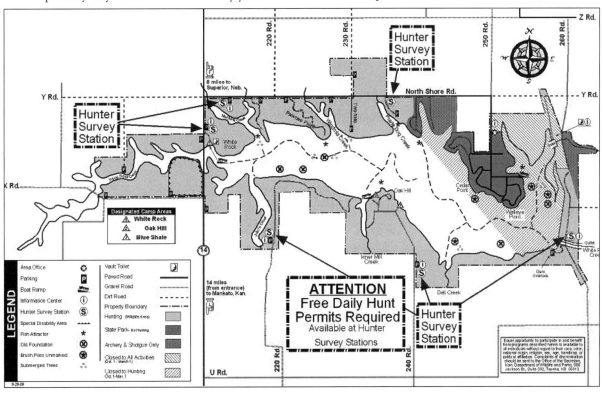

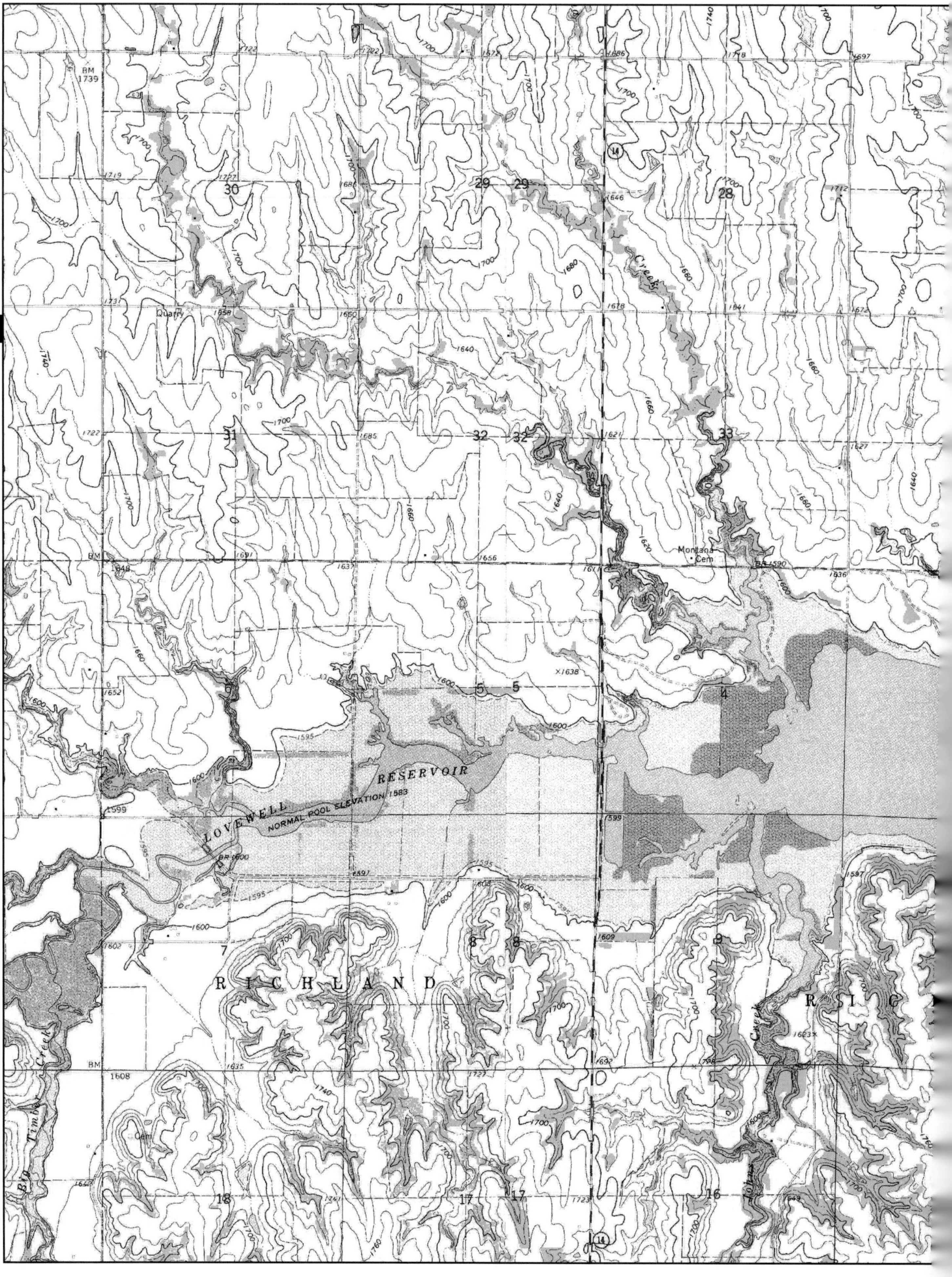
LOVEWELL
RESERVOIR
NORMAL POOL ELEVATION 1583
RICHLAND
Montana Cem
Quarry
Big Timber Creek
Creek
BM 1739
30
29
28
31
32
33
5
4
7
8
9
18
17
16

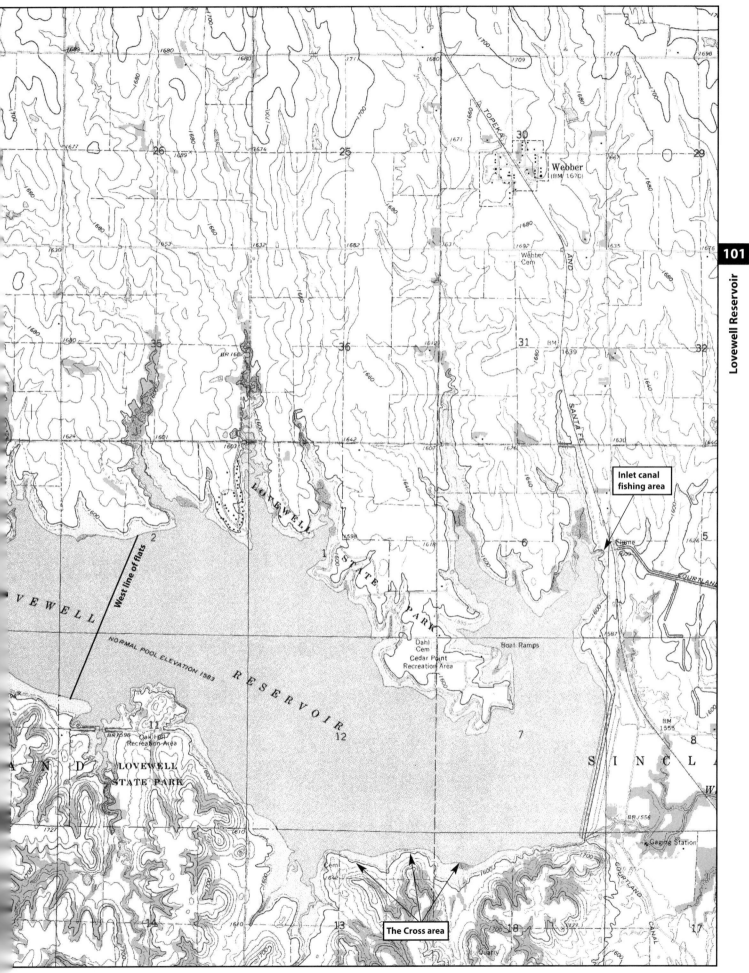

"I think it's one of the more scenic lakes in the state," says Gary Charbonneau, who, along with wife Lyndell, owns Lovewell Marina and Grill. Whenever he has the time, Charbonneau fishes. "I usually fish for walleye," he says, noting the lake is excellent for walleye. "And you can always catch a white bass out there, as well."

Feature Fish

Walleye: Scott Waters, the reservoir's fisheries biologist with the Kansas Department of Wildlife and Parks, calls the lake a good trip to catch many sport fish, including catfish, white bass, wipers, and crappie. It also is home to bluegill and largemouth bass. Lovewell, however, maybe best known for its walleye populations.

"The future of walleye angling at Lovewell is very bright," Waters says. So is the present. Walleye rank in the top five in terms of density, as well as lunker fish, according to Waters. "It looks like the walleye population is on the upswing. Good classes of fish have been produced over the past three years, and the numbers continue to climb."

Fishing is best from April through early June, with anglers drifting jig and nightcrawler combinations having the best success. Anglers have particularly enjoyed success around May along the 2-mile road located on the western end of the lake when the fish move to the flats, which is located west of GPS point N39 53.994' W98 04.010'. Walleye also congregate at a few of the lake's fish attractors.

After mid-June, Waters says, anglers might find walleye back toward the dam and Walleye Point area. "Most guys catch them trolling," he says, adding that at night, using floating lights off the dam and main points also can be successful.

In the fall, a longtime hot spot is the old roadbed in the Cabin Point area. "We caught tons of walleye

there in our fall netting," Waters says. "They're always there in those areas." If the lake is full, this spot typically sits in 8 feet of water, he adds.

White Bass: White bass is typically deemed excellent at Lovewell. It's normally rated as one of the top ten reservoirs in the state for density of whites, as well as lunker fish. According to Waters, the best time to fish for Lovewell whites is in the summer during peak irrigation releases from mid-June to mid-August. About 70–80 percent of the whites caught are in the inlet and outlet area.

"It's a popular hotspot," Waters says. "When there is water flowing in, that can be a really good place to catch fish." This is due to the fish moving up into the moving water, he explains.

While the inlet and outlet areas historically produce the vast majority of whites harvested, summer

---

Popular brush piles
GPS: N39 53.889 W98 02.025
East of state park: Not used as much as others, per KDWP, but can be very productive in low-water in fall and winter, especially for crappie. 10–12 feet deep at conservation pool.

GPS: N39 53.811 W98 04.319
Oak Hill brush pile: Favorite location for crappie and large-mouth bass in spring. Channel catfish and walleye in spring and summer. Depths range 6–15 feet at conservation pool. Marked by buoy.

GPS: N39 54.195 W98 03.594
Cabin Point south: Created August 2006. Cedars anchored with cinder blocks and other weights, per KDWP. 10–20 feet deep at conservation pool. Good for crappie throughout the year. Located on sharp drop-off and will concentrate walleye, white bass, and channel catfish. Marked by buoy.

GPS: N39 54.359 W98 03.636
Cabin Point north: 50 large cedars. 13–15 feet deep at conservation pool. Excellent for crappie. Largemouth bass and channel catfish fair. A variety of other species.

GPS: N39 89.5317 W98 04.8567
Cedar Point: Over 200 cedars anchored with cement blocks Depth is 20–25 feet. Very popular for crappie. Excellent fishing in fall and winter. Walleye and wipers decent in spring and early summer. Located just south of the boat ramp.

GPS: N39 53.934 W98 02.108
Marina Cove Point: Long popular among shoreline anglers due to location off the riprap, reports KDWP. In spring, before irrigation drawdown, 10–12 foot depth typical, and crappie excellent. Largemouth bass during the spawning period and early summer.

GPS: N39 53.985 W98 02.208
Marina Cove: Popular in higher water. Older brush pile with about 90 cedars. Crappie excellent in April and May during spawn. Channel catfish in summer. Marked by buoy. Located straight north of marina boat ramp. 11–12 feet deep.

topwater activity can also be productive. Also, Waters reports that night fishing using floating lights has been good in past years, and drifting or slabbing over submerged roadbeds, brush piles, and humps throughout the year is also an effective method for hooking into a nice stringer of whites.

Wiper: According to Waters, numbers are steady, and overall the lake typically has good numbers of keeper fish. Similar to white bass, decent numbers of wipers can be caught during the irrigation season as the fish migrate to the inlet and outlet areas. Other anglers report success catching bigger wipers trolling crank baits and deep-diving Rapalas along the north shore and the dam.

Catfish: Lovewell also has good numbers of both channel catfish and flatheads, Waters says. Lovewell ranks in the top ten among the state's reservoirs for density of channel catfish, and is one of the best lakes to catch some trophies.

According to Waters, channels and flatheads can be vulnerable in all arms of the reservoir, including Montana, Windmill, and Prairie Dog Creeks, as well as the Oak Hill area, the White Cross point, and up White Rock Creek near the K-14 bridge. "The inlet can be good for catfish, too," he says. During peak irrigation releases, catfish can readily be caught close to inlet and outlet structures and are susceptible along the dam and other rocky areas during spawn. They also congregate at several of the lake's brush piles.

Crappie: Crappie numbers fluctuate from year to year, but there can be some good fishing for those who find it. Waters says numbers were up considerably for the 2010 fishing season. While conditions are normally conducive to successful spawning in the spring months, extended irrigation draw downs in late summer and fall can eliminate available habitat. According to Waters' annual report, irrigation releases have been documented to remove up to 95 percent of the young crappie each year.

Several brush piles are maintained annually to help concentrate fish for anglers, including the Cabin Point and Cedar Point brush piles. Decent success can also be found fishing around the flooded vegetation in Montana Creek, Johns Creek, and other coves during late April and May when the fish are spawning. If a good amount of water is coming in through April, the inlet also is a good spot.

Waters says many use minnows. Others opt for jig fishing, which might be the best springtime technique for catching crappie.

Facilities

In all, 6,000 acres of hunting and fishing make up this complex of public lands. With its many trees, **Lovewell State Park** has excellent shade for camping. A historic limestone school hosts summer church services. An archery range is located north of the Cottonwood shower building. The park also has a baseball diamond, basketball courts, and picnic facilities. In total, the park offers: nearly 120 utility campsites; 306 primitive sites; and 6 cabins.

Lovewell has several annual special events during the year, including a Kids' Fishing Derby and free fishing weekend in June; fireworks and sandcastle contest in July; a Lovewell Fun Day, campfire cook-off, and campground Christmas in August; free park entrance in September; and several fishing tournaments.

GPS

Marina Boat Ramp: N39 53.943 W098 02.260

Shopping/Supplies

At the **Lovewell Marina & Grill,** Gary and Lyndell Charbonneau provide anglers with their fishing needs on one half of the outfit and smoked barbecue and drinks next door. Gary Charbonneau, who was raised in the area but eventually moved to Tennessee, traveled the country for 35 years and also worked internationally for his job. He moved back to the area in 2000. "In Tennessee, we did a lot of barbecuing," he says. "So, I thought, why not buy this place and open a barbecue grill." 67 Y Rd., Webber, 785-753-4351.

Colsons Plumbing and Electric, 120 Delaware St., Jewell, 785-428-3572; **Ike's Mini Mart,** North Shore Rd., Lovewell Lake, Webber, 785-753-4041; **Jewell County Clerk,** 307 N. Commercial St., Mankato, 785-378-4020; **Webbs Bait and Tackle,** 202 S. Center St., Mankato, 785-378-3980.

Marion Reservoir

SIZE: 6,160 acres

LOCATION: About 4 miles northwest of Marion on US 56

GPS LOCATION: N38 22 3.72 W97 5 22.07

CONTACT: U.S. Army Corps of Engineers, 620-382-2101

FEATURE FISH: Channel Catfish, Flathead Catfish, Crappie, Walleye, White Bass, Wiper

DAILY CREEL LIMIT/MINIMUM LENGTH: Largemouth Bass: 2 fish, 18 inches • Channel Catfish: 10 fish • Flathead Catfish: 5 fish • Crappie: 50 fish • Walleye: 5 fish, 18 inches • Wiper: 5 fish, 18 inches

AQUATIC NUISANCE SPECIES ALERT: Zebra Mussels (unlawful to possess alive)

A thunderstorm brewed in the distance on this early spring day—the perfect weather for fishing, Wichita aircraft worker Bob Bair said. It was a weekday he didn't have to go to work, and he couldn't imagine a better way to celebrate than fishing upstream of Marion Reservoir.

He stood on the bank of the Cottonwood River, not far from where the river flows into the Marion County impoundment, where the white bass run had commenced upstream. Bair doesn't miss the annual rite. "I've been fishing Marion Reservoir since I was a kid," he said, noting that on occasion he spends summer days trolling for walleye and white bass on the reservoir itself.

But it's not yet summer, he noted with a smile. "It's mid-April and that's why I'm here." And, with the front moving in, he had already caught two keepers.

The spot Bair was fishing is known as the Broken Bridge—a popular fishing location at GPS point N38 27.098 W97 11.236 on the Cottonwood where two concrete slabs that once connected are located. The slabs allow for handicapped-accessible fishing. There also is a boat ramp, parking, and restrooms. He was amid a dozen or so people on this day trying to catch white bass. Some fish the banks. Others put in small boats and trek up and down the river.

• • •

For John and I, Marion is one lake we're more familiar with. We've fished Marion together since we were married, whether it was on the dam during the walleye spawn, searching for wipers out on the water, or, like Bair, hitting the Broken Bridge area upstream in April, hoping to catch white bass.

John's fished the lake since childhood. He and his family and friends especially hit the Cottonwood upstream after a rain event, which is an outstanding time to reel in heavy catfish.

But on this spring day, our fishing was centered on the white bass. We fished with jigs and Mr. Twisters with plenty of success along the Cottonwood near the little town of Durham.

Beginning in late winter, white bass, along with wipers, begin congregating at the mouth of waterways in

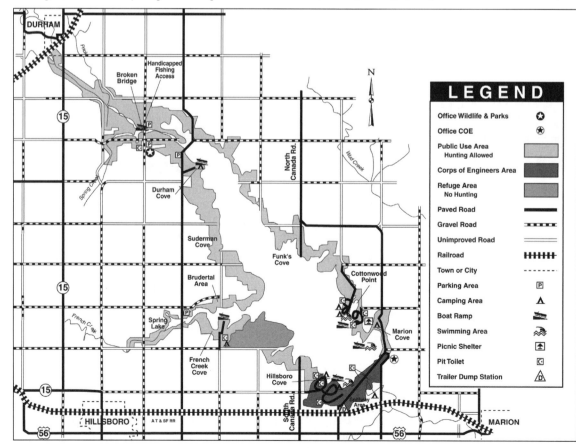

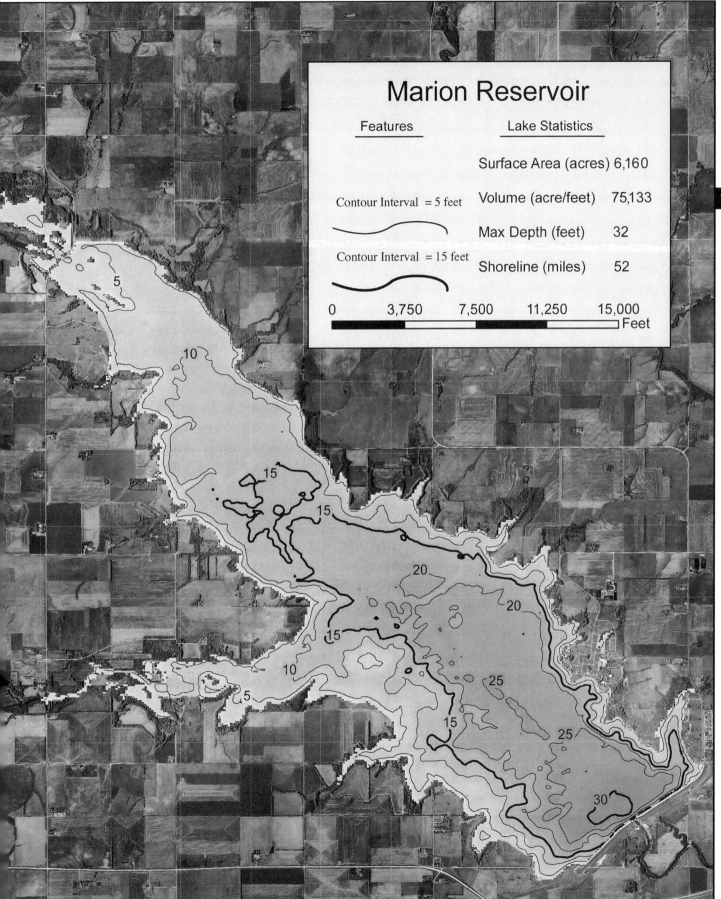

Marion Reservoir

Features	Lake Statistics	
	Surface Area (acres)	6,160
Contour Interval = 5 feet	Volume (acre/feet)	75,133
	Max Depth (feet)	32
Contour Interval = 15 feet	Shoreline (miles)	52

0   3,750   7,500   11,250   15,000 Feet

preparation for their spawning run. Unlike the large-mouth bass, which build nests and guard them during the reproduction process, white bass move out of lakes and reservoirs and into flowing rivers and creeks to lay their eggs on their run upstream. The trigger is a water temperature of 50–55 degrees. That's when avid anglers start to trudge the banks of the Cottonwood from the mouth of the reservoir to K-15 near Durham, a stretch of river that is surrounded by public land.

On most occasions, Bair says, fishing for whites, whether it's in the lake or the river, is excellent—making it a fine fishery for avid anglers. Yet white bass are just one species in this rich fishing lake.

Marion Reservoir, completed in 1968, was named after the town and county of Marion, which itself was named for General Francis Marion, who served during the American Revolution. The lake averages about 14 feet in depth, according to the Kansas Department of Wildlife and Parks, and is characterized by a shallow sloping shoreline, opening water, and relatively little variation in basin bottom.

And, of course, there are ample opportunities to catch fish. The lake is noted for walleye, crappie, white bass, wipers, and catfish, including channels and flatheads. Marion also has a few largemouth bass. Fish feeders are located in Hillsboro Cove and Cottonwood Point.

Water clarity is usually adequate for good fishing, and when water is being released from the reservoir, anglers have ample success below the dam and in the outlet channel. "The nice thing about it is it doesn't get the recreational traffic that other lakes get," says Mike Cook, who operates Four Lake Guides. "Most people who go to Marion go there to fish."

Feature Fish

Catfish: It may sound rather daunting to fish in July when the fishing is lazy. Yet, when the temperatures soar, the catfish start biting. Cook says that, of the four lakes he fishes in Kansas, he ranks Marion and Cheney number one for cat.

The mighty catfish is one of the species that rules at Marion. And, with Warren Kreutziger's stinky concoction, success typically ripples into the boat within minutes of the anchor hitting bottom. It's a meal of soured soybeans, which the catfish greedily eat up, along with the bait hook.

Kreutziger says he grew up fishing the Cottonwood River for catfish long before Marion was constructed. These days, he's fishing for the species in a little bigger water—a lake that rests just north of the little unincorporated town of Canada, where Kreutziger operates Canada Bait and Tackle, along with his catfish guiding service.

Kreutziger's method is called chumming, which is growing in popularity across Kansas reservoirs because of the quickness of reeling in fish and the increased catches it

brings. Some anglers use stink bait rather than soured soybeans when fishing with this method. Either way, it's a simple and effective way to attract and keep fish in a given area. Anglers say the best spots for chumming are drop-offs where catfish tend to congregate. Marion has several of these holes around the lake.

Cook says there are four prime chumming areas. Two are along the dam on the east and west sides coming off 15–18 feet of water. Another is located on the north end around Durham Cove, a spot around 5–8 feet in depth that comes out of 12–15 feet of water. The other is just north of French Creek Cove.

However, chumming isn't the only way to catch catfish. KDWP fisheries biologist Jessica Mounts says the catfish are nearly reservoir wide. And Cook, who says he doesn't do much chumming, does much of his channel cat fishing in extremely shallow water.

"I try to use the wind," Cook says. "The windier, the shallower I fish. On a normal day, when the wind is five to fifteen miles per hour, I fish in three feet. When it is windier, above fifteen, I fish in one to two feet of water."

Channel cats also congregate in French Creek and Durham Cove during the summer. One of Cook's favorite roadbed spots is near French Creek. Cook says Marion has underwater roadbeds that are good to target for several different species—roadbeds that could be 4–12 feet from the surface. Some of the old roadbeds have slab rock and rebar on them from the highway projects, giving the bait fish a place to hide.

"There is a point just south of French Creek," he says, "that actually has six of these roadbed jetties coming off that great big point, those things going out there three-hundred to four-hundred yards."

Another good place is the causeway, Cook says, but adds the water there is shallow for boaters. By July or

August, find the catfish in deeper water, Cook advises, but adds, "It's a tough time of year to fish. That's the time of year I switch to wipers." But there are summer hot spots on the river, especially at night, he notes. "The best way to find them is to fish the river at night under a light."

Cook uses stink bait, except in the winter, when he uses cut bait to fish for channel cats. Other options include drifting with whole shad, according to Mounts.

White bass: Marion is a regular fish hatchery when it comes to white bass, an impoundment that typically has excellent fishing. And, as Bair can attest, Marion has good numbers of white bass that spawn up the Cottonwood River each year. Also look for them in sandy beaches upstream from the mouth of French Creek Cove.

Whites like to spawn in brushy and rocky areas along riffles—typically staging in deeper water above and below these areas. A few areas to target: deep holes along stream bends, below brush piles, and around bridge supports. One factor controlling the white bass run is water flow, according to the KDWP. Without good stream flow, the fish can't make it upstream. Good flow, however, is generally the case at Marion.

Most anglers fishing for white bass use light- or medium-action spinning tackle and a 6- to 8-pound test line. Preferred baits include artificial lures like jigs, small spinners, and spoons. Live minnows also work well. Also, anglers report, try fishing with lures that mimic shad.

The average white bass weighs about a pound, but some can grow to 4 pounds. Mounts says to look for whites in their typical haunts—chasing shad around the lake and in coves. Cook says to find them on windblown points, as well, but adds the best time for white bass fishing, of course, is during the spawn. "People will line the river all the way to Durham," he says.

Wiper: Another excellent fishing opportunity for anglers who want a little reel action. Marion ranked number one in Kansas for this species in 2010. And Cook ranks Marion high on his list for wiper and white bass fishing, as well. It's what he fishes for when summer hits.

Mounts advises anglers to hit the dam and rocky points, as well as areas with standing timber at the north end of the lake. Look for the shad, and you'll almost always find wipers and whites.

Wipers can be caught mixed in with the whites on points and drops with crank baits and curly tailed grubs. Cook said he uses white, chartreuse, or any combination of curly tail grubs or soft-shad bodies on a jig for wipers, with the size of the jig dependent on the lake condition. "If it is going to be windy, I use a quarter-ounce jig head and a eighth-ounce if it is not windy."

He says the best advice he could give an angler: "Look for the boats."

Crappie: There's an abundance of crappie for the angling pleasure at Marion. "It's one of the best in the state, it really is," says Cook. "According to the KDWP testing, there is a ton of crappie in there."

Of course, spawn is one of the best times to catch crappie, largely because that's when they come the closest to shore. Crappie begin to spawn in late spring, when water temperatures reach the mid-50s. According to the

KDWP, crappie may spawn as shallow as 2 feet, with the fish being the most active at dawn and dusk, when light levels are low.

Fish typically spawn in brush and rock piles, weed beds, and rocky shorelines. Productive lures include small, colorful jigs. Small spoons, spinners, and crankbaits are effective, as well, throughout the year. Live minnows are also good crappie bait, especially during cool spells when fish aren't as active.

Cook says there is a resident population of crappie on the Cottonwood River all year long, and lots of fish on the dam. Meanwhile, Mounts says successful crappie anglers find fish on the dam and at windy points and in shallow areas using minnows for bait. Cook also says to target coves with timber.

Walleye: Of course, you can catch some walleye off the dam during the spring spawn. However, says Mounts, walleye don't spawn at this location like they do at other Kansas reservoirs. She says the shape of the dam underneath the water is different than most dams, making it not as lucrative of a location in April.

Also, KDWP officials milk the male walleye about this time. Marion is one of the lakes biologists use to retrieve male fish. Biologists net the walleye, take them to a hatchery and extract the sperm. Once the procedure is completed, the fish are then returned to the lake.

Still, walleye are rated as good to excellent in these waters.

Mounts says to try fishing from the bank and on points with the wind blowing into or across points. By May or June, walleye can be caught on a jig and night crawler combo on the flats, as well as in woody points or on summertime humps. Cook says he doesn't prefer fishing during the spawn, but noted anglers who do fish then use big rattletraps in hopes to hook a walleye. When guiding after the spawn, he fishes by drifting in and out of points using jig and night crawlers.

Cook notes silting in of the reservoir over the years has hurt Marion's flats, but adds anglers will still find walleye at his point south of French Creek where there are jetties and road beds. "That's just a really good spot," he says.

According to Mounts, the lake has strong recruitment, with a good fall netting in 2010. "This is a naturally reproducing lake and the fish are doing very well," she says. "The sampling showed fairly large fish—from 15 inches to 24 inches." She says that the walleye has certain things they like for spawning and that Marion gives them what they want.

Aquatic Nuisances

Marion has had blue-green algae since 2004. Sometimes, when conditions are worse, the U.S. Army Corps of Engineers will shut down the swimming beach. The Corps also recommends not wading in areas where there is an algae bloom. Blooms are a result of phosphorus in the water.

Zebra mussels were discovered in Marion Reservoir in 2008, Mounts says. "We don't want people moving them to other reservoirs," she says. (See "Aquatic Nuisances" in the Introduction, p. 16, for more information, including regulations.)

Also, a commercial fisherman has been removing buffalo carp from the lake. More than 300,000 pounds were removed in 2008, according to the KDWP. Cook says some anglers like to bow fish for carp at Marion, noting there are still plenty of these "trash fish." "When the cotton is hitting the water, floating on top of the water," he says, "you can see the carp and buffalo sucking up on it."

Facilities

Marion Reservoir is surrounded by another 6,000 acres of public lands, according to the Corps. This includes 4 Corps parks—**Cottonwood Point, Hillsboro Cove, Marion Cove,** and **French Creek Cove.** Altogether, they offer 171 campsites. Camping on the KDWP managed area is allowed only at **Durham Cove.** There is a hiking trail at the lake, as well as swimming beaches. Boaters must pay to use all Corps boat ramps except for two undeveloped ramps located at Durham Cove and Broken Bridge. There are fish feeders located in Hillsboro Cove and Cottonwood Point.

GPS

Broken Bridge Area: N38 27.098 W97 11.236

Shopping/Supplies

Alco, 615 N. Ash St., Hillsboro, 620-947-5548; **Canada Bait 'N' Tackle** (check to see if they have bait), 1942 Nighthawk Rd., Marion, 620-382-2931, canada@southwind.net; **Johnson's General Store,** 800 W. 5th St., Florence, 620-878-4611; **Marion County Clerk,** 200 S. 3rd St., Marion, 620-382-2185; **Peabody Hardware and Lumber,** 124 N. Walnut St., Peabody 620-983-2170.

Guide Service

Canada Bait 'N' Tackle, Canada, 620-382-2931; **Four Lake Guides,** Mike Cook, 316-655-1541.

Melvern Reservoir

SIZE: 7,000 acres

LOCATION: About 35 miles south of Topeka on US 75

GPS LOCATION: N38 31.72 W95 44.70

CONTACT: U.S. Army Corps of Engineers, Melvern Reservoir, 785-549-3318

FEATURE FISH: Largemouth Bass, Smallmouth Bass, Spotted Bass, Channel Catfish, Flathead Catfish, Crappie, Sauger, Walleye, White Bass, Wiper

DAILY CREEL LIMIT/MINIMUM LENGTH: Largemouth Bass: 6 fish, 18 inches • Smallmouth Bass: 6 fish, 18 inches • Spotted Bass: 6 fish, 18 inches • Blue Catfish: 10 fish • Channel Catfish: 10 fish • Flathead Catfish: 5 fish • Crappie: 20 fish, 10 inches • Sauger: 5 fish, 15 inches • Striped Bass: 2 fish, 18 inches • Walleye: 5 fish, 18 inches

On a hot July day in 2010, I found Emporia couple Fred and Audra Agin trailing lines behind their boat, searching for fish. Did I say it was hot? Make that scorching hot. Hot enough that there weren't many boats on the lake—either for recreation or for fishing. Some might even have said it was too hot to catch anything.

Yet when it comes to trolling the waters of Osage County's Melvern Reservoir, fed by the Marais des Cygnes River, for walleye, white bass, and crappie, call the Agins the masters. Their familiarity with the eastern Kansas lake was what led me to seek them out. In fact, I jumped at the chance to go out with a couple of lake experts.

John and I had spent the evening before camping on the shores of the lake—a rare outing without our girls. We met up with the Agins the next morning. Audra wanted to teach me the ins and outs of using a planer board, and she figured it'd be easier for me to understand the concept if she could show me in person.

They aren't your faint-hearted anglers. Audra laughed as she told how she taught her husband how to fillet fish when they first met during an outdoor club excursion at Emporia State University. She also laughed at the fact I was wearing shorts on this 90-plus-degree day—while she sported bib overalls.

But when it comes to trolling, Audra is serious. She has researched the subject thoroughly and refined the skill through lots of practice. Like dedicated walleye tournament anglers, Audra and Fred fish with an assortment of 7- to 12-foot long poles. They use line counter reels with clickers spooled with 10- to 12-pound line. They have drift socks. A global positioning system marks waypoints. And their tackle boxes are filled with any type of artificial lure imaginable. Fred jokes that when it comes to fishing, his wife fills the boat with everything but the kitchen sink.

Then again, they are successful.

"Some people think trolling is boring," Audra says, "but once you learn how to do it, it will keep you busy catching fish. This is an easy way to introduce a person to fishing." It's a method that doesn't appeal to everyone, but for the Agins trolling is sometimes the only way to catch fish consistently.

• • •

Lebo resident Terry Bivins had been telling me of Melvern's good fishing for quite a while. Bivins, who likes to fish for white bass, says he moved to the Coffey County town because of the prime fishing location—a

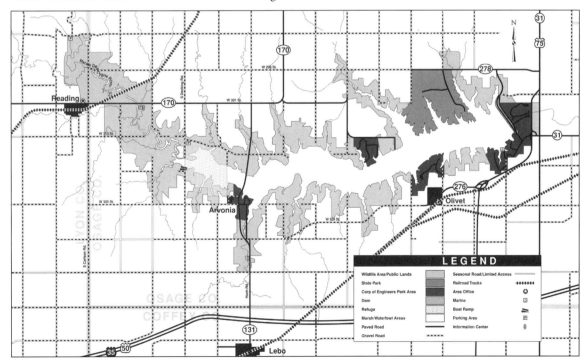

Rock Quarry
Cove

Lowman's
Cove

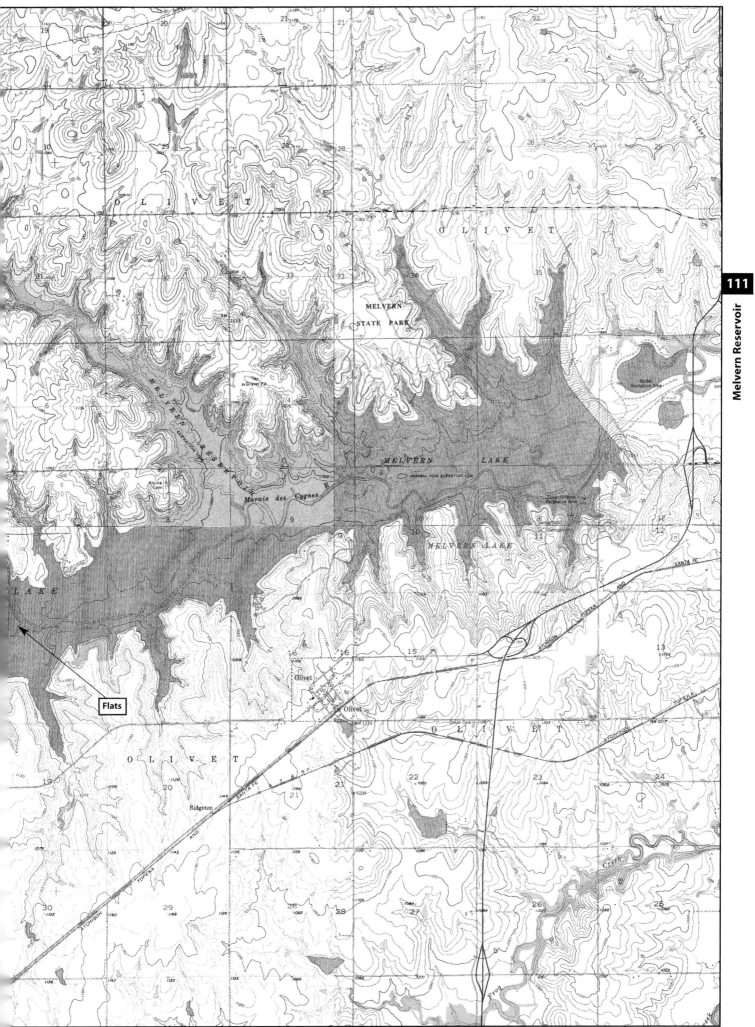

handful of lakes close to home. That includes Melvern, which, he says, is more than just a white bass hatchery.

Melvern Reservoir, built in 1954 for flood control and water recreation, covers nearly 7,000 acres of water fed by the Marias des Cygnes River. It also has 17,244 acres of adjacent land that serves as the nucleus of recreational and natural resource activities for more than 500,000 visitors annually, according to the U.S. Army Corps of Engineers.

The lake is known for a variety of fish. Melvern, after all, is one of Bivins' favorites. "You have tons of great walleye and white bass fishing," he says. "It has a tremendous amount of smallmouth. It's good for crappie, too."

Meanwhile, the Outlet Park River Pond just below the dam is a honey hole for anglers, according to Leonard Jirak, the Kansas Department of Wildlife and Parks fisheries biologist for Melvern. The pond was renovated in 1990 and 2001, and it has been managed intensively via game fish stocking, placement of habitat structure, and an aggressive feeding program. The pond's species include crappie, channel catfish, black bass, bluegill, and wiper.

"The river pond, it is one of the best channel cat fisheries in the state, with many of the channels weighing over 10 pounds," Jirak says. "It is excellent for bass fishing and has large bluegill. Most of the fishing is done from the bank."

It's good fishing, but also good scenery, says Shelia Albright, of Topeka, who was searching for walleye with her husband, Allen Jr., and grandkids, Logan and Kennedy, on a summer afternoon. "We come here several times a year," Allen said, noting it is a lake close by where the family can spend time together.

"And," Shelia said, "I like the solitude here. It's just me and my pole."

• • •

A farm girl from near Caney, Audra Agin grew up on a river and had two cane polls down on the water that would either have a catfish or turtle on them each morning. "We always kept catfish," she says. "We had fresh catfish all summer long."

She says her dad started her trolling on Bull Shoals Lake. Now that Audra and Fred are both retired, their expertise is trolling.

The Agins have a path they follow at Melvern. On this day, we started along the west shoreline of Turkey Point Cove, the long cove just west of Eisenhower State Park, then headed west along the north shore before turning around and following the same path again, but in a little deeper water.

Our hot summer trip proved successful, as we reeled in white bass after white bass, as well as crappie.

Audra, an excellent teacher, didn't just let me watch—by the end of the trip, I had nearly mastered the art of planer-board fishing. We used deep diving crankbaits, with water depths varying from around 15 to 30 feet, and the lures hitting depths of 12–15 feet. The Agins kept the boat speed at about 2.3–3 mph with the wind, but never stopped the boat to reel in fish.

"If you really want to target crappie, slow down your speed to 1.5 mph," Audra says.

Trolling with planer boards is effective because the boards allow anglers to get their lures away from the boat. It also allows the angler to go over waters the boat hasn't spooked, as well as to fish more rods while trolling. For instance, with one board out on each side of the boat at a minimum distance of roughly 25 feet in each direction, an angler's trolling path will be about 50 feet wide or more. That's a lot of water being covered.

Plus, it allows more fishing lines to troll simultaneously, efficiently, and without getting the worst tangled mess you could imagine. This, I must admit, is prone to happen when I'm in the boat. Or so my husband says.

The Agins note a few other areas they try to hit when they come to the lake. Audra pointed out a tiny cove just between Turkey Point campground and Eisenhower State Park. The north shore divot "is sometimes the only place we'll catch fish," she says. "That ditch goes a long way out."

Meanwhile, Fred says the cove in Coeur d'Alene campground is a good spot for crappie and walleye anglers who are using jigs and night crawlers. "That is where we caught a lot of nice crappie in March," Fred says. "We'd let the wind drift us."

Flats by Eisenhower State Park also are fruitful, including the east point of the state park, where Audra says one will find "humps and bumps and walleye hanging out." Also, the area around the boat ramp is good for crappie and smallmouth.

There are flats on the south side not far off from where Indian Hills Road intersects with the lake, Audra says. "Between those two coves, it's a gradual slope. When it's real windy from the south, it's a good place to get out of the wind. We catch walleye, but we talked to a fishing guide, and he loves to catch crappie over there."

Feature Fish

Crappie: Melvern is "one of the top consistent crappie fishery in the state," according to Jirak. "It doesn't necessarily have the biggest crappie, but it has good numbers all the time." Want proof? Just ask any crappie angler. "This lake gets fished for crappie 365 days of the year," Jirak says.

When they aren't spawning, Jirak says to look for them in 15–20 feet of water, where they will congregate around brush piles, points, and ledges. For bank fishermen, the marina and boat slips is a good spot to try.

Fred says one spot he never misses for crappie is a long cove just west of Eisenhower State Park. Another crappie hotspot is the old rock quarry cove, which Cable Creek feeds into. In the spring, bank fishermen will sit on a little bridge on the west side of the cove, jigging for crappie.

Meanwhile, Audra says to check out Lowman's Cove for crappie, as well. The cove, located on the south shoreline, has standing timber—maybe even the most standing timber of any cove on the lake. Also, Audra pinpointed on a map a small divot area just north and west of the Arrow Rock boat ramp. "That's a great crappie area for springtime spawning," she says.

Catfish: Channel catfish are ubiquitous, Jirak says. Look for them in the mouth of creeks after a rain, or along the riprap during the spawn. Fred says to try the Sun Dance Park area for channel cats, as well.

Chumming is a popular method for catching cats at Melvern. "A lot [of people] put out rotten soybeans in the summer time," Jirak says.

Melvern is also home to blue cats, with some weighing more than 30 pounds in 2010. There are also some heavy flatheads, which are typically caught by trotline fisherman, Jirak says. One good hangout includes the Turkey Creek channel, as well as the Marais des Cygnes, which winds across the entire lake.

Walleye: Jirak calls Melvern one of the better walleye lakes in the eastern half of the state. Find them spawning on the dam in April, then get out the jig and night

crawlers when the fish move to the flats in May and June. According to Jirak, that includes flats off Eisenhower Point, Turkey Creek, and Arrow Rock Cove.

"They'll be in anywhere from two to fifteen feet of water that time of year, depending on the time of day," Jirak says.

Audra also recommends a cove just west of Turkey Point for catching walleye. Or, she says, follow the river channel around the Coeur d'Alene campground shoreline. It's a spot where anglers will troll or jig for walleye.

Melvern has a special 30-acre pond where Jirak raises walleye up to 10 inches, then releases them into the reservoir.

White Bass: According to Jirak, whites are probably the second-most sought-after fish in Melvern. Depending on the spring, he says, anglers will find them running up to the low-water dam at Reading during the spawn. Otherwise, whites will spawn off rocky and gravel points. Some anglers have success along the north shore of Eisenhower Park, "especially when the wind is blowing in there," he says. And, from July on, find them hitting shad.

Try Marina Cove for another white bass hangout.

Black Bass: Melvern has all three species of black bass. "We have a really good smallmouth fishery," Jirak says, noting smallmouth density at Melvern ranks in the top five for Kansas reservoirs. He's been stocking the lake with smallmouth since the mid-1990s, and anglers catch and release between 6,000–8,000 smallmouth at the lake each year. The length limit is 18 inches.

Find smallmouth along the rocky bluffs and ledges. Fred notes one area like this is the Coeur d'Alene campground. Many anglers use spinner baits and jigs.

Jirak says a good place to try for spotted bass is in the Marina Cove area and inside the rocky coves. Preferred baits include crawdad lures and rubber worms. "They like clear water, deep water and rocks," he says.

As for largemouth fishing, Jirak calls it mediocre—although, on a hot summer day in July, Fred Agin caught one by trolling. Jirak says largemouth are found in the coves that have cover and a soft bottom, as well as around trees, flooded vegetation and brush piles. Fred also says hit the cove just east of the state park: "There's some largemouth in there."

Sauger: Jirak notes that "we still have the state record sauger at Melvern." Not many lakes have a sauger population, and this record is an older one. Jimmy Barnes, of Kansas City, caught a 4.80-pound, 23.75-inch sauger in November of 1996 using a rod and reel with a jig and minnow.

Find them in shallower water—anywhere from 1–10 feet, Jirak says.

Audra Agin's Guide to Expert Trolling

"If you like to eat a variety of fish, trolling can fill up your livewell," Emporia resident Audra Agin says.

On a recent summer day, she quipped a fishing proverb for walleye: "Wind from the east and north, jig fish. Wind from the south and west, troll." Most times when the wind is out of the east or north, use a slower presentation, she says—or just stay home. That's what she and her husband, Fred, do from spring until hunting season starts in the fall.

Audra, who wrote a paper on the effectiveness of planer boards, has this to say on why folks might want to use them (as well as some sage advice):

• Planer boards give the angler a better hookup with the fish. The board allows the line to give when a fish strikes the lure, and the lure has a better chance of not being yanked from the fish's mouth.

• Should you have to stop the boat to fight a fish on another pole, the board usually stays upright and helps to keep the line away from the area. And, with a little forward motion, you usually don't have to reel it in.

• If fish are in shallow water or there is not much wave action, the boat scares the fish out to the side of the boat into the path of the planer boards and lures. This is especially effective for fish that spook easily, such as walleye and crappie. The fish will spook right into the path of the oncoming lures being run off the planer boards. When using a shallow lure next to the shoreline, Audra says to put out 40–60 feet of line behind the board.

• "There have been times—when the lake is like glass—we put out four or five poles total, and two poles had planer boards, one on each side of the boat," she says. "Only the poles with the planer boards got the fish; the two inside poles got very few."

• Meanwhile, when the water is choppy, the Agins replace the boards and 9-foot rods with 12-foot rods held horizontal to the water.

• In areas where fishing pressure is intense, fish will close their mouths at the slightest disturbance. The knowledgeable planer board angler, however, who trolls the lure presentation overtop of suspended fish, or just overtop of structure with the boat a generous distance away—will prove that fish can be taken no matter the circumstances.

• With a wider spread of lines, the lines do not get tangled as often with the other lines. However, make sure your lures are running true, and adjust them. You also cover more area of water this way.

• The clicker on the reel helps you to hear if the line is being pulled out and you have a fish on. Set the clicker tension to the pull weight and drag of lure and planer board.

• Since the board is sitting in the water, your lure should go deeper than if on the pole by itself. So if you are used to running a certain lure 120 feet out, on the planer board go 100 feet behind the board.

• In the beginning of your fishing day, with multiple poles out, you should have a variation of lure depths and colors to try to figure out what the fish want.

• A special permit allows anglers to have 3 poles each.

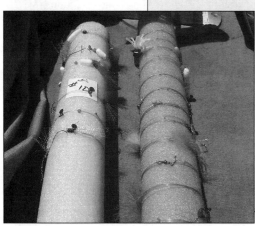

• Audra says to think of a planer board as a bobber, a line indicator. Study how it rides in the water. When a fish gets on, the board may move back a few feet, it may sit lower in the water, or the board may be tilted or water may be going over the front of the board. "You could also just have some junk on it, too," she says. "It could also be hitting bottom. Do you have other poles and lures out about the same depth? Are they hitting bottom?"

Audra admits she has received looks from other boaters while using planer boards—something rarely seen on some of the state's waters. "The only other time you will see anybody else using a planer board is the week prior to a walleye tournament," she says.

Facilities

Melvern Reservoir, along with 17,244 acres of adjacent land, serves as the nucleus of recreational and natural resource activities for more than 500,000 visitors annually. Six campgrounds are conveniently located around Melvern Reservoir. The Corps manages five out of the six campgrounds. They are: **Outlet, Coeur D'Alene, Arrow Rock, Sun Dance,** and **Turkey Point Parks.** The state of Kansas manages the **Eisenhower State Park** campground. The park has beaches, full-service marina, several boat ramps, nature trails, and an equestrian trail, as well as four modern and three primitive cabins.

GPS

Old Boat Ramp: Located in the river above the lake above the log jam. N38 30.544 W95 55.067

Arvonia Cemetery Boat Ramp: Located on the river below the log jam. N38 29.590 W95 53.728

Arrow Rock area and boat ramp: N38 29.8487 W95 44.834

Shopping/Supplies

Lakeview Bait & Tackle, 203 N. Main St., New Strawn, 620-364-8354; **Melvern Lake Marina,** 31271 Marina Parkway, Melvern, 620-256-6566; **Sports Mart,** RR 2, Lyndon, 785-828-3360; **Sundance Bait & Tackle,** 8145 W. 325th St., Lebo, 620-256-6061.

Milford Reservoir

SIZE: 16,200 acres

LOCATION: 5 miles northwest of Junction City on US 77

GPS LOCATION: N39 06.241 W96 53.682

CONTACT: Milford Project Office, U.S. Army Corps of Engineers, 785-238-5714

FEATURE FISH: Smallmouth Bass, Blue Catfish, Channel Catfish, Flathead Catfish, Crappie, Walleye, White Bass, Wiper

DAILY CREEL LIMIT/MINIMUM LENGTH: Largemouth Bass: 5 fish, 15 inches • Smallmouth Bass: 5 fish, 15 inches • Spotted Bass: 5 fish, 15 inches • Blue Catfish: 5 fish* • Channel Catfish: 10 fish* • Flathead Catfish: 5 fish • Crappie: 50 fish • Walleye: 5 fish, 18 inches • Wiper: 2 fish

* Blue Catfish and Channel Catfish in combination, with no more than 5 Blue Catfish. (All 10 fish can be channel cats, but only 5 can be blues.)

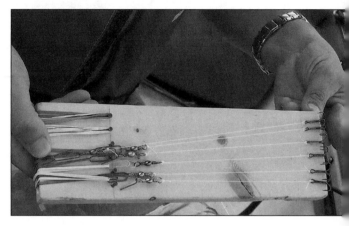

The Reverend Larry Brock will tell anyone that life doesn't get much better than a cloudless sky that stretches across an expanse of water. On Sundays, you'll find him behind the pulpit at Longford and Mizpah United Methodist Churches. But during the week, when time allows, this pastor angles channel catfish from his small boat at Milford Reservoir.

"I love to slip away here," Brock said one morning as we fished for catfish near Wakefield. And sometimes, he says, you'll find him with his parishioners out on the lake.

Brock is an old family friend of my husband's family—a guy who got hooked on fishing while chumming for catfish on Kanopolis Reservoir before he was called to preach closer to Milford. And, he said, it didn't take him long to find Milford was just as excellent for cat fishing as Kanopolis.

Not that Brock really needed to sell me on the fishing at Milford. This lake, after all, is the lake I grew up around since I was in diapers. Every Labor Day weekend, my parents, along with my two older siblings, would go to Milford for a long four-day weekend with a couple from our small Baptist church. Our activities included camping, skiing, and fishing.

I still recall one of the first fish I caught at Milford—along the shoreline not far from our campsite at Curtis Creek. I couldn't tell you what species it was, although I recall hooking it on a worm and bobber. I was so proud that I told my Grandpa we should cook it up that night.

Unbeknownst to me at the time, Grandpa threw the tiny fish back into the water.

It wouldn't be the last fish I'd catch at Kansas' largest impoundment. And I would find some actual keepers, too. Milford, known as the Fishing Capitol of Kansas, is home to solid populations of blue and channel catfish, as well as smallmouth bass, walleye, white bass, and wiper. With 163 miles of shoreline, including plenty of coves, rocky points, and drop offs, anglers can find many fishing locations.

So on my birthday weekend, I staked camp at Milford with my husband, John, and my brother, Scott, for a long weekend of fishing, just like we used to do when we were growing up. And, as always, it turned out to be another successful trip, with Brock leading us to the catfish in the northern part of the lake—plenty for supper. Later on, we explored both of Milford's wiper islands, reeling in a few of these fighters.

• • •

Milford began operating in 1967. On average, about 500,000 people visit Milford each year for boating, camping, hunting, and fishing, according to the U.S. Army Corps of Engineers. Besides the lake, there are 18,800 acres of public land.

"We're really fortunate," says Rick Dykstra, assistant director of the Geary County Convention and Visitors Bureau who, as an avid fisherman, had a local television fishing show for 13 years. "If you're looking for a lake with a lot of species and good fishing, you are hard-pressed to beat Milford Lake."

Feature Fish

Blue Catfish: Brock told me about Jim Leonard, whose home is not far from Milford's shore. He called Leonard the expert cat fisherman on Milford. And most call him by his self-proclaimed nickname, Catfish Fever. Leonard is a military man who went straight to fishing the reservoir upon retirement in 1975. Living by the lake, his adopted name graces his boat, his license tag, and even his clothing.

He fishes every season. When it's cold, he looks for catfish by the dam in 60 feet of water. In the summer, he follows the river channel for blues, as well as hitting other spots about which he is more secretive. He keeps a logbook with dates and GPS coordinates. He also follows a fish calendar.

"If the lake is not frozen, I'll fish," he says, then adds, "I'm not going to get out on the ice, though."

According to John Reinke, Milford's fisheries biologist with the Kansas Department of Wildlife and Parks, the lake

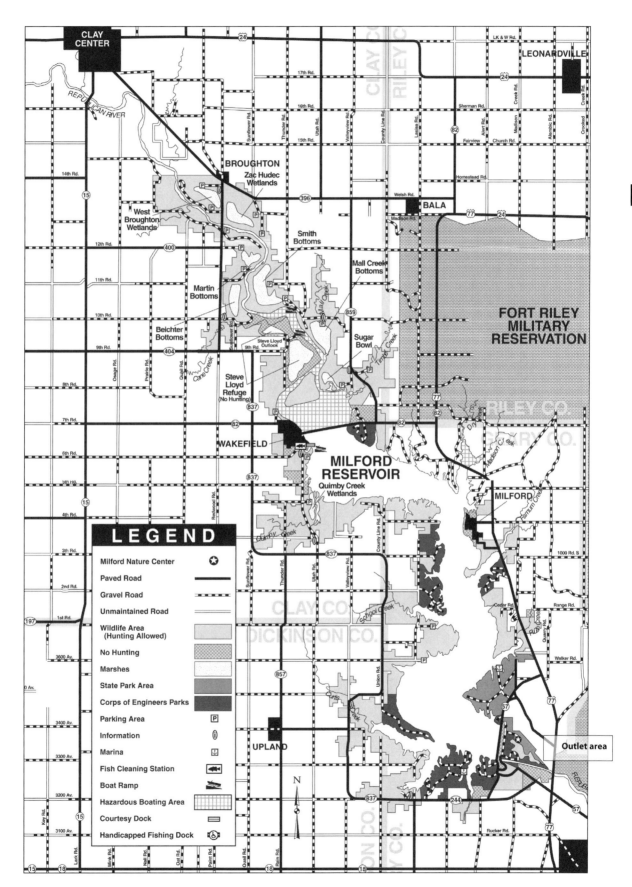

CLAY CENTER

LEONARDVILLE

LK & W Rd.

17th Rd.

16th Rd.

Sherman Rd.

Creek Rd.

Fairview

Church Rd.

82

15th Rd.

Homestead Rd.

14th Rd.

REPUBLICAN RIVER

BROUGHTON

Zac Hudec Wetlands

396

Welsh Rd.

BALA

77

24

West Broughton Wetlands

Madison Rd.

12th Rd.

400

Smith Bottoms

Mall Creek Bottoms

FORT RILEY MILITARY RESERVATION

11th Rd.

Martin Bottoms

859

10th Rd.

Belchter Bottoms

404

9th Rd.

Steve Lloyd Outlook

Sugar Bowl

77

8th Rd.

Carol Creek

Steve Lloyd Refuge (No Hunting)

82

7th Rd.

82

837

WAKEFIELD

MILFORD RESERVOIR

MILFORD

6th Rd.

Quimby Creek Wetlands

5th Rd.

837

4th Rd.

15

1000 Rd. S

3rd Rd.

LEGEND

Milford Nature Center	✪
Paved Road	
Gravel Road	
Unmaintained Road	
Wildlife Area (Hunting Allowed)	
No Hunting	
Marshes	
State Park Area	
Corps of Engineers Parks	
Parking Area	P
Information	
Marina	
Fish Cleaning Station	
Boat Ramp	
Hazardous Boating Area	
Courtesy Dock	
Handicapped Fishing Dock	

197

1st Rd.

3600 Av.

Cedar Rd.

Range Rd.

CLAY CO.
DICKINSON CO.

School Creek

3400 Av.

3300 Av.

857

Walker Rd.

UPLAND

N

57

Outlet area

3200 Av.

837

15

244

3100 Av.

Rucker Rd.

77

57

15

18

Lark Rd.

Mink Rd.

Nall Rd.

Oat Rd.

Paint Rd.

Quail Rd.

Rain Rd.

18

18

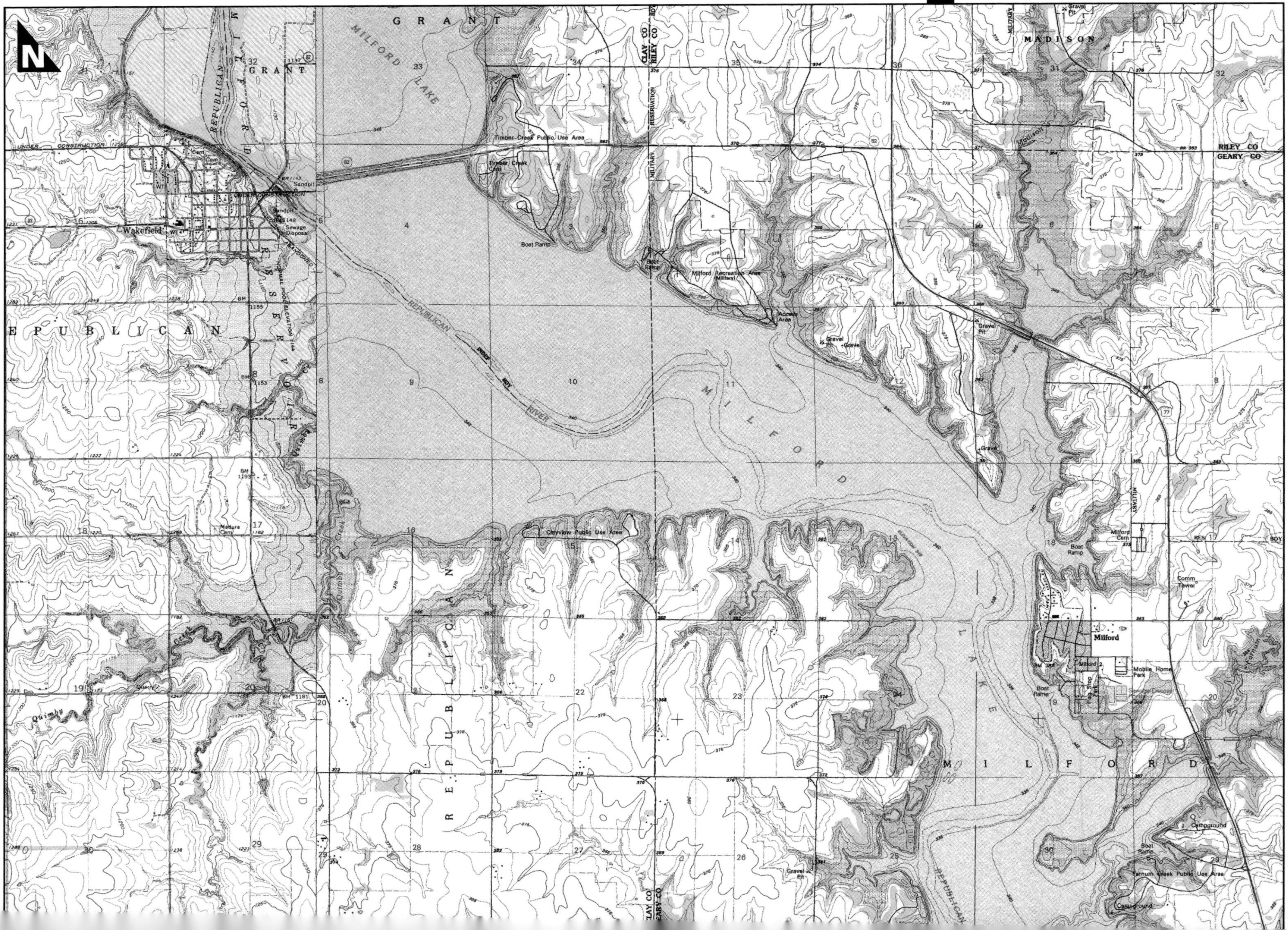
MILFORD LAKE
MILFORD RESERVOIR
REPUBLICAN RIVER
GRANT
MADISON
REPUBLICAN
Wakefield
Milford
Timber Creek Public Use Area
Timber Creek Cem
Boat Ramp
Milford Recreation Area (Military)
Access Area
Gravel Pit
Clayview Public Use Area
Madura Cem
Quimby Creek
Quarry
Sandpit
Sewage Disposal
NORMAL POOL ELEVATION 1144
Milford Cem
Comm Tower
Mobile Home Park
Campground
Farnum Creek Public Use Area
Madison Creek
CLAY CO
RILEY CO
GEARY CO
MILITARY RESERVATION

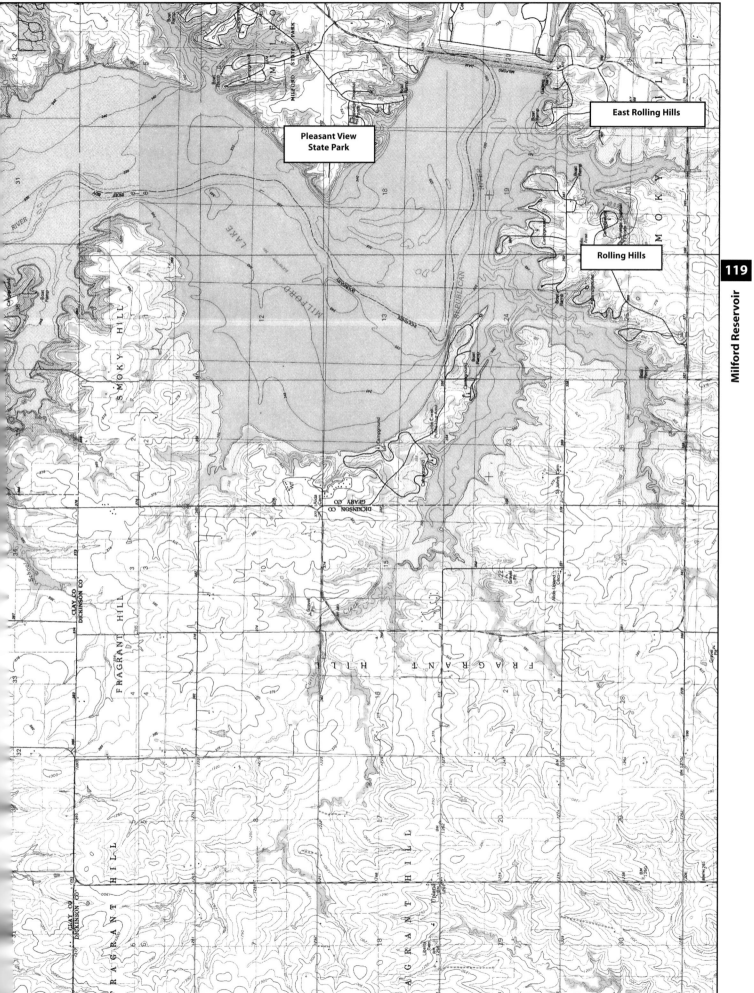

Pleasant View State Park

East Rolling Hills

Rolling Hills

typically ranks number one for blue cat populations and has good numbers of both channel and flathead catfish.

Wildlife officials first stocked blue cats in the early 1990s. "It was an experimental stocking to see how they would do," Reinke says. "We wanted to see if they would develop into a self-sustaining population, and they have."

He says that, more often than not, those wanting to reel in a legendary blue can find them in the river channels on the lake. There are some big 'ins, too. Reinke heard of a guy catching a 62-pounder in the spring of 2010, which would be a lake record.

Most anglers catch blues and channels on live shad, sunfish, and fresh cut bait.

A few hotspots include the north end of the lake in the spring, where the water is shallower. Anglers can also find blues in the Republican River during this time, Reinke says, noting one springtime spot is a 20-foot cliff called Highbanks, which drops right into the river channel. You'll also find blues deep into the lake's river channel during the heat of summer. The Madison Creek area is also a good spot for blues.

Channel/Flathead Catfish: According to Reinke, the upper end of the lake above the Wakefield causeway has traditionally offered the best cat fishing, but catfish are common throughout the reservoir. Catfish also like the standing timber in the upper end of the lake, where anglers catch them on setlines and live bait.

Look for flatheads around rocky points and the Wakefield causeway area, as well as Madison Creek—good night spots during the summer. Reinke says some anglers are catching flatheads of up to 50–60 pounds.

Wiper: Milford is home to the hatchery that produces many of the wipers stocked in the state's reservoirs every year. "Our wipers are so vicious, we're using lures that should be used in the ocean," Dykstra says, jovially comparing it to throwing a lure at a train and trying to hold on.

Well, maybe these fish aren't that strong, but there are some good-sized wipers to be caught at Milford. The reservoir, after all, has one of the best densities of this hybrid fish in Kansas, as well as having a fair amount of big ones, although it might seem daunting to try to find them in such a large reservoir.

Reinke, however, says they're not necessarily that hard to find. Some of the most popular spots are the north and south wiper islands, underwater humps where water depths go from 50 feet to 9 feet on the north hump, located at N39 06.973 W96 54.975, and around 20 feet on the south hump, located at N 39 06.029' W96 55.800. According to Reinke, these spots are hot in the summer and early fall. Anglers can catch wipers using live bait on the bottom, or, when the shad are spawning, using a surface-water bait like a chug bug.

"The two islands get quite a bit of attention," Reinke says. He adds, however, that when wipers are chasing shad

on the surface, "You can find them anywhere." He also recommends trying the face of the dam and rocky points throughout the year.

"Any of the main lake points are good," Reinke says, adding that on days when it is bright out, wipers will be easily caught trolling with crank baits in areas like Madison Creek, School Creek, and Curtis Creek—where these coves meet the main part of the lake.

Smallmouth Bass: Milford has all three species of black bass—smallmouth, largemouth, and spotted. However, the lake is best known for its smallmouth. In fact, the state record for this species was caught there in April 2010.

Frank Evans, Jr., of Salina, was fishing for walleye at Milford when he hooked and landed the fish of many bass anglers' dreams—a 6.88-pound smallmouth that he reeled in with jerk bait. Reinke says the huge smallie was 21.5 inches long with a girth of 16.5 inches. Evans bested another Salina resident, Jason Heis, who landed a monster smallmouth of 6.68 pounds at Milford in 2004.

Fishing was excellent through much of 2010, as well. Milford typically ranks in the top five for density of smallmouth. "They have caught several that have been close to a new record," Reinke says.

The best spots for smallmouth fishing include main lake rocky banks and points, as well as coves. In the spring, smallmouth usually stay in deep water, 30–35 feet deep, and spawn in gravel areas. They come up to the shallow water to hit topwater baits like chug bugs, Reinke says, but noted any topwater bait will work. "In the summer," he says, "they will catch them on topwater lures in deep water—when the water is clear."

The face of the dam also is prone to a high density of this fish—check it out in late spring and into the fall.

Walleye: Milford usually ranks in the top ten for density of walleye, according to the KDWP. Walleye concentrate along the dam during the early April spawn. Following the spawn, Reinke says, the fish move to the Farnum Creek flat, the mud flats near School Creek, as well as the flats near the military marina. In the heat of summer, how-

ever, Reinke recommends looking for them in 25–40 feet of water, and adds that they are best caught trolling crankbaits. Another good area for trolling is the shorelines.

White Bass: According to Reinke, white bass of all sizes are abundant in Milford—even trophy-sized whites. Fishing the Republican during the spawn in the spring, jigging and trolling in early summer, and fishing the top waters in the late summer and into the fall should be most productive. Anglers can also find them off the face of the dam in late spring after the spawn.

During the hot summer, night fishing under lanterns or floating lights yields good results. Reinke says one of the best places for night fishing is Madison Creek and along the Wakefield causeway. Madison Creek is a year-round spot, while the Wakefield causeway is more prime in the springtime when the whites go up and down the river. "School Creek is pretty good, too," Reinke says. "They'll be in and around the wipers."

Another recommendation: fish dropoffs and points, vertical jigging with slab spoons.

Crappie: Reinke recommends looking for these paper mouths around any of the creek areas when they are spawning. "Just about all the brush and rocky coves have crappie," he says. Good spots: the coves in the Rolling Hills and Curtis Creek areas. In the winter, anglers ice fish in the Curtis Creek area.

Facilities

The U.S. Army Corps of Engineers operates eight park areas at the **Milford Lake Project.** There also is **Milford State Park, Clay County Park,** and a park operated through the city of Milford. In total, seven campgrounds in the state park offer: 141 campsites with water and electric; 108 non-utility sites; and 5 cabins. Other cabins are available on the lake for renting, as well.

Milford has a dozen boat ramps, including at **Rolling Hills, Curtis Creek, School Creek, Farnum Creek, Thunderbird, Milford State Park, the city of Milford, Clay County Park** and **Timber Creek,** as well as a full-service marina, a large yacht club, swimming beaches, and a multi-purpose trails system. There's also a boat ramp area designated for military personnel. Four trail systems throughout the park allow visitors to hike, mountain bike, and horseback ride.

Nearby **Milford Nature Center** offers interpretative exhibits and live animal displays, including snakes, prairie dogs, birds of prey, and a bobcat. The nearby **Milford Fish**

Hatchery is the state's only warm-water, intensive-culture fish hatchery. Visitors can walk around the area at any time. Guided tours are offered April–September.

Annual events include a kids' fishing clinic and derby each June.

Shopping/Supplies

Army and Air Force Exchange Service, Building 2210, Trooper Dr., Fort Riley, 785-784-2210; **Big Mouth Bait Convenience Store,** 8106 Laurel Canyon Rd., Junction City, 785-238-2193; **BJ's 66,** 5410 N. US 77, Junction City, 785-238-5966; **Chapman Creek Fly & Tackle,** 2701 N. Marshall St., Chapman, 785-922-6630 ; **Clem's Convenience Corner,** 8508 N. US 77, Milford, 785-238-8955; **Dillons,** 618 W. 6th St., Junction City, 785-238-2141; **Flagstop Resort RV,** 302 Whiting St., Milford, 785-463-5537; **Geary County Clerk,** 200 E. 8th St., Junction City, 785-238-3912; **Orscheln Farm Home,** 1023 S. Washington St., Junction City, 785-762-4411; **Thunderbird Marina,** 4725 W. Rolling Hills Rd., Junction City, 785-238-5864 (during the season); **Walmart,** 521 E. Chestnut St., Junction City, 785-238-8229.

GPS Waypoints

East Rolling Hills area and boat ramp:
  N39 04.687 W96 54.459
West Rolling Hills area and boat ramp:
  N39 04.847 W96 55.492
Timber Creek area and boat ramp:
  N39 12.690 W96 58.358
Walnut Grove Boat Ramp: N39 7.217 W96 53.408
South Boat Ramp: N39 05.623 W096 54.145
Rush Creek Marina and Boat Ramp:
  N39 06.907 W096 53.954
Clay County Park: N39 12.835 W97 00.435
School Creek Boat Ramp: N39 08.236 W96 55.857
Farnum Creek Park with boat ramp:
  N39 09.303 W96 54.139

Contacts

Milford Lake Marina, 785-238-4010; **Milford Lake Project Office,** U.S. Army Corps of Engineers, 785-238-5714; **Milford Nature Center,** 785-238-5323; **Milford Wildlife Area,** 785-461-5402; **Milford State Park,** 785-238-3014.

Milford Reservoir

Perry Reservoir

SIZE: 11,630 acres

LOCATION: About 20 miles northeast of Topeka on I-70 and US 24

CONTACT: Perry Project Office, U.S. Corps of Engineers, 785-597-5144

FEATURE FISH: Largemouth Bass, Blue Catfish, Channel Catfish, Flathead Catfish, Crappie, Sauger, Walleye, White Bass, Wiper

DAILY CREEL LIMIT/MINIMUM LENGTH: Largemouth Bass: 5 fish, 18 inches • Blue Catfish: 5 fish, 35 inches • Channel Catfish: 10 fish • Flathead Catfish: 5 fish • Crappie: 20 fish, 10 inches • Sauger: 5 fish, 15 inches • Saugeye: 5 fish, 15 inches • Walleye: 5 fish, 15 inches

AQUATIC NUISANCE SPECIES ALERT: Zebra Mussels (unlawful to possess alive)

Perry Reservoir is known by several different names, depending on whom one asks. It's been called a "crappie factory" by those who know its history as a productive lake for slabs. It's also been called the Brown County Feed Lot and contains a feature affectionately called the Hog Trough by those who view the impoundment as among the best places in the state to "bean" for catfish in the summer. But the lake has more to offer anglers than crappie, catfish, and catchy names.

Perry is poised to become a good black bass fishery. Angling in the outlet continues to rival other shoreline fishing locations in Kansas, with an ample population of large wiper and walleye that spend their time in the Delaware River behind Perry, looking for easy meals in the churning tail waters. With more than 160 miles of shoreline, an active fish management plan, and clear water, Perry is a good place for any angler looking for plenty of different species of fish throughout the entire calendar year.

I've only visited Perry a few times, generally when I was on my way to somewhere else, stopping only for a short visit. During a trip to Perry while researching this book, I fished primarily on the shore, and spent my time talking to anglers at the lake, rather than put my boat in the water. Perry is a known hot spot for zebra mussels, yet several other lakes in the area have remained clear of the aquatic nuisance. I had plans to travel to several of those lakes within the same week, and I didn't feel good about putting in at Perry, and then traveling to other nearby waters without a week to let the boat dry out properly.

I can tell you what I did find at Perry. I found clear water, a great marina stocked with a lot of gear, and a lake loaded with impressive boats. I found a lot of shoreline areas with fishing jetties that make fishing from land much easier.

To be honest, I learned more about Perry by talking with the lake's biologist and local anglers. What they showed me is something I couldn't have learned on my visit—even if I had spent several days roaming the lake in my boat. I learned that this lake has a lot to offer anglers

throughout the year. There's no shortage of crappie, white bass, wipers, and black bass, and there's no shortage of hot spots to catch them.

Feature Fish

Crappie: Perry Reservoir is known as one of the top crappie lakes in the state. The impoundment consistently ranks among the top Kansas reservoirs for both density and size of crappie according to annual biologists reports.

The U.S. Army Corps of Engineers relies on Perry to provide downstream flood protection for the cities of Perry, Lawrence, Bonner Springs, and Kansas City. This flood plan often means an increase in the water level in the early spring, which provides plenty of flooded shoreline vegetation for crappie looking to spawn in May.

According to Kansas Department of Wildlife and Parks fisheries biologist Kirk Tjelmeland, Perry contains a lot of natural riprap along the lower end of the lake to attract spring crappie. "They'll move anywhere in the

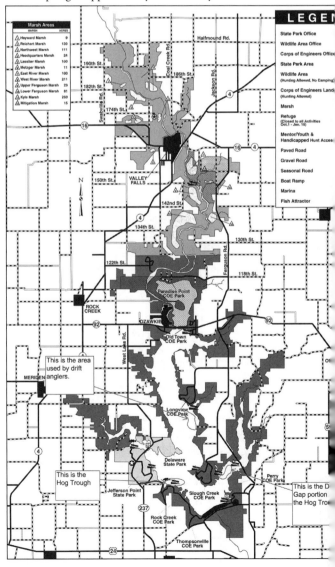

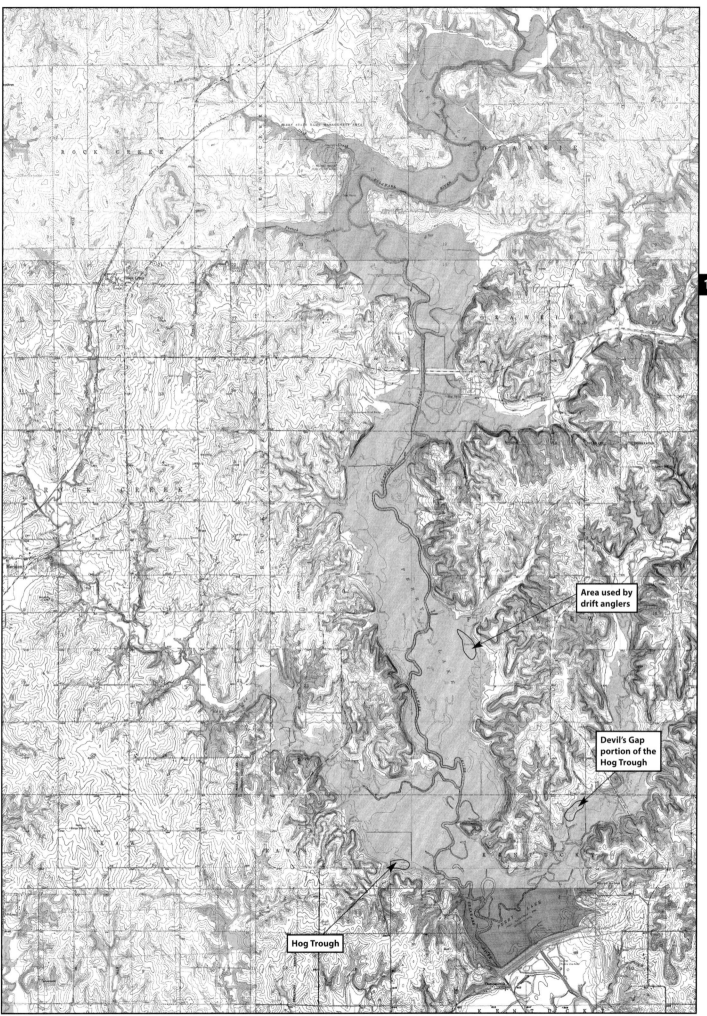

Area used by drift anglers

Devil's Gap portion of the Hog Trough

Hog Trough

reservoir and crash the bank," Tjelmeland says, adding that the fish can be found in as little as two feet of water.

Spring crappie anglers find success in Slough Creek, the lake's eastern arm, Rock Creek, the lake's western arm, around the marina, which is located near the dam, and around the causeway bridge on the lake's upper end, near the town of Ozawkie.

Most crappie anglers at Perry rely on small jigs, with blue holding favor. Tjelmeland says while some anglers use minnows, they're really not necessary. "Anything with fleck in it," Tjelmeland said of the popular baits at Perry. "They use all kinds of goofy colors."

In recent years, the KDWP has begun working on shallow water brush piles, and Tjelmeland said the crappie are starting to use that structure more frequently.

Clyde "The Guide" Holscher, who operates Guide Lines Guide Service out of Topeka, says anglers would be wise to not overlook the fall and winter fishing that's available at Perry. "This is a good winter fishing lake," Holscher says. "There will be as many boats on the lake in the winter as there are in the spring and summer combined."

As the crappie school up in the fall and winter—generally from September through November—they congregate around the deep water brush piles that have been established in the lake. Tjelmeland says there is plenty of such habitat. In addition to the KDWP, another 67 area residents are permitted to establish brush piles at Perry. Most of the brush is located in 20–30 feet of water, with the deepest brush pile resting 43 feet below the surface.

White Bass/Wiper: Perry Reservoir's wiper fishing has little to do with Perry itself, and more to do with Milford Reservoir, which lies more than an hour to the west along the Kansas River, for which Perry's Delaware River is a tributary. Milford is an excellent wiper fishery, while the waters inside Perry's shoreline aren't stocked with the fish. The Milford wipers, however, migrate toward the outlet waters of Perry, where water, and more importantly shad, are nearly always pouring from the lake.

In fact, the last state record wiper, which weighed over 22 pounds, was caught at the Perry spillway, and the new state record, which weighed in at 25 pounds, was also caught at the Perry spillway in the summer of 2010.

Tjelmeland says that both the spillway and the lake hold good numbers of white bass, and that the fishing can be productive, although it fluctuates from year to year.

Holscher says he likes to fish for Perry whites in the fall, after the Labor Day holiday, when the water starts to cool down once the cooler nights set in. "I always say that the fishing's best when you have to wear a hooded sweatshirt and the Chiefs are getting their butts kicked," he says.

As the water temperature begins to drop, Holscher works his way back to shallow water, casting small jigs, roadrunners, and Rattletraps in the feeder creeks and rivers, and along the windy points. In fact, Holscher says, the white bass can be found in the same places during the fall as they're found during the spring spawn.

During the summer months, Tjelmeland says, deep water breaks and humps around the creek and river channels hold the whites. Holscher says it's during this time of year that he spoons for white bass in 15–20 feet of water. Typically, from July 4 through Labor Day, Holscher uses ½–1-ounce jigs and spoons, vertically jigging them over breaks and channel edges in the lake.

In the spring, some whites move up the creeks and rivers to spawn, but Holscher says he's found plenty of spawning fish in the lake. "They'll just find the nearest riprap where their eggs can be agitated," Holscher says. "The rod and reel tells the truth more than anything else: Those white bass are main lake spawners."

Walleye/Sauger: Tjelmeland likes to joke that Perry has three walleye in the entire body of water. "Larry, Moe, and Curly," he laughs.

While Perry lacks a healthy walleye population, it does hold a decent number of the fish's relative—the sauger. Holscher says the lake is a good sauger fishery, yet doesn't generate the traffic that other lakes attract when the walleye bite is active.

The sauger mimics many of the walleye's seasonal patterns, so look for these fish to move toward the rocky points and the dam in the early spring, shortly after ice-out, before moving toward the mud flats after the spawn. Vertical jigging and a jig and crawler combination are successful after the spawn.

Catfish: If there's a place called the Hog Trough, and people gravitate toward it to spend a day fishing, it's a pretty good bet that you'll find catfish. For the past 30 years, anglers have spent the summer days "beaning" for catfish and having a good time doing it. The Hog Trough even caught the attention of *In-Fisherman* magazine and televised angler Babe Winkelman.

There are several areas that make up the Hog Trough. One is near the Delaware arm of Perry Reservoir, north of the Rock Creek Corps of Engineers park. Another is east of the Slough Creek park, just off of the Devil's Gap boat ramp. Another area, popular with anglers who like to drift fish, is just west of the Longview Corps park, south to Leopold Point.

Holscher says the preferred chumming bait is soured soybeans—and he makes the point that it's not rotten soybeans that draw in the fish. Anglers who "bean" all have their own recipes. However, the common ingredients are soybeans, water, sunlight, and time. As the soybeans begin to sour, they'll turn a golden brown color and begin to smell sour. Much longer in the sunlight, and those beans will start to mush and rot and the smell is nearly intolerable.

Tjelmeland says that since Kansas has a generally southern wind in the summer, many anglers simply drift through the area, sometimes with traditional catfish baits like liver and stink bait. Some anglers, however, are casting a net for shad, and drifting live bait through the cat fishing hotspot.

Perry also contains the much larger flatheads and blue catfish. Tjelmeland said anglers find the flatheads in the outlet behind the dam, and the upper part of the lake, by Ozawkie. The most often used bait for flatheads is a live green sunfish.

Black Bass: While the larger Delaware arm of Perry receives much attention for its cat fishing, it's the two smaller arms of the lake—Slough and Rock Creek—that hold the promise for black bass anglers. Tjelmeland says Perry has consistently been ranked high in the state, not for its numbers of bass, but for the size of those fish—many of which weigh upwards of six and seven pounds.

In addition to the robust largemouth population, an emerging population of smallmouth bass have gained the attention of local anglers. "It's getting to be a good smallmouth lake—and that's been substantiated," Holscher says. "They've been up and coming in the past couple of years."

Tjelmeland says smallmouth were introduced to the lake about three years ago, and that his sampling shows they're getting larger and showing some reproduction—despite concerns about a lack of the smallmouth's preferred prey, the crawdad. "The lake doesn't have very many crawdads," he says. "But the shad numbers in the lake are sufficient to sustain them."

The supply of shad, coupled with good habitat, has helped the smallmouth thrive in Perry. One of the best areas in the lake for smallmouth is along the Corps of Engineers' Thomsanville Park, which sits adjacent to the dam, on the west side of the lake.

For largemouth, Tjelmeland suggests fishing in the Slough Creek and Rock Creek areas, where brush piles and other underwater vegetation is located near shoreline riprap.

Ultimately, Holscher says it's the fish that will dictate how an angler at Perry will spend his or her day. "It's got white bass, channel cats, largemouth, smallmouth, and crappie," he says. "That's what will be your guide on what you'll fish for."

And if there's any question about what's biting, or where they're biting, Tjelmeland suggests looking for the boats on the water and not being too shy about pulling up alongside them—particularly in the infamous Hog Trough. "The guys on the beans are really friendly," Tjelmeland says. "Most of them are retired and they love to tell fishing stories."

Facilities

Perry State Park includes two areas that cover 1,250 acres. In total, the park offers: 102 campsites with water and electric; 200 non-utility sites; 4 rental cabins; 5 shower houses; 2 dump stations; 10 shelter houses; 10 boat ramp lanes; 2 courtesy docks; a marina available in non-park area; 1 fish cleaning station; and 1 swimming beach.

The U.S Army Corps of Engineers operates four campgrounds at Perry Reservoir.

Longview Park: A 316-acre park located on the east side of the lake. Facilities include 45 reservable campsites, 26 electric sites, shower houses, dump station, group shelter house, boat ramp, courtesy dock, hiking trails, and a picnic area.

Old Town: This 113-acre park on the east side of the lake, by K-92, is open May 1–September 30, and self-pay camping is also available October 1–April 31. Facilities include 75 campsites, including 33 with water and electric, shower houses, dump station, a day-use shelter house, a boat ramp, courtesy dock, and a picnic area.

Rock Creek: A 568-acre park on the west side of the lake that is open May 1–September 30. Self pay campsites are available October 1–April 30. Facilities include 108 designated campsites, 51 with water and electric, shower and latrine, dump station, group shelter house, boat ramp, courtesy dock, and playground.

Slough Creek: Open April 16–October 15, this 833 acre parks sits on the east side of the lake, west across the bridge over Slough Creek. Campground includes 271 campsites, 78 with water and electric, 41 with electric only, 2 group camp areas, 3 shower houses, 2 dump stations, a boat ramp, courtesy docks, fish cleaning stations, a picnic area, and playgrounds. Also includes 2.5-mile Thunder Ridge educational trail as well as access to the Perry Lake Trail.

Shopping/Supplies

The **Rock Creek Marina Resort** is a family-owned full-service marina. The marina offers a floating motel for guests, cabins, supplies for boating and fishing, and professional technicians on staff. **Mulligans** on the lake also offers a full menu at the marina—including barbecue. **The Rock Creek Ballroom** includes a full bar and live music on Saturday nights. 6049 W. Lake Rd., Ozawkie, 785-484-2656. **Route 92** sells fishing licenses, tackle, bait, food, and fuel. Open 5:00 a.m. to 10:00 p.m. daily. 409 Jefferson St., Oskaloosa, 785-863-2817.

Country Inn Service, 19944 K-4, Nortonville, 913-886-7480; **Lake Perry Yacht and Marina,** 10770 Perry Park Dr., Perry, 888-597-5796; **Perry State Park,** 5441 W. Lake Rd., Ozawkie, 785-246-3449; **Kangaroo Express,** 3522 US 24, Grantville, 785-246-1748.

Pomona Reservoir

SIZE: 4,000 acres

LOCATION: 25 miles south of Topeka on US 75

GPS LOCATION: N38 39.580 W95 36.012

CONTACT: Kansas Department of Wildlife and Parks, 785-828-4933

FEATURE FISH: Blue Catfish, Channel Catfish, Flathead Catfish, Crappie, Wiper, White Bass

DAILY CREEL LIMIT/MINIMUM LENGTH: Largemouth Bass: 5 fish, 15 inches • Channel Catfish: 10 fish • Flathead Catfish: 5 fish • Crappie: 50 fish • Walleye: 5 fish, 18 inches • Wiper: 2 fish, 18 inches

Terry Bivins spent years racing cars in the 1960s and 1970s. He even finished eighth in the Daytona 500. And while racing is still part of this Lebo man's life, many a Kansas day sees him with a rod and reel—no matter what Mother Nature is dishing out.

So it didn't surprise me the first few times I called Bivins only to find he was either at the shop working on his racecars or he was out at the lake searching for white bass. When we finally connected, the jovial angler gave me an earful about why he chose to move to the small Coffey County town of Lebo—a central location and short drive to his favorite honey holes.

That includes Pomona and Melvern Reservoirs—eastern Kansas lakes that Bivins calls quality fishing. On a spring day when the weather was cold, Bivins bragged that he caught and released nearly 80 white bass in one sitting at Pomona Reservoir. "Pomona can be hot with white bass if you know where to find them," he said happily.

Sometimes 90 percent of the lake's white bass might be schooled up in one location. Yet, he says, while finding fish is obviously a priority of a successful outing, catching them is what really counts. And catching them is Bivins' specialty. Which is why Bivins is known as one of the top anglers of the region—a jig expert.

• • •

Arriving at Pomona for a weekend of fishing with our twin daughters, my husband, John, and I found a lake with plenty of shade—conducive for a family with little children. There are plenty of activities, besides fishing, to be found in the surrounding 10,500 acres of public land, which includes picnic areas, swimming beaches, and nature trails. Also, bald eagles visit here in the winter.

And, of course, there are opportunities to catch fish in this hatchery of sorts. It wasn't tough for our family to find good angling—enough so to keep the girls satisfied. This, of course, is an important aspect when there are young children in the boat. So is having plenty of snacks, drinks, and coloring books—a sure bet to keep them somewhat occupied, as long as they aren't coloring on the boat seats.

We fished for everything from white bass to catfish—reeling in enough to have a shore luncheon around noon before heading back out for a few more hours to explore the lake.

• • •

Pomona Dam was completed in 1963 at a cost of $13 million. The Pomona water system is formed from 110-Mile Creek and two tributaries, Dragoon Creek and Valley Brook. As the three creeks come together and form the lake, the 110-Mile flows down the outlet channel where it meets the Marais des Cygnes River eight miles downstream. Fish feeders operate at the handicapped dock in Michigan Valley Park, at several locations around the rock quarry, and at Light House Bay Marina.

"Pomona Reservoir is well known for its great crappie, white bass, channel catfish, flathead catfish, and wiper and walleye fishing," says Don George, the reservoir's fisheries biologist with Kansas Department of Wildlife and Parks. "In fact, this reservoir has produced two past state records for wiper and flathead catfish." While the lake no longer holds those records, there are still some big fish to be caught, he says.

Pomona is also known for quality fish, according to Clyde Holscher, a 16-year fishing guide from Topeka who goes by the title "Clyde the Guide." The prime fishing he does at Pomona includes catfish, whites, and wipers. He warns, however, that the lake sometimes has turbidity issues.

Feature Fish

Crappie: According to George, crappie are plentiful in this lake and attract good crowds of anglers during the year—especially during the spring spawn. While spawning, these fish move into shallow water and are very accessible to shoreline and boat anglers.

Some anglers use jigs with white or red twister tail grubs. George recommends trying drifting bait in the early morning and evening hours. "Crappie anglers like to use an assortment of lures and baits," he says. "Use live minnows or jigs of chartreuse or dark blue colors, and you'll probably catch lots of crappie."

Crappie move off the shore after spawning and suspend. They are found in deeper bays and in the main lake near underwater structure, such as in the flat areas near dropoffs, as well as along deep shorelines and points.

During the fall, winter, or spring months, crappie often concentrate around underwater structure and fish attractors. Numerous fish attractors have been placed in desirable locations. George says an example of this fine work is just off of Adams Grove on the U.S. Army Corps of Engineers park area. "Find some brush piles, and you are in a good crappie hot spot," George says.

Early and late winter is the best time to ice fish at Pomona. Find crappie hanging out in 15 feet of water near the creek channel.

Wiper/White Bass: Bivins is a jig expert who can catch dozens of whites in just a few hours. "It is one of the good white bass and wiper lakes, and it also has some nice crappie," he said. "But it is really noted for the white bass and wiper fishing."

These fish are caught all year long, George says, but few things are as fun as watching and catching white bass and wipers when they are feeding on the surface.

During late July and August, forage fish like the gizzard shad are abundant, and schools of white bass and wiper push these bait fish to the surface. This makes for great surface action, and, according to George, the predators will strike anything resembling a gizzard shad. He also recommends using silver spoons, silver crank baits, and big jigs when these predators come up on top to feed.

On some outings, Bivins uses a 4-inch Turbo Shad Bass Assassin on a 3/8 lead-head jig. He also uses a small wire hook—"not those big hooks," he says. He uses this lure for bottom bouncing over humps and breaks.

Early in the spring, George says, white bass can be caught in large numbers along riffles in Dragoon Creek. Clyde the Guide says the white bass will also spawn in the upper ends of the lake to the dam. "Look for them on riprap on a northern windblown bank," Clyde says.

Clyde's proven setup includes fishing a 4–6-pound test line with jig and 2- or 3-inch yellow grub. For wipers, Clyde recommends a 3-inch swimbait. In the summer, he says, wipers and whites will hang out in humps and ridges adjacent to the main lake.

Bivins says one of the places he waypoints is the mouth of the creek directly to the right of the dam, in a spot between the beach and the marina. The area, about 8 feet deep, is where he has caught a few monster whites. "Other hot spots are subtle," Bivins says.

According to Bivins, there are a couple good places on the south side, including the first cove by the dam. "Just inside that cove is a great spot for them," he says. "There's a really good dropoff. It isn't a real big area, but these are spots they use."

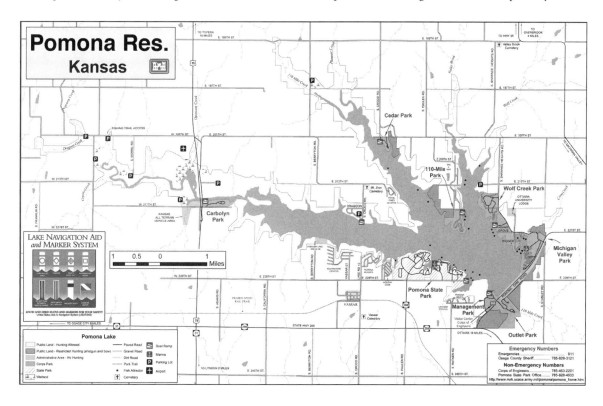

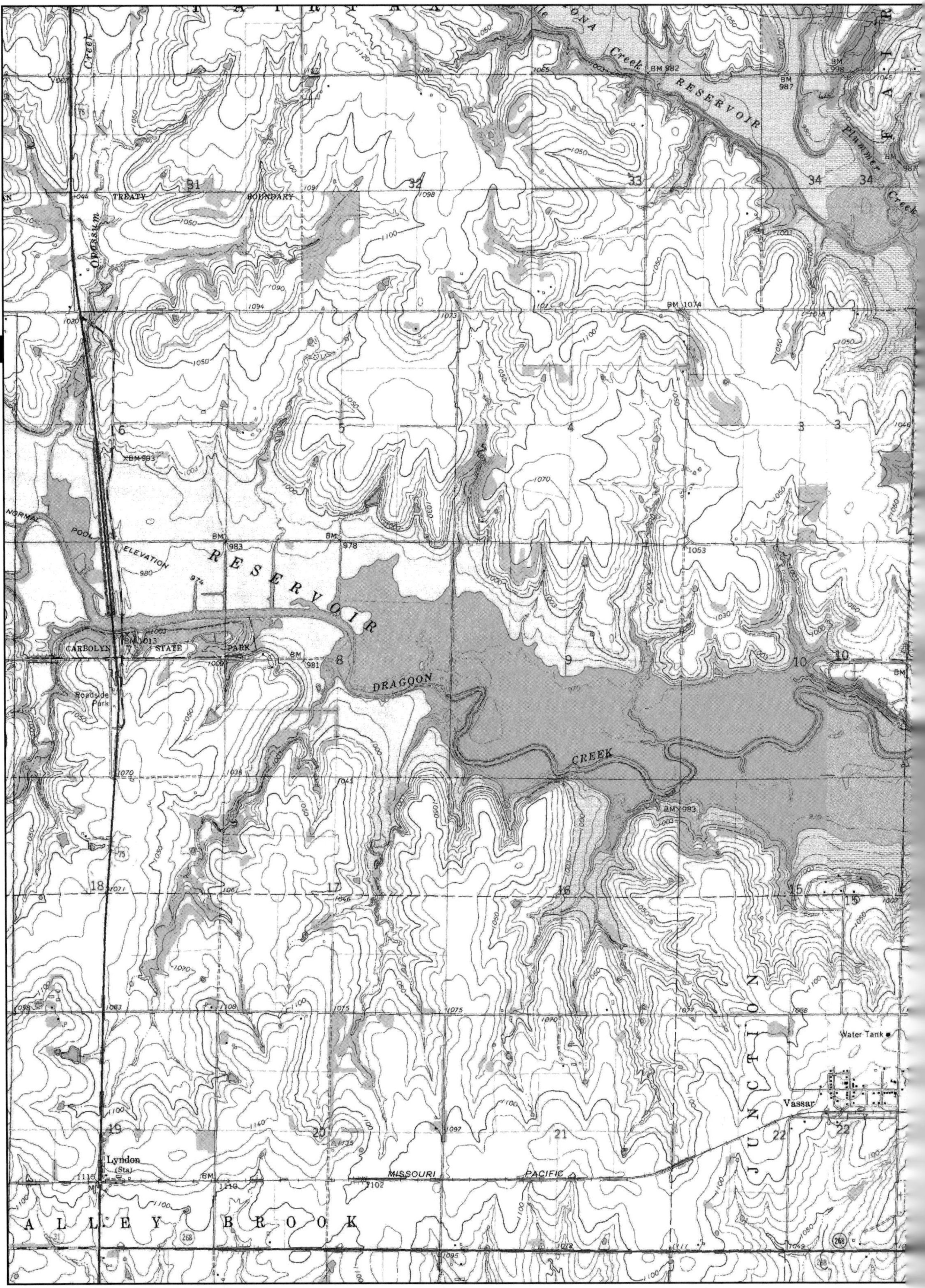
TREATY BOUNDARY
Opossum Creek
Creek
RESERVOIR
Plummer Creek
NORMAL POOL ELEVATION
RESERVOIR
CARBOLYN STATE PARK
Roadside Park
DRAGOON CREEK
Water Tank
Vassar
JUNCTION
Lyndon (Sta)
MISSOURI PACIFIC
ALLEY BROOK

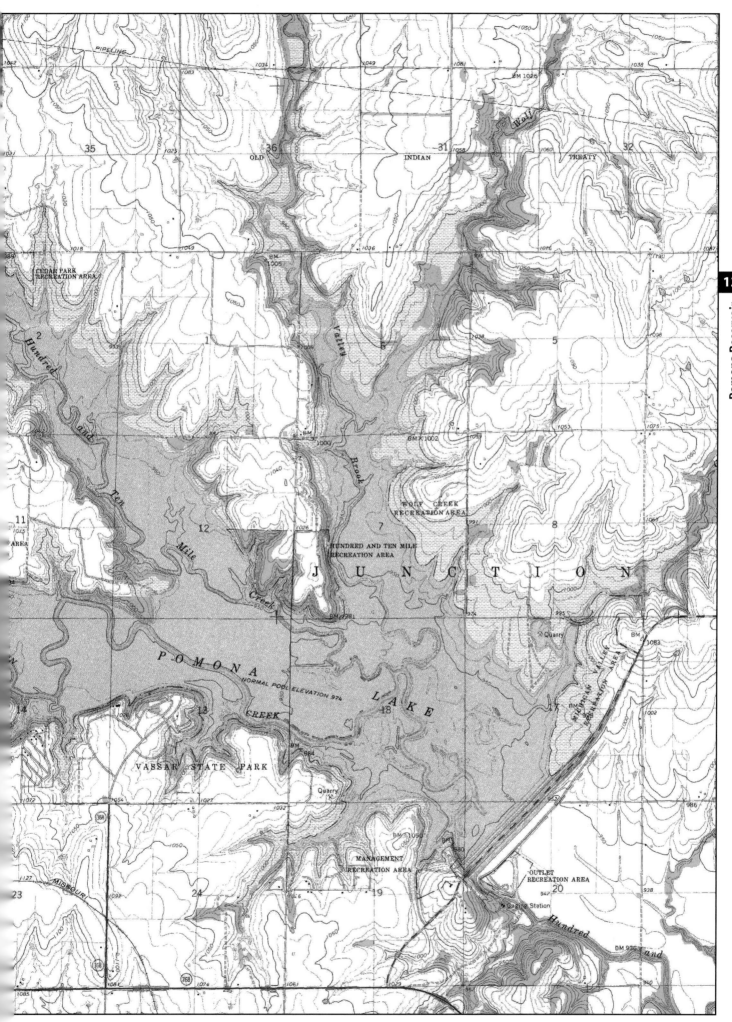

"I look for their supper tables," Bivins says. "If you go on a good day, 100 white bass is nothing. I can do that using one rod—that's how good the lake is when you find them."

Some favorite areas that George recommends include off of 110 Mile Park and any area off of the Pomona State Park. Meanwhile, Clyde says to look for the shad when fall hits—that's where the white bass will be gorging. Clyde adds that he and his clients caught a lot of 8–12-pound wipers in 2010.

Catfish: Channel catfish are easy to catch and are always biting at this lake. With the liberal creel limits, anglers can always catch some channel catfish for lunch. Favorite baits are always worms, chicken liver, and fresh or cut shad. But lots of fish are caught on prepared baits, George says.

Several floating fish feeders are strategically located for anglers around the lake. Floating fish feeders dispense fish food several times a day, during the warm months, to attract fish to shoreline areas of good angler access. These feeding events can be very exciting as large numbers of channel catfish and rough fish come up on top to eat the catfish chow. "It literally looks like a person could walk on the water there are so many fish," George says.

After a hard rain, try the upper ends of the reservoir where the creeks—Dragoon, 110 Mile, and Wolf Creeks, as well as Valley Brook—come into the main lake. High-water flows will carry lots of food, and the channel catfish will go up the creek on a feeding rampage.

Others spots include Cedar Park and the outlet channel. Located on the north side of the lake, Cedar Park has a lot of fish structure, making it an excellent area. Fishing the outlet channel is best when releases are high or when the release rate has just been cut back.

Flathead catfish are quite common, and the blue catfish are increasing in numbers each year. George says that most flathead and blue catfish are caught by anglers using trot lines, float lines, or set lines with goldfish or green sunfish for bait. "There are some very dedicated anglers who fish with setlines, and they caught very big fish," George says. "It is not uncommon to see fish over fifty pounds caught this way."

Jug or float lines are legal to use in this reservoir during the July 15–September 15 season. A $2.50 float line permit is required.

Other Fishing: Clyde says while the numbers aren't as plentiful, "Pomona isn't a bad black bass lake." But, he adds, "They are so spot specific."

"I'm not going to go here and catch, like in a community lake, eighty largemouth a day," he says. "But, there are quite a few in the two- to five-pound range."

Clyde says to find largemouth bass in rocky areas along banks, coves, and in weeds. Also, submerged timber is a traditional largemouth bass habitat.

Facilities

Seven campgrounds are located around the reservoir. The Corps manages six of these campgrounds: **Outlet, Michigan Valley, Wolf Creek, 110-Mile, Cedar,** and **Carbolyn.** The KDWP manages Pomona State Park campground. In total, the area offers: 142 utility sites; and more than 200 non-utility campsites. The KDWP also has two cabins.

The Corps has paved boat ramps at the following locations: Management Park, North Shore Marina, Adams Grove, 110–Mile Park, Carbolyn Park, and the Dragoon Access area. The Kansas Department of Wildlife and Parks operates several boat ramps within the Pomona State Park. An unimproved launch is located in Cedar Park.

Recreational opportunities include 3 hiking trails that offer 2.4 miles of hiking and biking, a swimming beach, day-use picnic areas that include volleyball courts and basketball courts, and a nine-hole disc golf course. The Corps also allows upland bird and waterfowl hunting at wildlife areas. Bald eagles visit the lake in the winter.

GPS

State Park and Marina area: N38 39.435 W 95 35.580

Shopping/Supplies

Blackwater Marine, 4009 Marina Rd., Vassar, 785-828-4777; **Lamont Hill Resort,** 22975 S. K-368, Vassar, 785-828-3131; **Lighthouse Bay Marina,** 4009 Marina Rd., Vassar, 785-828-4777; **Obryhim's Thriftway,** 205 Maple St., Overbrook, 785-665-7111; **Osage County Clerk,** 717 Topeka Ave., Lyndon, 785-828-4812; **Sports Mart,** 24131 S. US 75, Lyndon, 785-828-3360.

Contacts

Lighthouse Bay Marina, Pomona Lake, 4009 Marina Rd., Vassar, 785-828-4777; **Pomona Project Office,** U.S. Army Corps of Engineers, 5260 Pomona Dam Rd., Vassar, 785-453-2201; **Pomona State Park,** 22900 S. K-368, Vassar, 785-828-4933.

Toronto Reservoir

SIZE: 2,800 acres

LOCATION: 15 miles southwest of Yates Center on US 54 and K-105

CONTACT: U.S. Army Corps of Engineers, 620-658-4445

FEATURE FISH: Largemouth Bass, Channel Catfish, Flathead Catfish, Crappie, White Bass

DAILY CREEL LIMIT/MINIMUM LENGTH: Largemouth Bass: 5 fish, 15 inches • Spotted Bass: 5 fish, 15 inches • Channel Catfish: 10 fish • Flathead Catfish: 5 fish • Crappie: 50 fish

Toronto Reservoir, located in Woodson County in southeast Kansas, is sometimes a 2,800-acre lake, and other times it swells and becomes a much larger reservoir during the torrential downpours of spring. While those periods of high water—sometime "flashing" upwards of 20 feet higher than normal levels—are an inconvenience for anglers, it's the time in between those floods that have given Toronto its reputation as a crappie haven.

"It's a big crappie lake," says local angler Jim Bybee. "One of the best in Kansas, as far as I'm concerned."

Those high water events that make boat ramps and shorelines inaccessible, turn the water turbid, and shut down most of the fishing on the lake also serve to bring nutrients and habitat into Toronto—and that in turn keeps the lake rated as one of Kansas' top fisheries for crappie.

However, those who fish only the main body of Toronto Reservoir are likely missing out on some of the best fishing the area has to offer. The Verdigris River, which feeds the lake, and Walnut Creek, which flows into the lake from the west, are hot spots for a multitude of species, including crappie, largemouth bass, white bass, and catfish.

The back end of the Verdigris is also a productive spot for a variety of fish—particularly during those times when the U.S. Army Corps of Engineers is releasing water from the swollen reservoir.

"I fish in the river about 70 percent of the time," Bybee says. "There are a lot of lay downs, and a lot of willow trees that provide shade. I just fished the river (during a late August summer), and I was catching fish in a foot of water."

• • •

What I found at Toronto was a lake that didn't seem to be as devastated by the floodwaters that plagued southeast Kansas in 2007 and 2008. While Elk City and Fall River both suffered from high water, tangles of debris, and submerged boat ramps, the high water damage had largely subsided.

After visiting with park manager Kim Jones, I stopped at several locations around the lake to drop in a fishing line or simply explore the area. One of those locations was Cross Timbers State Park, near the Toronto Point area. Three cabins overlook the shoreline and water of Toronto Point, which is also one the best crappie hotspots in the lake. My trip took place in the middle of November, and the hardwood forests around the cabin were in the midst of their autumnal change, creating an astonishing backdrop to the lake.

In addition to the scenic views and productive fishing, Toronto also offers a backwoods hiking and camping adventure that's not often found in Kansas. The "yellow" and "red" loops of the Chautauqua Hills Trail extend away from the developed camping areas of Toronto Point. A special permit is required for backcountry camping,

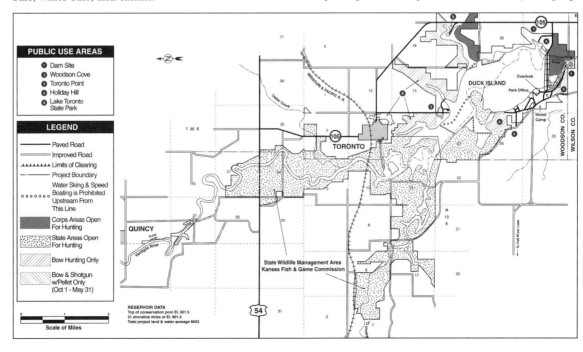

Disposal

Toronto

Quarries

NORMAL POOL ELEVATION 902

WALNUT GROVE

CREEK

RESERVOIR

PLEASANT GROVE

Oil Walls

GREENWOOD CO.
WOODSON CO.

TORONTO

Toronto
Public Us

Duck Is

INDIAN

Holid
Public

Carlisle
Cem

Sewage D

BM 1056

OIL
FIELD

PLEASANT GROVE

Branch

Carlisle

BM 1038

BM

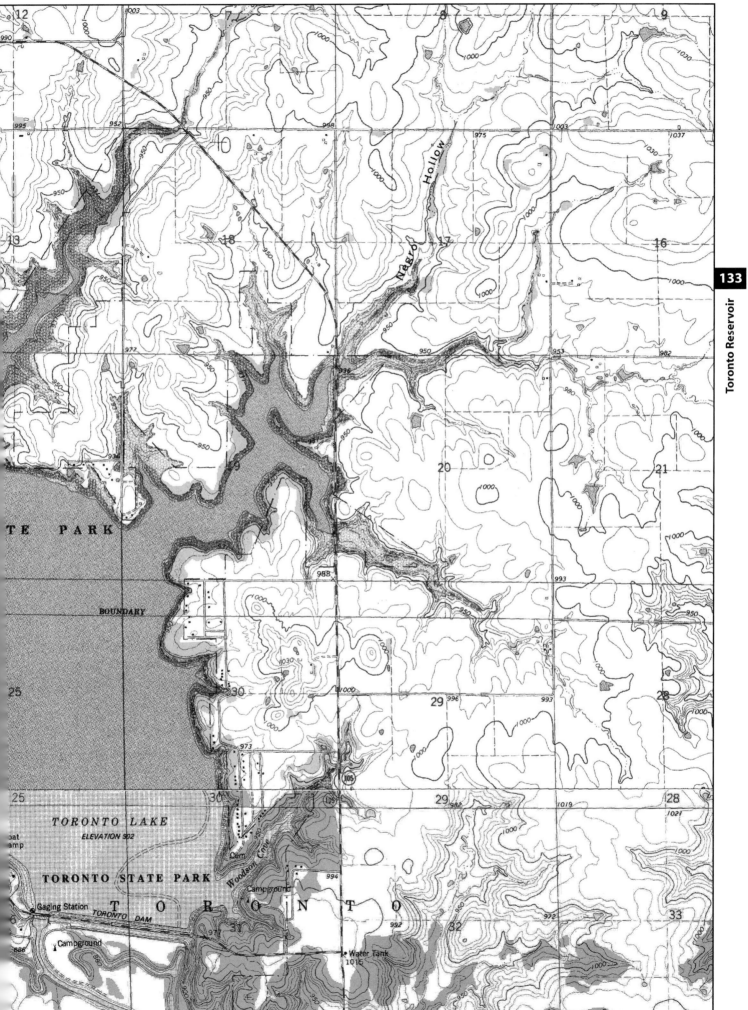

but there's little doubt that the paperwork would be well worth if for this uncommon Kansas experience.

Feature Fish

Crappie: Toronto has everything a crappie could want. The main body of the reservoir contains ample timber for shelter, vegetation and rocky shorelines for spawning, and a river that dumps nutrient-filled water into the lake. This combination gives crappie at Toronto the opportunity to grow large and grow fast—and in plentiful numbers.

Carson Cox, the Kansas Department of Wildlife and Parks fisheries biologist for Toronto, says the fish there nearly double in size from their second year to the sixth year. His sampling data shows that 2-year-old crappie measured 7.6 inches long, but had grown to 10.7 inches in length by their third year. Those crappie grew another two inches the next year, and by the time they reached six years the fish measured a healthy 15.4 inches long.

"There are high numbers of big fish, and they have a great growth rate," Cox says.

But it's not just the local biologist who can testify to the lake's big crappie. Bybee says he regularly catches 2-pound crappie from Toronto, and that it's not uncommon to catch fish over 15 inches in length. Plenty of fish also fall into the 10–14 inch range, he says.

In addition to the favorable conditions for crappie, Kim Jones, park manager for Toronto, says the floods that plagued the region in 2007 and 2008 have brought on an unexpected benefit to the crappie population—and those who fish for them. "It's reduced fishing pressure at the lakes," he says of both Toronto and Fall River.

During those years when the water level is relatively stable, Jones suggests anglers in search of spawning crappie should head to Mann's Cove, on the northeast side of the lake. He says the fish move into this area during April and May. The cove has timber, deep water areas, and rocky shorelines. However, he warns that anglers coming from the main body of the reservoir should use caution. The timber in the area can wreak havoc on hulls and props. A boat ramp near the back of the cove offers access to the spawning areas—without the danger of working through submerged timber.

Another spawning area is toward the back of Toronto Cove, which is on the north side of the lake, to the west of Mann's Cove. Toronto Cove has rocky bluffs along the shore, and Cox says there is a lot of timber in the area, particularly near the KDWP rental cabins in Cross Timbers State Park.

According to Cox, however, this area isn't just for

spring-time fishing. Toronto Cove is among the most popular spots for crappie anglers after Labor Day. "They even catch them up there in the winter, around the docks in four to six feet of water," Cox says.

Generally, though, Cox recommends looking for the fish in the shallows during the spring, and searching for the fish around deep water brush near rocky areas in the winter.

Yet another fish-holding portion of the lake can be found on the north side of Duck Island, located toward the southwestern shore of the reservoir, near the middle of the lake. According to Cox, debris that washes in from the Verdigris River and Walnut Creek often finds its way to this location. "Tree stumps stack up on the north side of the island," Cox says. "If the fish are shallow, look for them on the gravel around the island. If they're deep, look for them around the channel."

When it comes to crappie fishing, however, perhaps the best location at Toronto Reservoir isn't in the lake at all, but in Walnut Creek, which flows in from the west. From September 15 through mid-January, Cox says, the crappie at Toronto migrate up the river and over to Walnut Creek, where the clear water forms deep pockets for crappie to hide. It's during this time of year—when the lake's water level is low or stable and the air temperature is moderate, that the best fishing can be found at Toronto.

"There have been times when I check the water temperature in the lake, and it would be 48 or 49 degrees," Cox says. "Then I'd find that the temperature in the river or creek was 12 degrees warmer than the lake."

Anglers can move up the creek from the reservoir, or put a boat in at the Baker Bridge boat ramp—an area that Cox says is well known for holding crappie. "There is access in this area, but mostly people will fish from shore," Cox says. "A lot of people will camp in this area, and when the crappie get in there, it's really good."

Throughout the year, Bybee says, his preferred bait is a plain lead jig head, tipped with a white jig body.

Catfish: While crappie might dominate anglers' attention at Toronto, it's the catfish population that truly thrives in Toronto's waters. And unlike the crappie fishing, which is adversely affected by high water and seasonal flooding, catfish can be caught both before flood waters reach the reservoir and afterward, when the swollen lake releases millions of gallons of water downstream. Anglers looking for catfish have several productive approaches available, depending on the water level.

The convergence of the Verdigris River and Walnut Creek is located at the northern end of the lake and forms a shallow, silted river delta that draws catfish by the thousands. "Right at the mouth, just as the water comes in during the spring, it's a feeding frenzy," Cox says. "You can see the fish gather in there, and it's something to behold."

Cox warned, however, that fishing of this nature doesn't last long, so timing is important. To hit this spectacular cat fishing, he suggests monitoring upriver rainfall and stream flow. When the runoff water begins filling the lake, Cox says, anglers using stink bait, liver, shad sides, or live bait will likely catch all the fish they could want.

As the water level rises, however, this fishing will die down, and that's when it's time for anglers to head to the other end of the lake—fishing in the spillway below Toronto Dam. Jones says this area is among the best, and most popular, places for catfish anglers—particularly when the lake is high and the U.S. Army Corps of Engineers is releasing a lot of water, and, consequently, fish.

Cox says the lake employs a water management plan from July 4 through the fall. During this period, the reservoir collects rainwater Monday–Friday, and then releases that water on Saturday and Sunday. This hold-and-release method makes it easy for anglers to know the best times to fish the spillway. When the water is released, catfish flood the basin below the lake.

"You can always go below the spillway and catch fish," Cox says.

A bonus for catfish anglers is the apparent migration of blue cats from Oklahoma, which seem to be making their way up the Verdigris and establishing residency behind Toronto.

Another structure that holds catfish isn't as obvious or as striking as the inlet and outlet of the Verdigris River, but it's no less effective. An old railroad line, which lies below the water to the east of Duck Island, runs south toward the dam and stretches for nearly 200 yards. Cox says anglers will pick up this structure on their fish finders—look for an area of water roughly six feet deep, then a drop to deeper water (the old railroad ditch) that then moves to a plateau of roughly four feet before dropping off again to the deeper water on the alternate side of the track.

"In the fall, that is fantastic for channel cats," Cox says. "Channel cats hold on that, and it acts like a funnel."

Largemouth Bass: The largemouth bass population thrives in these waters—a fact proven by the exceptional growth documented by Cox. A bass just over 10 inches long in its second year had grown to over 17 inches by its fifth year of life—and continues to grow rapidly through its tenth year.

But unlike crappie, nearly all the bass in Toronto won't be found in the lake, but in Walnut Creek, near Baker Bridge. "There's tons of brush in the Walnut, and much of it doesn't come the surface," Cox says. "Many people will fish only the brush they see, but they're driving by a lot of structure because they don't see it." Additionally, the water is clear and warm, which also draws bass to this part of the creek.

To bass fish Walnut Creek, Cox suggests remaining parallel to the banks in the center of the creek, in the main channel, fishing toward the shallower shelves near the shoreline.

The primary forage in this area is shad, and Cox suggests that any lure that imitates those baitfish will be more successful than worms or crawfish. Favorites used by local anglers include white twister tail grubs and jigs, as well as shad-colored Rattletraps. The only exception to this approach would be in the hottest days of summer, when a plastic worm is more likely to pull a bass from its shaded hole.

"That's a honey hole up there," Cox says. "There's a large density of fish and this area holds both bass and crappie."

White Bass: Another species that keeps anglers' fishing rods bent over throughout the year is the white bass. This hard-fighting and seemingly always hungry fish also uses the waters of the Verdigris River and Walnut Creek, particularly during the spring spawning season, when they look for riffles in the water in which they can lay their eggs. While the first of such riffles is located off of public land on the Verdigris, the water in Walnut Creek holds both suitable structure for spawning whites and plenty of shoreline access for anglers.

Cox suggests looking for spawning whites at the delta, where the Walnut Creek flows into Toronto Reservoir, all the way to the Baker Bridge area. During this season, the white bass are chasing shad ahead of the spawn, and nearly any shad-oriented bait will draw a strike.

Once the spawn dies down, look for white bass to move to the mud flats on the upper end of Toronto, as well as to position off of windblown points, where they chase schools of shad. Try trolling crankbaits or Rattletraps during this time of year.

Facilities

Cross Timbers State Park, located 12 miles west of Yates Center in Woodson County, is a 1,075-acre park that covers five areas at Toronto Reservoir: Toronto Point, Mann's Cove, Woodson Cove, Holiday Hill, and Dam Site. Camping areas feature easy access to the lake, shaded campsites, rolling hills, and great scenery. In total, Cross Timbers offers: 15 campsites with water, sewer, and electric; 37 sites with water and electric; 10 sites with electric only; and 180 non-utility sites; 3 rental cabins; 5 shower houses; 1 dump station; 6 boat ramps; 2 courtesy docks; 2 fish cleaning stations; and a swimming beach located in the Toronto Point area.

Additionally, a network of trails are open to mountain biking, and backcountry hiking is available, with a permit, on the Chautauqua Hills Trail around Toronto Cove. The lake is also surrounded by a 4,600-acre wildlife area that provides habitat for deer, turkey, quail, squirrel, dove, and a variety of wildlife. The U.S. Army Corps of Engineers manages land behind the Toronto dam, as well as public land to the south of Mann's Cove.

Shopping/Supplies

Country Junction sells bait, tackle, groceries, fuel and deli food, open 7:00 a.m. to 7:00 p.m. daily. 153 US 54, Toronto, 620-637-2384. **Hilltop Bait/Grocery** sells food, bait, camping supplies, and "a little bit of everything." Also home of the **Hilltop Café.** Several cabins are available for rent—call ahead for information or reservations. Open 8:00 a.m. to 8:00 p.m. Thursday through Tuesday, 8:00 a.m. to 2:00 p.m. on Wednesday. 153 Westshore Rd., Toronto, 620-637-2700.

Alco, 501 W. US 54, Eureka, 620-583-7076; **Cross Timbers State Park,** 144 K-105, Toronto, 620-637-2213; **DJ Sporting Goods,** 200 W. River St., Eureka, 620-583-5211; **Fall River State Park,** 144 K-105, Toronto, 620-637-2213; **Johnson's General Store,** 205 W. River St., Eureka, 620-583-5672; **Johnson's General Store,** 201 W. Mary St., Yates Center, 620-625-2538; **Main Street Mini Mall,** 226 W. Main St., Madison, 620-437-2441.

Tuttle Creek Reservoir

SIZE: 12,500 acres

LOCATION: Just north of Manhattan on US 24

GPS LOCATION: N39 15.445' W96 34.77'

CONTACT: Tuttle Creek Project Office, U.S. Army Corps of Engineers, 785-539-8511

FEATURE FISH: Largemouth Bass, Blue Catfish, Channel Catfish, Flathead Catfish, Crappie, Saugeye, Trout, White Bass

DAILY CREEL LIMIT/MINIMUM LENGTH: Largemouth Bass: 5 fish, 18 inches • Blue Catfish: 10 fish • Channel Catfish: 10 fish • Flathead Catfish: 5 fish • Crappie: 50 fish • Saugeye: 5 fish, 15 inches • Trout: 5 fish • Walleye: 5 fish, 15 inches

It was an early morning in the spring—3:00 a.m. to be precise—and while most people were asleep across Kansas, Ron Harrison maneuvered his boat over the depths of Tuttle Creek Reservoir. Actually, he was the only fisherman on Tuttle this foggy day, which Harrison told me is typical. Several days a week, he launches his boat,

MARSHES

Olsburg 135 acres
Fancy Creek 39 acres
Irving 15 acres
Timber Creek 40 acres
Swede Creek 80 acres
Blk Vermillion 50 acres

LEGEND

Office Buildings	
Paved Road	
Gravel Road	
Unimproved Roads	
State Park Area	
State Wildlife Area Hunting Area	
Corps Managed Area	
Handicapped Hunting Area	
Marsh	
Boat Ramp	

and he sees few, if any, anglers on the water amid the morning's wee hours. But when he's done, he is usually lugging home some lunker catfish—as he did on this morning.

"I do things different than the average person," Harrison, of Manhattan, says. "I'm up at 2:00 or 3:00 a.m., and I'm done by 9:00 a.m. You'll catch more fish during those hours when it comes to catfish—it's the prime time they like to eat."

We hit Tuttle at daybreak as Harrison was getting off the water. Harrison reiterated what we already knew about this lengthy northeastern Kansas lake—our best bet was to find catfish. As for Harrison, it wasn't just any old catfish he wanted to hook—he was in search of those elusive blues.

Tuttle, after all, is sporadic when it comes to fishing for anything other than catfish. The Big Blue River flushes water from as far north as the farm fields of Nebraska, which is why Tuttle is muddy. With those high flooding events, this lake, to Harrison, is good for one thing.

"Fish like white bass and crappie, they don't survive well in that kind of atmosphere," he says. "It's primarily a catfish lake, with a little bit of white bass, crappie, and saugeye."

Yet, of those inflow events, he says, "It's the best time to catfish—when that water runs."

But John and I, not knowing the lake well, were skunked this summer day. The fog didn't help matters, either. It never lifted that morning. So, after a few hours of fruitless fishing, figuring the conditions were too dangerous to do much exploring, we headed home.

• • •

Nestled in the Flint Hills near my college town of Manhattan, in northeast Kansas, Tuttle Creek Reservoir is the state's second largest impoundment with 12,500 acres of water and 100 miles of rugged, wooded shoreline. In all, the lake extends about 16 miles above the dam, and averages a mile in width.

According to the U.S. Army Corps of Engineers, the reservoir plays a vital role in flood control within the Kansas River basin, impounding the Big Blue River. The Big Blue basin covers 9,628 square miles, with about three-fourths of the area in Nebraska. A basin reservoir was talked about for several years before actual work began in 1952. Work progressed on and off for a decade, with the lake finally complete and operational in 1962.

Sedimentation, however, is an issue, with the lake losing 40 percent of its capacity since its construction, according to the Kansas Water Office.

• • •

Fishing has suffered at Tuttle due to flooding events, says Ely Sprenkle, the reservoir's fisheries biologist with the Kansas Department of Wildlife and Parks. Fish are prone

to migrate downstream of the reservoir. "Luckily we have well-developed fisheries downstream," he says, noting that includes tail water tubes where a high harvest rate of crappie, channel catfish, flatheads, and saugeye can be had.

Typically, the reservoir is 10–15 feet above conservation pool on average at different times during the year. However, in 2010, the lake was 30 feet above conservation pool at one point. By comparison to Kansas' other 24 reservoirs, "Tuttle is kind of the sacrificial lamb," says Sprenkle. "When someone has to get flooded, Tuttle does."

Sprenkle notes that when the reservoir is drier, access to some boat ramps is limited. Meanwhile, when the reservoir is taking in water, boaters should be aware of trash like logs and brush washing in from upstream.

The reservoir is also a bow fishing site, Sprenkle says, with bow fishermen taking buffalo carp and gar throughout the lake.

Feature Fish

Catfish: A few days after a large rain event in the area, Harrison had his boat on the water in the northern end of the lake, where, he says, the blues stay in shallower depths during the spring. "You catch more of them early in the year," he says, adding that when the temperatures rise, the blues head to deeper water in the southern part of the lake.

He caught a 41-pounder earlier in the spring, which "is a big one for a blue in Tuttle Creek."

Blue catfish are the largest of North America's sundry catfish species. They're native to some eastern Kansas rivers and can survive in large impoundments like Tuttle.

If you go after a blue like you're fishing for channel catfish, Harrison says, you probably won't have luck. Blues like cut or live baits. You also won't find them in brush piles like a channel cat. Instead, spring fishing means looking for dropoffs, such as areas that go from 4 feet to 10 or 18 feet. "They kind of like to hang out on ledges," he says.

However, Tuttle's blue population isn't as multitudinous as that of nearby Milford Reservoir. "Blues didn't take off like they did in Milford," Sprenkle says. "We don't have good natural spawns."

However, he notes, at present, Tuttle is still second-best for blue cat fishing, albeit perhaps only until introduction of blues takes hold in a handful of other state reservoirs, when Tuttle might drop down on the list of hot blue cat waters.

Tuttle typically has excellent channel and flathead catfish fishing. Anglers can find them in the lake as well as the river above and below the lake. One hot spot, Sprenkle says, is one mile downstream of the dam at Rocky Ford, which is a good place not only for catfish but other species that migrate upstream to spawn. Another good spot is the outlet.

Anglers can also use float lines during daylight hours July 15–September 15 at Tuttle Creek Reservoir from the dam upstream to Blue Rapids.

According to Sprenkle, in mid- to late May, the channel catfish get up in the big rocks to spawn in a couple feet of water. A good place where anglers can find spawning channel catfish includes the Carnahan Creek area. During flooding events, look for them in freshly flooded vegetation or up in creeks.

Crappie: Tuttle Creek is known for good crappie fishing, Sprenkle says, but adds that crappie numbers are dependent on good water conditions during spawning periods, which varies year to year. Still, regardless of density, anglers can reap a good spring harvest when the fish come shallow to spawn.

As when fishing cats, Sprenkle recommends fishing around the tailwater tubes at the outlet as well as coves and brush piles, using jigs and live minnows. Meanwhile, Sprenkle says, Carnahan Creek Cove is a good spot year round, including for ice fishing anglers.

Other hot spots according to Harrison: Stockdale and McIntyre Coves—both are out of the wind and are fished for crappie, especially during the spawn.

Largemouth Bass: Fair numbers of largemouth bass are caught near standing timber and brush piles in coves in the southern third of the lake. The McIntyre Cove area tends to produce the better fishing. Check out the river pond, as well. "These areas tend to be the clearer, more stable habitat," Sprenkle says. "And McIntyre Cove is usually pretty good, the best spot to find largemouth."

White Bass: Fish for white bass off rocky points, the dam, and up the Big Blue in mid-April, during the spring spawn. Feeder waters can also be good in mid-April, including Fancy Creek.

White bass will be good starting in July, says Harrison. Shad hatch will be about an inch long at this time. "The whites will be following the shad," he says, noting to follow the wind and gulls. "Because of the feeding frenzy that goes on in July and August, it makes white bass fishing easier."

Saugeye: Most anglers aren't looking for saugeye in Tuttle, Sprenkle admits. "Usually, they are a bonus fish," he says. "The population fluctuates due to the high release rates. We can have exceptional years followed by a desert."

Saugeye can be taken off the face of the dam in late March–early April. Midway through June, this species will congregate at the mud flats, and the rest of the year they can be found around rocky points.

Trout: About 13,000 rainbow trout are stocked in Willow Lake in the fall and winter. A special trout stamp is required. The season runs October 15–April 15.

Facilities

The Corps manages two campgrounds (**Stockdale** and **Tuttle Creek Cove Parks**), KDWP manages 5 campgrounds, and Pottawatomie County manages 1 campground. In total, the area offers: 200 utility campsites; 500 non-utility sites; and 7 cabins. The Randolph area horse campground is still receiving improvements and will provide an additional 13 electric campsites with community water when completed. You'll also find several boat ramps around the lake. The Corps has ramps at Carnahan Park, Fancy Creek, Randolph, and Stockdale. The lake has a swimming beach and miles of trails for hikers, bicyclists, off-road vehicles, and horses. Tuttle also has a 12,200-acre wildlife area for hunting and wildlife viewing.

The area is home to several events, including an OK Kids Day during the summer, the Country Stampede, and several day-long outdoor concerts in June.

GPS Waypoints

ADA Fishing Dock: N39 15.287' W96 34.902'
Spillway with boat ramp: N39 28.135 W96 59.093
Fancy Creek area with boat ramp: N39 26.168 W96 45.138
Rocky Ford Fishing area: N39.23922 W96.58595

Shopping/Supplies

Ballard Sporting Goods, 1218 Moro St., Manhattan, 785-539-2441; **Chapman Creek Outdoors,** 2701 N. Marshall, Chapman, 866-922-6630; **Dara's Fast Lane,** 5321 Tuttle Creek Blvd., Manhattan, 785-320-6633; **Derick's Bait & Tackle,** 4700 Tuttle Creek Blvd., Manhattan, 785-587-9356; **Dillons,** 130 Sarber Ln., Manhattan, 785-776-9285; **Dillons,** 1000 Westloop Pl., Manhattan, 785-539-7631; **Fort Riley Conservation Division,** 1020 Huebner Rd., Fort Riley, 785-239-8579; **Ole Mikes Shooter Supply,** 1111 N. 3rd St., Manhattan, 785-537-9815; **Riley County Clerk,** 110 Courthouse Plaza, Manhattan, 785-537-6300; **Sharps Short Stop,** 118 W. Randolph St., Randolph, 785-293-5293; **Walmart Supercenter,** 101 Bluemont Ave., Manhattan, 785-776-4897; **Wildcat Marina,** Spillway State Park, 785-776-3113.

Contacts

Tuttle Creek Project Office, U.S. Army Corps of Engineers, 5020 Tuttle Creek Blvd., Manhattan, 785-539-8511; **Tuttle Creek River Pond Gate House,** 5800 A River Pond Rd., Manhattan, 785-743-2031; **Tuttle Creek State Park,** 5800 A River Pond Rd., Manhattan, 785-539-7941; **Tuttle Creek Wildlife Area,** 801 S. Main St., Blue Rapids, 785-363-7316.

Webster Reservoir

SIZE: 3,740 acres

LOCATION: About 8 miles west of Stockton on US 24

GPS LOCATION: N39 25.373 W099 26.141

CONTACT: Webster State Park, 913-425-6775 (area office), 785-628-8614 (regional office)

FEATURE FISH: Largemouth Bass, Channel Catfish, Flathead Catfish, Crappie, Walleye, Wiper, White Bass

DAILY CREEL LIMIT/MINIMUM LENGTH: Largemouth Bass: 5 fish, 15 inches • Smallmouth Bass: 5 fish, 15 inches • Channel Catfish: 10 fish • Flathead Catfish: 5 fish • Crappie: 50 fish • Trout: 5 fish • Walleye: 5 fish, 15 inches • Wiper: 2 fish

My husband John and I decided to venture on a lengthy four-day weekend trip to Webster Reservoir with our twin girls, Brett and Kaci, who were just 2 years old at the time. It would be our first trip fishing as a family. And, in our minds, we pictured a Norman Rockwell moment: a family of four with fishing poles in hand, listening to the waves splash against the boat and the sounds of birds and wildlife. We'd sleep in a tent, cook fish on the fire.

It sounded good, anyway, until the wails of toddlers hit.

Yup, welcome to my world of fishing. The girls weren't terrible. But they were toddlers. They thought a few hours in the boat was more than plenty, even if the fishing was hot. Brett wanted to pet the fish we caught. She even wanted to pet the "baby fishies"—lures with treble hooks, including crankbaits. Her eyes welled with tears when we sternly told her, "No."

I tried to explain it was for her own safety—that getting her finger hooked wouldn't be any fun. She still didn't understand. Moreover, she also became sad when we released the fish, not understanding why we couldn't take them home as pets.

Still, we'd get in a few hours of fishing before boredom hit too hard—the girls finding something to do for a while to keep them occupied. Kaci found the crayons and proceeded to color on the boat seats. Thankfully, they were washable. Brett liked to open the cooler and look at the fish we caught.

Kaci wanted to drive the boat. Brett liked to play with Mr. Twisters. Brett also had a habit of honking the horn when we weren't looking—just one of several happenings, I'm sure, that scared the fish away.

And there were proud moments, as well. They showed interest in the outdoors. Kaci even tried to help me fish. I think she's almost ready for her own rod.

No, it wasn't a perfect trip, by any means, but we made some memories. The girls experienced fresh fish over the campfire, as well as marshmallows. We slept in a tent and took showers at the bathhouse. We held up the line of people as Brett screamed when we tried to give her a shower.

And it really was one of the best Kansas fishing trips in the two years of traipsing the countryside for this book.

We found plenty of wipers—which made the girls laugh with delight. These were decent-sized fish, too, with the top one we caught weighing more than 8 pounds. It was quite tasty over a campfire later that night, by the way.

• • •

The Bureau of Reclamation built Webster Reservoir in 1958 for the purpose of flood control, according to the Kansas Department of Wildlife and Parks. Webster State Park was added to the Kansas park system in 1965.

Nestled in the Solomon River Valley in the Chalk Hills region of north-central Kansas, Webster Reservoir is known for its walleye and wiper population. Anglers can also catch largemouth bass, crappie, white bass, walleye, and catfish. And you can always take a moment to enjoy the scenery—a mixture of grass prairie and riparian trees and shrubs, along with plenty of wildlife.

• • •

It's not yet 6:00 a.m., but the bantering has begun at Blaine Baxter's bait shop. That's the way most days begin when the fishing is hot at Webster Reservoir. Some need lures, others fresh bait. Some just gather around the table for a game of cards and a morning cup of coffee. And Baxter turns on the light for them in the wee hours of the morning, seven days a week.

This is the ritual at Baxter's Bait and Tackle—a little shop along Main Street in Stockton, the Rooks County seat with a population of 1,500. Hundreds of other bait shops are scattered throughout Kansas. But while many come and go, Baxter's is distinctive. It's remained an anchor in the town's economy for more than 20 years, thanks to the good fishing at the nearby lakes, including Webster.

Leaning against the counter at the downtown store, Baxter talked matter-of-factly about his successful business. He pointed to a topographical map he keeps in the store—showing me a few places where anglers said the walleye and wipers were biting.

He knows, after all, despite only fishing when he has time—which is rare when running a bait and tackle shop. Still, he listens to the early morning banter—and always makes a daily trip to Webster just to see how the lake looks and how the fishing is going. "I go to the lake every day, just to look around," he said.

There's plenty to look at these days, too, he says. Compared to past years, when water levels dwindled because of low rainfall and irrigation, levels at the Rooks County lake rose over the past two years. Visitor numbers have been increasing.

"It's exciting," Baxter says, noting those folks frequent his shop. "I've heard guys tell me they're bringing in some quality fish."

The lake has seen its ups and downs, Baxter notes. Built mainly for flood control and irrigation, Webster's levels tend to fluctuate. Fishing was superior in the late 1990s when rainfall filled western Kansas' reservoirs, including Webster. Drought and irrigation, however, lowers the pool some years, such as during much of the 2000s.

In 2009 and 2010, water levels were higher thanks to Mother Nature, rising as much as 30 feet, KDWP biologist Mark Shaw says. Those waters flooded trees and brush, making this lake a fishing haven.

According to the KDWP, more than 50 trees were added to the south side fish attractors and 49 trees to the north side fish attractors in 2010. Keeping the lake a fishing haven is the goal, says Don Jenkins, Jr., a former park ranger and manager who now spends his summers as a camp host in between fishing for walleye.

That's why Webster is one of the top lakes in the state these days for walleye, crappie, white bass, and wipers, Jenkins says. He calls it a family-type atmosphere more devoted to fishing than jet skiing and boating. Moreover,

he adds, the higher levels of the lake have brought people far and wide for some angling, he said. While a well-kept secret to some in the eastern half of Kansas, the lake is well used by northwest Kansas locals, as well as visitors from as far as eastern Colorado and southern Nebraska, especially with Webster being centrally located to four other western Kansas lakes—Keith Sebelius, Kirwin, Glen Elder, and Cedar Bluff Reservoirs.

"Due to the low water in years past, we lost some habitat," Jenkins says. "But now it is starting to come back. With walleye, white bass, and wipers, we have a year-round fishery."

The boost in visitors has also helped the local economy, which is noticeable when one owns a bait shop. "I never figured I'd see the lake full like this," Baxter says.

Feature Fish

Wiper: Kansas fisheries biologists have been developing wiper-stocked reservoirs across the state, and Webster is no exception. Anglers have the chance to catch some of the biggest and feistiest fish in the form of this white bass–striped bass hybrid. "Western Kansas can have some big wipers," says Shaw. "Webster is no different."

Webster typically ranks in the top ten when it comes to density of wipers. However, if you're looking for big 'ins, Shaw says Webster is typically among the top few. In fact, in 2010, Webster ranked sixth among all reservoirs for density of wipers that were 12 inches or longer. Fish 20 inches or larger accounted for nearly half of the fall netting. Jenkins, meanwhile, says that in spring of the year, anglers were hooking wipers that weighed 10–12 pounds.

Shaw recommends casting bucktail jigs into the wind around corners of the dam. Wipers feed on shad, he says,

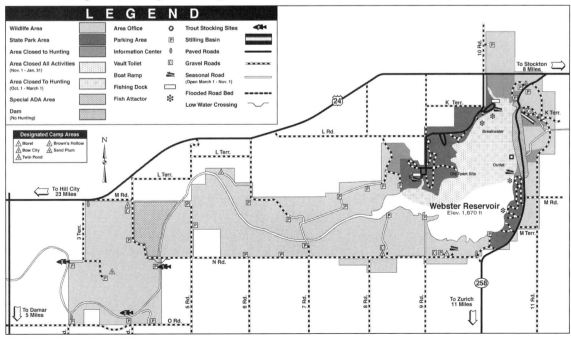

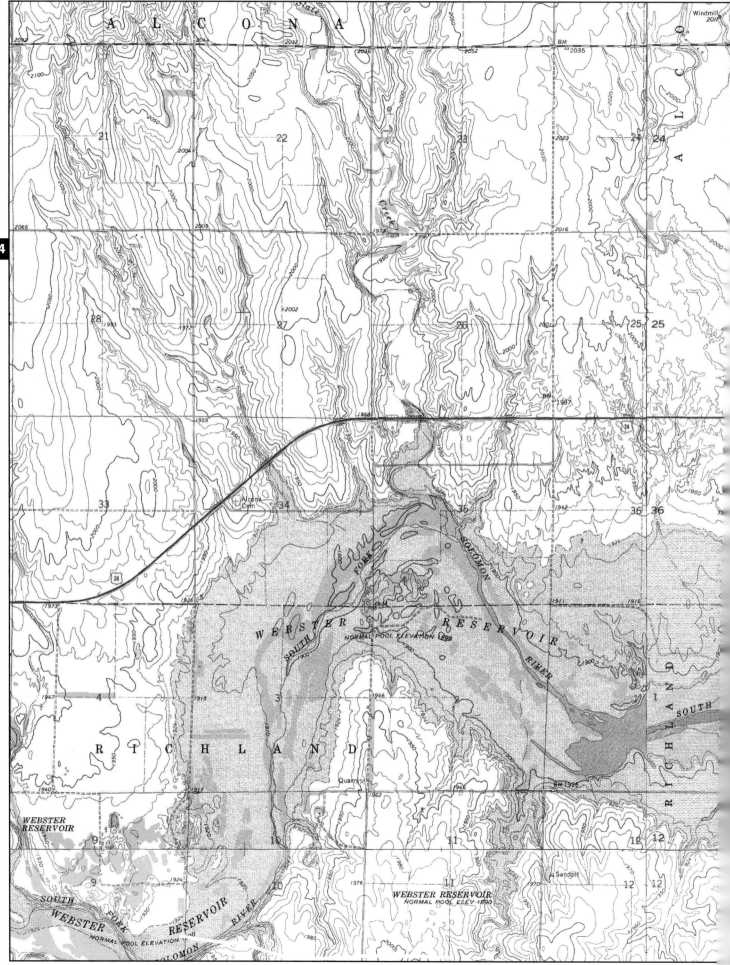

Webster Reservoir

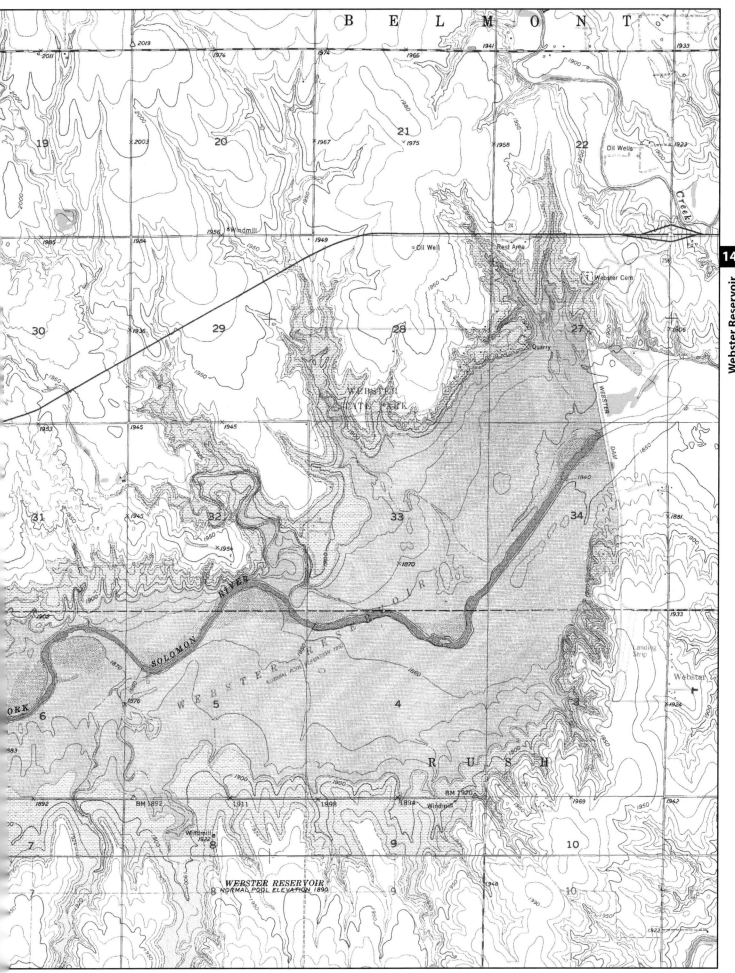

so find them where the gulls are located. Many a wiper is caught trolling down shorelines using crankbaits.

One hot spot Shaw recommends is the Methodist Camp Point, and he notes that the river channel goes just east of this area. Also, try just east of Old Marina Cove off Stump Point, where Shaw says there are a lot of big trees. "You can catch walleye along it, too," he says.

Shaw also recommends fishing around the outlet, as well as the old swim beach area. Mid-summer, look for them in deeper water where it is cooler.

Catfish: Webster typically is a fair lake for catfish, with some average-sized fish out there for the taking. Shaw says to look for them around the dam, north and south shore breakwaters, and along the bluffs. Moreover, when there are inflows coming into the lake from the South Fork of the Solomon River, anglers should find catfish up west and in the Bow City and Methodist Camp areas.

Shaw adds not to forget Webster's stilling basin, the fish feeders at Rock Point, as well as up the river. Most anglers use traditional baits like shad, shad gizzards, shrimp, dip and stink baits, as well as night crawlers. Another successful bait is green sunfish.

White Bass: According to Shaw, anglers have excellent opportunities throughout the reservoir for surface action during the summer when the whites chase shad around the lake. He says trolling with diving lures like Hot-N-Tots and casting roadrunners should be productive. "Keep an eye on the sky and follow the gulls," he says.

Look for them lake wide, as well as on the windward side of coves. When the water cools off, anglers might catch them while jigging for crappie.

Walleye: Jenkins, whose father was Webster's first park manager when the lake opened in 1965, says he grew up around these western Kansas waters. He served as a park ranger, then as park manager, at the lake before making a career change to law enforcement—eventually becoming the Stockton police chief.

Now somewhat retired, Jenkins says what he likes to fish best is walleye, which he tries to find time to fit into his busy schedule that includes his summer job at the park as well as coaching football, wrestling, and track at Stockton High School. And, on days when the fishing is hot, he says some anglers get their limit of walleye in just a few hours.

Webster typically ranks in the top five Kansas reservoirs for walleye, Shaw says. In 2010, his samplings found there to be a lot of 9–15-inch walleye, with the potential of catching keeper walleye.

As with all of Kansas' lakes that have walleye, find them up along the dam in March and April as they come into spawn. The best bait during this time is jigs, roadrunners, and crankbaits. When they move to the flats in May, Shaw says to get out the night crawlers.

Shaw recommends trying the south side of the lake. "You can also catch some in the submerged old roadbeds," he says. And, in August, look for them off the river channels by trolling deep or drifting with a jig and a worm off the breaks in between 12–30 feet of water. "I would say the majority is around 20 feet," he says.

Jenkins recommends the flats on the western end of the lake, where the old town of Webster once sat before it was covered with water. That's a spot most locals have marked as a waypoint on their GPS. Some also troll or drift for walleye here, as well as along the shoreline using diving lures like hot and tots.

In the fall, head back to the flats, Shaw says. Also try fishing the submerged farm fields on the south side of the reservoir when the reservoir is more full.

An angler named Darryl, who was fishing the reservoir on a spring day, recommended the north and south bluffs for walleye, as well as the old swimming beach. The beach area isn't just a hotbed for walleye, he says. Also expect to find some white bass and wipers here.

Crappie: Water level rises helped produce good crappie spawns, Shaw says, which may be why black crappie density rating is among the top five in the state.

Look for the crappie around brush, north and south shore fish attractors, break waters on both the north and south sides, and along the dam. Other hot spots include Rock Point Cove and Old Marina Cove. Shaw recommends using jigs, jigs with minnows under a bobber, and small slab spoons.

A concrete bridge that crosses one of the north-end coves is also a good place to find crappie and also some white bass, Jenkins says. Furthermore, anglers will walk along the breakwaters on the north side of the lake to jig for crappie. Be sure to check out the west end of the lake, as well, he adds, saying the brushy habitat is a popular crappie hangout.

Shaw says most of the ice fishing is around fish attractors, including by two on the north shore and two on the south side.

Largemouth Bass: Jenkins says Webster used to be a popular spot for bass tournaments, but the low water levels have hurt populations in the past. But, he adds, with the improved water levels and tree vegetation habitat available to help the species survive, largemouth bass fishing could see an upswing.

According to Shaw, reservoir populations in 2010 were young, but fish should be getting bigger and the angling better in years to come. KDWP stocked 19,000 fingerlings in 2008.

A few angling spots include Old Marina Cove and vegetative areas in the lake's west end, Jenkins says.

Trout: Anglers also have the opportunity to catch rainbow trout during winter months at the Webster stilling basin, as well as the South Fork of the Solomon River above the reservoir. The season runs October 15–April 15. The KDWP typically stocks about 2,000 trout in the middle of each month in the stilling basin and about 800 in the river, which extends from a half-mile downstream of the low water crossing on N Road to one mile upstream of the crossing.

Facilities

There are 5 camping areas at the lake. In total, the area offers: more than 70 utility campsites; more than 100 non-utility sites; 1 cabin; 5 boat ramps; 3 courtesy docks; an electric fish cleaning station on the north shore of the reservoir; and swimming beaches. There is also a hiking trail.

Moreover, the lake offers floating fishing docks, an easily accessible fishing pier at the nearby stilling basin, as well as 50 miles of shoreline for the angling pleasure. Meanwhile, the fish feeder located in Old Marina Cove just west of the Coyote shelter runs every 3 hours. The fish feeder in the stilling basin goes off at 7:00 a.m. and 8:00 p.m.

GPS Waypoints

Goose Flats Boat Ramp: N39 23.945 W99 25.448
Rock Point Boat Ramp: N39 24.944 W99 25.901
Old Marina Boat Ramp: N39 23.976 W99 27.339

Shopping/Supplies

Baxter's Bait and Tackle, 424 Main St., Stockton, 785-425-6321; **Mr. Quick Bait,** 1003 Main St., Hays, 785-628-1865; **Northshore Bait & Tackle,** 1201 9 Rd., Stockton, 785-425-7029; **Rooks County Clerk,** 115 N. Walnut St., Stockton, 785-425-6391; **Sport Haven,** 31094 K-147, Ellis, 785-726-4457.

Wilson Reservoir

SIZE: 9,040 acres

LOCATION: About 60 miles west of Salina on I-70 and K-232

CONTACT: Wilson Project Office, U.S. Army Corps of Engineers, 785-658-2551

FEATURE FISH: Largemouth Bass, Smallmouth Bass, Channel Catfish, Crappie, Striped Bass, Walleye, White Bass

DAILY CREEL LIMIT/MINIMUM LENGTH: Largemouth Bass: 5 fish, 15 inches • Smallmouth Bass: 5 fish, 15 inches • Spotted Bass: 5 fish, 15 inches • Blue Catfish: 5 fish, 35 inches • Channel Catfish: 10 fish • Flathead Catfish: 5 fish • Crappie: 50 fish • Striped Bass: 2 fish • Walleye: 5 fish, 15 inches

ACQUATIC NUISANCE SPECIES ALERT: White Perch and Zebra Mussels (Unlawful to possess alive).

Few people knew Wilson Reservoir better than "Big" Jim Smith, and few local anglers were talked about more than Smith—who lived just outside of Wilson, but could just as well have called Wilson Reservoir his home. Die-hard anglers at Wilson, Kanopolis, and Glen Elder knew him and talked about his ability to catch fish when no one else seemed to be doing much good at all. Bait shops and biologists threw out his name as the expert on where, and how, to find fish.

And when Ellsworth resident Paul Bahr broke the state record on May 14, 2010, by landing a 44-pound striper, Jim Smith was one of the people he publicly thanked for sharing his insights and years of experience. "He taught me a lot when I first started out," Bahr said of Smith. "He was one of those guys who wasn't afraid to share what he knew. I was lucky to start fishing with him 10 years ago."

For his part, Smith didn't brag about what he knew, but he spoke with a sense of certainty that can only come from years of repeated success. He would talk about stripers, and where they'd be found at different times of the year. Or he might have talked about how important it is to put the bait right in front of crappie, and how it has to be

presented in the right manner. Whatever it was, Smith fished for it, and over time he developed an encyclopedia of knowledge about how to catch them.

My past fishing trips to Wilson could have benefited with a little help from people like Smith and Bahr. I've never been too successful at finding monster stripers, and a good number of the times I've traveled to the lake, some sort of storm seems to have traveled with me.

But there are few lakes in Kansas that can offer the natural beauty of Wilson. The water is deep and clear and reflects a dark blue against the reds and oranges of the sandstone cliffs.

More importantly, Wilson gives anglers a lot of places, and species, to try. One of my favorite areas is Hell Creek, toward the south side of the lake. This area features cove after cove of wind-sheltered water to fish—and moving into those coves with an electric trolling motor almost makes it feel as if you're the only angler on the lake. It's a good area for just about every species at one time of the year or another, and the scenery has a way of dulling the pain of an unsuccessful fishing trip.

(Author's note: Sadly, "Big" Jim Smith, pictured to the left, passed away in December 2010.)

Feature Fish

Stripers: Stripers were an area of expertise for Smith. "The fish will be close to the river channel," Smith said of summertime striper fishing. "That river is like a highway, and humps are like restaurants—they'll run up and down that channel until they're hungry and then they'll chase the shad up the humps." According to fisheries biologist Tommie Berger, Wilson's clarity creates an ideal environment for predators such as stripers, who take advantage of the clear water when chasing their prey.

Wilson is the state's premier striper fishery, and the previous state record stripers all hail from the lake. In addition to the clear water, the feeding Saline River helps stripers thrive at Wilson. Wilson's water has "a slight salt content," says Berger, which helps these native saltwater fish fare well in Wilson.

Like Cheney in south-central Kansas, the invasive white perch was accidentally introduced into Wilson. Unlike at Cheney, however, the white perch haven't become as big of a nuisance—something Berger attributes to the striper's voracious feeding habits.

Although the white perch have supplanted some of the white bass population, according to Smith the fish provide an exciting and easy opportunity to get kids hooked on fishing, and the fillets offer good eating. Smith said that it's not uncommon to catch white perch in the 8–12 inch range.

"The white perch have made it a little harder to catch stripers than it used to be," Smith added. "There's an abundance of white perch, and they have a lot to eat." But the striper fishing is still plenty good, as Bahr's state record suggests.

Early in the spring, even before the ice has fully melted from the lake, Smith boated his way to the upper end of the lake and into the backs of the coves at Hell Creek. During this time of year, the stripers move toward shallow water in search of shad struggling to survive after the winter.

"They go shallow," Smith said of early spring stripers. "I've thrown spoons into the weeds in a foot and a half or two foot of water. They'll come up with their mouths open and look like a largemouth busting the water." Smith had also found success with bucktail jigs and curly tail jigs cast into the shallow water. It's not uncommon to start catching white bass and white perch using this approach.

And though the time of year suggests that the bait should be fished slow, Smith said that he'd caught fish with a fast retrieve, sometimes buzzing the bait through those shallow areas.

During the summer months, the stripers generally head to deep water—and that's when Smith fished the deep-water striper highway of the original river channel. He looked for humps located near the river channel—in places where the water depth changes from 60–65 feet to around 40 feet. He'd anchor over the 40-foot water and drop a sunfish or live shad in the transition and wait for the fish to move out of the channel.

In the fall, Smith said, smaller stripers can be found chasing shad to the surface, much like white bass do during the early morning and late evening hours of the summer months. With stripers, however, the action can sometimes last all day.

"The birds show up where the fish are," Smith said. "You don't even need a graph—you can follow the birds. It's really a cat and mouse game, but it's fun to do."

Smith said the birds might leave, but the fish are likely to linger for a while longer, waiting in deeper water for the crippled shad to fall in front of them. He used lighter tackle than is needed for the deep summer fishing, and would drop a spoon to the stripers' depth and "pop" it until the fish hit.

When the action stops, and the birds are hitting the water in another area, Smith moved on for another round. But don't leave before the action stops. "If I'm still catching fish, there's no need to leave fish to find fish," he said.

Bahr's state record striper was caught in the spring by trolling a planer board to the shoreline side of his boat, with a free-line shad rigged underneath. He commonly works the shoreline area slowly, moving only one or one-and-a-half miles per hour, until he finds a group of stripers.

Around 7:00 p.m., Bahr hooked into a fish that kept "going and going." "I thought he was around 20 pounds," Bahr says, "but the first time I saw him I thought, 'Man, this may be in the high 30s.'" When he checked the weight on his scale, the fish was 45 pounds, with the official weight at 44 pounds—enough to knock off the old state record.

Like Smith, Bahr begins late-winter days on the west end of the lake, where the water warms quickest, and gradually makes his way toward the Hell Creek area as the temperature rises. The approach is a proven one. Aside from Bahr's state record, his daughter landed a 40-pound fish and his son landed a striper that weighed in at over 30 pounds—all in the same year.

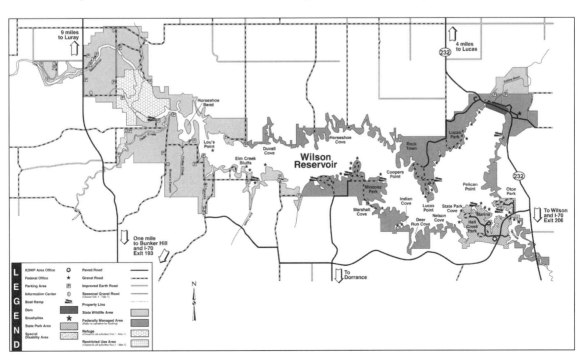

LURAY
LURAY
SALINE
RIVER
Creek
ELEVATION
RESERVOIR
SALINE
RIVER
WIL
Boat Ramp
Spring
Elm
CENTER
BM 1545
BM 1570
BM 1520
BM 1543
BM 1742

Bahr's suggestion for anglers new to Wilson is to practice patience. While there are a lot of striper in Wilson, and plenty of big ones, not every trip is successful and not every hole produces fish on every trip. "Just stay with it," Bahr says. "They could be anywhere, but that mid-May time seems to be the best window to catch a big one."

Smith, too, said the lake can be hard to fish simply because of its volume. With more than 100 miles of shoreline and depths of up to 70 feet, there are a lot of places fish could be hiding. Success comes through not only knowing where those fish might be, but in putting something in front of them that looks like what they're used to eating. "Figure out what size the shad are in the lake," Smith said, "and use something that's the same size."

During the summer months, use live shad or sunfish for bait. In the fall and spring seasons, spoons and bucktail jigs work well. The wade fishermen like windblown points in the fall, right up into November, fishing with white bucktail jigs.

Black Bass: Wilson is a productive fishery for largemouth and smallmouth bass. In fact, fisheries biologist Tommie Berger anticipates that in the coming years Wilson will become a popular stop on bass fishing tournaments, thanks to an explosion in the number of black bass at the lake. "We've been surprised at Wilson," Berger says. "The black bass have come on better than we anticipated. There are lots of guys catching them."

Berger suggests fishing in the flooded vegetation near the shoreline, as well as the rocky areas in Hell Creek. Topwater baits work well, as well as soft plastics tossed toward the shoreline.

Walleye: The most fished-for species at Wilson is walleye. Smith said the walleye fishing at the lake is feast or famine. Look for walleye to head toward the dam in the spring spawning season before heading to the flat area around Lucas Road, to the east of Lucas Point. A jig and crawler works well. In the fall, look for the walleye in the Hell Creek area and toward the upper end of the lake, west of Minooka Point. Also try fishing the flats around the Elm Creek/Duval roadbed, Alfalfa Flats, the old Lucas swim beach area, Pelican Point, and just west of Hell Creek State Park.

Crappie: Berger says the crappie fishing is tough, but that the population is gaining ground and should improve in the years to come. Look for crappie to move toward the vegetation-lined coves during the spawning season, and in deep water brush piles during the fall. Smith said successful crappie fishing depends on finding them, getting your depth right, and presenting the bait. Generally crappie set above the brush, and you have to put it in front of them if they're not in a feeding frenzy. Additionally, Smith reckoned most people move their bait too fast. "Just flip the bait and let it settle down," Smith said. "About the time you're ready to flip it again, wait about another 15 seconds because those fish will sit there and eyeball it."

White Bass: Although white bass numbers have declined significantly since the white perch showed up, there are still some nice white bass in the lake. Look for them in the upper end in the spring, scattered around the lake in the summer, and chasing shad in the fall. Most of the white bass taken from Wilson are caught by anglers fishing for other species.

Catfish: Though catfish don't gain much attention at Wilson, they are there, and Berger says many anglers overlook this fishing opportunity. Wilson ranks in the upper tier of Kansas reservoirs in density of channel catfish, and they can be found in many areas throughout the lake. In addition to channel cats, biologists have been stocking blue cats for the past several years at a rate of about five fish per acre to serve as another predator on white perch and zebra mussels.

Facilities

Wilson sits in one of the most scenic areas of the state. This 945-acre state park includes the **Hell Creek** and **Otoe** areas, both on the south end of the lake. In total, the area offers: 4 campsites with water, sewer, and electric; 99 sites with water and electric; 36 sites with electric only; 100 non-utility sites; 4 rental cabins; 5 shower houses; 3 dump stations; 4 shelter houses; 5 boat ramp lanes; 2 courtesy docks; a marina with boat rental available; 1 fish cleaning station; and 2 swimming beaches. The U.S. Army Corps of Engineers manages three federal parks at Wilson—**Minooka, Sylvan,** and **Lucas.**

It's important to know that at Wilson, shade is at a premium. Campers looking for groves of trees in which to set up camp will have to find them early, as they're not that numerous.

Shopping/Supplies

Located at the entrance to the **Hell Creek Park** area, **Knotheads** sells licenses and permits, as well as bait and some tackle, and camping supplies. 785-658-2166. **Lake Wilson Marina** in Wilson State Park is open April 1–November 1. Supplies include live bait, tackle, camping supplies, and groceries. Slips are available for rent, and rental boats are available. Fuel also sold on the water. 785-658-2392.

Bring the Kids Fishing Opportunities for Youths

In Kansas, a kid's ability to enjoy the outdoors and spend a little time fishing is really limited only by his or her desire and motivation. There are plenty of kid-friendly waters in the state, and more often than not there's someone willing to tag along for the fun.

Take 13-year-old Lucas Schwiegert for example. There's nothing Stewart likes more than fishing. During the summer he pleads with his parents to load up the boat and head to one of the lakes near his home in Hutchinson. If that doesn't work, he angles for a chance to hit a farm pond or one of the local public ponds. If he's still unsuccessful, he'll grab his rod and reel and walk the short distance to the nearby storm-water drainage canal—where, surprisingly, he has managed to catch a number of bluegill and sunfish.

"I won't ever give up fishing," Schwiegert says. "I want to run a bait shop when I grow up."

It's not something he takes lightly, either. He has a tackle box brimming with gear, including a jointed Rapala crankbait and something he calls "space monkeys," which resemble crawdads and are deadly on large-mouth bass. He's been fishing since he was 3 years old, but he got "serious" when he was about 10 or 11, after he won a rod and reel combo at a local fishing derby.

To hone his skills, he tied on a sinker and practiced casting in the yard. "I got hung up on the power line in the front yard," Lucas says. "Then I did it again on the power line in the alley." He wasn't discouraged, though, and he continued to hone his casting skills.

I felt much the same way when I was Lucas' age. I've been fishing for about as long as I can remember, and it was the crappie spawn at Cheney that got me hooked. My dad would anchor the boat in some shallow cove or near a rock formation, and we'd catch crappie by the buckets full. When I wasn't at the lake with my dad, I'd head to "Maxine's Pond" just outside my hometown with my best friend Nate.

Maxine's Pond was little more than a wide spot in a creek, but it was full of bluegill, sunfish, crappie, and bullhead catfish. Those bullheads never were much for eating, but Nate and I would keep a line in the water all day long, waiting for our chance to catch a couple.

We'd work up the creek to the dam and keep our precious fish inside the impoundment. We'd haul rocks from scattered locations throughout the pond to create good breeding grounds for our fishery. Before we knew there were rules against such a thing, we'd catch fish at another pond or a lake and haul them to Maxine's Pond in the hope of increasing the water's diversity.

The same sorts of fishing memories from childhood have stayed with Nick Butler, who helps run the Flint Hills Bass Association and its Junior division, the Topeka Junior Hawgs. When he was a teenager, fishing

provided a way for him to get away from his parents when times were tense. "When I was inside, I got into trouble with my parents," Butler says. "Fishing was a way for me to get out of the house."

But fishing also taught him patience, a trait that would stay with him throughout his life. "There are so many other things that kids can do that can get them in trouble," Butler says. "Technology is a bigger part of their lives now, even more than 10 years ago. There's a lot to keep people from being outdoors."

Through the Flint Hills Bass Association, Butler and others like him are able to share their passion for fishing with the next generation. At least once a year, the older club members load up their boats with junior members and take them out for a guided fishing trip. Throughout the year, the Flint Hills members help organize and sponsor junior tournaments at smaller lakes within an hour of the Topeka area.

"A couple of the kids think we're superstars," Butler says. "We're not. We're just regular guys who like fishing. We come from all walks of life."

The Flint Hills group isn't alone: Other angling groups, many with a focus on helping children learn about the fun of fishing, are active throughout Kansas.

Emporia outdoorsman and youth hunting and fishing advocate Phil Taunton works with a number of those youth hunting and fishing programs, striving to help introduce youth to fishing. "Fishing is an individual character builder," Taunton says.

Bassmasters' CastingKids program teaches youth to flip, pitch, and cast with accuracy. Big Brothers Big Sisters has a program called Pass it On that teams up adult outdoors mentors with children who want to experience the outdoors. Meanwhile, a regional program implemented in Johnson County called Cops n' Bobbers teams up law enforcement with kids for fishing clinics and derbies.

There are even some schools in Kansas that have fishing in the curriculum, Taunton said.

Many groups have youth fishing tournaments at Kansas reservoirs and community lakes, and the Kansas Department of Wildlife and Parks hosts a free fishing weekend every year to encourage families to give fishing a try. Several state parks include fishing ponds that are well stocked and reserved for youth fishing.

Additionally, every state park in Kansas plays host to one-day outdoors events called OK Kids Day, sponsored by Kansas Wildscape. OK Kids Day events typically include a fishing clinic and derby to help educate and expose kids to fishing. Fisheries biologists also hold local clinics at kids ponds or community lakes throughout the summer. Often, rods, reels, tackle, and bait are provided for those events.

Throughout the state, KDWP helps provide fishing holes for kids through its Community Fishing Assistance Program, which leases public ponds and stocks them with fish, and the Urban Fishing Program, which stocks fish every two weeks in heavily fished waters in Kansas cities and towns. These programs give another generation of children the chance to experience what Butler, Taunton, and I did when we were younger, and what 13-year-old Schwiegert experiences today.

It also gives us a chance to enjoy a family activity with our children and grandchildren.

"I used to do sports in high school and college," Taunton says. "But it's been a long time since I ran 100 yards. Fishing is just a big part of family and getting out with kids. It's something they can continue on with their entire life."

Urban Fishing Program Lakes

Atchison County: Atchison State Fishing Lake

Butler County: Lake George, Andover; Benton Poling Lake, Benton

Douglas County: Lake Henry in Clinton State Park; Mary's Lake, Lawrence

Finney County: Sandsage Bison Range and Wildlife Area, Garden City

Johnson County: Cedar Lake, Olathe; Frisco Lake, Olathe; Olathe East High School Pond, Olathe; Mahaffe Farmstead Pond, Olathe; Waterworks Lake, Olathe; Kingston Lake, Overland Park; Regency Lake, Overland Park; South Lake, Overland Park; Prairie Center Pond, Olathe; Rose's Pond, Lenexa; Tomahawk Parkway Middle Pond, Leawood; Tomahawk Parkway South Pond, Leawood

Leavenworth County: Jerry's lake, Leavenworth; Lansing City Lake, Lansing

Lyon County: Camp Alexander Lake, Emporia; Peter Pan Park, Emporia; Jones Park Ponds, Emporia

Ottawa County: Ottawa State Fishing Lake, 5 miles north and 1 mile east of Bennington

Pottawatomie County: Pottawatomie State Fishing Lake No. 2, 1.5 miles east and 2.5 miles north of Manhattan

Reno County: Dillon Nature Center, Carey Park Pond, Hutchinson

Riley County: 7 mile pond, Fort Riley; Breakneck Lake, Fort Riley; Pritchard Pond, Fort Riley; Moon Lake, Fort Riley

Saline County: Lakewood Lake, Salina; Indian Rock Lake, Salina; Saline State Fishing Lake, Salina

Sedgwick County: Chisholm Ridge Lake, Clearwater; High Park, Derby; Rainbow Valley Lake, Derby; Stone Creek Park, Derby; Haysville City Lake, Haysville; South Hampton Lake, Kechi; Cedar Brook Lake, Mulvane Sports Complex; Chisholm Pointe, Park City; McLaughlin Pond, Valley Center

Sedgwick County, Wichita: Sedgwick County Park, East KDOT Lake, West KDOT lake, Buffalo Park Lake, Chisholm North Park, Emery Park Lake, Northwest Water Reclamation Plant, South Lake, Watson Park, Dillon's Pond, Harrison Lake, Cruiser Lake, Chisholm Island Pond

Shawnee County: Governor's East Pond, Topeka; Cedar Crest Pond, Topeka; Governor's West Pond, Topeka; Shawnee Jr.; Shawnee State Fishing Lake; Karl's Lake; Westlake, Topeka; Central Park Lake, Topeka; Clarion Lake, Topeka

Wyandotte County: Big 11 Lake; Pierson Park Lake; North Park Lake, Bonner Springs; New Pond

Kids Fishing Ponds (local regulations posted on site)

Kanopolis State Park Pond

Glen Elder State Park

Clinton State Park

Elk City State Park

Scott State Park, trout pond

Tuttle Creek State Park, Willow Lake

Wilson State Park

Eisenhower State Park pond at Melvern Reservoir

Fall River State Park Kid's Pond: 1 acre, 2 fish daily catfish creel limit.

Pratt kid's fishing pond: 2 miles east, 1 miles south of Pratt. Fishing hours from 6:00 a.m. to 10:00 p.m. Children 10 and under must be accompanied by a person 16 or older. Two fish daily creel limit.

Yates Center Kid's Pond: 1 acre

Lebo Kid's Pond: 2 acres

Overbrook Kid's Pond: 5 fish daily creel limit for largemouth bass, 15 inch length limit; 10 fish daily creel limit for catfish; 2 fish daily creel limit for wipers.

River Fishing

"If a man goes fishing every day, he will be a good fisherman," Catdaddy Shumway quips, as if it were an old Chinese proverb. So, it shouldn't come as a surprise that almost daily Shumway, of Topeka, pushes off from a dock on the Kansas River, spending hours searching for the big ones.

No, Shumway says, Kansas doesn't have the mountain streams of Colorado or the rivers of Minnesota. But that's okay. An expert at fishing the rivers of Kansas, especially the Kansas River, he knows his terrain like the back of his hand. There aren't many places a fish can hide from him.

Renne R. "Catdaddy" Shumway, after all, calls himself a river rat. He's a man who sports bib overalls

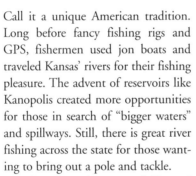

on most days and whose burly arms are strong enough to hoist big fish across his boat. As long as it is his species of choice, that is—and which species shouldn't come as a surprise.

"The only thing that goes in my boat has whiskers," he says.

• • •

Call it a unique American tradition. Long before fancy fishing rigs and GPS, fishermen used jon boats and traveled Kansas' rivers for their fishing pleasure. The advent of reservoirs like Kanopolis created more opportunities for those in search of "bigger waters" and spillways. Still, there is great river fishing across the state for those wanting to bring out a pole and tackle.

I've floated some of Kansas' rivers, on occasion, in search of catfish. That includes the Smoky Hill River, near where my husband, John, grew up, which can be a fishing paradise on a lazy summer day. Catfish still find refuge beneath the surface, just as they always have. When doing this, we're usually not looking for trophies—just some nice-sized catfish for the supper table. We also enjoy taking in the quiet beauty of the Kansas outdoors, without the fast-paced atmosphere.

We have the river to ourselves, after all—except, of course, for the elusive catfish.

I've also spent time angling from the shores of the Cottonwood, just upstream of Marion Reservoir, during the annual spring white bass spawn.

• • •

Kansas Department of Wildlife and Parks Fisheries Chief Doug Nygren calls Kansas' waterways an excellent opportunity for anglers. There are more than 10,000

miles of streams and river in Kansas, according to the KDWP. And, says Nygren, that includes the state's three public, navigable waterways—the Arkansas, the Kansas, and the Missouri—although one must have permission to access these rivers through private land.

While the rest of the rivers remain private, according to Nygren, there are several that have public access—whether they are upstream of a reservoir, meander through a city, or are leased from the landowner through KDWP's Fishing Impoundment and Stream Habitats program.

For those without a boat, it doesn't cost much to set up trot lines off the banks of a river to catch catfish, or to find a good spot to stand and cast for white bass during the spring run upstream. Also, rivers in the east and southeast part of Kansas may also provide opportunities to catch spotted bass, largemouth bass, and crappie.

• • •

George Stuck of Emporia says it isn't uncommon to see the Soden's Grove Park river bridge over the Cottonwood at Emporia packed with anglers. "Most of them are cat fishing," says Stuck, who used to own a bait shop in town. He says anglers catch several types of catfish in the eastern Kansas river system, including channels, flatheads, blues, and yellow cats.

"They'll catch some that are over 30 pounds, some even over the 50-pound mark." The biggest he's caught, a 50-pound flathead, he says, was with a rod and reel using worms.

Moreover, he says, you can fish the river year round if you want. "You can catch them through the ice if you are dedicated enough," he says of catfish. "Use those smelly old shad sides then, and when the ice goes off you can still use shad sides or go with the shad entrails."

• • •

Kansas' rivers are where Catdaddy prefers to throw his line. "The river, you are free down there on the river," he says. "There is just more fishing opportunities. There is crappie, bass, walleye, spoonbill, yellow cats, blue cats, a smorgasbord of fish.

"If a person is wanting to fish for a huge, big fish," he adds, "the best bet is to go to the river."

River Fishing Regions
Predominately, catfish are found in Kansas' flowing waters—largely in the eastern half of the state, where the flow is less intermittent than the waters of the west. For instance, the Arkansas River as far east as Edwards County has been dry for years—only flowing a few times in that period due to high rain events. But, in the eastern two-thirds of the state, river-angling opportunities abound—for sundry sportfish.

In the southeastern part of the state, for example, there are spotted bass for the catching. Meanwhile, according to Mike Miller, the KDWP's information chief and editor of the agency's magazine, white bass spawn upstream of the state's reservoirs each spring. That includes Marion, Kanopolis, and Fall River, among others, he says.

And while Kansas isn't a mountain state, Miller says, there are places to find clear, rocky streams with a good current—especially in southeast Kansas. "The Elk River above Elk City, that stretch is really pretty," he says.

Meanwhile, by the little town of Galena on K-66, Shoal Creek is another stream with an Ozark feel. There are three access points on the Spring River near Baxter Springs.

"These are pristine areas that many don't think about being in Kansas," Miller says.

Feature Fish

While this listing is not nearly complete, we have tried to highlight some places where you will find good river fishing for these species.

White Bass: Beginning in late winter at many of Kansas' reservoirs, white bass, along with wipers, begin congregating at the mouth of waterways in preparation for their spawning run. Typically, whites move out of lakes and reservoirs and into flowing rivers and creeks to lay their eggs on their run upstream. The trigger is a water temperature of 50–55 degrees, which brings avid anglers to trudge the banks of these successful spawning areas.

When the water in the rivers is warming, some males will move upstream earlier to wait for females. As the days get longer, the females start to move, and around April and early May, anglers will start catching big females.

At Marion Reservoir, that includes a several-mile stretch of the Cottonwood River that is surrounded by public land, from the mouth of the reservoir to K-15 near Durham.

At Toronto Reservoir, most of the fish go up the Walnut River, says Carson Cox, the area's KDWP fisheries biologist.

Other good spots include the rivers above Kanopolis, Glen Elder, and Cedar Bluff.

Cox also says to look for white bass up to the riffles of Fall River. "They particularly like a place where Otter Creek meets Fall River," he says. "We did a study up there and couldn't find the fish in the lake—by February, they left the lake. The fish really keyed in on that riffle."

Meanwhile, at John Redmond Reservoir, a logjam in the river at the head of the lake is a good spot, says Loy Hall, a fisherman who owns a The Bait Shop in Burlington. The logjam on the Neosho River stops the whites from venturing much farther upstream. Thus, many bass spawn along the logjam.

Upstream of John Redmond also can be a good angling spot, says Emporia's George Stuck, telling a story of how he caught a whopper in 1977. "We decided

we weren't going to keep a white bass, and we never put a white bass on a stringer that was under 3 pounds," he says. "That day, one weighed 4.25 and one weighed 4.5. There were some big white bass in there."

In fact, the state record white bass was caught in the river above John Redmond. According to the KDWP, in April of 2002 Marvin Gary, of Peculiar, Missouri, used a rod and reel with a roadrunner lure to bring in a 5.67-pound, 20-3/8-inch white bass. An average white bass will weigh about a pound.

But what's the best method during the spring run? White bass prefer to spawn in rocky or brushy areas along riffles and stage in deeper water above and below these areas. Brush piles can be good, also.

During this time they'll bite on just about anything, Cox says. A lot of anglers use a white twister tail; if it's muddy they'll use a chartreuse color. Others use jigs, small spinners, and spoons. Live minnows can work well, too. According to the KDWP, a light or medium action spinning tackle and 6- to 8-pound test line is the preferred equipment.

While many white bass anglers wade streams during the spring spawning run, some use boats on larger rivers.

Crappie: In the late winter, according to Cox, many anglers head up to Ladd's Bridge on the Fall River to fish for crappie. For those who venture to the southeast Kansas river, Cox says there's a deep hole near the bridge that people fish a lot. "That is somewhat spotty, though," he says, "as it can be good one day and then no good the next. Then, in the spring, it floods, and they disappear, and sometimes the river stays high all summer."

Cox says, however, that when conditions allow, crappie can be caught in the river in the summer when the species is chasing shad. "A lot of people will put in at Ladd Bridge," he says. "The water is cool, it's oxygenated, and there are deep holes, timber, and willow trees on both sides of the river to provide shade for fish. You'll find them under those trees trying to hide in the shade. There are also two brush piles in the area."

Black Bass: While largemouth bass are native to several eastern Kansas rivers, those searching for this species of black bass can find them in the La Cygne River above La Cygne Reservoir, as well as at Pillsbury Crossing near Manhattan and the Kansas River.

Meanwhile, anglers can find largemouth bass in Fall River, as well, Cox says, noting most anglers fish above the Ladd Bridge area. "Here, there are lots of trees, and there is a lot of debris, and the fish are chasing shad up here in the clear water of the river."

Catching 5-pound bass is common, Cox says. The density isn't great, but the fish are there.

Up in the river, try fishing with plastic worms, rattletraps, or anything that looks like shad in the spring. In the summer, use a jig and pig or crankbaits that look like shad.

Meanwhile, Miller says, spotted bass are common in parts of southeast Kansas to as far north as Council Grove and as far west as Butler County. "The first one

Public Access for River Fishing (see Region map, page 165)

Region 1
Saline River: low-water dam at Lincoln
Saline River: Wilson Reservoir Wildlife Area
Smoky Hill River: Kanopolis Reservoir Wildlife Area
Smoky Hill River: Salina
Solomon River: Beloit
Solomon River (north fork): Glen Elder Reservoir Wildlife Area
Solomon River (south fork): Glen Elder Reservoir Wildlife Area
Solomon River: Low-water dam at Minneapolis
Solomon River (south fork): Webster Wildlife Area

Region 2
Big Blue River: Rocky Ford Dam below Tuttle Creek Reservoir
Big Blue River: Tuttle Creek Reservoir Wildlife Area
Big Blue River: Tuttle Creek State Park River Pond Area
Delaware River: Perry Reservoir Wildlife Area, Valley Falls
Kansas River: Cedar Creek
Kansas River: De Soto
Kansas River: Edwardsville
Kansas River: Lawrence
Kansas River: Topeka
Kansas River: at mouth of Big Blue River, Manhattan
Marais des Cygnes River: low-water dam at Osawatomie
Marais des Cygnes River: low-water dam at Ottawa
Missouri River: Atchison
Missouri River: city parks in Doniphan, Leavenworth, and Wyandotte Counties
Republican River: Milford Reservoir Wildlife Area
Rock Creek: Clinton Reservoir Wildlife Area
Wakarusa River: Eudora
Wakarusa River: Clinton Reservoir Wildlife Area

Region 3
Arkansas River: at Cottonwood Falls, 1 mile south, ½ mile east of Coolidge
Ninnescah River (south fork): 2 miles east, 1 mile south of Pratt
Ninnescah River (south fork): Lemon Park, Pratt

Region 4
Arkansas River: Kaw Wildlife Area
Arkansas River: Arkansas City
Arkansas River: Low-water dam at Oxford
Arkansas River: Wichita 71st St. South (63rd St. South and Grove, then Sand E to River
Arkansas River: Wichita Chapin Park (S side of Hydraulic Ave. Bridge, First road E)

Arkansas River: Wichita Garvey Park (S Washington and 38th Street S)
Arkansas River: Wichita Herman Hill Park
Arkansas River: Wichita Lincoln Street Bridge
Arkansas River: Wichita Downtown
Arkansas River: Wichita 21st Street bridge (Big Ark River Park)
Arkansas River: Hutchinson Carey Park
Arkansas River: Sterling, 3.5 miles west of Sterling
Arkansas River: Alden, 3 miles south of Alden
Arkansas River: Raymond, 1 mile south of Raymond
Chikaskia River: Drury Dam, 5½ miles south of South Haven
Cottonwood River: Cottonwood Falls
Cottonwood River: Marion Reservoir Wildlife Area
Grouse Creek: Silverdale
Little Arkansas River: Through Wichita
Neosho River: Council Grove Wildlife Area
Walnut River: Arkansas City
Walnut River: Winfield

Region 5
Caney River: Federal Land above Hula Reservoir
Cottonwood River: Emporia, Peter Pan Park
Cottonwood River: Emporia, Soden Park
Elk River: Elk City Reservoir Wildlife Area
Fall River: Low-water dam at Fredonia
Fall River: Fall River Reservoir Wildlife Area
Marais des Cygnes River: Marais des Cygnes Wildlife Area
Marais des Cygnes River: Melvern Reservoir Wildlife Area
Marmaton River: Low-water dam at Fort Scott
Neosho River: Low-water dam at Burlington
Neosho River: Low-water dam at Chanute
Neosho River: Low-water dam at Chetopa
Neosho River: Low-water dam at Hartford
Neosho River: Low-water dam at Iola
Neosho River: Low- water dam at Neosho Falls
Neosho River: Low-water dam at Oswego
Neosho River: On the Neosho Wildlife Area
Neosho River: John Redmond Reservoir Wildlife Area
110-Mile Creek: Above Pomona Reservoir
Shoal Creek: Galena
Spring River: Low-water dam at Baxter Springs
Spring River: Southeast of Riverton below Empire Lake
Spring River: Off K-96 near the Kansas–Missouri state line
Verdigris River: Low-water dam at Coffeyville
Verdigris River: Low-water dam at Independence
Verdigris River: Low-water dam at Neodesha
Verdigris River: Toronto Reservoir Wildlife Area

I ever caught was in El Dorado Reservoir when it was just filling."

Trout: The trout season runs October 15 to April 15. During this season, some of the state's waters are stocked with trout, including Kansas' rivers.

A few of the spots include the Solomon River near Webster Reservoir and the Kanopolis Seep Stream—which gives fly-fishing anglers an opportunity similar to that of the mountain creek.

The Kanopolis seep stream draws cold water from the deepest part of the lake and winds its way behind the dam before entering the outlet waters. Along the way, there are several pools that the KDWP has constructed to concentrate fish along the small waterway. The main pool, closest to the outlet, is the largest and experiences the most fishing pressure. Many anglers, however, will work their way upstream to the smaller pools.

Bait fishing is allowed only in the pools at each

end of the seep stream; the middle pools are reserved for artificial lure fishing.

Kanopolis is one of the few locations that stocks brown trout in addition to rainbow trout. The KDWP stocks trout in nearly 30 locations throughout Kansas as part of the trout program. Popular baits include corn, Powerbait, and salmon eggs, while lure anglers prefer small spoons and Rooster Tails.

Catfish: According to Shumway, when it comes to producing robust catfish, Kansas' flowing waters—primarily found in the eastern half of the state—offer some of the best opportunities to land a lunker.

And when Catdaddy talks about catfish, he talks about monsters. He has the photos to prove it, too. He caught an 88-pound flathead on a rod and reel in the Kansas River, as well as an 85.8-pound blue cat on a limb line—roughly 8 pounds shy of breaking the state record. Shumway used a 3-pound carp as bait to bring in this massive blue.

Coincidently, James Edmiston of Shawnee caught the state record, a 94-pound, 57-inch blue cat on the Kansas River in July of 2000. He used a rod and reel with shad as bait.

Catdaddy grew up on the Kansas, or Kaw as the Native Americans called it. He fished off the banks as a youngster. He also learned a few tricks while frequenting his father's Topeka bait shop, listening to clients' stories and inspecting their tackle. It took him a while, but Catdaddy eventually followed in his father's footsteps. "I gave up one day and decided I was going to become a guide," he said, noting he made the career change in the mid-1980s.

His customers range from day-tripper anglers to those who want an overnight campout at several of the state's rivers, as well at area reservoirs. He starts fishing the Kansas River in late February or early March, when the fish feed in the early spring. He throws out fresh-cut shad and shad guts; "You want to feed the fish what they are used to," he says.

When fishing for big 'ins on lines into the summer and fall, he says the best baits are bullheads, perch, and carp, usually in the 3- to 5-pound range. The best pole bait, however, he says, is skipjack herring. Of course, Shumway goes to Tennessee to get this bait. Those who don't have access to herring can try using 8–10-inch shad. "I use every bit of 10 inches," he says.

That's how he targets the big blues, which are native to his Kansas River, as well as the Missouri.

One area he finds blue cats is in clam mussel beds, along the clay banks of the river. "Blue cats go insane over these things," Shumway says. "They'll go in there like hogs and root them with their nose." He notes that this is one reason KDWP staff has stocked reservoirs with blues—in hopes the fish might control the invasive zebra mussel populations.

Good fishing also abounds when the river is on the rise. "When you go out there after a really high rain, look for them in the dead spots," he says. "They are tired, they get out of the current, and that is where you go to set the lines and stuff like that.

"But you can really catch some nice fish out there, even when the water is not rising," Shumway says. For instance, a high-pressure storm front puts pressure on catfish bladders and forces them to feed, he says. "But when you have a falling barometer, they won't move."

Fishing for catfish gets harder mid-summer, when the water temperature increases. That's when, according to Shumway, you'll find them in a river's deeper water, and even in the muddy holes of a river.

In the dog days of summer, when it is unbearably hot, dip bait is a good choice, he says. He uses Buck's Cat Slayer dip bait, and he notes the best times to fish are early mornings or late in the evenings.

During the fall, he catches catfish during their feeding frenzy. "They are a like an old bear," he says. "They get all fattened up for the winter. The last part of September, October, and November can be some excellent fishing."

Catdaddy also successfully chums holes and riffles in Kansas' rivers. He goes to a local woodshop and collects chips. He has access to turkey blood, and fills a barrel halfway full of blood.

"Then I'll let the flies procreate in that blood until they get a good mass of maggots in the barrel of blood. I'll take all those woodchips and stir it up, freeze it off, and then put it in five or six different buckets. Then I'll go up the river on the current side and throw a can out."

The mixture is heavier than the water, he says. The woodchips get stuck in the sand and mud and the blood oozes out. This is especially useful on a river with a good current. "You'll be catching fish all day long," he says. "It's on those hard, rough days when you're not supposed to catch fish that chumming comes in handy."

However, he noted with a laugh, "You have to have a strong stomach."

Meanwhile, he says, you don't need an expensive rod and reel to be successful. Technique is the answer. "A lot of people will buy all this gear, a $600 to $700 rod and reel," he says. "I don't care what kind of rod and reel you have, it's all in the knot. If your knot ain't right, you're not going to catch much."

He uses a Palomar, he says, noting he learned to tie it during Boy Scouts.

Still, despite it all, Shumway's business survives on his ability to lead folks to a few catfish on any given day. It's also about introducing anglers to a piece of Kansas' natural beauty—the river.

"It's totally majestic," he says of the Kansas River. "It is a beautiful river. I've fished other rivers—the Missouri—but the Kansas River is what I do best. It is really quite serene. I see deer and turkey, all kinds of critters. In the morning I hear the opera—all the birds, it's just fantastic.

"I'm doing something I love, and I thoroughly love it," he said. "I'm in seventh heaven."

Small Lakes

The scenery along K-96 in western Kansas offers motorists a long view of the horizon—a view most often filled with wheat or cattle. There aren't many hills or valleys, and for the most part the landscape is barren and uninspiring. But there's a prairie oasis of sorts nestled in a historic valley in Scott County, where the land changes from one of flat vistas to limestone canyons and spring-fed creeks that in turn feed tall cottonwood trees that shelter the shoreline.

It's here that Scott State Lake sits, serving as a secret fishing and water sports attraction for those who call the arid western Kansas plains home. Fed by natural springs that help keep its 100-acre water level up even in years of drought, Scott State Lake offers anglers an abundance of fishing opportunities—from crappie, largemouth bass, walleye, and catfish to the rainbow trout, which are stocked in the lake every winter and early spring.

"You can catch all the bass you want," avid angler and Scott City resident Jesse Carlson says.

Scott Lake might be one of the most surprising of Kansas' small lakes because of its location in western Kansas, but it's certainly not unique in the angling opportunities it offers. From the high plains of the west to the wooded hills of southeast Kansas, smaller lakes and ponds dot the landscape—in remote areas and in the heart of towns and cities.

The Kansas Department of Wildlife and Parks manages dozens of state fishing lakes to create exciting fishing opportunities. Most are managed with the shoreline angler in mind—so brush piles are often located within casting distance of the bank, and fishing jetties jut out into the water at many locations. Through the state's Urban Fishing Program, more than 70 city lakes and ponds are stocked every two weeks from April through September with catfish, sunfish, and wipers.

Additionally, through the KDWP's Community Fisheries Assistance Program, the department leases and manages more than 200 community lakes in Kansas. In exchange, those lakes agree to provide free fishing opportunities to the public.

These small lakes in the state are also managed with families in mind. The consumption of alcohol is prohibited at most of them, and camping is plentiful and reasonably priced. In addition to the largemouth bass and crappie that sport anglers prefer, most of these smaller lakes have ample populations of catfish and bluegill for younger anglers.

I've fished a number of these smaller lakes over the years, and I've always found these trips to be relaxing and relatively hassle free. While using a boat is the best bet at a reservoir, lakes such as Scott, McPherson County, and Kingman State Fishing Lake are easy to fish with little more than a line, sinker, and hook. Additionally, these smaller lakes often are less crowded than their larger counterparts. Most have "no wake" rules in effect, too, which keeps boat traffic under control.

When I visited Scott State Lake, it was no different in that respect. Families gathered on the shoreline, eager for some movement on the end of their line. Others congregated on the beach for an afternoon swim, while the smell of barbecue grills permeated the air.

If you're looking for a relaxing day of fishing, don't overlook some of the state's smaller bodies of water, like Scott Lake. (For more on Scott State Lake, see p. 161.)

Clark State Fishing Lake (Region 3)

SIZE: 300 acres

LOCATION: 8.5 miles south and 1 mile west of Kingsdown

DAILY CREEL LIMIT/MINIMUM LENGTH: Largemouth Bass: 5 fish, 15 inches • Channel Catfish: 5 fish • Flathead Catfish: 5 fish • Crappie: 50 fish • Walleye: 5 fish, 15 inches

AQUATIC NUISANCE SPECIES ALERT: Eurasian Watermilfoil

In an area of flat farmland and pastures on the semiarid southwest Kansas plains, new visitors might be surprised when they come upon Clark State Fishing Lake. This lake, after all, appears out of nowhere, nestled in the bottom of Bluff Creek's canyon—scenic mirage.

But for Alan Finkeldei, of Dodge City, who spoke as he cleaned a stringer of walleye he caught trolling the lake using a crankbait, the lake's beauty is just as good as its fishing. "It's a good lake that's close by," he said of the roughly 40-mile trip. "And usually, I always have good luck here."

He calls the lake a well-kept secret, but admits he likes it that way. Clark State Fishing Lake contains good populations of channel catfish, largemouth bass, walleye, white bass, crappie, bluegill, and carp. It's one of the top state fishing lakes in Kansas for channel catfish, and channels are stocked yearly to maintain the populations and typically are caught in the upper end of the lake and at the inflow during summer months.

Walleye also are stocked yearly, with numbers moderate and fish up to 9 pounds. Find summertime walleye on the points and flats using artificial lures like Wiggle Warts, Hot-n-Tots and Shad Raps. Otherwise, good success is always found using jigs and night crawlers fishing over humps or off ledges.

The prolific white bass is increasing at the Clark County lake, with a good number of 1 to 2 pounders in 2010. After the spawn, look for the shad and try using small jigs, Rattletraps and crankbaits, as well as any topwater bait.

Crappie also are common to this rock-lined lake. Find them along dropoffs and around brush piles using jigs and minnows. In the heat of the summer, find them on deep dropoffs and brush.

Largemouth bass like the timber around the lake and also can be found in small tributaries. During the summer, the best time to fish is early mornings and later in the evenings using topwater bait during these low-light times of day. If fishing during the heat of the day, use jigs and worms or crankbaits near banks and dropoffs.

Horsethief Reservoir (Region 3)

SIZE: 450 acres

LOCATION: 8 miles west of Jetmore on K-156

DAILY CREEL LIMIT/MINIMUM LENGTH: Largemouth Bass: 5 fish, 15 inches • Channel Catfish: 10 fish • Crappie: 50 fish • Walleye: 5 fish, 15 inches

Sitting in his small fishing boat at Hodgeman County's Horsethief Reservoir, Garden City resident Marvin Frizzell reeled in several channel catfish on a hot July morning. He noted that he couldn't think of much negative about his new fishing hole.

"Except for the rattlesnakes," he says.

Yet, a couple of rattlers haven't been enough to deter Frizzell from coming to Horsethief—less than an hour east of his home in Garden City—especially when he's catching 2- to 3-pound catfish just one month after the reservoir's grand opening in late June 2010.

"This is a much needed thing for this part of the state because, otherwise, we have no water," Frizzell said of southwest Kansas. With a semiarid landscape, there are no reservoirs in southwest Kansas and many small lakes are dry. Even the mighty Arkansas River hasn't flowed in years.

Building a 450-acre impoundment in Hodgeman County isn't a new idea. It was a lengthy process. The Pawnee is the largest watershed district in the U.S., containing more than 1.5 million acres. A lake at Horsethief's present site has been part of the discussion since at least the early 1970s. The idea finally became a reality in 2005, when voters in Ford, Finney, Hodgeman, and Gray Counties passed a sales tax increase to help fund the $21 million project.

The lake is named after the original Horsethief Canyon not far from the site of the dam—a box canyon where horse thieves would hide their loot back in the day. The reservoir's dam is more than 7,200 feet long, which is almost as long as Tuttle Creek Reservoir's dam. Campsites at the reservoir were completed in fall 2010.

Meanwhile, fishing can only get better, according to Horsethief manager Josh Hobbs. Since September 2009, the Kansas Department of Wildlife and Parks biologists have been stocking everything from bluegill and minnows to largemouth bass, walleye, and keeper catfish here.

Camping at Horsethief Reservoir opened April 15, 2011, with 42 camping sites with water and electric. A primitive camping area is also available.

Shopping/Supplies

Horsethief Reservoir Benefit District, 514 W Hwy 156, Jetmore, 620-357-6420; **Presto Convenience Store,** 222 Main, 620-357-8369; **Jetmore Food Center,** 100 E. Wash, 620-357-6554; **Jetmore Lumber Co.,** 418 Main, 620-357-8341.

Scott State Lake (Region 3)

SIZE: 115 acres

LOCATION: 11 miles north of Scott City on US 83, turning northwest onto K-95.

CONTACT: KDWP area office, 620-872-2061

FEATURE FISH: Largemouth Bass, Channel Catfish, Crappie, Rainbow Trout, Walleye

DAILY CREEL LIMIT/MINIMUM LENGTH: Largemouth Bass: 5 fish, 15 inches • Channel Catfish: 5 fish • Crappie: 50 fish • Trout: 5 fish • Walleye: 5 fish, 15 inches

Scott State Lake isn't as deep as some of the larger reservoirs in Kansas, with its deepest depth being less than 20 feet, near the dam, but the spring channel that runs the length of the lake provides cool water where fish retreat during the hot summer months of July and August. The upper end of the lake, where the impoundment's width and depth decrease significantly, becoming more like a river than a lake, is lined with cattails and reeds that provide ample shelter for fish. Additionally, the Kansas Department of Wildlife and Parks has worked to establish brush piles in various locations throughout the lake, which attract and hold schools of game fish, particularly crappie.

One such brush pile, just east of the dam near a camping area on the east side of the lake, is a favorite spot for Scott City resident Jesse Carlson, who often anchors his boat near the structure and fishes for crappie. He generally uses small tube jigs—white, yellow, and chartreuse are his preferred colors—either jigging them above the brush pile or letting them dangle from a slip bobber.

Rick Harp, who operates the Beach House bait and supply store at Scott Lake, says that's one of the most popular crappie holes in the lake, but explains that other structure throughout the lake also provides a good place for anglers to set up for a day of fishing. "If you can find the crappie and where they're hitting, you can fill up a bucketful," he says.

Harp, whose store is located on the swimming beach at Scott Lake and is open 8:00 a.m.–6:00 p.m. Friday–Monday, says the lake is filled with an abundance of good sized fish, but that not a lot of people know about the lake's potential. "It's a hidden little spot," Harp said. "And there are some big fish out there—some that will straighten your hook."

According to Harp, two of the most popular fish at the lake are catfish and largemouth bass. Most anglers will use nightcrawlers, plastic worms, or topwater baits in the morning and evening hours to hook into bass, Harp says. Recently, the KDWP has increased the number of bass stocked in the lake, which should keep the numbers up and the fishing good for years to come.

Carlson says he finds bass around the vegetation along the shoreline, mostly using assorted jigs and a shad Powerbait minnow. During the late summer, as moss begins to build up around the lake's shoreline, Carlson said he rigs the Powerbait without a weight, which allows the bait to fall slowly and allows him to retrieve the bait as if

it were an injured bait fish. A twister tail jig, also worked around the shoreline vegetation, has also brought Carlson success.

It wouldn't do to talk about Kansas fishing without mentioning the ubiquitous catfish—particularly the channel cat. With a preference for silty bottoms and tolerance for warm water, the catfish thrives like no other fish in Kansas. In Scott Lake, the species does as well as anywhere, and anglers after a good-tasting fish likely won't have much trouble finding success.

Anyone with a rod, reel, fishing line, and hook can haul in decent numbers of cats with standard baits like worms, chicken livers, or shad sides. Carlson, however, employs a technique that still attracts fish but keeps his bait intact. He'll tie a piece of nylon stocking, filled with chicken livers, onto his fishing line, with a treble hook on the terminal end of the line. The stocking, Carlson says, allows the scent of the liver to escape while keeping it secured in one piece on his line.

Many people look for catfish at night, when the air and water both cool slightly, but that's also a good time to find groups of crappie at Scott Lake. Anglers often will use floating lights on the water to attract bait fish, which in turn draws game fish. Carlson often fishes for crappie with a minnow below a bobber or with jigs. During the day, he'll use brighter colors, while at night he'll switch to darker browns and blacks. To increase his chances, he'll sometimes reach for tube jigs that have been scented ahead of time with cinnamon oil. "There's something about that scent that seems to work," Carlson says.

While the population of walleye at Scott Lake isn't as plentiful as crappie and bass, there are enough of this tasty species to justify spending some time drifting a worm harness across the lake bottom. Harp said anglers often find the walleye in the deeper parts of the lake, particularly in May and June. Some anglers have been surprised, Harp says, at the size of the walleye that can be found in this small body of water.

"I've seen a 9-pound walleye taken out of this lake," Harp says.

For the angler who loves to fish year-round, even when the snow is falling and the wind is blowing, the October–March trout season provides a winter respite. Carlson begins the winter fishing season by working the upper end of the lake, using small, yellow or chartreuse jigs to entice the cold-water fish.

The addition of winter fishing gives Carlson, as well as other anglers, an excuse to spend even the bitterly cold winter months wetting a line and enjoying all the opportunities Scott State Fishing Lake has to offer—even if those opportunities remain unknown to those outside of western Kansas.

"I've been fishing that lake on and off for 42 years," Carlson says. "Every time I can get out there, I go."

Chase State Fishing Lake (Region 4)

SIZE: 109 acres

LOCATION: 2.5 miles west of Cottonwood Falls

DAILY CREEL LIMIT/MINIMUM LENGTH: Largemouth Bass: 5 fish, 13–18 inches slot limit • Smallmouth Bass: 5 fish, 15 inches • Spotted Bass: 5 fish, 15 inches • Channel Catfish: 5 fish, 15 inches • Flathead Catfish: 5 fish • Crappie: 50 fish • Saugeye: 5 fish, 18 inches • Walleye: 5 fish, 18 inches

Chase State Fishing Lake is situated amid one of the last vestiges of tallgrass prairie in the Kansas Flint Hills. According to Craig Johnson, the KDWP fisheries biologist who manages fish populations at the Chase County lake, it has some excellent fishing.

Chase's lake has a steep to shallow rocky shoreline with shallow mudflats on the upper end, according to KDWP. Surrounded by the area's natural rock terrain, water clarity is usually good.

The lake is set up for good fishing, after all, with eight fishing piers and many rocky islands and brush fish attractors to enhance angling for channel catfish, largemouth and spotted bass, saugeye, crappie, white bass, and bluegill. Fish feeders also go off every morning and evening.

The best crappie fishing usually occurs in April and May during the spawning period, with anglers finding them close to shore and along the face of the dam, according to KDWP. Brush piles and the islands also are excellent places to find spawning fish.

Channel cats are most often caught from June through September off the face of the dam and the fishing piers, using live bait and shad sides. Also find excellent cat fishing at the lake's feeder creek after a heavy rain. When the stream is running strong, the catfish move into the stream channel to feed.

Largemouth fishing peaks during mid- to late May when the fish move into shallow water to spawn. The best places to look for these black bass is in the shallow corners of the dam and other shallow shorelines near a dropoff.

The lake includes plenty of scenery in its surrounding 383 acres, including wildflowers, wildlife, and even a waterfall below the lake's spillway. The lake has a boat ramp, toilets, and a swim beach. Camping is allowed in designated areas along the north shore.

Shopping/Supplies
Cottonwood Mercantile, 328 Broadway St., Cottonwood Falls, 620-273-8100.

Marion County Lake (Region 4)

SIZE: 153 acres

LOCATION: About 1 mile east of Marion on US 56, then south about 3 miles on Upland Road

CONTACT: Marion County Park and Lake, 620-382-3240

DAILY CREEL LIMIT/MINIMUM LENGTH: Largemouth Bass: 5 fish*, 18 inches • Smallmouth Bass: 5 fish*, 18 inches • Spotted Bass: 5 fish*, 15 inches • Channel Catfish: 5 fish • Flathead Catfish: 5 fish • Crappie: 50 fish • Saugeye: 5 fish*, 18 inches • Walleye: 5 fish*, 18 inches • Wiper: 2 fish, 18 inches

* Largemouth, Smallmouth, and Spotted Bass in combination. Walleye and Saugeye in combination.

Among the small lakes that anglers can find in Kansas, few stand out quite like Marion County Lake. While it's only 153 acres in size, this small body of water that is managed by Marion County acts like it's a full-sized reservoir. There's a full-service bait and tackle store on site, complete with a ranger office. Brush piles and other man-made fish attractors dot the water along the lake's shoreline. There are fishing docks and jetties, and the lake is filled with some species one would expect to find only in some of the state's larger bodies of water.

In fact the state record Spotted Bass was caught at Marion County Lake, a record that has stood since 1977.

One of the best attractions, and the best-known locally, is the heated dock at Marion County. No matter how cold the weather outside, the temperature inside the covered fishing area is always warm, and the water is always open. More often than not, the fish are there, too, basking in the warmest water of the lake.

Marion County Lake is a developed fishery, with plenty of access for local anglers. Most of the shoreline and underwater structure is rocky, creating great habitat

for bass and crappie. This rocky make up, however, leaves the lake susceptible to the invasive zebra mussels. To combat this potential problem, all boats that come to Marion County must undergo an inspection before launch. It's something the staff takes very seriously, and disregard for this rule will result in a $1,000 fine.

Brian Thiessen, assistant lake superintendent, says the lake is fed from an underground spring, which helps stabilize water levels. The lake features many boat docks. Unlike most lakes, though, the docks are available for use by any angler.

Marion County Lake is also part of the KDWP's Community Fisheries Assistance Program, which leases waters for public fishing and helps keep the waters stocked with fish throughout the spring and summer months.

Thiessen says some of the most popular species include bass, catfish, crappie, walleye, saugeye, and white bass. Crankbaits, jigs, and spinner baits are among the most popular artificial baits, while a worm and hook remains among the most popular live bait at Marion.

I don't make regular stops at Marion County, but it's a lake that I tend to visit on a whim, when I feel like fishing a productive water without the hassle of loading up the boat or a lot of gear. I can take a trip to Marion—about an hour from my home—and almost always find fish with very little trouble. In the winter, when the fishing bug bites, Marion and its heated dock is one of the first places that comes to my mind. I've always had good luck at Marion, and there are enough fishing holes to keep me fishing all day long.

For anglers with small children, there's not likely to be a better fishery than Marion County. Kids can set up and fish in front of a variety of brush piles, and there are enough bluegill and catfish in the water to keep even the most impatient kid sitting in front of his pole, waiting for the next bite.

Shopping/Supplies

Hudson's Bait Shop, located at the park office at Marion County Lake, offers bait, tackle, groceries, supplies and licenses.

Facilities

Camping is available throughout the area around Marion County Lake. This is decidedly a family friendly lake, and as such there are several regulations with family campers in mind. Regulations prevent the use of generators after 11:00 p.m. and before 6:30 a.m., and children under 17 cannot camp without an adult. Alcohol is prohibited at the lake, and the park superintendent actively works to ensure the comfort and enjoyment of the park's visitors—and those who aim to disturb visitors are dealt with accordingly.

Coffey County Lake (Region 5)

SIZE: 5,000 acres

LOCATION: 2 miles north and 1 mile east of Burlington off US 75

DAILY CREEL LIMIT/MINIMUM LENGTH: Largemouth Bass: 1 fish, 21 inches • Smallmouth Bass: 2 fish, 16–20 inches slot limit • Blue Catfish: 10 fish • Channel Catfish: 10 fish • Flathead Catfish: 5 fish • Crappie: 2 fish, 14 inches • Walleye: 2 fish, 18–24 inches slot limit • White Bass: 12 inches • Wiper: 1 fish, 21 inches

Ask an angler in these parts about this power-plant water body, and they'll tell you it's "the crown jewel of Kansas fisheries." Excellent fishing for a sundry of species, they say. Throw a lure in the water and you'll surely come up with something.

Well, if you know what you're doing, anyway.

According to Kansas Department of Wildlife and Parks fisheries biologist Leonard Jirak, Coffey County Lake is "known for walleye, smallmouth bass, white bass, and crappie." In fact, Coffey County ranks as the number one smallmouth bass fishery in the entire state for density and also ranks high for lunker-sized fish, Jirak says. And in the past few years, it's excelled as a white bass haven.

Built in 1980, Coffey County Lake provides cooling water for Wolf Creek nuclear power plant. The lake water helps cool steam to turn it back into water, which is then reheated to once again make steam.

In 1996, the lake was opened to public fishing, and it's now dedicated exclusively for this purpose. Known for its fishing quality, Coffey County has even been featured on national television programs such as *Jimmy Houston's Outdoors* and *Bill Saiff's Rod and Reel*, according to the Coffey County Chamber of Commerce.

That's because the lake offers some excellent structure, as well as miles of riprap that provide top-notch fishing opportunities for many a species, especially white bass, says Terry Bivins, a Lebo local who fishes Coffey County regularly. There are times he's left these waters after a day of catching and releasing dozens upon dozens of whites, he says, noting it's one of his favorites.

The predator to prey balance also means prime fishing, Bivins says. Wolf Creek officials try to manage the number of shad to keep them from clogging its intake screens, which means Coffey County Lake offers one of the best predator to prey ratios in the country. One guide even says Coffey County's shad constitute only about 2 to 6 percent of the total fishery weight.

During cold weather, of course, the warm-water discharge area often is best, especially for bass and catfish. One thing to note: While the hot water outlet area can register around 60 degrees on the coldest of days, most of the lake averages the same temperatures as any Kansas lake.

Meanwhile, look for largemouth and crappie in the lake's brush and timber. Moreover, the miles of riprap make it a good smallmouth lake about any time of the year according to Bob Hammond, a local angler and an environmental supervisor at Wolf Creek. Rocky shorelines also are a prime spot for smallmouth, which are especially hot when the wind is blowing into them.

Bivins himself uses bass assassins. Others troll or cast with crankbaits or jerk baits.

According to Jirak, white bass are one of the most numerous fish caught in the hot water area in the winter, and wipers are also abundant at the same time. During the summer, find them in deeper holes and open water.

In the past two years walleye numbers have decreased at Coffey County Lake, but there are now some larger size walleye, Jirak says. Fishing for walleye, many use jigs tipped with minnows or nightcrawlers, and some even have success casting crankbaits along windblown rocky points. Find them in their spawning grounds along the riprap and rock-lined shores in March and April before they move to the flats in May.

Coffey's average depth is about 22 feet, and its deepest spot is more than 60 feet deep, according to the Kansas Department of Wildlife and Parks.

While good fishing abounds, lake officials, however, have a few rules: Boaters must always wear a life jacket; the lake is open 30 minutes after sunup to 30 minutes before sundown; no camping allowed; the lake is closed during winter under certain weather conditions. That includes on days with high winds.

For additional information, call the lake's gatehouse at 620-364-2475.

Shopping/Supplies

Lakeview Bait & Tackle, 203 N. Main St., New Strawn, 620-364-8354; **Pamida,** 300 Cross St., Burlington, 620-364-2924; **Sundance Bait & Tackle,** 8145 W. 325th St., Lebo, 620-256-6061.

Elm Creek Lake (Region 5)

SIZE: 106 acres

LOCATION: 1 mile east and 2 miles north of Hiattville in Bourbon County

DAILY CREEL LIMIT/MINIMUM LENGTH: Largemouth Bass: 2 fish, 21 inches • Smallmouth Bass: 2 fish, 18 inches • Channel Catfish: 2 fish, 15 inches • Crappie: 50 fish • Saugeye: 2 fish, 18 inches • Walleye: 2 fish, 18 inches

Elm Creek Lake has been producing wonderful fishing trips since it reopened to fishing in January of 2005. The fishery at this lake is good for walleye and smallmouth and largemouth bass, and it's exceptional for channel catfish. The lake supports good shoreline access for shore anglers and a boat ramp for boat anglers. Fish feeders operate many times a day to enhance and attract channel catfish to the areas of good shoreline access. Bourbon County operates a park around this lake that provides camping and shelter houses.

Linn County Lakes (Region 5)

Critzer Lake

SIZE: 220 acres

LOCATION: 8483 Jennison Rd., west of Mound City

DAILY CREEL LIMIT/MINIMUM LENGTH: Look for local regulations when the lake opens in May 2011.

This new lake contains about 180 acres of standing timber. Critzer has been stocked with walleye, largemouth and smallmouth bass, channel catfish, crappie, redear, and bluegill sunfish. Access to this lake is about completed and the lake is tentatively scheduled for opening around May of 2011.

Mound City Lake

SIZE: 148 acres

LOCATION: About 7 miles west of Mound City

DAILY CREEL LIMIT/MINIMUM LENGTH: Largemouth Bass: 5 fish, 13–18 inches slot limit • Channel Catfish: 2 fish, 15 inches • Crappie: 50 fish • Walleye: 2 fish, 18 inches

Mound City Lake is primarily a boat angling lake, but special management activities improve the shoreline angler's success. This lake produces great channel catfish, largemouth bass, bluegill, and crappie fishing. The recent introduction of blue cats should eventually ensure an additional trophy fish for anglers. Fall anglers will be mesmerized by the brilliant fall colors of the hardwood forest surrounding parts of the lake. This lake is a CFAP cooperator and doesn't require a special permit.

Pleasanton City Lake West

SIZE: 127 acres

LOCATION: West side of the City of Pleasanton

DAILY CREEL LIMIT/MINIMUM LENGTH: Largemouth Bass: 2 fish, 21 inches • Smallmouth Bass: 2 fish, 15 inches • Spotted Bass: 5 fish, 15 inches • Channel Catfish: 2 fish, 15 inches • Crappie: 50 fish

Pleasanton City Lake was renovated several years ago to improve access for shoreline anglers, particularly those looking for largemouth bass and channel catfish. There are 5 earthen piers, improved fish habitats, and fish feeders that release food throughout the day. Some anglers use a boat, but just as many anglers fish from the shoreline—and thanks to the design of this lake, both do very well. This CFAP lake has been ranked in the top ten for bass and channel catfish for many years.

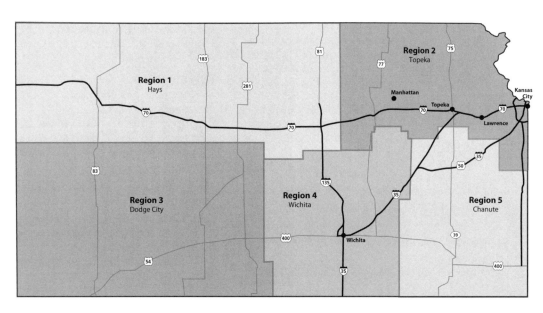

Small Lakes Listing

Fishing Impoundments and Stream Habitats waters
DAILY CREEL LIMIT/MINIMUM LENGTH: Largemouth Bass: 2 fish, 18 inches • Channel Catfish: 2 fish • Flathead Catfish: 5 fish • Crappie: 50 fish • Walleye: 5 fish, 15 inches • Wiper: 2 fish

Fishing Impoundments and Stream Habitats stream sites
DAILY CREEL LIMIT/MINIMUM LENGTH: Largemouth Bass: 5 fish, 15 inches • Channel Catfish: 10 fish • Flathead Catfish: 5 fish • Crappie: 50 fish • Walleye: 5 fish, 15 inches • Wiper: 2 fish

REGION 1
State Fishing Lakes and Other Waters
Jewell State Fishing Lake
SIZE: 57 acres.
LOCATION: About 6 miles southwest of Mankato. Surrounded by 108 acres of land. Some primitive camping.
DAILY CREEL LIMIT/MINIMUM LENGTH: Largemouth Bass: 5 fish, 21 inches • Channel Catfish: 5 fish, 15 inches • Flathead Catfish: 5 fish • Crappie: 50 fish • Saugeye: 5 fish, 15 inches • Walleye: 5 fish, 15 inches

Kanopolis State Park Pond
SIZE: 2 acres.
LOCATION: Near Kanopolis Reservoir in McPherson County.
DAILY CREEL LIMIT/MINIMUM LENGTH: Largemouth Bass: 2 fish, 18 inches • Channel Catfish: 2 fish • Crappie: 50 fish • Wiper: 2 fish

Logan State Fishing Lake
SIZE: 60 acres.
LOCATION: 2 miles north and 2 miles west of Russell Springs in Logan County. This lake is full three years out of ten—more dry than full. Camping is allowed in two areas.
DAILY CREEL LIMIT/MINIMUM LENGTH: Largemouth Bass: 5 fish, 15 inches • Channel Catfish: 5 fish

Ottawa State Fishing Lake
SIZE: 138 acres.
LOCATION: Northeast of Bennington. Includes camping as well as a cabin.
DAILY CREEL LIMIT/MINIMUM LENGTH: Largemouth Bass: 5 fish, 15 inches • Channel Catfish: 5 fish • Flathead Catfish: 5 fish • Crappie: 50 fish • Saugeye: 5 fish, 18 inches • Wiper: 2 fish, 18 inches
AQUATIC NUISANCE SPECIES ALERT: Eurasian Watermilfoil

Rooks State Fishing Lake
SIZE: 67 acres.
LOCATION: Southwest of Stockton. Periodically dry.
DAILY CREEL LIMIT/MINIMUM LENGTH: Largemouth Bass: 5 fish, 18 inches • Channel Catfish: 5 fish

Saline State Fishing Lake
SIZE: 38 acres.
LOCATION: Northwest of Salina. Periodically dry. The lake is closed October 1–March 31.
DAILY CREEL LIMIT/MINIMUM LENGTH: Channel Catfish: 5 fish

Sheridan State Fishing Lake
SIZE: 67 acres.
LOCATION: 12 miles east and 3/4 mile north from Hoxie. Primitive camping.
DAILY CREEL LIMIT/MINIMUM LENGTH: Largemouth Bass: 5 fish, 15 inches • Channel Catfish: 5 fish • Flathead Catfish: 5 fish • Crappie: 50 fish • Saugeye: 5 fish, 15 inches • Wiper: 2 fish
AQUATIC NUISANCE SPECIES ALERT: Eurasian Watermilfoil

Sherman State Fishing Lake
SIZE: Varies because it is periodically dry, but 210 acres when full.
LOCATION: About 12 miles south and west of Goodland in Sherman County. Periodically dry, this lake includes channel cats, crappie, and largemouth bass. No boat access.
DAILY CREEL LIMIT/MINIMUM LENGTH: Largemouth Bass: 5 fish, 15 inches • Channel Catfish: 5 fish • Crappie: 50 fish

St. Francis Sand Pits
SIZE: 1 acre (north pit), 2 acres (south pit).
LOCATION: 1 mile west and 2 miles south of St. Francis, adjacent to the Republican River in Cheyenne County. The north pit has a maximum depth of 12 feet. The south pit has a maximum depth of 8 feet. No boat access.
DAILY CREEL LIMIT/MINIMUM LENGTH: Largemouth Bass: 5 fish, 15 inches • Channel Catfish: 5 fish • Crappie: 50 fish

Community Lakes
Atwood Lake
SIZE: 55 acres.
LOCATION: Rawlins County. Periodically dry.
DAILY CREEL LIMIT/MINIMUM LENGTH: Largemouth Bass: 2 fish, 18 inches • Channel Catfish: 5 fish, 15 inches • Saugeye: 5 fish, 15 inches • Wiper: 2 fish

Belleville City Lake (Rocky Pond)
SIZE: 27 acres.
LOCATION: Near Belleville.
DAILY CREEL LIMIT/MINIMUM LENGTH: Largemouth Bass: 5 fish, 15 inches • Channel Catfish: 5 fish, 15 inches • Crappie: 50 fish • Walleye: 5 fish, 15 inches

Colby: Villa High Lake
SIZE: 1 acre.
LOCATION: Colby. City runoff fills lake. No boat access.
DAILY CREEL LIMIT/MINIMUM LENGTH: Largemouth Bass: 5 fish, 15 inches • Channel Catfish: 5 fish • Crappie: 50 fish

Ellis City Lake
SIZE: 100 acres.
LOCATION: Ellis, in Ellis County.
DAILY CREEL LIMIT/MINIMUM LENGTH: Largemouth Bass: 5 fish, 15 inches • Channel Catfish: 5 fish • Flathead Catfish: 5 fish • Crappie: 50 fish • Saugeye: 5 fish, 15 inches • Wiper: 2 fish

Graham County: Antelope Lake
SIZE: 80 acres.
LOCATION: 2 miles west and 1 mile north of Morland.
DAILY CREEL LIMIT/MINIMUM LENGTH: Largemouth Bass: 5 fish, 13–18 inches slot limit • Channel Catfish: 5 fish • Crappie: 50 fish • Saugeye: 2 fish, 18 inches • Wiper: 2 fish
AQUATIC NUISANCE SPECIES ALERT: Eurasian Watermilfoil

Jewell City Lake (Emerson Lake)
SIZE: 6 acres.
LOCATION: On the west edge of Jewell. No boat access.
DAILY CREEL LIMIT/MINIMUM LENGTH: Largemouth Bass: 5 fish, 18 inches • Channel Catfish: 5 fish, 15 inches

Logan City Lake
SIZE: Roughly 25 acres.
LOCATION: Near Logan.
DAILY CREEL LIMIT/MINIMUM LENGTH: Largemouth Bass: 5 fish, 18 inches • Channel Catfish: 5 fish, 15 inches • Flathead Catfish: 5 fish

Plainville Township Lake
SIZE: 200 acres.
LOCATION: 2 miles west of Plainville in Rooks County. Periodically dry.
DAILY CREEL LIMIT/MINIMUM LENGTH: Largemouth Bass: 5 fish, 15 inches • Channel Catfish: 5 fish • Flathead Catfish: 5 fish • Crappie: 50 fish • Wiper: 2 fish, 18 inches

Salina: Indian Rock Lake
SIZE: 2 acres.
LOCATION: Northeast Salina. No boat access.
DAILY CREEL LIMIT/MINIMUM LENGTH: Largemouth Bass: 5 fish, 18 inches • Channel Catfish: 5 fish • Flathead Catfish: 5 fish • Crappie: 50 fish

Salina: Lakewood Lake
SIZE: 6 acres.
LOCATION: North end of Salina.
DAILY CREEL LIMIT/MINIMUM LENGTH: Largemouth Bass: 5 fish, 18 inches • Channel Catfish: 5 fish • Flathead Catfish: 5 fish • Crappie: 50 fish • Saugeye: 5 fish, 15 inches • Walleye: 5 fish, 15 inches • Wiper: 2 fish • Trout: 5 fish

Sherman County: Smoky Gardens
SIZE: 11 acres.
LOCATION: Goodland. Periodically dry.
DAILY CREEL LIMIT/MINIMUM LENGTH: Largemouth Bass: 2 fish, 18 inches • Channel Catfish: 5 fish, 15 inches • Saugeye: 2 fish, 18 inches • Rainbow Trout: 5 fish

St. Francis: Keller Lake
SIZE: 3 acres.
LOCATION: Northwest edge of St. Francis in Cheyenne County. No boat access.
DAILY CREEL LIMIT/MINIMUM LENGTH: Largemouth Bass: 5 fish, 15 inches • Channel Catfish: 5 fish • Crappie: 50 fish

REGION 2
State fishing lakes and other waters
Atchison State Fishing Lake
SIZE: 66 acres.
LOCATION: 2 miles north and 2 miles west of Atchison. The area has extensive shallow water in the west end. The rest of the lake is characterized by flats on the northwest side and gradual to steep dropoffs to 15–30 feet over the rest of the area. Primitive camping is available, as well as a cabin.
DAILY CREEL LIMIT/MINIMUM LENGTH: Largemouth Bass: 2 fish, 18 inches • Smallmouth Bass: 2 fish, 18 inches • Channel Catfish: 2 fish, 15 inches • Flathead Catfish: 5 fish • Crappie: 20 fish • Walleye: 2 fish, 18 inches

Brown State Fishing Lake
SIZE: 62 acres.
LOCATION: 8 miles east and 1 mile north of Hiawatha. Characterized by gradual sloping shoreline with average depth of 8 feet. A 188-acre wildlife area adjoins the lake. Primitive camping allowed.
DAILY CREEL LIMIT/MINIMUM LENGTH: Largemouth Bass: 2 fish, 18 inches • Channel Catfish: 2 fish, 15 inches • Flathead Catfish: 5 fish • Crappie: 20 fish • Walleye: 2 fish, 18 inches

Browning Oxbow
SIZE: 100 acres.
LOCATION: Just north of Elwood.
DAILY CREEL LIMIT/MINIMUM LENGTH: Largemouth Bass: 5 fish, 15 inches • Blue Catfish: 10 fish • Channel Catfish: 10 fish • Crappie: 50 fish • Sauger: 5 fish, 15 inches • White Bass: 30 fish
AQUATIC NUISANCE SPECIES ALERT: Asian Carp (unlawful to possess alive)

Clinton State Park: Lake Henry
SIZE: 3 acres.
LOCATION: 0.3 mile south of Clinton State Park. No boat access.
DAILY CREEL LIMIT/MINIMUM LENGTH: Largemouth Bass: 5 fish, 18 inches • Channel Catfish: 2 fish • Crappie: 50 fish • Rainbow Trout: 5 fish

Clinton State Park: Picnic Area Pond
SIZE: 0.5 acres.
LOCATION: Clinton State Park. No boat access.
DAILY CREEL LIMIT/MINIMUM LENGTH: Largemouth Bass: 5 fish, 18 inches • Channel Catfish: 2 fish • Crappie: 50 fish

Douglas State Fishing Lake
SIZE: 180 acres.
LOCATION: Just northeast of Baldwin. Primitive camping.
DAILY CREEL LIMIT/MINIMUM LENGTH: Largemouth Bass: 2 fish, 18 inches • Channel Catfish: 5 fish, 15 inches • Flathead Catfish: 5 fish • Crappie: 50 fish • Saugeye: 2 fish, 15 inches

Geary State Fishing Lake
SIZE: 97 acres.
LOCATION: Southwest of Junction City. Primitive camping.
DAILY CREEL LIMIT/MINIMUM LENGTH: Largemouth Bass: 5 fish, 15 inches • Smallmouth Bass: 5 fish, 15 inches • Channel Catfish: 5 fish • Flathead Catfish: 5 fish • Crappie: 50 fish • Saugeye: 5 fish, 18 inches

Jeffrey Energy Center
Access is limited to these water bodies northwest of St. Mary's.
SIZE: Auxillary Make-up Lake 460 acres; Make-up Lake 125 acres.
LOCATION: 5 miles north and 3 miles west of St. Mary's
DAILY CREEL LIMIT/MINIMUM LENGTH: Largemouth Bass: 5 fish, 15 inches • Smallmouth Bass: 5 fish, 15 inches • Channel Catfish: 5 fish • Flathead Catfish: 5 fish • Crappie: 50 fish • Walleye: 5 fish, 18 inches • Wiper: 2 fish

Leavenworth State Fishing Lake
SIZE: 160 acres.
LOCATION: Near Tonganoxie. Surrounded by 340 acres of wildlife area. Primitive camping allowed.
DAILY CREEL LIMIT/MINIMUM LENGTH: Largemouth Bass: 5 fish, 13–18 inches slot limit • Smallmouth Bass: 2 fish, 18 inches • Channel Catfish: 2 fish, 15 inches • Flathead Catfish: 5 fish • Crappie: 50 fish • Sauger: 2 fish, 15 inches • Saugeye: 2 fish, 15 inches • Walleye: 2 fish, 15 inches • Wiper: 5 fish, 18 inches

Louisburg: Middle Creek

SIZE: 280 acres.

LOCATION: 7 miles south of Louisburg, in Miami County. Surrounded by 220 acres of upland hunting habitat. Primitive camping is available.

DAILY CREEL LIMIT/MINIMUM LENGTH: Largemouth Bass: 2 fish, 18 inches • Channel Catfish: 5 fish, 15 inches • Flathead Catfish: 5 fish • Crappie: 50 fish • Saugeye: 2 fish, 18 inches • Wiper: 2 fish, 18 inches

Miami State Fishing Lake

SIZE: 101 acres.

LOCATION: Southeast of Osawatomie. Bounded by about 150 acres of timbered hillsides and the Marais des Cygnes River. Some primitive camping allowed.

DAILY CREEL LIMIT/MINIMUM LENGTH: Largemouth Bass: 2 fish, 18 inches • Channel Catfish: 2 fish, 15 inches • Flathead Catfish: 5 fish • Crappie: 50 fish

Milford Hatchery Water Supply Pond

SIZE: Roughly 100 acres.

LOCATION: Below Milford Dam.

DAILY CREEL LIMIT/MINIMUM LENGTH: Largemouth Bass: 2 fish, 15 inches • Smallmouth Bass: 2 fish, 15 inches • Spotted Bass: 2 fish, 15 inches • Channel Catfish: 2 fish • Crappie: 10 fish • Sauger: 2 fish, 15 inches • Saugeye: 2 fish, 15 inches • Walleye: 2 fish, 15 inches • Wiper: 2 fish

Milford State Park Pond

SIZE: 2 acres.

LOCATION: Milford State Park. No boat access.

DAILY CREEL LIMIT/MINIMUM LENGTH: Channel Catfish: 5 fish

Nebo State Fishing Lake

SIZE: 38 acres.

LOCATION: Near Holton in Jackson County. Characterized by gradual sloping shoreline, with a shallow west end. There are 25 acres of land adjoining the lake. Primitive camping permitted.

DAILY CREEL LIMIT/MINIMUM LENGTH: Largemouth Bass: 2 fish, 18 inches • Channel Catfish: 2 fish, 15 inches • Flathead Catfish: 5 fish • Crappie: 50 fish

Nemaha Wildlife Area

SIZE: 18 acres.

LOCATION: Near Seneca.

DAILY CREEL LIMIT/MINIMUM LENGTH: Largemouth Bass: 5 fish, 15 inches • Channel Catfish: 10 fish • Crappie: 50 fish

Pottawatomie 1

SIZE: 24 acres.

LOCATION: 5 miles north of Westmoreland. Primitive camping available.

DAILY CREEL LIMIT/MINIMUM LENGTH: Largemouth Bass: 5 fish, 15 inches • Channel Catfish: 5 fish, 15 inches • Flathead Catfish: 5 fish • Crappie: 50 fish

Pottawatomie 2

SIZE: 75 acres.

LOCATION: Just a few miles northeast of Manhattan. Primitive camping available.

DAILY CREEL LIMIT/MINIMUM LENGTH: Largemouth Bass: 5 fish, 15 inches • Smallmouth Bass: 5 fish, 15 inches • Channel Catfish: 5 fish • Flathead Catfish: 5 fish • Crappie: 50 fish • Walleye: 5 fish, 15 inches

Shawnee State Fishing Lake

SIZE: 135 acres.

LOCATION: About 7 miles northeast of Silver Lake. The 400 acres of the Shawnee Wildlife Area is used for hunting in certain season. Primitive camping allowed.

DAILY CREEL LIMIT/MINIMUM LENGTH: Largemouth Bass: 5 fish, 15 inches • Channel Catfish: 5 fish • Flathead Catfish: 5 fish • Crappie: 50 fish • Walleye: 5 fish, 15 inches

Tuttle Creek: Willow Lake

SIZE: 10 acres.

LOCATION: Tuttle Creek State Park River Pond Area, below the Tuttle Creek Dam.

DAILY CREEL LIMIT/MINIMUM LENGTH: Largemouth Bass: 5 fish, 18 inches • Channel Catfish: 10 fish • Crappie: 50 fish • Rainbow Trout: 5 fish

Washington State Fishing Lake

SIZE: 65 acres.

LOCATION: 7 miles north and 3 miles east of Washington. Surrounded by 352 acres of public hunting land.

DAILY CREEL LIMIT/MINIMUM LENGTH: Largemouth Bass: 5 fish, 15 inches • Channel Catfish: 5 fish • Flathead Catfish: 5 fish • Crappie: 50 fish • Saugeye: 5 fish, 18 inches

AQUATIC NUISANCE SPECIES ALERT: Eurasian Watermilfoil

Community Lakes

Alma City Lake

SIZE: 80 acres.

LOCATION: Southeast of Alma in Wabaunsee County. Boat access.

DAILY CREEL LIMIT/MINIMUM LENGTH: Largemouth Bass: 5 fish, 18 inches • Smallmouth Bass: 5 fish, 18 inches • Channel Catfish: 10 fish • Flathead Catfish: 5 fish • Crappie: 50 fish • Walleye: 5 fish, 18 inches

Atchison City Lakes 1–4, 6–9, 24

SIZE: 51 acres.

LOCATION: Just southwest of Atchison in Atchison County. No boat access.

DAILY CREEL LIMIT/MINIMUM LENGTH: Largemouth Bass: 5 fish, 15 inches • Channel Catfish: 5 fish, 15 inches • Flathead Catfish: 5 fish • Crappie: 50 fish

Atchison County Lake

SIZE: About 60 acres.

LOCATION: 5 miles west of Huron. No boat access.

DAILY CREEL LIMIT/MINIMUM LENGTH: Largemouth Bass: 5 fish, 15 inches • Channel Catfish: 5 fish, 15 inches • Crappie: 50 fish

Atchison Warnock (City Lake 23)

SIZE: Roughly 39 acres.

LOCATION: Near Atchison off of US 59.

DAILY CREEL LIMIT/MINIMUM LENGTH: Largemouth Bass: 5 fish, 15 inches • Channel Catfish: 5 fish, 15 inches • Flathead Catfish: 5 fish • Crappie: 50 fish

Baldwin: Spring Creek Lake

SIZE: 7 acres.

LOCATION: Near Baldwin in Douglas County. No boat access.

DAILY CREEL LIMIT/MINIMUM LENGTH: Largemouth Bass: 5 fish, 15 inches • Channel Catfish: 10 fish • Flathead Catfish: 5 fish • Crappie: 50 fish

Bonner Springs: North Park Lake

SIZE: 3 acres.

LOCATION: South of 134th St. and Kansas Ave. in Wyandotte County. No boat access.

DAILY CREEL LIMIT/MINIMUM LENGTH: Largemouth Bass: 5 fish, 15 inches • Channel Catfish: 2 fish • Crappie: 50 fish • Saugeye: 5 fish, 15 inches • Wiper: 2 fish

Centralia City Lake

SIZE: 400 acres.

LOCATION: 2 miles south and 1 mile west of Centralia in Nemaha County. Boat access.

DAILY CREEL LIMIT/MINIMUM LENGTH: Largemouth Bass: 5 fish, 18 inches • Channel Catfish: 5 fish, 15 inches • Flathead Catfish: 5 fish • Crappie: 50 fish • Saugeye: 5 fish, 18 inches • Walleye: 5 fish, 18 inches

Douglas County: Lonestar Lake

SIZE: 195 acres.

LOCATION: 4 miles southwest of Lawrence. Boat access.

DAILY CREEL LIMIT/MINIMUM LENGTH: Largemouth Bass: 2 fish, 18 inches • Smallmouth Bass: 2 fish, 18 inches • Channel Catfish: 10 fish, 15 inches. Flathead Catfish: 5 fish • Crappie: 50 fish • Wiper: 5 fish, 18 inches

Edgerton: Bridgewater Lake

SIZE: Nearly 3 acres.

LOCATION: Near Edgerton in Johnson County.

DAILY CREEL LIMIT/MINIMUM LENGTH: Largemouth Bass: 5 fish, 15 inches • Channel Catfish: 10 fish, 15 inches

Edgerton City Lake

SIZE: Roughly 5 acres.

LOCATION: Edgerton in Johnson County. No boat access.

DAILY CREEL LIMIT/MINIMUM LENGTH: Largemouth Bass: 5 fish, 15 inches • Channel Catfish: 10 fish • Flathead Catfish: 5 fish • Crappie: 50 fish

Eskridge: Lake Wabaunsee

SIZE: 214 acres.

LOCATION: 4 miles west of Eskridge. Boat access. Requires local permit to fish.

DAILY CREEL LIMIT/MINIMUM LENGTH: Largemouth Bass: 5 fish, 18 inches • Smallmouth Bass: 5 fish, 18 inches • Channel Catfish: 10 fish • Flathead Catfish: 5 fish • Crappie: 50 fish • Saugeye: 5 fish, 18 inches • Walleye: 5 fish, 18 inches

Gardner City Lake

SIZE: 100 acres.

LOCATION: 1 mile north of Gardner in Johnson County. Boat access.

DAILY CREEL LIMIT/MINIMUM LENGTH: Largemouth Bass: 5 fish, 15 inches • Channel Catfish: 2 fish, 15 inches • Flathead Catfish: 5 fish • Crappie: 50 fish • Saugeye: 2 fish, 18 inches

Harveyville City Lake

SIZE: 25 acres.

LOCATION: 1 mile north and 1 mile west of Harveyville in Wabaunsee County. No boat access.

DAILY CREEL LIMIT/MINIMUM LENGTH: Largemouth Bass: 5 fish, 18 inches • Channel Catfish: 10 fish • Crappie: 50 fish • Saugeye: 5 fish, 18 inches • Walleye: 5 fish, 18 inches

Herington: Father Padilla Pond

SIZE: 2 acres.

LOCATION: N. Broadway St. and E. Vine St. in Herington in Dickinson County. No boat access.

DAILY CREEL LIMIT/MINIMUM LENGTH: Largemouth Bass: 5 fish, 18 inches • Channel Catfish: 5 fish

Herington City Lake: New

SIZE: 555 acres.

LOCATION: About 3 miles west of Herington in Dickinson County. Boat access.

DAILY CREEL LIMIT/MINIMUM LENGTH: Largemouth Bass: 5 fish, 18 inches • Channel Catfish: 10 fish • Flathead Catfish: 5 fish • Crappie: 50 fish • Walleye: 5 fish, 18 inches • Wiper: 2 fish

Herington City Lake: Old

SIZE: 367 acres.

LOCATION: Just southwest of Herington in Dickinson County. Boat access.

DAILY CREEL LIMIT/MINIMUM LENGTH: Largemouth Bass: 5 fish, 18 inches • Channel Catfish: 10 fish • Flathead Catfish: 5 fish • Crappie: 50 fish

Hiawatha City Lake

SIZE: 7 acres.

LOCATION: 1 mile south of Hiawatha in Brown County. No boat access.

DAILY CREEL LIMIT/MINIMUM LENGTH: Largemouth Bass: 2 fish, 18 inches • Channel Catfish: 5 fish, 15 inches

Holton: Elkhorn Lake

SIZE: 4 acres.

LOCATION: Holton, in Jackson County. No boat access.

DAILY CREEL LIMIT/MINIMUM LENGTH: Largemouth Bass: 2 fish, 18 inches • Channel Catfish: 5 fish, 15 inches • Crappie: 10 fish

Holton City (Prairie) Lake

SIZE: 78 acres.

LOCATION: Just northwest of Holton in Jackson County. Boat access.

DAILY CREEL LIMIT/MINIMUM LENGTH: Largemouth Bass: 2 fish, 18 inches • Channel Catfish: 5 fish, 15 inches • Crappie: 50 fish

Horton: Little Lake

SIZE: 10 acres.

LOCATION: East of Horton on K-20. Boat access.

DAILY CREEL LIMIT/MINIMUM LENGTH: Largemouth Bass: 2 fish, 18 inches • Channel Catfish: 5 fish, 15 inches • Flathead Catfish: 5 fish • Crappie: 50 fish • Wiper: 2 fish, 18 inches

Horton: Mission Lake

SIZE: 125 acres.

LOCATION: Horton, in Brown County. Boat access.

DAILY CREEL LIMIT/MINIMUM LENGTH: Largemouth Bass: 2 fish, 15 inches • Channel Catfish: 5 fish, 15 inches • Flathead Catfish: 5 fish • Crappie: 50 fish

Jackson County: Banner Creek Reservoir

SIZE: 535 acres.

LOCATION: 1 mile west of Holton on K-16. Boat access.

DAILY CREEL LIMIT/MINIMUM LENGTH: Largemouth Bass: 2 fish, 18 inches • Smallmouth Bass: 2 fish, 18 inches • Channel Catfish: 5 fish, 15 inches • Flathead Catfish: 5 fish • Crappie: 20 fish • Sauger: 2 fish, 18 inches • Walleye: 2 fish, 18 inches

Johnson County: Antioch North & South Ponds

SIZE: 1 acre.

LOCATION: 6501 Antioch Rd., Shawnee Mission. No boat access. Requires a local permit to fish.

DAILY CREEL LIMIT/MINIMUM LENGTH: Largemouth Bass: 2 fish, 18 inches • Channel Catfish: 2 fish, 15 inches • Crappie: 50 fish

Johnson County: Heritage Park Lake

SIZE: 20 acres.

LOCATION: 159th St. and Pflumm Rd., Olathe. No boat access. Requires a local permit to fish.

DAILY CREEL LIMIT/MINIMUM LENGTH: Largemouth Bass: 5 fish, 15 inches • Channel Catfish: 10 fish • Crappie: 50 fish

Johnson County: Kill Creek North Pond

SIZE: 1 acre.

LOCATION: 2.5 miles south and 0.5 mile east of K-10 and Kill Creek Rd. No boat access. Requires a local permit to fish.

DAILY CREEL LIMIT/MINIMUM LENGTH: Largemouth Bass: 5 fish, 18 inches • Channel Catfish: 10 fish

Johnson County: Kill Creek Park Lake

SIZE: 28 acres.

LOCATION: 2.5 miles south and 0.5 mile east of K-10 and Kill Creek Road. Boat access. Requires a local permit to fish.

DAILY CREEL LIMIT/MINIMUM LENGTH: Largemouth Bass: 2 fish, 18 inches • Smallmouth Bass: 2 fish, 18 inches • Channel Catfish: 2 fish, 15 inches • Crappie: 50 fish • Walleye: 2 fish, 18 inches • Wiper: 2 fish

Johnson County: Kill Creek South Pond

SIZE: 1 acre.

LOCATION: Near other Kill Creek locations. No boat access. Requires a local permit to fish.

DAILY CREEL LIMIT/MINIMUM LENGTH: Largemouth Bass: 5 fish, 18 inches • Channel Catfish: 10 fish

Johnson County: Shawnee Mission Park Lake

SIZE: 121 acres.

LOCATION: W. 79th St. and Renner Rd., Shawnee Mission. Boat access. Requires a local permit to fish.

DAILY CREEL LIMIT/MINIMUM LENGTH: Largemouth Bass: 2 fish, 18 inches • Channel Catfish: 2 fish, 15 inches • Crappie: 50 fish • Wiper: 2 fish

Johnson County: Shawnee Mission Pond

SIZE: 1 acre.

LOCATION: W. 79th St. and Renner Rd., Shawnee Mission. No boat access. Requires a local permit to fish.

DAILY CREEL LIMIT/MINIMUM LENGTH: Largemouth Bass: 2 fish, 18 inches • Channel Catfish: 2 fish, 15 inches

Johnson County: Stoll Park

SIZE: 2 acres.

LOCATION: 12500 W. 119th St., Overland Park. No boat access. Requires a local permit to fish.

DAILY CREEL LIMIT/MINIMUM LENGTH: Largemouth Bass: 5 fish, 15 inches • Channel Catfish: 10 fish

Johnson County: Sunflower Park

SIZE: 2 acres.

LOCATION: 4 miles west of DeSoto on Lexington Ave. No boat access. Requires a local permit to fish.

DAILY CREEL LIMIT/MINIMUM LENGTH: Largemouth Bass: 5 fish, 15 inches • Channel Catfish: 10 fish

Junction City: Bluffs

SIZE: 5 acres.

LOCATION: Caroline Ave. and Goldenbelt Blvd.

DAILY CREEL LIMIT/MINIMUM LENGTH: Largemouth Bass: 5 fish, 15 inches • Channel Catfish: 10 fish

Junction City: Homer's Pond (Rim Rock Lake)

SIZE: 5 acres.

LOCATION: 100 block of S. Eisenhower Dr. No boat access.

DAILY CREEL LIMIT/MINIMUM LENGTH: Largemouth Bass: 5 fish, 15 inches • Channel Catfish: 5 fish

Junction City: Riverwalk

SIZE: 7 acres.

LOCATION: Just off of I-70 at exit 298.

DAILY CREEL LIMIT/MINIMUM LENGTH: Largemouth Bass: 5 fish, 15 inches • Channel Catfish: 10 fish

Junction City: Wetland Park

SIZE: 2 acres.

LOCATION: Just off of I-70 at exit 298. No boat access.

DAILY CREEL LIMIT/MINIMUM LENGTH: Largemouth Bass: 5 fish, 15 inches • Channel Catfish: 5 fish

Lansing City Lake

SIZE: 1 acre.

LOCATION: East edge of Lansing in Leavenworth County.

DAILY CREEL LIMIT/MINIMUM LENGTH: Largemouth Bass: 2 fish, 15 inches • Channel Catfish: 2 fish • Crappie: 50 fish

Lawrence: Mary's Lake

SIZE: 6 acres.

LOCATION: 0.5 mile east of Haskell Ave. and W. 31st St. No boat access.

DAILY CREEL LIMIT/MINIMUM LENGTH: Largemouth Bass: 5 fish, 15 inches • Channel Catfish: 2 fish • Flathead Catfish: 5 fish • Crappie: 50 fish • Saugeye: 5 fish, 15 inches • Wiper: 2 fish

Lawrence: Pat Dawson Billings North & South

SIZE: 10 acres.

LOCATION: W. 27th St. and Crossgate Dr. No boat access.

DAILY CREEL LIMIT/MINIMUM LENGTH: Largemouth Bass: 5 fish, 15 inches • Channel Catfish: 2 fish • Crappie: 50 fish • Walleye: 5 fish, 15 inches

Leawood: Ironwoods Park Pond

SIZE: Nearly 2 acres.

LOCATION: Ironwood Ct. and Mission Rd., in Johnson County. No boat access.

DAILY CREEL LIMIT/MINIMUM LENGTH: Largemouth Bass: 5 fish, 15 inches • Channel Catfish: 10 fish

Leawood: Tomahawk Parkway Middle Pond

SIZE: 1 acre.

LOCATION: W. 119th St. and Tomahawk Creek Parkway, in Johnson County. No boat access.

DAILY CREEL LIMIT/MINIMUM LENGTH: Largemouth Bass: 5 fish, 15 inches • Channel Catfish: 2 fish

Leawood: Tomahawk Parkway North Pond

SIZE: 3 acres.

LOCATION: W. 119th St. and Tomahawk Creek Parkway, in Johnson County. No boat access.

DAILY CREEL LIMIT/MINIMUM LENGTH: Largemouth Bass: 5 fish, 15 inches • Channel Catfish: 2 fish

Leawood: Tomahawk Parkway South Pond

SIZE: 1 acre.

LOCATION: W. 119th St. and Tomahawk Creek Parkway, in Johnson County. No boat access.

DAILY CREEL LIMIT/MINIMUM LENGTH: Largemouth Bass: 5 fish, 15 inches • Channel Catfish: 2 fish • Wiper: 2 fish

Lenexa: Lake Lenexa

SIZE: 30 acres.

LOCATION: 1 mile south of W. 83rd St. on Monticello Rd. in Johnson County. Boat access.

DAILY CREEL LIMIT/MINIMUM LENGTH: Largemouth Bass: 5 fish, 15 inches • Channel Catfish: 10 fish

Lenexa: Mize Boulevard Lake

SIZE: 5 acres.

LOCATION: North of K-10 on Cedar Creek Parkway in Johnson County. No boat access.

DAILY CREEL LIMIT/MINIMUM LENGTH: Largemouth Bass: 5 fish, 15 inches • Channel Catfish: 2 fish

Lenexa: Resurrection Pond

SIZE: About 2 acres.

LOCATION: Within Resurrection Catholic Cemetery at W. 83rd St. and Quivira Rd. in Johnson County. No boat access.

DAILY CREEL LIMIT/MINIMUM LENGTH: Largemouth Bass: 5 fish, 15 inches • Channel Catfish: 10 fish

Lenexa: Rose's Pond

SIZE: About 2 acres.

LOCATION: W. 87th St. and Lackman Rd. No boat access.

DAILY CREEL LIMIT/MINIMUM LENGTH: Largemouth Bass: 5 fish, 15 inches • Channel Catfish: 2 fish • Saugeye: 5 fish, 15 inches • Wiper: 2 fish

Louisburg: Lewis Young Park Lake

SIZE: 2 acres.

LOCATION: W. 263rd St. and US 69. No boat access.

DAILY CREEL LIMIT/MINIMUM LENGTH: Largemouth Bass: 5 fish, 15 inches • Channel Catfish: 10 fish • Crappie: 50 fish

Louisburg City Lake

SIZE: 23 acres.

LOCATION: Southeast edge of Louisburg on Metcalf Rd., in Miami County. No boat access.

DAILY CREEL LIMIT/MINIMUM LENGTH: Largemouth Bass: 5 fish, 15 inches • Channel Catfish: 10 fish • Crappie: 50 fish • Saugeye: 5 fish, 15 inches • Wiper: 2 fish

Manhattan: Anneberg Park Pond

SIZE: 6 acres.

LOCATION: Anderson Ave. No boat access.

DAILY CREEL LIMIT/MINIMUM LENGTH: Largemouth Bass: 5 fish, 15 inches Channel Catfish: 10 fish • Crappie: 50 fish •

Marysville Country Club Lake

SIZE: 10 acres.

LOCATION: East end of Marysville on US 36, in Marshall County. Boat access.

DAILY CREEL LIMIT/MINIMUM LENGTH: Largemouth Bass: 5 fish, 15 inches • Channel Catfish: 10 fish • Crappie: 50 fish

Ogden City Lake

SIZE: 24 acres.

LOCATION: Ogden, in Riley County. Boat access.

DAILY CREEL LIMIT/MINIMUM LENGTH: Largemouth Bass: 5 fish, 15 inches • Channel Catfish: 5 fish • Flathead Catfish: 5 fish • Crappie: 50 fish

Olathe: Black Bob Park Pond

SIZE: 1 acre.

OCATION: 14500 W. 151 St. No boat access.

DAILY CREEL LIMIT/MINIMUM LENGTH: Largemouth Bass: 5 fish, 15 inches • Channel Catfish: 2 fish • Wiper: 2 fish

AQUATIC NUISANCE SPECIES ALERT: Hydrilla

Olathe: Cedar Lake

SIZE: 56 acres.

LOCATION: S. Lone Elm Rd., 0.5 mile south of W. 151st St. No boat access.

DAILY CREEL LIMIT/MINIMUM LENGTH: Largemouth Bass: 5 fish, 18 inches • Channel Catfish: 2 fish • Flathead Catfish: 5 fish • Crappie: 50 fish • Saugeye: 5 fish, 15 inches • Wiper: 2 fish, 18 inches

Olathe: East High School Pond

SIZE: 1 acre.

LOCATION: W. 127th St. and Pflumm Rd. No boat access.

DAILY CREEL LIMIT/MINIMUM LENGTH: Largemouth Bass: 5 fish, 15 inches • Channel Catfish: 10 fish

Olathe: Frisco Lake

SIZE: 12 acres.

LOCATION: E. Dennis Ave. and S. Sunset Dr. No boat access.

DAILY CREEL LIMIT/MINIMUM LENGTH: Largemouth Bass: 5 fish, 15 inches • Channel Catfish: 2 fish • Crappie: 50 fish

Olathe: Heatherstone Park Pond

SIZE: 1 acre.

LOCATION: 12310 Pflumm Rd. No boat access.

DAILY CREEL LIMIT/MINIMUM LENGTH: Largemouth Bass: 5 fish, 15 inches • Channel Catfish: 10 fish

Olathe: Lake Olathe

SIZE: 172 acres.

LOCATION: 2 miles west of Olathe on W. Dennis Ave. Boat access.

DAILY CREEL LIMIT/MINIMUM LENGTH: Largemouth Bass: 5 fish, 18 inches • Channel Catfish: 10 fish • Flathead Catfish: 5 fish • Crappie: 50 fish • Saugeye: 5 fish, 15 inches • Wiper: 2 fish, 18 inches

Olathe: Mahaffie Farmstead Pond

SIZE: 1 acre.

LOCATION: S. Ridgeview Rd. and E. Kansas City Rd. No boat access.

DAILY CREEL LIMIT/MINIMUM LENGTH: Largemouth Bass: 5 fish, 15 inches • Channel Catfish: 2 fish • Crappie: 50 fish

Olathe: North Waterworks Park Lake

SIZE: 1 acre.

LOCATION: E. Sheridan St. and S. Curtis St.

DAILY CREEL LIMIT/MINIMUM LENGTH: Largemouth Bass: 5 fish, 15 inches • Channel Catfish: 2 fish • Wiper: 2 fish

Olathe: Oregon Trail Pond

SIZE: 2 acres.

LOCATION: S. Robinson St. and Old US 56.

DAILY CREEL LIMIT/MINIMUM LENGTH: Largemouth Bass: 5 fish, 15 inches • Channel Catfish: 10 fish, 15-inch length limit

Olathe: Prairie Center Park Pond

SIZE: 1 acre.

LOCATION: West of ball fields in Prairie Center Park. No boat access.

DAILY CREEL LIMIT/MINIMUM LENGTH: Largemouth Bass: 5 fish, 15 inches • Channel Catfish: 2 fish • Crappie: 50 fish

Olathe: Prairie Center Pond

SIZE: 5 acres.

LOCATION: W. 135th St. and S. Cedar Niles Rd. No boat access.

DAILY CREEL LIMIT/MINIMUM LENGTH: Largemouth Bass: 5 fish, 15 inches • Channel Catfish: 2 fish • Crappie: 50 fish • Saugeye: 5 fish, 15 inches • Wiper: 2 fish

Olathe: Stagecoach Park Pond

SIZE: 5 acres.

LOCATION: E. Kansas City Rd. and S. Ridgeview Rd.

DAILY CREEL LIMIT/MINIMUM LENGTH: Largemouth Bass: 5 fish, 15 inches • Channel Catfish: 10 fish, 15 inches

Olathe: Waterworks Lake

SIZE: 6 acres.

LOCATION: E. Sheridan St. and S. Curtis St. No boat access

DAILY CREEL LIMIT/MINIMUM LENGTH: Largemouth Bass: 5 fish, 15 inches • Channel Catfish: 2 fish • Crappie: 50 fish • Wiper: 2 fish

Osawatomie: Beaver Lake

SIZE: 6 acres.

LOCATION: 1.5 miles north and 2.3 miles west of Osawatomie. No boat access.

DAILY CREEL LIMIT/MINIMUM LENGTH: Largemouth Bass: 5 fish, 13–18 inches slot limit • Channel Catfish: 5 fish, 15 inches • Crappie: 50 fish

Osawatomie City Lake

SIZE: 21 acres.

LOCATION: 0.5 mile north, 2 miles west of Osawatomie in Miami County. Boat access.

DAILY CREEL LIMIT/MINIMUM LENGTH: Largemouth Bass: 5 fish, 13–18 inches slot limit • Channel Catfish: 5 fish, 15 inches • Flathead Catfish: 5 fish • Crappie: 50 fish

Overland Park: Amesbury Lake

SIZE: Roughly 4 acres.

LOCATION: North of W. 143rd St. and Westgate St. No boat access.

DAILY CREEL LIMIT/MINIMUM LENGTH: Largemouth Bass: 5 fish, 15 inches • Channel Catfish: 2 fish, 15 inches

Overland Park: Kingston Lake

SIZE: 8 acres.

LOCATION: W. 151st St. and US 69. No boat access.

DAILY CREEL LIMIT/MINIMUM LENGTH: Largemouth Bass: 2 fish, 15 inches • Channel Catfish: 2 fish

Overland Park: Regency Lake

SIZE: 3 acres.

LOCATION: North of W. 151st St. and Horton St. No boat access.

DAILY CREEL LIMIT/MINIMUM LENGTH: Largemouth Bass: 2 fish, 15 inches • Channel Catfish: 2 fish

Overland Park: South Lake

SIZE: 5 acres.

LOCATION: West of Metcalf Ave. on W. 83rd St. and south on Valley View Dr. No boat access.

DAILY CREEL LIMIT/MINIMUM LENGTH: Largemouth Bass: 2 fish, 15 inches • Channel Catfish: 2 fish • Crappie: 50 fish

Overland Park: Summercrest Lake

SIZE: About 1 acre.

LOCATION: W. 112th St. and Riley St. No boat access.

DAILY CREEL LIMIT/MINIMUM LENGTH: Largemouth Bass: 5 fish, 15 inches • Channel Catfish: 2 fish, 15 inches

Overland Park: Wilderness Lake

SIZE: 3 acres.

LOCATION: East of W. 161st St. and Rosewood St. No boat access.

DAILY CREEL LIMIT/MINIMUM LENGTH: Largemouth Bass: 5 fish, 15 inches • Channel Catfish: 2 fish, 15 inches

Paola: Lake Miola

SIZE: 220 acres.

LOCATION: Just north and east of Paola in Miami County. Boat access.

DAILY CREEL LIMIT/MINIMUM LENGTH: Largemouth Bass: 2 fish, 18 inches • Channel Catfish: 10 fish • Flathead Catfish: 5 fish • Crappie: 50 fish • Saugeye: 2 fish, 15 inches • Walleye: 2 fish, 15 inches • Wiper: 5 fish

Pottawatomie County Cross Creek Lake

SIZE: 49 acres.

LOCATION: 6 miles south and 1.5 miles west of Havensville. Boat access.

DAILY CREEL LIMIT/MINIMUM LENGTH: Largemouth Bass: 5 fish, 13–18 inches slot limit • Channel Catfish: 5 fish • Flathead Catfish: 5 fish • Crappie: 50 fish

Sabetha: Pony Creek Lake

SIZE: 171 acres.

LOCATION: 2 miles north of Sabetha on US 75 in Nemaha County. Boat access.

DAILY CREEL LIMIT/MINIMUM LENGTH: Largemouth Bass: 2 fish, 18 inches • Smallmouth Bass: 2 fish, 18 inches • Channel Catfish: 5 fish, 15 inches • Flathead Catfish: 5 fish • Crappie: 20 fish • Walleye: 2 fish, 18 inches • Wiper: 2 fish, 18 inches

Sabetha City Lake

SIZE: About 100 acres.

LOCATION: 6 miles west of Sabetha in Nemaha County. No boat access.

DAILY CREEL LIMIT/MINIMUM LENGTH: Largemouth Bass: 2 fish, 18 inches • Channel Catfish: 5 fish, 15 inches • Flathead Catfish: 5 fish • Walleye: 2 fish, 18 inches

Shawnee: Monticello Springs Lake

SIZE: 1.5 acres.

LOCATION: Monticello Springs Park, 1 mile north of Monticello Rd. and W. 83rd St., Shawnee.

DAILY CREEL LIMIT/MINIMUM LENGTH: Largemouth Bass: 5 fish, 15 inches • Channel Catfish: 10 fish

Shawnee County: Karl's Lake

SIZE: 1 acre.

LOCATION: 0.5 mile east of Cedar Crest parking lot, Topeka.

DAILY CREEL LIMIT/MINIMUM LENGTH: Largemouth Bass: 5 fish, 15 inches • Channel Catfish: 2 fish • Crappie: 50 fish

Shawnee County: Lake Shawnee

SIZE: 416 acres.

LOCATION: 3139 SE. 29th St. in Topeka. Boat access.

DAILY CREEL LIMIT/MINIMUM LENGTH: Largemouth Bass: 5 fish, 13–18 inches slot limit • Smallmouth Bass: 2 fish, 18 inches • Channel Catfish: 10 fish • Flathead Catfish: 5 fish • Crappie: 50 fish • Rainbow Trout: 5 fish • Walleye: 2 fish, 15 inches • Wiper: 5 fish, 18 inches

Shawnee County: Shawnee Jr.

SIZE: 2 acres.

LOCATION: West of Lake Shawnee (above). Boat access.

DAILY CREEL LIMIT/MINIMUM LENGTH: Largemouth Bass: 5 fish, 15 inches • Channel Catfish: 2 fish • Flathead Catfish: 5 fish • Crappie: 50 fish

Spring Hill City Lake

SIZE: 38 acres.

LOCATION: US 169 and S. Lone Elm Rd., Spring Hill. No boat access.

DAILY CREEL LIMIT/MINIMUM LENGTH: Largemouth Bass: 5 fish, 15 inches • Channel Catfish: 10 fish • Crappie: 50 fish

Spring Hill: Woodland Ridge Pond

SIZE: 2.5 acres.

LOCATION: Just southeast of W. 207th St. and Barker Rd. No boat access.

DAILY CREEL LIMIT/MINIMUM LENGTH: Largemouth Bass: 5 fish, 15 inches • Channel Catfish: 2 fish, 15 inches • Crappie: 50 fish

Topeka: Cedar Crest Pond

SIZE: 3 acres.

LOCATION: I-70 and SW. Fairlawn Rd. No boat access.

DAILY CREEL LIMIT/MINIMUM LENGTH: Largemouth Bass: 5 fish, 15 inches • Channel Catfish: 2 fish • Flathead Catfish: 5 fish • Crappie: 50 fish

Topeka: Central Park Lake

SIZE: 3 acres.

LOCATION: 1534 SW. Clay St. No boat access.

DAILY CREEL LIMIT/MINIMUM LENGTH: Largemouth Bass: 5 fish, 15 inches • Channel Catfish: 2 fish • Crappie: 50 fish

Topeka: Clarion Lake

SIZE: 4 acres.

LOCATION: SW. 37th St. and SW. Fairlawn Rd. No boat access.

DAILY CREEL LIMIT/MINIMUM LENGTH: Largemouth Bass: 5 fish, 15 inches • Channel Catfish: 2 fish • Crappie: 50 fish

Topeka: Freedom Valley Lake

SIZE: 1 acre.

LOCATION: 14th St. and Locust St. No boat access.

DAILY CREEL LIMIT/MINIMUM LENGTH: Largemouth Bass: 5 fish, 15 inches • Channel Catfish: 2 fish

Topeka: Governor's Ponds East & West

SIZE: 1 acre.

LOCATION: I-70 and SW. Fairlawn Rd. No boat access.

DAILY CREEL LIMIT/MINIMUM LENGTH: Largemouth Bass: 5 fish, 15 inches • Channel Catfish: 2 fish • Flathead Catfish: 5 fish • Crappie: 50 fish

Topeka: Horseshoe Bend Park Pond

SIZE: 1 acre.

LOCATION: Horseshoe Bend Dr. just north of 45th St. No boat access.

DAILY CREEL LIMIT/MINIMUM LENGTH: Largemouth Bass: 5 fish, 15 inches • Channel Catfish: 10 fish

Topeka: West Lake

SIZE: 6 acres.

LOCATION: SW 6th Ave. and SW. Gage Blvd., Gage Park. No boat access.

DAILY CREEL LIMIT/MINIMUM LENGTH: Largemouth Bass: 5 fish, 15 inches • Channel Catfish: 2 fish • Flathead Catfish: 5 fish • Crappie: 50 fish • Saugeye: 5 fish, 15 inches • Wiper: 2 fish

Troy: 4-H Lake

SIZE: 5 acres.

LOCATION: 0.5 mile southwest of Troy in Doniphan County. Boat access.

DAILY CREEL LIMIT/MINIMUM LENGTH: Largemouth Bass: 2 fish, 18 inches • Channel Catfish: 5 fish, 15 inches • Flathead Catfish: 5 fish • Crappie: 10 fish

Wamego City Lake

SIZE: 5 acres.

LOCATION: Wamego. No boat access.

DAILY CREEL LIMIT/MINIMUM LENGTH: Largemouth Bass: 5 fish, 15 inches • Channel Catfish: 10 fish • Crappie: 50 fish

Waterville City Lake

SIZE: 9 acres.
LOCATION: 1 mile west and 1 mile north of Waterville in Marshall County. No boat access.
DAILY CREEL LIMIT/MINIMUM LENGTH: Largemouth Bass: 5 fish, 15 inches • Channel Catfish: 10 fish • Crappie: 50 fish

Wyandotte County: Big Eleven Lake

SIZE: 3 acres.
LOCATION: N. 11th St. and State Ave., Kansas City. No boat access. Requires a local permit to fish.
DAILY CREEL LIMIT/MINIMUM LENGTH: Largemouth Bass: 5 fish, 15 inches • Channel Catfish: 2 fish • Crappie: 50 fish

Wyandotte County: Pierson Park Lake

SIZE: 12 acres.
LOCATION: S. 55th St. and Douglas Ave., Kansas City. No boat access. Requires a local permit to fish.
DAILY CREEL LIMIT/MINIMUM LENGTH: Largemouth Bass: 5 fish, 15 inches • Channel Catfish: 2 fish • Crappie: 50 fish

Wyandotte County Park Pond (Bonner Lake)

SIZE: 7 acres.
LOCATION: N. 126th St. and State Ave., Bonner Springs. No boat access.
DAILY CREEL LIMIT/MINIMUM LENGTH: Largemouth Bass: 2 fish, 15 inches • Channel Catfish: 2 fish • Wiper: 2 fish

Wyandotte County Lake

SIZE: 407 acres.
LOCATION: Leavenworth Rd. and N. 91st St., Kansas City. Boat access. Requires a local permit to fish.
DAILY CREEL LIMIT/MINIMUM LENGTH: Largemouth Bass: 5 fish, 15 inches • Smallmouth Bass: 5 fish, 18 inches • Channel Catfish: 5 fish • Flathead Catfish: 5 fish • Crappie: 50 fish • Walleye: 2 fish, 18 inches • Wiper: 2 fish, 18 inches

YMCA Camp Hammond

SIZE: 15 acres.
LOCATION: 6329 SE. Stubbs Rd., Tecumseh, in Shawnee County. Also known as Lake Hammond.
DAILY CREEL LIMIT/MINIMUM LENGTH: Largemouth Bass: 5 fish, 15 inches • Channel Catfish: 10 fish

REGION 3
State Fishing Lakes and Other Waters

Barber State Fishing Lake: Lower

SIZE: 51 acres.
LOCATION: Just north of Medicine Lodge. Camping is allowed, as well as hunting in the northern 80 acres of the wildlife area.
DAILY CREEL LIMIT/MINIMUM LENGTH: Largemouth Bass: 5 fish, 15 inches • Channel Catfish: 5 fish • Walleye: 5 fish, 15 inches

Barber State Fishing Lake: Upper

SIZE: 26 acres.
LOCATION: Near the lower lake, north of Medicine Lodge. Camping allowed.
DAILY CREEL LIMIT/MINIMUM LENGTH: Largemouth Bass: 5 fish, 15 inches • Channel Catfish: 5 fish • Crappie: 50 fish

Clark State Fishing Lake

SIZE: 300 acres.
LOCATION: 8.5 miles south and 1 mile west of Kingsdown. Primitive camping.
DAILY CREEL LIMIT/MINIMUM LENGTH: Largemouth Bass: 5 fish, 15 inches • Channel Catfish: 5 fish • Flathead Catfish: 5 fish • Crappie: 50 fish • Walleye: 5 fish, 15 inches
AQUATIC NUISANCE SPECIES ALERT: Eurasian Watermilfoil

Concannon State Fishing Lake, and Finney State Fishing Lake

These lakes were dry in 2010

Ford State Fishing Lake

SIZE: 48 acres.
LOCATION: 3 miles north and 5 miles east of Dodge City. Camping allowed in designated areas.
DAILY CREEL LIMIT/MINIMUM LENGTH: Largemouth Bass: 5 fish, 15 inches • Channel Catfish: 5 fish • Flathead Catfish: 5 fish • Crappie: 50 fish • Saugeye: 5 fish, 15 inches

Goodman State Fishing Lake

SIZE: 40 acres.
LOCATION: 5 miles south and 2.5 miles east of Ness City. Includes 225-acre upland wildlife area. Primitive camping is allowed
DAILY CREEL LIMIT/MINIMUM LENGTH: Largemouth Bass: 5 fish, 13–18 inches slot limit • Channel Catfish: 5 fish • Crappie: 50 fish

Hain State Fishing Lake

SIZE: 53 acres.
LOCATION: 5 miles west of Spearville. Periodically dry, the lake is primarily used for waterfowl hunting, but is stocked with fish when conditions are good. No boat access. Camping allowed, but no restroom facilities available.
DAILY CREEL LIMIT/MINIMUM LENGTH: Largemouth Bass: 5 fish, 15 inches • Channel Catfish: 5 fish

Hamilton State Fishing Lake

This lake was dry in 2010.

Hodgeman State Fishing Lake

SIZE: 87 acres.
LOCATION: 4 miles east and 2 miles south of Jetmore. Periodically dry. Camping sites available.
DAILY CREEL LIMIT/MINIMUM LENGTH: Largemouth Bass: 5 fish, 15 inches • Channel Catfish: 5 fish

Kiowa State Fishing Lake

SIZE: 21 acres.
LOCATION: Northwest corner of Greensburg. The city pumps the lake and keeps it full. Fish feeders on the lake go off at 7:00 a.m., noon, and 7:00 p.m. Camping allowed.
DAILY CREEL LIMIT/MINIMUM LENGTH: Largemouth Bass: 5 fish, 15 inches • Channel Catfish: 5 fish • Flathead Catfish: 5 fish • Crappie: 50 fish • Wiper: 2 fish, 18 inches

Meade State Fishing Lake

SIZE: 80 acres.

LOCATION: 8 miles south and 5 miles west of Meade on K-23. Surrounded by a 360-acre wildlife area. The lake includes camping and swimming, and is also home to a hatchery.

DAILY CREEL LIMIT/MINIMUM LENGTH: Largemouth Bass: 5 fish, 13–18 inches slot limit • Channel Catfish: 5 fish • Flathead Catfish: 5 fish • Crappie: 50 fish

Pratt Centennial Pond

SIZE: 3 acres.

LOCATION: 2 miles east and 1 mile south of Pratt.

DAILY CREEL LIMIT/MINIMUM LENGTH: Rainbow Trout: 2 fish • all other species are catch and release only

Sandsage Bison Range & Wildlife Area

SIZE: 5 acres.

LOCATION: South edge of Garden City. Periodically dry, stocked with trout in the winter when there is water in it. No boat access.

DAILY CREEL LIMIT/MINIMUM LENGTH: Largemouth Bass: 2 fish, 15 inches • Channel Catfish: 5 fish • Rainbow Trout: 5 fish

Scott State Lake

SIZE: 115 acres.

LOCATION: Scott State Park, 11 miles north of Scott City.

DAILY CREEL LIMIT/MINIMUM LENGTH: Largemouth Bass: 5 fish, 15 inches • Channel Catfish: 5 fish • Crappie: 50 fish • Saugeye: 5 fish, 15 inches • Rainbow Trout: 5 fish • Walleye: 5 fish, 15 inches

AQUATIC NUISANCE SPECIES ALERT: Eurasian Watermilfoil, Rudd

Community Lakes

Cimarron Grasslands Fishing Pits

SIZE: 15 acres.

LOCATION: 8 miles north of Elkhart. No boat access.

DAILY CREEL LIMIT/MINIMUM LENGTH: Largemouth Bass: 5 fish, 15 inches • Channel Catfish: 5 fish • Crappie: 50 fish • Rainbow Trout: 5 fish

Coldwater City Lake

SIZE: 250 acres.

LOCATION: 1 mile south and 1 mile west of Coldwater. Boat access.

DAILY CREEL LIMIT/MINIMUM LENGTH: Largemouth Bass: 5 fish, 15 inches • Channel Catfish: 5 fish • Crappie: 50 fish • Wiper: 5 fish

Dodge City: Lake Charles

SIZE: 1 acre.

LOCATION: Dodge City Community College. No boat access.

DAILY CREEL LIMIT/MINIMUM LENGTH: Largemouth Bass: 2 fish, 18 inches • Channel Catfish: 5 fish • Crappie: 50 fish • Rainbow Trout: 5 fish

Dodge City: Mariah Hills Golf Course

SIZE: 2 acres.

LOCATION: Dodge City. No boat access.

DAILY CREEL LIMIT/MINIMUM LENGTH: Largemouth Bass: 5 fish, 15 inches • Channel Catfish: 5 fish • Crappie: 50 fish

Great Bend: Stone Lake

SIZE: 50 acres.

LOCATION: Southwest of Great Bend. No boat access.

DAILY CREEL LIMIT/MINIMUM LENGTH: Largemouth Bass: 5 fish, 15 inches • Channel Catfish: 5 fish • Crappie: 50 fish • Wiper: 2 fish, 18 inches

Great Bend: Veteran's Park

SIZE: 13 acres.

LOCATION: Great Bend. Boat access.

DAILY CREEL LIMIT/MINIMUM LENGTH: Largemouth Bass: 5 fish, 15 inches • Channel Catfish: 5 fish • Crappie: 50 fish • Saugeye: 5 fish, 15 inches • Rainbow Trout: 5 fish

Horsethief Reservoir

SIZE: 450 acres.

LOCATION: 8 miles west of Jetmore on K-156. Boat access, swimming beach. Campsites.

DAILY CREEL LIMIT/MINIMUM LENGTH: Largemouth Bass: 5 fish, 15 inches • Channel Catfish: 10 fish • Crappie: 50 fish • Walleye: 5 fish, 15 inches

Jetmore City Lake

SIZE: 106 acres.

LOCATION: 2 miles south, 3 miles west of Jetmore. Periodically dry. Boat access.

DAILY CREEL LIMIT/MINIMUM LENGTH: Largemouth Bass: 5 fish, 13–18 inches slot limit • Channel Catfish: 5 fish • Wiper: 2 fish, 18 inches

LaCrosse: Warren Stone Memorial Lake

SIZE: About 30 acres.

LOCATION: 2 miles east of LaCrosse. Periodically dry. Boat access.

DAILY CREEL LIMIT/MINIMUM LENGTH: Largemouth Bass: 5 fish, 15 inches • Channel Catfish: 5 fish

Larned City Pond

SIZE: 2 acres.

LOCATION: Southwest of Larned. No boat access.

DAILY CREEL LIMIT/MINIMUM LENGTH: See local regulations.

Liberal: Arkalon Recreation Area

SIZE: 5 acres.

LOCATION: 10 miles east of Liberal. No boat access.

DAILY CREEL LIMIT/MINIMUM LENGTH: Channel Catfish: 10 fish

Pratt County Lake

SIZE: 51 acres.

LOCATION: 2.5 miles east of Pratt. Boat access.

DAILY CREEL LIMIT/MINIMUM LENGTH: Largemouth Bass: 2 fish, 18 inches • Channel Catfish: 2 fish, 15 inches • Crappie: 50 fish • Walleye: 2 fish, 18 inches • Wiper: 2 fish, 18 inches

Syracuse: Sam's Pond

SIZE: 50 acres.

LOCATION: 1 mile south of Syracuse on K-27.

DAILY CREEL LIMIT/MINIMUM LENGTH: Largemouth Bass: 5 fish, 15 inches • Channel Catfish: 10 fish

Ulysses City Lake

SIZE: 17 acres.

LOCATION: East side of Ulysses.

DAILY CREEL LIMIT/MINIMUM LENGTH: Largemouth Bass: 5 fish, 15 inches • Channel Catfish: 10 fish

REGION 4
State fishing lakes and other waters
Black Kettle State Fishing Lake
SIZE: 8-acre borrow pit.
LOCATION: 2 miles north and 0.5 mile east of Moundridge. Boat access.
DAILY CREEL LIMIT/MINIMUM LENGTH: Largemouth Bass: 5 fish, 18 inches • Channel Catfish: 5 fish, 15 inches • Flathead Catfish: 5 fish • Crappie: 50 fish

Butler State Fishing Lake
SIZE: 124 acres.
LOCATION: 3 miles west and 1 mile north of Latham. Boat access. Primitive camping.
DAILY CREEL LIMIT/MINIMUM LENGTH: Largemouth Bass: 5 fish, 15 inches • Channel Catfish: 2 fish, 15 inches • Flathead Catfish: 5 fish • Crappie: 50 fish • Walleye: 5 fish, 15 inches

Chase State Fishing Lake
SIZE: 109 acres.
LOCATION: 2.5 miles west of Cottonwood Falls. Primitive camping is allowed along the north shore. Boat access.
DAILY CREEL LIMIT/MINIMUM LENGTH: Largemouth Bass: 5 fish, 13–18 inches slot limit• Smallmouth Bass: 5 fish, 15 inches • Spotted Bass: 5 fish, 15 inches • Channel Catfish: 5 fish, 15 inches • Flathead Catfish: 5 fish • Crappie: 50 fish • Saugeye: 5 fish, 18 inches • Walleye: 5 fish, 18 inches

Cowley State Fishing Lake
SIZE: 84 acres.
LOCATION: 13 miles east of Arkansas City on US 166. Boat access. Camping is allowed. Vehicle access is limited to the north side of the lake.
DAILY CREEL LIMIT/MINIMUM LENGTH: Largemouth Bass: 5 fish, 15 inches • Channel Catfish: 5 fish, 15 inches • Flathead Catfish: 5 fish • Crappie: 50 fish • Walleye: 5 fish, 15 inches

Kingman State Fishing Lake
SIZE: 144 acres.
LOCATION: 7 miles west of Kingman. Home to northern pike. A waterfowl refuge is maintained on the eastern two-thirds of the lake, including the campground area. The lake and surrounding wildlife area are ranked in the top 13 areas for wildlife viewing in Kansas. Boat access.
DAILY CREEL LIMIT/MINIMUM LENGTH: Largemouth Bass: 5 fish, 18 inches • Channel Catfish: 2 fish, 15 inches • Flathead Catfish: 5 fish • Crappie: 50 fish • Northern Pike: 2 fish, 30 inches • Walleye: 5 fish, 18 inches
AQUATIC NUISANCE SPECIES ALERT: White Perch (unlawful to possess alive)

McPherson State Fishing Lake
SIZE: 46 acres.
LOCATION: Maxwell Wildlife Refuge, 6 miles north of Canton. The 2,800-acre refuge in the natural prairie in the Smoky Hills is home to bison and elk. Primitive camping is available at the lake, as well as one cabin. Boat access.
DAILY CREEL LIMIT/MINIMUM LENGTH: Largemouth Bass: 5 fish, 13–18 inches slot limit • Channel Catfish: 2 fish, 15 inches • Flathead Catfish: 5 fish • Crappie: 50 fish • Saugeye: 5 fish, 18 inches

Community Lakes
Andover: Lake George
SIZE: 3 acres.
LOCATION: 1607 E. Central Ave. No boat access.
DAILY CREEL LIMIT/MINIMUM LENGTH: Largemouth Bass: 2 fish, 18 inches • Channel Catfish: 2 fish

Anthony City Lake
SIZE: 156 acres.
LOCATION: 1 mile north and 0.5 mile west of Anthony. Boat access.
DAILY CREEL LIMIT/MINIMUM LENGTH: Largemouth Bass: 5 fish, 15 inches • Channel Catfish: 10 fish • Flathead Catfish: 5 fish • Crappie: 50 fish

Arkansas City: Knebbler #1
SIZE: 16 acres.
LOCATION: US 77 Bypass and US 166. No boat access.
DAILY CREEL LIMIT/MINIMUM LENGTH: Largemouth Bass: 5 fish, 15 inches • Channel Catfish: 5 fish • Crappie: 50 fish

Arkansas City: Knebbler #2
SIZE: 5 acres.
LOCATION: US 77 Bypass and US 166. No boat access.
DAILY CREEL LIMIT/MINIMUM LENGTH: Largemouth Bass: 5 fish, 15 inches • Channel Catfish: 5 fish

Arkansas City: Sixth Street Pond
SIZE: 16 acres.
LOCATION: S. Sixth St. and W. Taylor Ave. No boat access.
DAILY CREEL LIMIT/MINIMUM LENGTH: Largemouth Bass: 5 fish, 15 inches • Channel Catfish: 5 fish • Flathead Catfish: 5 fish • Crappie: 50 fish

Benton: Poling Lake
SIZE: 2 acres.
LOCATION: SW. 20th St. and Prairie Parkway. No boat access.
DAILY CREEL LIMIT/MINIMUM LENGTH: Largemouth Bass: 2 fish, 18 inches • Channel Catfish: 5 fish

Clearwater: Chisholm Ridge Lake
SIZE: 5 acres.
LOCATION: 1 mile east of Clearwater. No boat access.
DAILY CREEL LIMIT/MINIMUM LENGTH: Largemouth Bass: 2 fish, 18 inches • Channel Catfish: 5 fish

Colwich City Lake
SIZE: 10 acres.
LOCATION: Colwich. No boat access.
DAILY CREEL LIMIT/MINIMUM LENGTH: Largemouth Bass: 2 fish, 15 inches • Channel Catfish: 2 fish

Council Grove City Lake
SIZE: 434 acres.
LOCATION: 3 miles west of Council Grove on US 56, then north 1 mile. Boat access.
DAILY CREEL LIMIT/MINIMUM LENGTH: Largemouth Bass: 5 fish, 13–18 inches slot limit • Spotted Bass: 5 fish, 15 inches • Channel Catfish: 5 fish • Flathead Catfish: 5 fish • Crappie: 20 fish • Walleye: 5 fish, 18 inches

Derby: High Park

SIZE: 4 acres.

LOCATION: 2700 E. Madison Ave., Derby. No boat access.

DAILY CREEL LIMIT/MINIMUM LENGTH: Largemouth Bass: 2 fish, 18 inches • Channel Catfish: 5 fish

Derby: Rainbow Valley

SIZE: 2-acre pond.

LOCATION: 1442 E. Warren Ave., Derby. No boat access.

DAILY CREEL LIMIT/MINIMUM LENGTH: Largemouth Bass: 2 fish, 18 inches • Channel Catfish: 5 fish

Derby: Stone Creek

SIZE: 2-acre pond.

LOCATION: 2712 N. Button Bush St. and E. 63rd St. S. No boat access.

DAILY CREEL LIMIT/MINIMUM LENGTH: Largemouth Bass: 2 fish, 18 inches • Channel Catfish: 5 fish

El Dorado: East Park Pond

SIZE: 1 acre.

LOCATION: El Dorado.

DAILY CREEL LIMIT/MINIMUM LENGTH: See local regulations.

AQUATIC NUISANCE SPECIES ALERT: Zebra Mussels (unlawful to possess alive)

Harvey County: Camp Hawk

SIZE: 2 acres.

LOCATION: Southwest of Newton. No boat access.

DAILY CREEL LIMIT/MINIMUM LENGTH: Largemouth Bass: 2 fish, 21 inches • Channel Catfish: 2 fish, 15 inches

Harvey County: East Lake

SIZE: 254 acres.

LOCATION: 7 miles east of Newton. Boat access.

DAILY CREEL LIMIT/MINIMUM LENGTH: Largemouth Bass: 5 fish, 13–18 inches slot limit • Channel Catfish: 5 fish • Crappie: 50 fish • Saugeye: 2 fish, 18 inches • Walleye: 2 fish, 18 inches

Harvey County: West Lake

SIZE: 15 acres.

LOCATION: 4 miles north and 3 miles west of Halstead. Boat access.

DAILY CREEL LIMIT/MINIMUM LENGTH: Largemouth Bass: 2 fish, 18 inches • Channel Catfish: 5 fish, 15 inches • Flathead Catfish: 5 fish • Crappie: 50 fish • Saugeye: 2 fish, 18 inches

Haysville: Riggs Lake

SIZE: 1 acre.

LOCATION: 525 Sarah Ln., Haysville. No boat access.

DAILY CREEL LIMIT/MINIMUM LENGTH: Channel Catfish: 2 fish

Haysville: South Hampton

SIZE: 2 acres.

LOCATION: Meridian St. and 71st St. No boat access.

DAILY CREEL LIMIT/MINIMUM LENGTH: Largemouth Bass: 2 fish, 18 inches • Channel Catfish: 5 fish

Hutchinson: Carey Park Lagoon & Pond

SIZE: 5 acres.

LOCATION: South end of Main St. in Carey Park. No boat access.

DAILY CREEL LIMIT/MINIMUM LENGTH: Largemouth Bass: 5 fish, 15 inches • Channel Catfish: 5 fish • Flathead Catfish: 5 fish • Crappie: 50 fish

AQUATIC NUISANCE SPECIES ALERT: White Perch (unlawful to possess alive)

Hutchinson: Dillon Nature Center

SIZE: 3 acres.

LOCATION: Northeast of Hutchinson. No boat access.

DAILY CREEL LIMIT/MINIMUM LENGTH: Largemouth Bass: 5 fish, 15 inches • Channel Catfish: 5 fish • Flathead Catfish: 5 fish • Crappie: 50 fish • Rainbow Trout: 5 fish

Kechi Lake

SIZE: 1 acre.

LOCATION: 6300 N. Oliver St., Kechi. No boat access.

DAILY CREEL LIMIT/MINIMUM LENGTH: Largemouth Bass: 2 fish, 18 inches • Channel Catfish: 2 fish

Kingman: Hoover Pond

SIZE: 1 acre.

LOCATION: Riverside Park, Kingman. No boat access.

DAILY CREEL LIMIT/MINIMUM LENGTH: Largemouth Bass: 5 fish, 15 inches • Channel Catfish: 10 fish

AQUATIC NUISANCE SPECIES ALERT: White Perch (unlawful to possess alive)

Marion County Lake

SIZE: 153 acres.

LOCATION: 2 miles east and 2 miles south of Marion. Boat access. Campsites.

DAILY CREEL LIMIT/MINIMUM LENGTH: Largemouth Bass: 5 fish*, 18 inches • Smallmouth Bass: 5 fish*, 18 inches • Spotted Bass: 5 fish*, 15 inches • Channel Catfish: 5 fish • Flathead Catfish: 5 fish • Crappie: 50 fish • Saugeye: 5 fish*, 18 inches • Walleye: 5 fish*, 18 inches • Wiper: 2 fish, 18 inches

* Largemouth, Smallmouth, and Spotted Bass in combination. Walleye and Saugeye in combination.

Mount Hope: Oak Street Park Pond

SIZE: 2 acres.

LOCATION: Mt. Hope. No boat access.

DAILY CREEL LIMIT/MINIMUM LENGTH: Largemouth Bass: 2 fish, 18 inches • Channel Catfish: 2 fish

Mulvane Sports Complex

SIZE: 1 acre.

LOCATION: 1900 E. 111th St. S., Mulvane. No boat access.

DAILY CREEL LIMIT/MINIMUM LENGTH: Largemouth Bass: 2 fish, 18 inches • Channel Catfish: 2 fish

North Newton: Sunfield Pond

SIZE: 2 acres.

LOCATION: City of North Newton. No boat access.

DAILY CREEL LIMIT/MINIMUM LENGTH: See local regulations.

Park City: Chisholm Pointe

SIZE: 3 acres.

LOCATION: 2516 N. Grove St. No boat access.

DAILY CREEL LIMIT/MINIMUM LENGTH: Largemouth Bass: 2 fish, 18 inches • Channel Catfish: 5 fish

Renwick USD 267 Pond

SIZE: 1.5 acres.
LOCATION: Andale.
DAILY CREEL LIMIT/MINIMUM LENGTH: See local regulations.

Sedgwick County: Lake Afton

SIZE: 258 acres.
LOCATION: 25 miles southwest of Wichita. Boat access.
DAILY CREEL LIMIT/MINIMUM LENGTH: Largemouth Bass: 5 fish, 18 inches • Channel Catfish: 5 fish • Flathead Catfish: 5 fish • Saugeye: 2 fish, 21 inches • Walleye: 2 fish, 21 inches • Wiper: 2 fish, 21 inches
AQUATIC NUISANCE SPECIES ALERT: White Perch and Zebra Mussels (unlawful to possess alive)

Sedgwick County Park Lakes

SIZE: 63 acres.
LOCATION: 6501 W. 21st St. N., Wichita. No boat access.
DAILY CREEL LIMIT/MINIMUM LENGTH: Largemouth Bass: 2 fish, 18 inches • Channel Catfish: 5 fish • Crappie: 50 fish • Rainbow Trout: 5 fish (Artificial flies only on Slough Creek) • Wiper: 2 fish, 21 inches
AQUATIC NUISANCE SPECIES ALERT: White Perch (unlawful to possess alive)

Sterling City Lake

SIZE: 10 acres.
LOCATION: E. Garfield Ave. and Lake St., Sterling. Boat access.
DAILY CREEL LIMIT/MINIMUM LENGTH: Largemouth Bass: 5 fish, 15 inches • Channel Catfish: 10 fish • Wiper: 2 fish

Valley Center: Arrowhead Park Lake

SIZE: 5.4 acres.
LOCATION: Valley Center. No boat access.
DAILY CREEL LIMIT/MINIMUM LENGTH: See local regulations.

Valley Center: McLaughlin Pond

SIZE: 3 acres.
LOCATION: 716 McLaughlin Dr. No boat access.
DAILY CREEL LIMIT/MINIMUM LENGTH: Largemouth Bass: 2 fish, 18 inches • Channel Catfish: 2 fish

Wellington: Hargis Creek Lake

SIZE: 65 acres.
LOCATION: East edge of Wellington. No boat access.
DAILY CREEL LIMIT/MINIMUM LENGTH: Largemouth Bass: 2 fish, 18 inches • Channel Catfish: 5 fish, 15 inches • Flathead Catfish: 5 fish • Crappie: 50 fish • Saugeye: 2 fish, 18 inches

Wellington City Lake

SIZE: 674 acres.
LOCATION: 5 miles west and 1.5 miles south of Wellington. Boat access.
DAILY CREEL LIMIT/MINIMUM LENGTH: Largemouth Bass: 2 fish, 18 inches • Channel Catfish: 5 fish, 15 inches • Flathead Catfish: 5 fish • Crappie: 20 fish • Saugeye: 5 fish, 18 inches • Walleye: 5 fish, 18 inches • Wiper: 2 fish, 18 inches

Wichita: Buffalo Park Lake

SIZE: 12 acres.
LOCATION: West of Wichita. No boat access.
DAILY CREEL LIMIT/MINIMUM LENGTH: Largemouth Bass: 2 fish, 18 inches • Channel Catfish: 5 fish • Crappie: 10 fish • Saugeye: 2 fish, 18 inches • Wiper: 2 fish, 18 inches
AQUATIC NUISANCE SPECIES ALERT: Eurasian Watermilfoil

Wichita: Chisholm Island Pond

SIZE: 5 acres.
LOCATION: N. Woodlawn St. and E. 29th St. N., Great Plains Nature Center. No boat access.
All fishing shall be with artificial flies and lures only, except for during KDWP sponsored fishing clinics. All species are catch and release only.

Wichita: Chisholm North Lake

SIZE: 23 acres.
LOCATION: N. Woodlawn St. and K-96 Bypass. No boat access.
DAILY CREEL LIMIT/MINIMUM LENGTH: Largemouth Bass: 2 fish, 18 inches • Channel Catfish: 5 fish • Crappie: 10 fish • Saugeye: 2 fish, 18 inches • Walleye: 2 fish, 18 inches • Wiper: 2 fish, 18 inches

Wichita: Cruiser Lake

SIZE: 35 acres.
LOCATION: Southeast of I-35 and K-96 Bypass. No boat access.
DAILY CREEL LIMIT/MINIMUM LENGTH: Largemouth Bass: 2 fish, 18 inches • Channel Catfish: 5 fish • Crappie: 10 fish

Wichita: Dillon's Pond

SIZE: 2 acres.
LOCATION: 10515 W. Central Ave. and N. Maize Rd. No boat access.
DAILY CREEL LIMIT/MINIMUM LENGTH: Largemouth Bass: 2 fish, 18 inches • Channel Catfish: 5 fish • Crappie: 10 fish

Wichita: East KDOT

SIZE: 7 acres.
LOCATION: Access at N. Hydraulic Ave. and E. 45th St. No boat access.
DAILY CREEL LIMIT/MINIMUM LENGTH: Largemouth Bass: 2 fish, 18 inches • Channel Catfish: 5 fish • Crappie: 10 fish • Rainbow Trout: 5 fish • Wiper: 2 fish, 18 inches

Wichita: Emery Park Pond

SIZE: 7 acres.
LOCATION: 2325 E. MacArthur Rd. No boat access.
DAILY CREEL LIMIT/MINIMUM LENGTH: Largemouth Bass: 2 fish, 18 inches • Channel Catfish: 5 fish

Wichita: Harrison Park Lake

SIZE: 1 acre.
LOCATION: 1300 S. Webb Rd. No boat access.
DAILY CREEL LIMIT/MINIMUM LENGTH: Largemouth Bass: 2 fish, 18 inches • Channel Catfish: 2 fish

Wichita: South Lake

SIZE: 17 acres.
LOCATION: W. 55th St. S. and S. Seneca St. No boat access.
DAILY CREEL LIMIT/MINIMUM LENGTH: Largemouth Bass: 2 fish, 18 inches • Channel Catfish: 5 fish • Crappie: 10 fish • Saugeye: 5 fish, 15 inches

Wichita: Blackbird Pond

SIZE: 4 acres.

LOCATION: 4182 N. 135th St. W. No boat access.

DAILY CREEL LIMIT/MINIMUM LENGTH: Largemouth Bass: 2 fish, 18 inches • Channel Catfish: 5 fish

Wichita: Sunflower Pond

SIZE: 8 acres.

LOCATION: 4182 N. 135th St. W. No boat access.

DAILY CREEL LIMIT/MINIMUM LENGTH: Largemouth Bass: 2 fish, 18 inches • Channel Catfish: 5 fish

Wichita: Watson Park Lake

SIZE: 42 acres.

LOCATION: 3055 S. Old Lawrence Rd. No boat access.

DAILY CREEL LIMIT/MINIMUM LENGTH: Largemouth Bass: 2 fish, 18 inches • Channel Catfish: 5 fish • Flathead Catfish: 5 fish • Crappie: 10 fish • Saugeye: 2 fish, 18 inches • Wiper: 2 fish, 18 inches

Wichita: West KDOT

SIZE: 10 acres.

LOCATION: Access is near N. Hydraulic Ave. and E. 45th St. No boat access.

DAILY CREEL LIMIT/MINIMUM LENGTH: Largemouth Bass: 2 fish, 18 inches • Channel Catfish: 5 fish • Crappie: 10 fish • Wiper: 2 fish, 18 inches

Windom City Pond

SIZE: 1 acre.

LOCATION: South end of Main St. Boat access.

DAILY CREEL LIMIT/MINIMUM LENGTH: Largemouth Bass: 5 fish, 15 inches • Channel Catfish: 10 fish

Winfield City Lake

SIZE: 1,200 acres.

LOCATION: 10 miles northeast of Winfield. Boat access.

DAILY CREEL LIMIT/MINIMUM LENGTH: Largemouth Bass: 5 fish, 15 inches • Spotted Bass: 5 fish, 15 inches • Channel Catfish: 10 fish • Flathead Catfish: 5 fish • Crappie: 20 fish • Walleye: 5 fish, 18 inches • Wiper: 2 fish, 18 inches

AQUATIC NUISANCE SPECIES ALERT: Zebra Mussels (unlawful to possess alive)

Winfield: Island Park Lake

SIZE: 7 acres.

LOCATION: North of Winfield.

DAILY CREEL LIMIT/MINIMUM LENGTH: See local regulations

REGION 5
State Fishing Lakes and Other Waters
Big Hill Wildlife Area

SIZE: 14 acres between 2 ponds.

LOCATION: 6 miles east of Cherryvale in Montgomery County. Surrounded by 1,320 acres of land. Fishing opportunites for black bass and channel catfish. Primitive campsites available. No boat access.

DAILY CREEL LIMIT/MINIMUM LENGTH: Largemouth Bass: 5 fish, 21 inches • Channel Catfish: 10 fish • Flathead Catfish: 5 fish • Crappie: 50 fish

Bourbon State Fishing Lake

SIZE: 103 acres.

LOCATION: 4 miles east of Elsmore. About 270 acres of land surrounds the lake. Campsites available. Boat access.

DAILY CREEL LIMIT/MINIMUM LENGTH: Largemouth Bass: 5 fish, 15 inches • Spotted Bass: 5 fish, 15 inches • Channel Catfish: 2 fish, 15 inches • Crappie: 50 fish • Saugeye: 2 fish, 18 inches • Walleye: 2 fish, 18 inches

Crawford State Fishing Lake

SIZE: 150 acres.

LOCATION: 9 miles north and 1 mile east of Girard. The 500-acre park features 6 campgrounds with electrical hookups and primitive camping. Boat access.

DAILY CREEL LIMIT/MINIMUM LENGTH: Largemouth Bass: 2 fish, 18 inches • Spotted Bass: 5 fish, 15 inches • Channel Catfish: 5 fish, 15 inches • Flathead Catfish: 5 fish • Crappie: 50 fish • Saugeye: 2 fish, 18 inches • Striped Bass: 2 fish, 18 inches • Walleye: 5 fish, 18 inches

Fall River Toe Drain

LOCATION: Below the dam at Fall River State Park, 4 miles northeast of the town of Fall River.

DAILY CREEL LIMIT/MINIMUM LENGTH: Blue Catfish: 2 fish • Channel Catfish: 2 fish

Lyon State Fishing Lake

SIZE: 135 acres.

LOCATION: 13 miles north of Emporia on K-99. A fairly clear lake. Camping is allowed in designated areas. Boat access.

DAILY CREEL LIMIT/MINIMUM LENGTH: Largemouth Bass: 5 fish, 13–18 inches slot limit • Channel Catfish: 5 fish • Crappie: 50 fish

Marais des Cygnes Wildlife Area

SIZE: 1,967 acres of land with many lakes.

LOCATION: 7 miles north of Pleasanton on US 69. These waterfowl-management lakes are open to fishing on April 15. Many pools are good angling when draining. During draining, some pools are open to public fish salvage. Boat access. Primitive camping.

DAILY CREEL LIMIT/MINIMUM LENGTH: Largemouth Bass: 5 fish, 15 inches • Blue Catfish: 10 fish • Channel Catfish: 10 fish • Flathead Catfish: 5 fish • Crappie: 50 fish

Melvern River Pond

SIZE: 90 acres.

LOCATION: 0.5 mile south of Melvern Reservoir. No boat access.

DAILY CREEL LIMIT/MINIMUM LENGTH: Largemouth Bass: 2 fish, 13–18 inches slot limit • Channel Catfish: 2 fish, 15 inches • Flathead Catfish: 5 fish • Crappie: 10 fish, 10 inches • Rainbow Trout: 2 fish • Walleye: 2 fish, 18 inches • Wiper: 2 fish, 18 inches

Mined Land Wildlife Area

SIZE: 1,500 acres.

LOCATION: Crawford, Cherokee, and Labette Counties. The property is comprised of 1,500 acres of water and 13,000 acres of land. Camping allowed. Boat access. The site also has a modern cabin.

DAILY CREEL LIMIT/MINIMUM LENGTH: Largemouth Bass: 5 fish, 13–18 inches slot limit • Spotted Bass: 5 fish, 15 inches • Channel Catfish: 5 fish, 15 inches • Crappie: 50 fish • Brown Trout: 1 fish, 20 inches • Rainbow Trout: 5 fish • Walleye: 5 fish, 18 inches • Wiper: 2 fish, 18 inches

AQUATIC NUISANCE SPECIES ALERT: Eurasian Watermilfoil

Montgomery State Fishing Lake

SIZE: 105 acres.
LOCATION: 3 miles south and 1 mile east of Independence. Primitive camping. Boat access.
DAILY CREEL LIMIT/MINIMUM LENGTH: Largemouth Bass: 5 fish, 13–18 inches slot limit • Channel Catfish: 5 fish, 15 inches • Crappie: 50 fish

Neosho State Fishing Lake

SIZE: 92 acres.
LOCATION: 6 miles south and 1 mile west of St. Paul. The lake has 3 sites designated for primitive camping, 18 fishing piers, 1 cement ramp, 3 automatic fish feeders, and 3 walking trails.
DAILY CREEL LIMIT/MINIMUM LENGTH: Largemouth Bass: 5 fish, 18 inches • Channel Catfish: 5 fish, 15 inches • Crappie: 50 fish

Neosho Wildlife Area

SIZE: 800 acres.
LOCATION: 1 mile east of St. Paul on K-57.
DAILY CREEL LIMIT/MINIMUM LENGTH: Largemouth Bass: 5 fish, 15 inches • Channel Catfish: 5 fish, 15 inches • Crappie: 50 fish

Osage State Fishing Lake

SIZE: 140 acres.
LOCATION: Just southeast of Carbondale. Primitive camping. Boat access.
DAILY CREEL LIMIT/MINIMUM LENGTH: Largemouth Bass: 2 fish, 18 inches • Smallmouth Bass: 2 fish, 18 inches • Channel Catfish: 2 fish, 15 inches • Flathead Catfish: 5 fish • Crappie: 10 fish • Walleye: 2 fish, 15 inches • Wiper: 2 fish, 18 inches

Riverton: Empire Lake

SIZE: 840 acres.
LOCATION: Southeast of Riverton. No boat access.
DAILY CREEL LIMIT/MINIMUM LENGTH: Largemouth Bass: 5 fish, 15 inches • Spotted Bass: 5 fish, 15 inches • Channel Catfish: 10 fish • Flathead Catfish: 5 fish • Crappie: 50 fish • Walleye: 5 fish, 15 inches

Wilson State Fishing Lake

SIZE: 110 acres.
LOCATION: Just west of Chanute. Surrounded by 172 acres of wildlife haven. There are 4 solar-powered fish feeders at various locations on the lake. Boat access and primitive camping available.
DAILY CREEL LIMIT/MINIMUM LENGTH: Largemouth Bass: 5 fish, 15 inches • Spotted Bass: 5 fish, 15 inches • Channel Catfish: 5 fish, 15 inches • Flathead Catfish: 5 fish • Crappie: 50 fish • Walleye: 5 fish, 18 inches

Woodson State Fishing Lake

SIZE: 180 acres.
LOCATION: About 6 miles east of Toronto. The lake has 7 solar-powered fish feeders. Boat access and paid and primitive camping available.
DAILY CREEL LIMIT/MINIMUM LENGTH: Largemouth Bass: 2 fish, 13–18 inches slot limit • Smallmouth Bass: 2 fish, 18 inches • Channel Catfish: 2 fish, 15 inches • Flathead Catfish: 5 fish • Crappie: 10 fish, 10 inches • Walleye: 2 fish, 15 inches • Wiper: 2 fish, 18 inches

Community Lakes

Altamont City Lake

SIZE: 34 acres.
LOCATION: 4 miles south of Altamont. Boat access.
DAILY CREEL LIMIT/MINIMUM LENGTH: Largemouth Bass: 5 fish, 13–18 inches slot limit • Channel Catfish: 5 fish, 15 inches • Crappie: 50 fish

Arma City Lake

SIZE: About 1 acre.
LOCATION: Hookie Park, Arma. No boat access.
DAILY CREEL LIMIT/MINIMUM LENGTH: Largemouth Bass: 2 fish, 18 inches • Channel Catfish: 2 fish, 15 inches • Crappie: 50 fish

Blue Mound City Lake

SIZE: 19 acres.
LOCATION: 1 mile north and 2 miles west of Blue Mound. Boat access.
DAILY CREEL LIMIT/MINIMUM LENGTH: Largemouth Bass: 5 fish, 15 inches • Channel Catfish: 2 fish, 15 inches • Crappie: 50 fish

Bone Creek Reservoir

SIZE: 540 acres.
LOCATION: 7 miles north and 5 miles east of Girard. Boat access.
DAILY CREEL LIMIT/MINIMUM LENGTH: Largemouth Bass: 5 fish, 13–18 inches slot limit • Channel Catfish: 5 fish, 15 inches • Crappie: 10 fish • Walleye: 2 fish, 18 inches

Bourbon County: Cedar Creek

SIZE: 220 acres.
LOCATION: 4 miles west and 3 miles south of Fort Scott. Boat access.
DAILY CREEL LIMIT/MINIMUM LENGTH: Largemouth Bass: 2 fish, 21 inches • Smallmouth Bass: 2 fish, 18 inches • Channel Catfish: 2 fish, 15 inches • Crappie: 50 fish • Walleye: 2 fish, 18 inches

Bourbon County: Elm Creek Lake

SIZE: 106 acres.
LOCATION: 1 mile east and 2 miles north of Hiattville. Boat access.
DAILY CREEL LIMIT/MINIMUM LENGTH: Largemouth Bass: 2 fish, 21 inches • Smallmouth Bass: 2 fish, 18 inches • Channel Catfish: 2 fish, 15 inches • Crappie: 50 fish • Saugeye: 2 fish, 18 inches • Walleye: 2 fish, 18 inches

Carbondale East Lake

SIZE: 265 acres.
LOCATION: 2 miles east of Carbondale. Boat access.
DAILY CREEL LIMIT/MINIMUM LENGTH: Largemouth Bass: 2 fish, 18 inches • Smallmouth Bass: 2 fish, 18 inches • Spotted Bass: 2 fish, 15 inches • Blue Catfish: 2 fish • Channel Catfish: 2 fish, 15 inches • Flathead Catfish: 5 fish • Crappie: 50 fish • Sauger: 2 fish, 15 inches • Saugeye: 2 fish, 15 inches • Walleye: 2 fish, 18 inches • Wiper: 2 fish, 18 inches

Chanute City Lake (Santa Fe Lake)

SIZE: 80 acres.
LOCATION: South edge of Chanute. Boat access.
DAILY CREEL LIMIT/MINIMUM LENGTH: Largemouth Bass: 2 fish, 15 inches • Spotted Bass: 2 fish, 15 inches • Channel Catfish: 2 fish, 15 inches • Flathead Catfish: 5 fish • Crappie: 50 fish • Saugeye: 2 fish, 18 inches

Chanute: Highland Park Pond
SIZE: Roughly 1 acre.
LOCATION: Chestnut and Kansas St., Chanute.
DAILY CREEL LIMIT/MINIMUM LENGTH: See local regulations.

Cherryvale City Lake (Tanko)
SIZE: 11 acres.
LOCATION: 1.5 miles south of Cherryvale. Boat access.
DAILY CREEL LIMIT/MINIMUM LENGTH: Largemouth Bass: 5 fish, 18 inches • Channel Catfish: 5 fish, 15 inches • Crappie: 50 fish

Coffey County Lake
SIZE: 5,000 acres.
LOCATION: 2 miles north and 1 mile east of Burlington off US 75. Boaters must always wear a life jacket. Open 30 minutes after sunup to 30 minutes before sundown.
DAILY CREEL LIMIT/MINIMUM LENGTH: Largemouth Bass: 1 fish, 21 inches • Smallmouth Bass: 2 fish, 16–20 inches slot limit • Blue Catfish: 10 fish • Channel Catfish: 10 fish • Flathead Catfish: 5 fish • Crappie: 2 fish, 14 inches • Walleye: 2 fish, 18–24 inches slot limit • White Bass: 12 inches • Wiper: 1 fish, 21 inches

Coffeyville: LeClere Lake
SIZE: 7 acres.
LOCATION: Coffeyville. No boat access.
DAILY CREEL LIMIT/MINIMUM LENGTH: Largemouth Bass: 5 fish, 15 inches • Channel Catfish: 10 fish • Crappie: 50 fish

Columbus: VFW Pond
SIZE: 2 acres.
LOCATION: 1 mile south of junction US 69/160 and K-7.
DAILY CREEL LIMIT/MINIMUM LENGTH: Largemouth Bass: 2 fish, 15 inches • Channel Catfish: 2 fish, 15 inches

Critzer Lake
SIZE: 220 acres.
LOCATION: 8483 Jennison Rd., west of Mound City
DAILY CREEL LIMIT/MINIMUM LENGTH: Look for local regulations when the lake opens in May 2011

Edna City Lake
SIZE: 11 acres.
LOCATION: 2 miles west and 1 mile south of Edna. No boat access.
DAILY CREEL LIMIT/MINIMUM LENGTH: Largemouth Bass: 5 fish, 18 inches • Channel Catfish: 5 fish, 15 inches • Crappie: 50 fish

Elm Creek Lake
SIZE: 106 acres.
LOCATION: 1 mile east and 2 miles north of Hiattville in Bourbon County
DAILY CREEL LIMIT/MINIMUM LENGTH: Largemouth Bass: 2 fish, 21 inches • Smallmouth Bass: 2 fish, 18 inches • Channel Catfish: 2 fish, 15 inches • Crappie: 50 fish • Saugeye: 2 fish, 18 inches • Walleye: 2 fish, 18 inches

Emporia: Jones Park Ponds
SIZE: 3 acres.
LOCATION: Emporia. No boat access.
DAILY CREEL LIMIT/MINIMUM LENGTH: Largemouth Bass: 5 fish, 15 inches • Channel Catfish: 2 fish, 15 inches • Flathead Catfish: 5 fish

Emporia: Peter Pan Park
SIZE: 2 acres.
LOCATION: Emporia. No boat access.
DAILY CREEL LIMIT/MINIMUM LENGTH: Largemouth Bass: 5 fish, 15 inches • Channel Catfish: 2 fish, 15 inches • Flathead Catfish: 5 fish

Eureka City Lake
SIZE: 259 acres.
LOCATION: 4 miles north of Eureka on State St. Boat access.
DAILY CREEL LIMIT/MINIMUM LENGTH: Largemouth Bass: 5 fish, 18 inches • Spotted Bass: 5 fish • Channel Catfish: 5 fish, 15 inches • Flathead Catfish: 5 fish • Crappie: 50 fish • Saugeye: 5 fish, 18 inches • Walleye: 5 fish, 18 inches

Fort Scott: Gunn Park Lake East (Fern Lake)
SIZE: 2 acres.
LOCATION: Northwest corner of Fort Scott. No boat access.
DAILY CREEL LIMIT/MINIMUM LENGTH: Largemouth Bass: 2 fish, 18 inches • Channel Catfish: 2 fish, 15 inches • Flathead Catfish: 5 fish • Crappie: 50 fish • Rainbow Trout: 5 fish

Fort Scott: Gunn Park Lake West
SIZE: 11 acres.
LOCATION: Northwest corner of Fort Scott. No boat access.
DAILY CREEL LIMIT/MINIMUM LENGTH: Largemouth Bass: 2 fish, 18 inches • Channel Catfish: 2 fish, 15 inches • Flathead Catfish: 5 fish • Crappie: 50 fish

Fort Scott: Lake Fort Scott
SIZE: 350 acres.
LOCATION: 2 miles south, 3 miles west of Fort Scott. Boat access.
DAILY CREEL LIMIT/MINIMUM LENGTH: Largemouth Bass: 2 fish, 18 inches • Smallmouth Bass: 2 fish, 18 inches • Spotted Bass: 2 fish, 15 inches • Channel Catfish: 2 fish, 15 inches • Crappie: 50 fish • Walleye: 2 fish, 18 inches

Fort Scott: Rock Creek Lake
SIZE: 75 acres.
LOCATION: Just southwest of Ft. Scott. Boat access.
DAILY CREEL LIMIT/MINIMUM LENGTH: Largemouth Bass: 5 fish, 15 inches • Channel Catfish: 5 fish • Flathead Catfish: 5 fish • Crappie: 50 fish

Fort Scott Community College Lakes
SIZE: 2 acres.
LOCATION: Fort Scott Community College. Boat access.
DAILY CREEL LIMIT/MINIMUM LENGTH: Largemouth Bass: 2 fish, 18 inches • Channel Catfish: 2 fish, 15 inches • Crappie: 50 fish

Frontenac City Lake
SIZE: 5 acres.
LOCATION: N. Cherokee St.
DAILY CREEL LIMIT/MINIMUM LENGTH: Largemouth Bass: 2 fish, 18 inches • Channel Catfish: 2 fish, 15 inches • Crappie: 10 fish, 10 inches

Garnett: Cedar Valley Reservoir
SIZE: 350 acres.
LOCATION: 6 miles south and 2 miles west of Garnett. Boat access.
DAILY CREEL LIMIT/MINIMUM LENGTH: Largemouth Bass: 5 fish, 18 inches • Channel Catfish: 5 fish • Flathead Catfish: 5 fish • Crappie: 20 fish • Walleye: 2 fish, 18 inches • Wiper: 2 fish, 18 inches

Garnett City Lake: North

SIZE: 55 acres.

LOCATION: North edge of Garnett. Boat access.

DAILY CREEL LIMIT/MINIMUM LENGTH: Largemouth Bass: 2 fish, 13–18 inches slot limit • Smallmouth Bass: 2 fish, 18 inches • Channel Catfish: 2 fish, 15 inches • Flathead Catfish: 5 fish • Crappie: 10 fish, 10 inches • Walleye: 2 fish, 18 inches • Wiper: 2 fish, 18 inches

Garnett City Lake: South (Crystal Lake)

SIZE: 25 acres.

LOCATION: South edge of Garnett. Boat access.

DAILY CREEL LIMIT/MINIMUM LENGTH: Largemouth Bass: 5 fish, 13–18 inches slot limit • Channel Catfish: 2 fish, 15 inches • Flathead Catfish: 5 fish • Crappie: 10 fish, 10 inches • Walleye: 2 fish, 18 inches • Wiper: 2 fish, 18 inches

Greenbush Community Lake

SIZE: 5 acres.

LOCATION: 7 miles west of Girard. No boat access.

DAILY CREEL LIMIT/MINIMUM LENGTH: Largemouth Bass: 2 fish, 18 inches • Channel Catfish: 2 fish, 15 inches • Crappie: 50 fish

Gridley City Lake

SIZE: Over 30 acres.

LOCATION: 1 mile north of Gridley on Emmer Ln. Requires a local permit to fish.

DAILY CREEL LIMIT/MINIMUM LENGTH: Largemouth Bass: 2 fish, 13–18 inches slot limit • Channel Catfish: 2 fish, 15 inches • Crappie: 10 fish, 10 inches • Walleye: 2 fish, 18 inches • Wiper: 2 fish, 18 inches

Howard: Polk Daniels Lake

SIZE: 69 acres.

LOCATION: 1 mile east of Howard.

DAILY CREEL LIMIT/MINIMUM LENGTH: Largemouth Bass: 5 fish, 15 inches • Spotted Bass: 5 fish, 15 inches • Channel Catfish: 5 fish • Flathead Catfish: 5 fish • Crappie: 50 fish

Independence Community College: Campus Pond

SIZE: Very small.

LOCATION: Independence.

DAILY CREEL LIMIT/MINIMUM LENGTH: Largemouth Bass: 5 fish, 15 inches • Channel Catfish: 10 fish

Lebo City Lake

SIZE: 70 acres.

LOCATION: Just northeast of Lebo.

DAILY CREEL LIMIT/MINIMUM LENGTH: Largemouth Bass: 2 fish, 13–18 inches slot limit • Smallmouth Bass: 2 fish, 18 inches • Channel Catfish: 2 fish, 15 inches • Flathead Catfish: 5 fish • Crappie: 10 fish, 10 inches • Walleye: 2 fish, 18 inches • Wiper: 2 fish, 18 inches

AQUATIC NUISANCE SPECIES ALERT: Eurasian Watermilfoil

Linn County Strip Pits

SIZE: Roughly 20 acres.

LOCATION: Northeast of Prescott. No boat access.

DAILY CREEL LIMIT/MINIMUM LENGTH: Largemouth Bass: 2 fish, 13–18 inches slot limit • Channel Catfish: 2 fish, 15 inches • Crappie: 50 fish

Madison City Lake

SIZE: 114 acres.

LOCATION: 2 miles south of Madison on K-99. Boat access.

DAILY CREEL LIMIT/MINIMUM LENGTH: Largemouth Bass: 5 fish, 13–18 inches slot limit • Spotted Bass: 5 fish • Channel Catfish: 5 fish • Flathead Catfish: 5 fish • Crappie: 50 fish • Saugeye: 5 fish, 15 inches

Moline City Lake (New)

SIZE: 185 acres.

LOCATION: 1 mile north of Moline. Boat access.

DAILY CREEL LIMIT/MINIMUM LENGTH: Largemouth Bass: 5 fish, 13–18 inches slot limit • Channel Catfish: 5 fish • Flathead Catfish: 5 fish • Crappie: 50 fish

Moline City Lake (Old)

SIZE: 65 acres.

LOCATION: 1 mile west of Moline on US 160. Boat access.

DAILY CREEL LIMIT/MINIMUM LENGTH: Largemouth Bass: 5 fish, 13–18 inches slot limit • Channel Catfish: 5 fish • Flathead Catfish: 5 fish • Crappie: 50 fish

Mound City Lake

SIZE: 148 acres.

LOCATION: 4 miles west of Mound City.

DAILY CREEL LIMIT/MINIMUM LENGTH: Largemouth Bass: 5 fish, 13–18 inches slot limit • Channel Catfish: 2 fish, 15 inches • Crappie: 50 fish • Walleye: 2 fish, 18 inches

Mulberry Park Lake

SIZE: 3 acres.

LOCATION: North side of Mulberry.

DAILY CREEL LIMIT/MINIMUM LENGTH: Largemouth Bass: 2 fish, 15 inches • Channel Catfish: 2 fish, 15 inches

New Strawn City Lake

SIZE: 3 acres.

LOCATION: New Strawn. No boat access.

DAILY CREEL LIMIT/MINIMUM LENGTH: Largemouth Bass: 2 fish, 21 inches • Smallmouth Bass: 2 fish, 18 inches • Channel Catfish: 2 fish, 15 inches • Crappie: 10 fish • Walleye: 2 fish, 15 inches • Wiper: 2 fish, 18 inches

Olpe: Jones Park Pond

SIZE: 1 acre.

LOCATION: Olpe. No boat access.

DAILY CREEL LIMIT/MINIMUM LENGTH: Largemouth Bass: 5 fish, 15 inches • Channel Catfish: 2 fish

Olpe City Lake

SIZE: 90 acres.

LOCATION: Just southwest of Olpe. Boat access.

DAILY CREEL LIMIT/MINIMUM LENGTH: Largemouth Bass: 5 fish, 15 inches • Channel Catfish: 5 fish • Flathead Catfish: 5 fish • Crappie: 50 fish • Saugeye: 5 fish, 15 inches • Wiper: 2 fish

Osage City Lake

SIZE: 49 acres.

LOCATION: Almost 2 miles south of Osage City. Boat access.

DAILY CREEL LIMIT/MINIMUM LENGTH: Largemouth Bass: 2 fish, 18 inches • Channel Catfish: 2 fish, 15 inches • Crappie: 10 fish • Walleye: 2 fish, 18 inches • Wiper: 2 fish, 18 inches

Overbrook City Lake

SIZE: 3 acres.

LOCATION: Northeast side of Overbrook along US 56. No boat access.

DAILY CREEL LIMIT/MINIMUM LENGTH: Largemouth Bass: 2 fish, 13–18 inches slot limit • Smallmouth Bass: 2 fish, 18 inches • Channel Catfish: 2 fish, 15 inches • Crappie: 10 fish, 10 inches • Walleye: 2 fish, 15 inches • Wiper: 2 fish, 18 inches

Parker City Lake

SIZE: 7 acres.

LOCATION: Just southwest of Parker. No boat access.

DAILY CREEL LIMIT/MINIMUM LENGTH: Largemouth Bass: 2 fish, 13–18 inches slot limit • Channel Catfish: 2 fish, 15 inches • Crappie: 50 fish

Parsons City Lake

SIZE: Nearly 1,000 acres.

LOCATION: 4 miles north and 3.5 miles west of Parsons. Boat access.

DAILY CREEL LIMIT/MINIMUM LENGTH: Largemouth Bass: 5 fish, 15 inches • Channel Catfish: 5 fish, 15 inches • Flathead Catfish: 5 fish • Crappie: 50 fish • Saugeye: 5 fish, 18 inches

Parsons: Tolen Creek Pond

SIZE: 5 acres.

LOCATION: Just southeast of US 59 and US 400.

DAILY CREEL LIMIT/MINIMUM LENGTH: See local regulations.

Parsons: West Pond

SIZE: 1 acre.

LOCATION: 32nd St. and Chess Ave.

DAILY CREEL LIMIT/MINIMUM LENGTH: See local regulations.

Pittsburg: Lakeside Park Lake

SIZE: 4 acres.

LOCATION: 4 blocks east of US 69 bypass on Quincy Ave., then 5 blocks north on Catalpa Ave.

DAILY CREEL LIMIT/MINIMUM LENGTH: Largemouth Bass: 2 fish, 15 inches • Channel Catfish: 2 fish, 15 inches • Crappie: 50 fish

Pittsburg: Lincoln Park Lake

SIZE: 1 acre.

LOCATION: 710 W. 9th St.

DAILY CREEL LIMIT/MINIMUM LENGTH: Largemouth Bass: 2 fish, 15 inches • Channel Catfish: 2 fish, 15 inches

Pittsburg: University Lake

SIZE: 2 acres.

LOCATION: 1701 South Broadway.

DAILY CREEL LIMIT/MINIMUM LENGTH: Largemouth Bass: 5 fish, 15 inches • Channel Catfish: 10 fish • Crappie: 50 fish

Pittsburg: Wilderness Pond

SIZE: 3 acres.

LOCATION: West of Parkview Dr. on Atkinson Rd.

DAILY CREEL LIMIT/MINIMUM LENGTH: Largemouth Bass: 2 fish, 15 inches • Channel Catfish: 2 fish, 15 inches

Pleasanton City Lake: East

SIZE: 127 acres.

LOCATION: 1 mile north and 0.5 mile east of Pleasanton. Boat access.

DAILY CREEL LIMIT/MINIMUM LENGTH: Largemouth Bass: 2 fish, 21 inches • Smallmouth Bass: 2 fish, 15 inches • Channel Catfish: 2 fish, 15 inches • Crappie: 50 fish • Saugeye: 2 fish, 18 inches • Striped Bass: 2 fish, 18 inches • Walleye: 2 fish, 18 inches • Wiper: 2 fish, 18 inches

Pleasanton City Lake: West

SIZE: 32 acres.

LOCATION: Just west of Pleasanton. Boat access.

DAILY CREEL LIMIT/MINIMUM LENGTH: Largemouth Bass: 2 fish, 21 inches • Smallmouth Bass: 2 fish, 15 inches • Spotted Bass: 5 fish, 15 inches • Channel Catfish: 2 fish, 15 inches • Crappie: 50 fish

Prescott City Lake

SIZE: 25 acres.

LOCATION: Just southeast of Prescott. No boat access.

DAILY CREEL LIMIT/MINIMUM LENGTH: Largemouth Bass: 5 fish, 15 inches • Channel Catfish: 5 fish • Crappie: 50 fish

Richmond City Lake

SIZE: 21 acres.

LOCATION: 1 mile south and 1.5 miles east of Richmond. Boat access.

DAILY CREEL LIMIT/MINIMUM LENGTH: Largemouth Bass: 2 fish, 13–18 inches slot limit • Channel Catfish: 2 fish, 15 inches • Crappie: 50 fish • Walleye: 2 fish, 18 inches

Sedan City Lake: North

SIZE: 55 acres.

LOCATION: 3.5 miles west and 2 miles north of Sedan on K-99. Boat access.

DAILY CREEL LIMIT/MINIMUM LENGTH: Largemouth Bass: 5 fish, 13–18 inches slot limit • Channel Catfish: 5 fish • Flathead Catfish: 5 fish • Crappie: 50 fish • Saugeye: 5 fish, 15 inches

Sedan City Lake: South

SIZE: 70 acres.

LOCATION: 2 miles north of Sedan on K-99. Boat access.

DAILY CREEL LIMIT/MINIMUM LENGTH: Largemouth Bass: 5 fish, 13–18 inches slot limit • Channel Catfish: 5 fish • Flathead Catfish: 5 fish • Crappie: 50 fish • Saugeye: 5 fish, 15 inches

Severy City Lake

SIZE: 10 acres.

LOCATION: 2 miles west of Severy.

DAILY CREEL LIMIT/MINIMUM LENGTH: Largemouth Bass: 5 fish, 15 inches • Channel Catfish: 5 fish • Flathead Catfish: 5 fish

Thayer City Lake (New)

SIZE: 45 acres.

LOCATION: Just southwest of Thayer. Boat access.

DAILY CREEL LIMIT/MINIMUM LENGTH: Largemouth Bass: 5 fish, 13–18 inches slot limit • Channel Catfish: 5 fish, 15 inches • Crappie: 10 fish

Thayer City Lake (Old)

SIZE: 30 acres.
LOCATION: Just southwest of Thayer.
DAILY CREEL LIMIT/MINIMUM LENGTH: Largemouth Bass: 5 fish, 13–18 inches slot limit • Channel Catfish: 5 fish, 15 inches • Crappie: 10 fish

Uniontown School Pond

SIZE: 2 acres.
LOCATION: Uniontown.
DAILY CREEL LIMIT/MINIMUM LENGTH: Largemouth Bass: 2 fish, 18 inches • Channel Catfish: 2 fish, 15 inches

Yates Center City Lake

SIZE: 200 acres.
LOCATION: 2 miles west and 3 miles south of Yates Center.
DAILY CREEL LIMIT/MINIMUM LENGTH: Largemouth Bass: 5 fish, 13–18 inches slot limit • Channel Catfish: 2 fish, 15 inches • Crappie: 10 fish, 10 inches • Walleye: 2 fish, 15 inches • Wiper: 2 fish, 18 inches
AQUATIC NUISANCE SPECIES ALERT: Eurasian Watermilfoil

Yates Center: South (Owl)

SIZE: 250 acres.
LOCATION: 0.5 mile south of Yates Center. Boat access.
DAILY CREEL LIMIT/MINIMUM LENGTH: Largemouth Bass: 5 fish, 13–18 inches slot limit • Channel Catfish: 2 fish, 15 inches • Crappie: 10 fish, 10 inches • Walleye: 2 fish, 15 inches • Wiper: 2 fish, 18 inches